Third Edition

Contemporary Group Work

Charles D. Garvin
The University of Michigan

Allyn and Bacon
Boston • London • Toronto • Sydney • Tokyo • Singapore

Managing Editor, Social Work: Judy Fifer
Executive Editor: Karen Hanson
Series Editorial Assistant: Jennifer Jacobson
Marketing Manager: Joyce Nilsen
Editorial-Production Service: Shepherd, Inc.
Composition Buyer: Linda Cox
Manufacturing Buyer: Megan Cochran
Editorial-Production Administrator: Donna Simons

Copyright © 1997 by Allyn & Bacon
A Simon & Schuster Company
Needham Heights, MA 02194

Library of Congress Cataloging-in-Publication Data

Garvin, Charles D.
    Contemporary group work / Charles D. Garvin. — 3rd ed.
        p.   cm.
    Includes bibliographical references and index.
    ISBN 0–205–19877–5
    1. Social group work—United States.   I. Title.
HV45.G37   1996
361.4—dc20   96–1227
                                                            CIP

Printed in the United States of America

10   9   8   7   6   5   4   3   2   1   00   99   98   97   96

Dedicated to
Beth Glover Reed, who has taught me how feminist ideas can contribute to group work theory and practice, and to Charlene Anderson, with whom I have worked for many years facilitating groups, and who has taught me by example many things about how to be a sensitive and effective group worker.

Brief Contents

Contents

Preface

This is intended as an introductory text on group work. As such its purpose is to help the reader understand how to select members for groups, facilitate the development of groups through beginning, middle, and ending phases, and evaluate with the members the impact of the group experience. Groups are used for many reasons in such settings, and no one book can convey the range of approaches required for all of these. We, therefore, focus much of our attention on groups established to enhance the functioning of individual members. However, a broad, rather than a narrow, conception of enhancing functioning is intended, so as not to preclude this book's application to work with a variety of groups. Interest groups, committees, educational groups, and representative groups can all have this as a major thrust. In our last chapter we focus on task groups such as committees. We have, consequently, included content applicable to all of these situations.

The selection of content for this book has also been guided by several of the author's convictions. First, the actions of the group worker should be to help the group and its members attain mutually agreed-on goals. The first major task of the worker and the members is to determine such goals, then to guide subsequent events by these goals or to revise them accordingly. This premise leads to the second preposition that movement toward goals should be monitored and that the worker and the group should acquire the means to do this. Third, the worker's actions should be based on an understanding of research and theory from the social sciences, and throughout this book we have included content on monitoring changes and on relevant social science material. Fourth, we believe that social workers with groups should use any effective means consistent with social work values and purposes. We, therefore, have incorporated many ideas from other disciplines and professions.

An important approach taken in this book is that learning requires an experiential element that includes carefully structured observations. To assist with this, many chapters conclude with a structured exercise or an observational guide. Throughout the book, we present many practice illustrations and detailed practice examples.

While extensive discussions of concepts are presented later, it should be noted that the author utilizes many systemic notions. Thus the idea of the worker as a mediator among members, between members, and the group-as-a-whole, and between the group and external institutions, is a view maintained throughout the book. Also relevant is a group dynamics approach that views group changes in terms of interactions of forces within, as well as outside of the group. Finally, we hold a sociobehavioral view that individual behavior is a consequence of social forces and interactions. Cognitive factors are not overlooked, however, as the author is committed to an approach in which group members determine their own destinies by being guided to awareness of group forces as they affect individual behavior.

The ideas of the author about group work have increasingly become influenced by feminist ideas. He sees these as relevant to the above convictions regarding the complementary activity of the worker and group members in determining goals, the vital importance of attention to and respect for processes among the members, the centrality of learning from experience and using experience to inform theory (praxis), and the attention to be paid to societal issues (the personal is political). Furthermore, feminist ideas have helped the author deepen his understanding of power and oppression as these affect group goals and processes, an understanding that he hopes enriches this book. Thus while the author lays no claim to having written a feminist text, as such, due to the limits of his own experiences and understanding, he hopes that this book has been strengthened by his current comprehension of feminist thought and experience.

The organizing principles of the book are twofold: first, a group developmental approach is taken that views worker and member tasks as occurring differently at each stage of group development. Second, a "functional" approach is taken that sees group development as affected by group purposes and agency functions. For this reason, a typology of such purposes is presented early in the book and forms the major basis for the final chapters.

Acknowledgements

Throughout my years as a practicing group worker, supervisor of this practice, and trainer of social work students, the ideas of a number of people have greatly benefited me. First, I wish to acknowledge my debt to my first supervisors of group work practice, Edna Hansen and Rose Cohn; second, to such writers as Robert Vinter and William Schwartz, who on many occasions encouraged and supported my development and who undoubtedly found places where I benefited as well as strayed from their contrasting inputs. The work of preparing the previous edition of this book was greatly helped by the constructive suggestions of Beulah Rothman, Stella Wong, University of Hawaii, and Helen Guthrie, Nazareth College.

As indicated by my dedication of this book, in recent years I have gained a great deal from my collaboration with two women. Beth Reed of the University of Michigan School of Social Work and I have worked together on many group work projects such as an edited volume on gender issues in group work, a small group experiment on the influence of race and gender of leader on group process, and several papers on feminist approaches to work with groups. My ability to introduce feminist ideas into this book is largely due to this collaboration. In addition, I have worked with a group for a number of years with Charlene Anderson, as well as joining her and others in creating the Michigan Center for Groups. Her skill and understanding in work with groups have taught and inspired me a great deal.

Chapter *1*

Contemporary Group Work

An Overview

Group work, as a social work method, has evolved and changed in the three-quarter century since its origin. These changes result from altered circumstances, increased knowledge, and an expansion in the number and variety of practice settings. A consensus has developed during this period as to what constitutes social work with groups, although different practice models have been created and coexist within this broad consensus.

In the first two chapters of this book, we shall provide information of the history of group practice so the reader might better understand the ideas that unify as well as divide practitioners of this social work method. This chapter will present our approach to group work and how it relates to other workers, from both inside and outside the field of social work.

In a recent article, Middleman and Goldberg describe the essential elements of social work with groups.[1] The first element is that the worker "must focus on helping members to become a system of mutual aid." The main source of help for each group member comes from other members, individually and collectively. A major task of the social worker, then, is to help members understand this and to create a group where mutual aid can occur. The worker's specific techniques will be described throughout the book.

The second element of social work with groups is that the worker understands and makes use of group processes and helps the members do the same. We shall have much more to say about group process later in the book. At this point, the reader should understand that we are speaking of the unfolding of events in the group as members solve problems together, express feelings to and toward each other, evolve a pattern of relationships, and influence each other. Group processes can be powerful forces for the members and may or may not help members attain their goals. The tasks of the workers are to support beneficial processes, to diminish those that are not, and to help members of the group do the same.

The third element cited by Middleman and Goldberg is that the worker helps the members to function more autonomously as individuals and as a group. They view the worker as easing him or her "out of a job." To function autonomously may be feasible in some situations, as when groups continue wholly on a "self-help" basis; in other situations this may not be possible, at least in the short run during the "life" of the group.

Middleman and Goldberg cite a fourth element, which helps members to "re-experience their groupness at the point of termination." We view this as part of the third element in that all of life's experiences have beginnings, middles, and endings, and members are helped to understand and to cope with this when they become conscious of the unfolding of these phases of the group. We believe, therefore, that members should be helped to understand their group experience as a means of dealing with the many other group experiences they face in their lives.

The Organizational and Environmental Approach

Our practice model was initially developed from the model generated by Vinter and his colleagues at the University of Michigan.[2] This extension of the ideas of Vinter and others is originally described by Glasser and Garvin, who sought to develop principles to guide effective practice in the broad variety of social welfare agencies that now sponsor group services.[3] Their model, termed "an organizational and environmental approach," incorporates a diversity of practice procedures by declaring that the purpose or purposes for which the group is established determines the way the members will respond to their group experience and the way the worker will work with the group.

Clarification of Purpose

The organizational and environmental approach to group purpose recognizes that the ultimate fulfillment of the purpose will result from interactions involving the agency, the workers, the members, and others in the environment. In certain situations, for instance when the agency recruits members for the group, the agency's view of group purpose will affect even the selection of the worker and the members. In current terms, then, this model is a social-ecological one.

To help the worker understand group purposes and to use this understanding in making decisions, we have developed a typology of group purposes. While this will be discussed fully in the next chapter, we describe it briefly here. Our categorization takes into consideration whether the group is meant to enhance the social development of members who have joined the group voluntarily and whose development is viewed as proceeding normally (*socialization groups*), or whether the group is to remedy the social development of members whose previous socialization is viewed, sociologically, as deviant and where group participation is often a consequence of some form of social pressure (*resocialization groups*). Each of these purposes is subdivided further, which shall also be described in the following chapter.

The categorization of group purpose allows us to offer one resolution of an important concern of group work practice as well as of all social work: to present appropriate ways of modifying both individual and environmental circumstances to attain individual goals. For each type of purpose we identify, singly or in combination, there are relevant targets of change related to the individual member, the group, and the larger social environment.

Elsewhere, when we criticized the unfortunate tendency to dichotomize the choice of *either* individual or environmental targets, we made the following statements.

> *The use of groups is seen either as a means to achieve social goals in a community context or as a method to encourage individual growth and change in an educational or rehabilitative context. It may be argued that this is consistent neither with modern social science theory nor with common sense. A broad view sees the social environment as a source of individual behavior patterns, as influential in maintaining such patterns, and as a useful tool in altering them. On the other hand, the individual—often together with others—can play a significant role in making more constructive use of his environment or change it in ways that will provide greater satisfaction of his or her needs.[4]*

Whether the purpose of the group is to facilitate the socialization or resocialization of the member, we view all member goals as related to optimal *social functioning.* This concept refers to the way individuals seek to cope with their social situations by modifying themselves, their environment, or both to achieve the best fit among individual needs and capacities and environmental opportunities.

We have found role concepts useful in analyzing social functioning because they describe individual behaviors as responses to social circumstances. Thus the ways wives and husbands function in their marital roles, their children in their child roles, the parents in their work roles, and all family members in their community roles (for example, student, church member, or member of friendship groups) are examples of social functioning.

Problems in social functioning occur when people's roles do not fit their needs and capacities, when they are not satisfied with their enactment of their roles, when the way one person performs his or her role is in conflict with the actions of others, or when others are critical of one's actions in relationship to roles. Problems can also occur when the environment fails to provide resources for role performance or hinders such performance in other ways.

Social work clients may seek to modify their role performances through acting differently, feeling differently, or thinking about their situations in new ways. They may also seek to change their environment so it affects their role-related activities differently.

Social workers can enhance social functioning on many levels by working solely with the individual concerned or with that individual in concert with family members, friends, and so forth. People may help each other with problems in social functioning in group situations which is what this book is about. Individual social functioning can also be enhanced by changes brought about on a community level or in national social policies. Such changes in the environment may be sought by the individual, often with the help of social workers, or may be sought by social workers on behalf of individuals, whether known to them personally or as members of such classes as the disabled or ethnic groups.

Group workers have helped alleviate many social functioning problems. For example, groups can provide people with recreational and educational resources, or groups members can join together to obtain these. Groups can also help people "at risk" such as adolescents facing developmental stresses, parents who fear that their stresses may provoke them to mistreat their children, or unemployed people who seek ways to regain employment.

Focus on Goals

Our approach also emphasized individual goal specification and attainment—the goal being enhanced social functioning. A *goal* relates to a group member's condition, situation, or both that the member and the worker agree should be changed through group experience. A goal should be expressed in concrete terms so the member will be able to recognize it when it has been reached. To achieve member goals, the goals regarding group and environmental conditions must also be clearly specified. Later we shall present in detail procedures and examples regarding such goal specifications.

A Mutual Aid System

Although we see group work as facilitating individual goal attainment, we, like all group workers, view the group as a mutual aid system. Many approaches to groups describe the worker as interacting with individuals in the context of the group. While we see this as a necessary activity of group workers from time to time, we join other group work theorists in emphasizing how the group worker helps the members help one another achieve their individual and collective aspirations.

Evaluation of Practice

The goal attainment of the members in this approach to practice should be assessed at regular intervals for several reasons: first, the effectiveness of the group process and the worker's facilitation of this process should be determined so that the individual members, the group, and the worker can, when necessary, change group conditions; second, the member, when goals have been achieved, should either leave the group or select new goals; third, the agency and the worker should gather evidence as to the effectiveness of group services. Throughout this book, therefore, we shall present ways of measuring changes in individual, group, and environmental conditions.

Worker Tasks

The worker's actions to help members achieve their goals and to create a group to accomplish this are specified in this practice model. Since the worker with and on behalf of the members is sometimes required to seek changes in the environment outside the group, this is also detailed. Although other models do not necessarily present worker behaviors in this way, ours does because group workers should be able to generate and test propositions about the effects of different kinds of worker actions; effective ways of helping the member can then be identified and taught to others.

Values

In this discussion of values, we shall first describe two broad ideological positions that inform our approach to practice. We shall then indicate specific values that serve as foundations for our thinking about group work.

Our first ideological position is that all social work practice should seek the empowerment of both workers and clients. This stems from our view that a major part of social work should be to work with and on behalf of people oppressed because of their economic status, class position, gender, culture, ethnicity, sexual orientation, or physical or mental disabilities. These characteristics often require that such individuals learn to empower themselves to enhance their social functioning.

Our view of empowerment is consistent with Solomon's:

> *a process whereby the social worker engages in a set of activities with the client . . . that aim to reduce the powerlessness that has been created by negative valuations based on membership in a stigmatized group. It involves identification of the power blocks that contribute to the problem as well as the development and implementation of specific strategies aimed at either the reduction of the effects from indirect power blocks or the reduction of the operations of direct power blocks.*[5]

The second ideological position is derived from our conviction that contemporary feminist ideas can contribute a great deal to our approach to group work. We strongly endorse Walters's succinct statement of the major components of a feminist perspective as this bears upon practice:

> *Any feminist perspective in therapy has, I believe, four major components. . . . These components are (1) the conscious inclusion, in both theory and practice, of the experience of women growing up; developing; relating to each other; to men, and to social institutions; raising families; working; and growing old in a culture largely shaped and defined by male experience; (2) a critique of therapy practices and the theoretical constructs on which they are based, that lend themselves to a devaluing of women, and of the particular social and familial roles of women—in other words, a critique of those practices and ideas commonly identified as sexist; (3) the integration of feminist theory, and the information derived from women's studies, into a knowledge based of psychological theory, as well as of methodological—and even pedagogical—framework; and (4) the use of female modes and models in the continuing expansion and development of theory and practice in the field.*[6]

Throughout this book, as we discuss various practice principles, we shall endeavor to link these to feminist perspectives such as that of Walters.

In addition to these ideological positions, three specific values are basic to our practice approach. First, our approach to group work shares with others in social work a commitment to respect the worth of all people; the importance placed on self-determination is derived from this, as is the importance placed on the right of individuals to obtain support from society to achieve their maximum potential. In this sense, we also define our approach as humanistic while recognizing that other group workers might define this term differently.

Self-determination requires that we uphold voluntary participation in groups and insist on a "contract" between the worker and members, and the worker and the group-as-a-whole that specifies goals and member and worker tasks. The worker should negotiate these tasks with members and renegotiate them whenever changes take place. A related principle is that workers may intervene in the group in ways that do not benefit all members, but must not intervene in ways that can harm any member, even if it benefits others.

The second social work value inherent in group work is the value placed on human life. This means not only the biological preservation of the individual but the nurturance of growth toward maximum utilization of capacities. Thus an alcoholic accelerates the approach of biological death and psychological impairment, and the latter, in at least a metaphorical sense, is death. Similarly, the adolescent who embarks on a criminal career also has chosen a psychological death in terms of killing his or her prosocial talents to contribute to society, even if the crimes do not threaten biological existence.

The third value issue addressed by our model arises from priorities for developing and staffing services. Social work has always had a commitment to serve those who, as a result of being the most exploited, the most needy, or the most vulnerable, are, or may become, impaired in their social functioning. Group workers have always worked with the poor, the ethnically oppressed, the immigrants, and those with grievances related to urban conditions. In a later period of group work history, workers served other oppressed groups such as mental patients, children in conflict with their schools, and prisoners. The oppression of women has also concerned group workers.

Some writers argue that it is not the obligation or prerogative of the profession or its educational institutions to influence the practitioner's choice of settings. We do not agree with this position. For example, health care institutions are often enjoined to provide medical care to people deprived of such service, and lawyers are increasingly expected to advocate for persons treated unjustly by the criminal justice system. As much, if not more than these professions, social work has a mandate to serve socially oppressed persons.

A major problem for the practitioner seeking to function ethically is that following some of the values mentioned can conflict with others. In later chapters we shall discuss responses to this issue.

Differing Approaches to Practice

In the following discussion, our model will be compared to other contemporary approaches to group work to place it in both historical and contemporary contexts. One of the earliest comparisons of these approaches was that of William Schwartz, who identified three models.

> There was a kind of "medical" model in which "the steps of the helping process are described by assuming a sequence of movements through which the worker investigates, diagnoses, and treats the problem under consideration." There was a "scientific" model "in which the steps in the helping process resemble closely the problem solving sequence by which the scientific worker moves from the unknown to the known." And there was a "model of the organic system in which the total helping situation is viewed as a network of reciprocal activity, and in which it is impossible to describe accurately any part of the system without describing its active relationship to the other moving parts."[7]

A year later, Vinter described three orientations to group work that he believed succeeded each other historically. The first emphasized "democratic decentralization," the second "socialization," and the third "rehabilitation."[8]

A paper that defined group work models for at least a decade and is still influential today was prepared by Papell and Rothman for the 1966 meeting of the Council on Social Work Education.[9] In their presentation the "social goals," "remedial," and "reciprocal" models were identified.

The social goal approach, perhaps the oldest, is clearly the outcome of the democratic decentralization orientation referred to by Vinter. This model, because of its view of social work as a "cause" and because of its relevance to contemporary struggles for human rights, continues to influence all of social work practice as well as its group work component.

The remedial model emerged during the movement of group work into rehabilitation settings. It focused on treatment goals for individuals, with the group viewed as a means and content to attain such goals. This model is the one out of which our approach emerged.

The reciprocal model sought to identify and enhance the process whereby individuals, groups, and larger social systems engaged each other to undertake activities of mutual benefit. The worker, therefore, was described as a "mediator," involved, for example, in the ways a group's member sought to use the group, the demands the group placed on the members to ensure its own survival, the pressures the group placed on the agency, and the agency requirements transmitted to the group and its members.

The assumption that group work practice included three models was influential for a number of years; the editors of two consecutive editions of the *Encyclopedia of Social Work* in 1971 and 1977 commissioned three articles to present the state of group work theory: one by William Schwartz, the exponent of the reciprocal model; one by Garvin and Glasser, who wrote in the tradition of Vinter's remedial model; and the third, "The Developmental Approach" by Emmanuel Tropp, which although not identified by its author as the "social goals" models, was described as "starting with a strong emphasis on the common group goals and the democratic process of group involvement."[10]

As one would expect, a movement is occurring toward an integration of models and a reaffirmation of the core ideas of what constitutes social work with groups. The two most recent editions of the *Encyclopedia of Social Work* have returned to presenting one article on group work that emphasizes its central ideas.[11]

The most recent effort to codify models of group work was the publication of *Theories of Social Work with Groups*. This volume was planned as a companion to *Theories of Social Casework*[12] with the expectation that the "single systems theoretical models" (that is, casework, group work, family treatment) "will serve as the major building blocks of multi-system integrated practice theories.[13]

It was quite clear to Roberts and Northen, who edited the group work volume, that the papers included did not represent distinct approaches to group work, although some authors' values or other foundations of their theories contrasted sharply. In a final review chapter, Roberts and Northen compared the articles on such dimensions as behavioral science foundations, target populations, criteria for group member selection, and worker activity. They found that authors with a similar position on one of these dimensions often had different postures on another. Clearly, while the authors may claim, with some justification, to have internally consistent models, all seek to achieve this by assembling a basic set of practice elements in different ways.

We encourage the reader to choose appropriate strategies for group composition or group formation from among various alternatives. It is premature to assemble all group work ideas into a master plan in which the group circumstances and the array of group work approaches can be totally accommodated, although some have tried.[14] In this book, therefore, while we do favor one model, we shall often identify alternative approaches. Whatever else may be argued, all groups have beginnings, middles, and endings, even though different ideas exists as to how to approach these events.

Influences beyond Social Work

Criteria for Use

Group activities for personal growth are proliferating and include many elements not included in the social work models just described. Group workers in social work, as well as their counterparts in psychiatry, psychology, nursing, and education, do not live in a vacuum. Professionals read each other's works and borrow ideas across institutional boundaries. When new ideas such as gestalt therapy or cognitive-behavioral therapy are promoted, practitioners from all disciplines hear of them through books and workshops and seek to utilize what they have learned. Clearly, then, no set of techniques fully distinguishes any profession's work with groups, and goals and methods overlap.

The social worker with groups will, therefore, utilize techniques from any source if they are (1) compatible with social work values; (2) helpful to those customarily served by social workers; (3) appropriate to the institutions that employ social workers; and (4) encompassable in the educational program prescribed for social work. Those techniques easily integrated into the practitioner's model will be the most utilized.

Needs of Social Work Clients.   Any discussion of the use of nonsocial work approaches must begin with a reiteration that social work focuses on individual-environmental transaction. Thus social work approaches should be concerned with enhancing not only the behavior of individuals but the way environments meet their needs. In a sense this is inevitable in group work since the group has been widely viewed as a social microcosm that can reflect many of the forces the individual copes with in other situations. The group is one aspect of the member's environment. It is possible, of course, to use groups so that the social component is minimized. Group workers sometimes use the phrase "case work in the group" to describe groups that primarily focus on worker-member communications rather than on member-member communications. Approaches from outside of social work that operate in a similar way are inappropriate to group work in social work because of its concern for social functioning.

Requirements of Social Work Agencies.   An even more difficult issue is to determine approaches appropriate to the institutions that employ social workers. The following organizational variables have implications for this:

1. Social work agencies often have limited budgets. Approaches that require training well beyond that usually received by social workers, expensive equipment, several workers working simultaneously, or high-paid consultants may be unfeasible.
2. Social work organizations should emphasize voluntary participation, personal freedom, and noninfliction of pain. Some approaches have limited applicability in such agencies because of their use of compulsion or of aversive measures. Even the strong

confrontation style sometimes used in correctional and drug programs may be unacceptable to many social work agencies.

3. Social workers may have less power over their organizational environments than members of other professions. Approaches that require control over broad aspects of that environment may also not be feasible for group workers.

4. A few approaches require more training than can be encompassed in a social work curriculum for the worker to acquire even minimally acceptable competence. Some social workers, after receiving their degrees, may secure such training. The purpose of this text, however, is to portray ways of working that can be taught to social workers in the normal course of a professional program. Thus, for example, the full scope of gestalt therapy or analytic group psychotherapy cannot be offered in a social work program. Nevertheless, there are techniques and concepts, drawn from these treatment systems, that can be so incorporated.

The following discussion describes some of the major approaches to work with groups developed outside of social work. In presenting each approach, we shall note those aspects that can be integrated into social work practice and taught in a social work curriculum. We shall focus on eleven approaches, grouped into four clusters, that we believe incorporate most of the major contemporary trends in work with groups for personal growth and change. Some of this material shall be elaborated on in later chapters when we discuss practice issues. We omit ideas (for example, rational emotive therapy and reality therapy) which, while they had group applications, are not conceived of primarily as ways of working with groups.[15]

Approaches Utilizing or Originating from Psychoanalysis

Gestalt Therapy.   The framework of gestalt therapy owes its origin and much of its development to Fritz Perls.[16] Its theoretical foundations are drawn from gestalt psychology, particularly the idea that perception is organized around attention to some aspect of a total situation (figure) with the balance (the ground) forming a context. A particularly important concept for the gestalt therapist, then, is *awareness* inasmuch as one's needs and feelings may often be blocked and remain as *ground* and, thus, out of awareness. These concepts are also closely related to the notion that one may deny aspects of one's own desires, potentialities, or experiences that might be drawn upon to enhance one's life.

Techniques developed by Perls and his colleagues to increase awareness and subsequent integration of rejected aspects of one's self include drawing a person's attention to body positions and movements, and role playing components of one's own body, dreams, fantasies, or attitudes. The individual may then actually hold a "dialogue" among these aspects, while "occupying" what is referred to as the "hot seat." The worker in a gestalt group may also use "exercises" to help members increase self-awareness.

Perls involved group members to a very limited degree with each other, as the person in the "hot seat" worked primarily with the therapist. Many contemporary gestalt therapists, however, use awareness exercises in which group members interact with each other; they may also encourage the group to discuss the individual issues raised while in the "hot seat."

Whether or not group workers fully understand gestalt therapy, they can use gestalt exercises to promote awareness. For example, exercises can be used at the beginning and ending of the group to elicit feelings about these phases. Group workers can also use these techniques to help members "own" beliefs and feelings such as anger or rejection, which they project onto others. Ambivalence, also, is a very frequent problem that inhibits decision making, and gestalt approaches such as double chairing are useful in exploring issues around alternative choices facing members.

Group workers have used nonverbal activities in groups. These are drawn upon to enhance relationships, encourage expressiveness, and build skills. The gestalt concepts regarding awareness may help group workers add another dimension to their understanding and use of program experiences.

Transactional Analysis.   Eric Berne, the founder of transactional analysis, like Fritz Perls, was originally trained and experienced in psychoanalytic therapy.[17] His system is based on an analysis of how transactions among people are affected by their "ego states," which are defined by Berne "as a set of coherent behavior patterns; or pragmatically, as a system of feelings which motivates a related set of behavior patterns." Most readers are probably familiar with the ego states that Berne has labeled as the *child, parent,* and *adult.* Through the writings of Berne and his followers, the indicators of these ego states and many subtypes of each ego state have been identified. These concepts are used in the transactional analysis therapy situation to analyze transactions of the individual with others.

Such transactions are also found in more complex interactions, and Berne developed ways of conceptualizing these. One technique examines sequences that substitute for "intimacy," which Berne called *games.* Long-lasting interactional patterns in life are labeled *scripts,* and means have evolved for identifying these. The intent of this conceptual frame work is to help people examine transactions so that both immediate interactions and lifelong patterns may be consciously modified.

In the group therapy situation, members are trained in the analysis of ego states, games, and scripts. Subsequently, with the help of the therapist and each other, they apply this analysis to behavior in the group and to the environment outside the group.[18]

Within the social work group, it is often essential to examine the transactions between the worker and the members or among members. There are many approaches to this, ranging from those that call attention to what is taking place to those that utilize a generalized set of concepts as in transactional analysis. Without any research on how effective one approach is compared to another, the worker will have to draw upon what seems most appropriate to the population represented.

Psychoanalytic Group Therapy.   With the exception of some early experiments with tubercular patients and World War I veterans, group psychotherapy was developed within a psychoanalytic framework. The early group psychotherapists adopted many approaches to group therapy drawn from individual psychoanalysis, including free association and the analysis of transference. One group of writers, namely Foulkes, Ezriel, Whitaker, and Lieberman, sought to understand how affects and drives are related to group forces.[19] The following are some of the propositions from these analytically oriented theories:

1. Members of groups will identify common ideational and emotional reactions among themselves and direct their discussion to these. These often relate to individual drives and psychological states.

2. Reactions to therapists include both realistic elements as well as distortions determined by members' past experiences (i.e., transference).
3. Conflicts occur between a desire to fulfill individual needs and a fear of the consequences of striving to meet these needs, and these are often shared by members. The consensus reached as to the resolution of such conflicts may be compatible with the goals of therapy or may be a hindrance on both group and individual levels.

The role of the therapist is to stimulate examination of these issues and to make the kinds of interpretations that will bring about conflict resolution through reality-oriented therapist-member interactions. Common psychological themes can be dealt with and resolved in ways that help members with their individual difficulties.

The application of these concepts is dependent on the therapist's understanding of psychoanalytic theory and how it illuminates group phenomena. Group workers have not had such training in depth, but are usually taught basic information on human development, often from a psychoanalytic (usually ego psychological) perspective.

Many group work clients are not motivated to engage in the long-term verbally and psychologically oriented activities that group analytic approaches require. Nevertheless, an understanding that members may distort the reality of the worker and each other and that such distortions may hinder group and individual problem solving is important to effective work with groups. The worker's ability to identify group themes and to analyze the meaning of these in terms of affects and drives is also useful to "make sense" out of the many pieces of information provided by group members. Workers should have a point of view with regard to members' personality manifestations and the meaning of their behavior, and psychoanalytic and ego psychological theory certainly provides one such system.

The Tavistock Approach.   When we refer to the *Tavistock approach,* we have in mind primarily the work of Wilfred Bion.[20] Bion was psychoanalytically trained and subsequently became impressed with group phenomena. One of Bion's major ideas was that groups often avoid "work" by operating according to "basic assumptions." A major reason for responding to a basic assumption is to react to the authority of the leader. Basic assumptions include dependence on the leader, fight-flight responses, and pairing among members. Typically, in a Tavistock group, the leader, who is analogous to the psychoanalyst with individuals, remains relatively inactive so that the basic assumptions, as they emerge, do so presumably out of the members' needs rather than worker reality.

This model may be useful for people seeking to understand these emotional processes in groups. The short-term, more focused nature of social work groups militates against this as a central framework. Nevertheless, to work toward their goals, all groups must be helped to free themselves from emotional reactions that are hindering, especially those toward leadership. The leader who has participated in a Tavistock-type experience will be particularly sensitive to this issue and will be able to impart this understanding to group members.

Approaches Utilizing or Originating from Social Psychological Theories

Guided Group Interaction.   The Guided Group Interaction approach has been utilized primarily with delinquent adolescents in institutional settings.[21] One of the earliest studies of the guided group interactions concepts, published in 1958, reported on its use in a New Jersey institution, Highfields.[22] A related approach has been called *positive peer culture.*[23]

Guided Group Interaction was designed by sociologists who believed that delinquent behavior was determined in the main by peer group rather than psychological processes. Efforts to encourage change must, therefore, be directed at these social processes. Interventions in the guided group approach require frequent, usually daily, interactions among group members, who are also aware of each other's extra group behavior, usually within an institutional program.

The group is given considerable salience for the youth in that major decisions regarding current privileges and future plans are evaluated there. These decisions are based on whether members have identified and worked on *problems*. A terminology for such problems is either developed by the group or, as in positive peer culture, taught to it. This "language" describes problems in direct, often colloquial, ways.

A major norm developed in the group is one of *candor* (as opposed to *conning*). Staff members motivated the members to develop such norms by creating initial ambiguity regarding the group, by confronting the group, and by fostering the dependency of members on the group. As one text on Guided Group Interaction states, a program based on sociological theory will have to concentrate on "changing reference group and normative orientations; utilizing ambivalent feelings resulting from the conflict of conventional and delinquent standards; and providing opportunities for recognition and achievement in conventional pursuits."[24]

In some ways, these ideas can be drawn upon by group workers; in others, they are problematic. Those most usable relate to how the group shapes norms and how workers can mold this process, since group workers *do* work with people branded by society as deviant and placed in institutions involuntarily. On the other hand, the manipulative style and the type of confrontation encouraged pose value dilemmas to social workers.

Self-Help Groups. A recent discussion of self-help groups estimated a membership of 7.5 million in the United States.[25] The actual number is much larger if all the local affiliates of such organizations as Alcoholics Anonymous, Weight Watchers, and Parents Anonymous are considered. The range of concerns addressed by such groups is vast and includes addictions (Synanon, Alcoholics Anonymous), aggressive behavior (Parents Anonymous), mental illness (Recovery, Inc.) disability (Emphysema Anonymous), loss of children (Compassionate Friends), loss of spouse (Parents without Partners), gamblers (Gamblers Anonymous), weight control (Weight Watchers), and sexual orientation (Gay Liberation Front).

This type of group activity is classified as a sociological approach for several reasons: the emphasis of the groups is on interpersonal support rather than on psychological uncovering; a major component of what such groups offer is successful role models; and these groups often have social action goals such as securing better services or overcoming the stigma directed at group members. The use of these groups is also an outgrowth of social forces as members are likely to have been rejected by mental health professionals and are often viewed as deviant.

Several similarities are found among the groups, although vast differences in programs exist. These include procedures to provide support for members between sessions, an opportunity to tell one's full "story" in an accepting atmosphere, an occasion to enhance one's self-esteem by helping others, and the availability of successful role models. The groups are also, with a few exceptions such as Parents Anonymous, without professional leadership and, in fact, are often suspicious of it. While supportive, many of the groups at times are quite direct and confronting in their style; it is presumed that those who take this stance have earned the right by having shared and overcome similar problems.

The importance of the approaches to group work used in self-help groups is several-fold. These groups remind us of the great value of peer helping, and this challenges professional self-importance. Even in professionally led groups, the techniques of peer support, as well as confrontation, can be cultivated to a greater degree than usual. There is value in nonprofessionally led groups because of the sense of competence they nurture. The task of the group worker is to support and offer consultation to such groups without taking them over.

Psychodrama. The psychodrama approach has been associated largely with the work of one man—J. L. Moreno.[26] Many of the techniques now in use, particularly gestalt and encounter sessions, were anticipated or even stimulated by Moreno's work. We classify this approach as social psychological because of Moreno's stress on the "public" aspects of one's activities rather than on the psychological components.

The methods of psychodrama include casting the individual into a problematic role and other individuals present into related roles and then enacting actual and potential scenes. Out of this, insights are elicited, emotional catharsis is secured, and other group members benefit through discussion as well as vicariously.

Moreno also developed another concept, sociodrama, which focuses on social factors such as intercultural conflict. In fact, Moreno was interested in applying his techniques to the resolution of issues raised by the civil rights movement.

Dramatic devices have always had a place in group work; nevertheless, the type of emotional expression and confrontation brought about in psychodrama is not usually elicited by social work practitioners. The emergence of gestalt and encounter techniques, however, has probably made us less apprehensive about such events, although lack of proof of their effectiveness may sometimes create skepticism.[27] Because of this effectiveness issue, group workers will benefit by an examination of the carefully specified and illustrated techniques developed by Moreno and his successors.

Approaches Developed from Educational-Psychological Frameworks

Behavior Modification in Groups. One of the greatest impacts on the human service field today comes from the contemporary behaviorists. Drawing from the laboratory work of many people, particularly experimental psychologists, a vast array of behavioral procedures has emerged for treatment of the same problematic conditions at which other approaches are directed. It is not surprising, therefore, that behavioral therapists, like other practitioners, saw the potential of group contexts for behavioral treatment.

Behavioral therapy in groups shares several features with individual behavioral therapy, including a commitment to precise goal specification and initial (baseline) and subsequent measurement of the behaviors to be modified. These changes in behavior are obtained using interventions planned as applications of the principles of conditioning,[28] such as those having to do with behavior resulting from antecedent or consequent events (operant conditioning) or as a conditioned response (respondent conditioning). Such behavior may consist of thoughts or actions or both. The precise procedures to be used are selected after an analysis to determine the controlling conditions for the relevant behaviors.

Vast strides have taken place in recent years in the development of what has come to be known as *cognitive behavior modification*.[29] A number of social work writers, such as Rose and LeCroy, have made considerable use of the principles of this approach in extending their ideas about group work.[30] Rose and his colleagues incorporate these ideas into a model of group work that, like other social work approaches, also draws upon small group theory and principles of mutual aid. Cognitive behavioral approaches recognize the function of thought processes as stimuli of behavior and view these thought processes as targets of change. In groups, therefore, members are assisted to help one another to examine the relationships between thoughts and behavior and to alter dysfunctional thoughts.

Group settings offer a number of additional possibilities for the applications of the principles of behavioral therapy. Members can help each other assess behaviors and can reinforce one another for change. In addition, since many of the behaviors to be modified occur in interpersonal contexts, members can engage in assessment and change activities related to behaviors occurring in the group.

The group worker can draw on many behavioral techniques in social work groups, and new behavioral approaches are being developed to facilitate this. Specific procedures such as assertiveness training, social skill training, and communicational training draw on behavioral concepts and are frequently and appropriately utilized in a variety of social work groups.

Laboratory Training (T-Groups).   While behavior modification grew out of an effort to apply psychological principles that had first been studied in laboratories to therapeutic situations, laboratory training evolved serendipitously from observations of "natural" group situations. Specifically, the laboratory training approach developed out of experiences of members of the staff of the Research Center on Group Dynamics at a workshop held in 1946 to help community leaders implement the Fair Employment Practices Act. Evening sessions were held at which interactions that occurred during the day were analyzed. To the participants attending, it became apparent that a powerful force for change was unleashed as members examined their behavior in the group and the reactions of others to it. Initially, the intent of the participants was to mold an effective social action device, but soon the major emphasis was placed on individual learning.[31]

Laboratory training typically takes place as a two-week residential experience where the individuals are isolated from their usual activities. In the beginning of the period, few instructions are given and the members struggle with this ambiguity. After such efforts, members are helped to examine the interpersonal behaviors elicited by this situation. The learning thus induced was utilized to develop applications to real-life situations outside the laboratory. Some of the key ideas of the trainers who facilitated this experience are that participants in groups can learn "how to learn" from experience; that this learning is facilitated by a "here and now focus"; and that feedback from members on their reactions to each other's behavior is an essential condition for interpersonal learning.

The ideas generated by laboratory training, selectively employed, can enrich all work with groups. Giving and receiving feedback is an important tool when used appropriately, but it can produce a great deal of anxiety if introduced into the wrong group or at the wrong time. Members can also be seduced into avoiding the very real purposes of groups by too extensive a focus on internal process. Nevertheless, some attention to process is valuable in all groups and essential in therapeutic groups. Group workers involved in training and program development may recommend to staffs and professional groups that they examine their group process when problems in group functioning occur.

Approaches Developed from Social Movements

Social Change Movements.   In discussing some approaches, the designation *social movement* is relevant. By this phrase, we mean an organized set of people dedicated to a social ideal often viewed as "radical" by status groups in the society. The term "radical" is justified by the principles embodied in the movement as well as by the efforts usually directed against specified ills of the society, sometimes even to create a society devoid of such problems. In this respect, it is important to reflect that during the early period of its history, group work had many of the characteristics of a social movement, as did the entire profession of social work.

Other movements also have developed approaches relevant to social group work. Black, Chicano, and similar ethnic groups have formed organizations that emphasize themes of group pride and conduct activities consistent with these themes. Social workers often work with ethnic group members whose problems relate strongly to lack of social support for their identities. A similar phenomenon is found among women's movement groups in their approaches to consciousness raising, group support, and confrontation of sexism as ways of meeting members' needs. This also has relevance for groups conducted by social workers. Even political groups committed to specific ideologies provide important normative climates and supports for their members that have parallels in social work situations. The programs of these groups utilize techniques similar to those employed by "grass roots" community organizations. Group workers should become familiar with these techniques.

The Encounter Movement.   So-called encounter groups probably form a continuum with those identified as sensitivity groups. Many encounter groups quite clearly present at least the rudiments of a social movement and have been so characterized by many writers.

The movement aspect of encounter groups, according to Shaffer and Galinsky, is "designed to put the normally alienated individual into closer contact—or encounter with himself, with others, and with the world of nature and pure sensation."[32] The socially critical stance of writers on encounter groups stems from their charge that our society and its institutions alienate individuals from themselves and their bodies. Values such as spontaneity, honesty in interactions, and the validity of one's own feelings are offered as a basis for the encounter experience. As with many other aspects of the "counterculture," authority is downgraded, particularly that based on the training and certification of the group leader. Instead, there is an emphasis on what can be gained from the creation of a sense of community.

Workers in encounter groups usually come from sensitivity groups, psychoanalytic, and psychotherapeutic backgrounds and are often influenced by writers such as Wilhelm

Reich who stress the relationship between physiological and emotional states. They inevitably recruit group members who hold social values different from those who enter traditional psychotherapies.

The techniques used in encounter groups include encouragement of direct emotional expression, physical exercises, physical interaction among participants (for example, hugging, arm wrestling, communicating by touch), and exercises drawn from approaches such as gestalt. The leader is active in introducing these procedures and is often a participant, thus lessening social distance between the leader and group members.

Some of the techniques used in encounter groups will not be accepted by social work clients from working class, as opposed to academic and professional, backgrounds and who seek help with specific circumstances and behaviors. On the other hand, the lowering of social barriers may be accepted by many clients of social work groups, particularly children and young people. Also, clients who are inhibited in emotional expression can be helped by various nonverbal exercises, and clients with bodily tensions can profit from learning ways to relax these. Finally, many clients do seek ways to develop closer ties with others by freeing themselves from various restraints and seeking new life styles.

Similarities and Differences among Approaches

A number of similarities such as the following can be found among virtually all group work writers.

1. Purposes.   All approaches to group work incorporate the professional purposes of preventing breakdown of social functioning, providing resources to meet human needs, helping people to utilize their strengths, and rehabilitating individuals whose functioning has been impaired. Some writers focus on one or another of these purposes, but none deny the legitimacy of social work's responsibility for all of these purposes and the contribution that group work can make to each.

2. Knowledge and Theory.   All approaches to groups work draw from a common source of knowledge from the behavioral sciences. Some lean more heavily upon one kind of knowledge than others, but all utilize small group theory as it describes group development, group leadership, group problem solving, and other group conditions. All also utilize an understanding of individual development and ways of coping, primarily related to participation in small groups. Role concepts abound in the group work literature and are used to describe positions occupied by group members such as leader, expert, or scapegoat. Role concepts are also used to discuss the processes of socialization as affected by group participation.

Group work writers will differ, however, in the degree to which they draw on concepts from ecological theory, behavioral theory, systems theory, or ego psychology. In these, the differences among group workers parallel those among all human services professionals.

3. Problem Solving.   Although differing somewhat on how the problems confronting groups and their members are to be analyzed, group workers are usually problem focused.

As Somers states, "Problem solving characterized the formulations of social group work practice across the spectrum of fifty years."[33] Somers explains this focus, not only in terms of the intellectual history of group work, but also because "The social and intellectual history of the United States is replete with examples of the pragmatic philosophy and experimental approach that form the matrix in which problem solving is embedded, and that provide the source of its essence and continuing energy."[34]

4. Intervention.   Different group work writers describe many similar worker interventions. These actions, which shall be discussed thoroughly in subsequent chapters, include enhancing program activities, eliciting the expression of affect, and supporting honest presentation of one's experiences and beliefs. Workers help members to try out roles in the group to rehearse for their performance outside the group and to give suggestions and feedback to one another regarding their behavior *both* in and out of the group.

A number of ideas have been developed and used more extensively by the adherents of one approach than another. We shall now summarize some of these.

William Schwartz

William Schwartz, the initiator of what he has called the *interactionist approach,* draws more strongly than others from systems concepts to portray members, groups, agencies, and other complex environments in interaction with each other and in a constant process of mutual adaptation. The social worker facilitates this process by functioning as a *mediator*.[35]

The interactionist model focuses on the process whereby individuals engage with others to meet mutual needs. This approach emphasizes the quality of the process rather than the long-term consequences (goals), although Schwartz emphasizes attention to "preferred outcomes." Schwartz's analysis of process enriches all of group work practice, particularly his portrayal of phases[36] and the tasks of group workers in relationship to such phases.[37]

Robert Vinter

Robert Vinter developed some of the major aspects of what he referred to as a *social treatment* or a *problem oriented* model, although others have referred to it as either the *remedial* or *preventive and rehabilitative approach*.[38] This work is based on the idea that the individual group member is the focus of change and the group is the means and context of such change. Vinter and his colleagues' ideas contrast with those of Schwartz in that they place a strong emphasis on establishing individual goals, often long-term in nature, that are precise and operational.

This model calls for an empirical base for practice: practice principles should be scientifically tested for effectiveness and used for goal attainment. Philosophically, therefore, this framework is closer to a positivist rather than an existential stance. The writings of Vinter and related theorists have been of value in the development of group work because of their efforts to specify group worker activities and their effects: these include worker acts (1) at different phases of group development.[39] (2) in relationship to different group processes,[40] (3) for various program approaches,[41] and (4) toward the social environment.[42]

Emanuel Tropp

Emanuel Tropp considers his approach as in the "mainstream" of the development of group work in social work; he regards many other group work writers as "special off-shoots."[43] Tropp sees the mainstream as stressing the principle that "group self-direction toward a common goal is the most effective group vehicle for the social growth of its members."[44] The individual is helped to achieve growth through participation in establishing and accomplishing the group's goal or purpose. Because Tropp sees the group as the vehicle of such growth, he described the worker (or "leader") as helping to establish and attain group goals.

In sharp contrast to Vinter's conceptualization, Tropp does not seek to articulate his model with social science and other research findings. He believes that these endeavors have not created, and are not likely to create, a basis for social work practice. Rather, he finds the empirical evidence for group work in the experiences of its practitioners.

Finally, Tropp does not describe group work as "treatment" and its beneficiaries as "abnormal or pathological." As he states, "All are seen as people who face stressful developmental stages, life situations, challenges, and crises with which they must cope in some way."[45] Thus Tropp has made major contributions to an understanding of how workers function when their intent is to provide the group context for individual growth experiences.

Alan Klein

Alan Klein, whose books on group work span almost three decades (the most recent published in 1972),[46] like Tropp, emphasizes the potential of group experience to help individuals acquire interpersonal skills. Klein, however, refers to his model as a "matching" one in which individual needs are related to environmental opportunities. Klein, as well as Tropp, places strong emphasis on the role of the group in nurturing and encouraging the freedom and autonomy of the group member. In this respect, Klein and Tropp draw on the extensive heritage in group work of analyses of the democratic process.

Margaret Hartford

Margaret Hartford has developed concepts that place group work in the context of generic practice,[47] in that the worker "uses the methodological approaches most appropriate for the given situation." She sees common as well as unique elements to all social work with groups and for this reason has developed a typology of the full range of such services. Her classifications include, for example, work focused on individual participants, problem solving or task achievement, the group context, and the institution outside the group or the wider society.[48] In this respect, Hartford differs from other writers who might see only one function of workers wherever they are located (for example, as mediators) or who limit their model to selected functions (for example, prevention and rehabilitation). Hartford describes "stances" for group workers depending on the type of group and the specific circumstances of the group (for example, stage of development). These stances include directing, facilitating, permissive, and flexible postures.

Boston University School of Social Work

The work of Saul Bernstein and others associated with the Boston University School of Social Work has also been influential for current practice.[49] Their impact is due to their identification of key practice issues. Their approaches and solutions are drawn from extensive experience as well as from theory—examples of which are their discussions of workers activities in different stages of group development, in group conflict situations, and in decisions on group purpose.

Helen Northen

Helen Northen has incorporated systems theory into group work to provide a theoretical foundation for the *psychosocial* model.[50] She employs concepts regarding individual assessment and goal setting that are also used in the preventive and rehabilitative model. Her model also emphasizes the concepts of group development and the ways worker tasks vary in relationship to the group's developmental stages. She presents a comprehensive review of the way changes in group conditions and member behaviors relate to the process of goal setting, interpersonal relationship development, confrontation, and feedback.

Behavioral Group Work

A rapidly developing approach to group work is derived from both behavioral theory and cognitive-behavioral theory (described earlier in this chapter). An important figure in this development is Sheldon Rose, [51] who has written a number of books and articles on this approach, as well as educated several generations of group work scholars who continue in this tradition such as Jeff Edelson, Richard Tolman, Randy Magen, Karen Subramenian, and Edith Lewis.

The behavior modification approach, like the preventive and rehabilitative model, focuses on individual behavior change to achieve mutually agreed-on goals. Procedures for achieving such changes are usually introduced by the worker and are derived theoretically from conditioning concepts. Change is carefully monitored and data is used as feedback for modifying the procedures. Rose's work differs from that of many behaviorists, however, in that it incorporates small group theory and describes how group conditions (for example, cohesiveness, leadership, deviance) may be modified to enhance individual goal attainment[52] These writers, as well as many others who use behavior modification in social work with groups, had been closely associated at one time or another in their careers with Vinter, Glasser, and Garvin at the University of Michigan.

Task-Centered Group Work

Garvin, as an extension of the organizational and environmental model, has contributed extensively to a task-centered model of group work practice.[53] This model was developed initially by William Reed and Laura Epstein.[54] The idea behind this approach was to offer social workers an effective short-term practice model. The intent of the model is to help clients achieve their goals through defining and executing tasks that consist of specific goal-oriented activities. The group work application is based on workers helping members to help each other select their goals, define their tasks, and carry out these tasks.

Feminist Group Work

A new and important development in group work is the introduction of feminist ideas, both in the United States and in other countries.[55] We have also been extensively involved in this development.[56] These feminist ideas provide new insights into ways that oppression and privilege occur in groups to the detriment of members. They also suggest ways that members and workers can strive to overcome oppression and the blindness due to privilege, ways we shall seek to portray throughout this book. These include analyses of gendering processes, of barriers to relationships, and of racism and sexism, as well as ways of combatting these through consciousness raising, resistance to oppression, challenges to power and status, and attention to political and personal dynamics.

Summary

In Chapter 1, we presented the model of group work to be utilized in this text, which included an explanation of how this model seeks to be relevant to the many settings in which group work is practiced through the use of a typology of group purposes. Each of these purposes requires adaptations of the model, including variations in procedures directed at individual members, the group, and the extra-group environment. Other features of the model that were discussed include the following: the view of the group as a mutual aid system; the requirement that goals and means of achieving them be specified behaviorally; and, that outcomes be evaluated. The professional values embedded in the model were enumerated.

Endnotes

1. Ruth Middleman and Gale Goldberg, "Social Group Work," in *Encyclopedia of Social Work* (New York: National Association of Social Workers, 1987): 714.

2. Martin Sundel, Paul H. Glasser, Rosemary Sarri, and Robert Vinter, eds., *Individual Change Through Small Groups*, 2nd ed. (New York: Free Press, 1985).

3. Paul H. Glasser and Charles D. Garvin, "An Organizational Model," in *Theories of Social Work with Groups*, eds. Robert W. Roberts and Helen Northen (New York: Columbia University Press, 1976): 75–115.

4. Paul H. Glasser and Charles D. Garvin, "Social Group Work: The Organizational and Environmental Approach," in *Encyclopedia of Social Work* (New York: National Association of Social Workers, 1977), II: 1338.

5. Barbara B. Solomon, *Black Empowerment: Social Work in Oppressed Communities* (New York: Columbia University Press, 1976): 19.

6. Marianne Walters, "A feminist perspective in family therapy," in *Gender and Power in Families,* eds. Rosine Jozef Perelberg and Ann C. Miller (London and New York: Tavistock/Routledge, 1990): 13.

7. William Schwartz, "Social Group Work: The Interactionist Approach," in *Encyclopedia of Social Work* (New York: National Association of Social Workers, 1971), II: 1255.

8. Robert D. Vinter, "Social Group," in *Encyclopedia of Social Work* (New York: National Association of Social Workers, 1965): 715–24.

9. Catherine P. Papell and Beulah Rothman, "Social Group Work Models: Possession and Heritage," *Journal of Education for Social Work* 2, no. 2 (Fall 1966): 66–77.

10. Emmanuel Tropp, "Social Group Work: The Developmental Approach," in *Encyclopedia of Social Work* (New York: National Association of Social Workers, 1977): 1322.

11. Middleman and Goldberg, "Social Group Work.". J. Schopler and M. Galinsky (1995) "Group Practice Overview; in *Encyclopedia of Social Work,*"Vol. II: 1129–1142 (Washington, DC, NASW).

12. Robert W. Roberts and Robert Nee, eds., *Theories of Social Casework* (New York: Columbia University Press, 1970).

13. Robert W. Roberts and Helen Northen, eds., *Theories of Social Work with Groups* (New York: Columbia University Press, 1976), p. xi. The volume includes the work of the same authors from the *Encyclopedia of Social Work* (Tropp, Schwartz, Garvin, and Glasser) and, in addition, proponents of still other group work practice theories. Some wrote group work texts (Northen, Hartford); one is a proponent of the "functional" (Rankian) approach; several were associated with casework models with group work applications (McBroom on socialization groups, Parad and colleagues on crisis intervention in groups, Garvin, Reed, and Epstein on task-centered groups). A chapter by Gertrude Wilson on group work history and by Mary Louise Somers on approaches to problem solving in groups completed the volume.

14. See, for example, Norma Lang, "A Broad Range Model of Practice with the Social Work Group," *Social Services Review* 46 (1972): 76–89. Also see the concept of a "Mainstream" model in C. Papell and B. Rothman (1980) relating the mainstream model of social work with groups to group psychotherapy and the structured group approach, *Social Work with Groups*, 3 (2): 5–23.

15. For a thorough discussion of many of the approaches commented on here, see John B.P. Shaffer, and David Galinsky, *Models of Group Therapy and Sensitivity Training,* 2nd ed (Englewood Cliffs, N.J.: Prentice Hall, Inc., 1989.

16. Fritz Perls, R. F. Hefferline, and Paul Goodman, *Gestalt Therapy* (New York: Julian Press, 1951).

17. For Berne's own explication of his system, see Eric Berne, *Transactional Analysis in Psychotherapy* (New York: Grove Press, 1961).

18. Ibid.: 165–87.

19. H. Ezriel, "Psychoanalytic Group Therapy," in *Group Therapy,* eds. L. R. Wolberg and E. K. Schwartz (New York: Intercontinental Medical Book Corporation, 1973); S. H. Foulkes, *Therapeutic Group Analysis* (New York: International Universities Press, 1965); and Dorothy Stock Whitaker and Morton A. Lieberman, *Psychotherapy Through the Group Process* (New York: Lieber-Atherton, Inc., 1965).

20. W. R. Bion, *Experiences in Groups* (New York: Basic Books, 1959).

21. LaMar T. Empey and Maynard L. Erickson, *The Provo Experiment: Evaluating Community Control of Delinquency* (Lexington, Mass.: Heath, 1972).

22. Lloyd W. McCorkle, Albert Elias, and F. Lovell Bixby, *The Highfields Story* (New York: Holt, Rinehart & Winston, 1958).

23. Harry Vorrath and Larry Brendtro, *Positive Peer Culture*, 2nd ed. (Chicago: Aldine Publishing Co., 1985).

24. Empey, and Erickson, *The Provo Experiment*: 7.

25. Morton A. Lieberman and Lonnie R. Snowden, "Problems in Assessing Prevalence and Membership Characteristics of Self-Help Group Participants," in *Understanding the Self-Help Organization: Frameworks and Findings,* ed Tomas J. Powell (Thousand Oaks, Calif., 1994): 32–49.

26. J. L. Moreno, *Psychodrama* (Beacon, N.Y.: Beacon House, Inc., 1964).

27. For research on the effects of these groups, see M.A. Lieberman, I. Yalom, and M. Miles, *Encounter Groups: First Facts* (New York: Basic Books, 1973).

28. For a discussion of such principles, see Garry Martin and Joseph Pear, *Behavior Modification: What It Is and How to Do It,* 4th ed. (Englewood Cliffs, N.J.: Prentice Hall, 1992).

29. Donald Meichenbaum, *Cognitive-Behavior Modification: An Integrative Approach* (New York: Plenum Press, 1977); Michael J. Mahoney, *Cognition and Behavior Modification.* (Cambridge, Mass.: Ballinger Publishing Co., 1974).

30. S. Rose and C. LeCroy, "Group Treatment Methods," *Helping People Change*, 4th ed., eds F. Kanfer and A. Goldstein (New York: Pergamon Press, 1991): 422–453.

31. This discussion of laboratory training draws heavily on Shaffer and Galinsky, *Models of Group Therapy:* 183–200.

32. Shaffer and Galinsky, *Models of Group Therapy:* 202–203.

33. Mary Louise Somers, "Problem Solving in Small Groups," in *Theories of Social Work with Groups*, eds. Roberts and Northen: 331.

34. Ibid.: 333.

35. William Schwartz, "Between Client and System: The Mediating Function," in *Theories of Social Work with Groups*, eds. Roberts and Northen: 178.

36. Ibid.: 186–94.

37. William Schwartz, "The Social Worker in the Group," in *New Perspectives on Service to Groups* (New York: Columbia University Press, 1961).

38. For writing on this approach, see Sundel, Glasser, Sarri, and Vinter, eds., *Individual Change Through Small Groups.*

39. Rosemary C. Sarri and Maeda Galinsky, "A Conceptual Framework for Group Development," in *Individual Change Through Small Groups*, eds. Sundel, Glasser, Sarri, and Vinter: 70–86.

40. Charles D. Garvin, "Group Process: Usage and Uses in Social Work Practice," in *Individual Change Through Small Groups,* eds. Sundel, Glasser, Sarri, and Vinter: 203–25.

41. Robert D. Vinter, "Program Activities: An Analysis of Their Effects on Participant Behavior," in *Individual Change Through Small Groups,* eds. Sundel, Glasser, Sarri, and Vinter: 226–36.

42. Charles Garvin and others, "Group Work Intervention in the Social Environment," in *Individual Change Through Small Groups,* eds. Sundel, Glasser, Sarri and Vinter: 277–93.

43. Emmanuel Tropp, "Developmental Theory," in *Theories of Social Work with Groups,* eds. Roberts and Northen: 198–99.

44. Ibid.

45. Ibid.: 213.

46. Alan F. Klein, *Effective Group Work* (New York: Association Press, 1972).

47. Margaret Hartford, "Group Methods and Generic Practice," in *Theories of Social Work with Groups,* eds. Roberts and Northen, pp. 45–74. Also see her effort to portray knowledge about groups for all social workers, in *Groups in Social Work* (New York: Columbia University Press, 1972).

48. Margaret Hartford, "Group Methods and Generic Practice,": 54–55.

49. Saul Bernstein, ed., *Exploration in Group Work* (Boston: Boston University School of Social Work, 1965).

50. A recent statement of her model is in Helen Northen, "Psychosocial Practice in Small Groups," in *Theories of Social Work with Groups,* eds. Roberts and Northen, pp. 116–52. An extensive presentation of her ideas is found in Helen Northen, *Social Work with Groups* 2nd ed. (New York: Columbia University Press, 1988).

51. Sheldon D. Rose, *Working with Adults in Groups: Integrating Cognitive Behavioral and Small Group Strategies* (San Francisco: Jossey-Bass, 1989); Sheldon D. Rose, *Working with Children and Adolescents in Groups* (San Francisco: Jossey-Bass, 1987).

52. Sheldon Rose, *Working with Adults in Groups.*

53. Eleanor Reardon Tolson, William J. Reid, and Charles D. Garvin, *Generalist Practice: A Task-Centered Approach* (New York: Columbia University Press, 1994). See especially Chapters 10–13, which deal with task-centered group work.

54. William Reid and Laura Epstein, *Task-Centered Casework* (New York: Columbia University Press, 1972).

55. Some British examples are Jalna Hanmer and Daphne Statham, *Women and Social Work* (Houndmills, Basingstoke, Hampshire and London: Macmillan Education Ltd., 1988) and S. Butler and C. Wintram, *Feminist Groupwork* (London: sage, 1991). American examples are C. M. Brody, ed. *Women's Therapy Groups: Paradigms of Feminist Treatment* (New York: Springer, 1987) and E. Lewis (1992), "Regaining Promise: Feminist Perspectives for Social Group Work Practice," in *Social Work with Groups,* 15 (2/3): 217–284.

56. Charles D. Garvin and Beth G. Reed, "Small Group Theory and Social Work Practice: Promoting Diversity and Social Justice or Recreating Inequities," in *Human Behavior Theory: A Diversity Framework,* ed. Roberta R. Greene (New York: Aldine de Gruyter, 1994); Charles D. Garvin and Beth G. Reed, "Sources and Visions for Feminist Group Work: Reflective Processes, Social Justice, Diversity, and Connection," in *Feminist Visions for Social Work,* ed. Nan Van den Bergh (Silver Springs, Md.: NASW, 1995).

C h a p t e r 2

Group Work Activities and Settings

The Significance of the Agency

Most group work as well as social work is practiced under the auspices of social agencies. These agencies have been established either by government or private citizens to meet a variety of social needs such as those related to physical and mental health, to specified populations (children, the aged), to resource deficits (financial assistance), or to the enhancement of the quality of life (education and the use of leisure time).

Chapter 2 will discuss the agency settings in which group work is practiced and how these settings affect the group. It will be followed by a summary of the history of group work to help the reader understand its scope and diversity.

Some social workers, including group workers, engage in private practice in which the worker directly recruits clients who then pay a fee. Private practice, therefore, tends to serve the more affluent. Because our model emphasizes service to the oppressed, we do not discuss private practice, although many group work principles do apply to it.

The agencies that offer group services include those in the public sector such as departments of welfare or community mental health, state institutions for the mentally ill, and schools. Those maintained by private boards (often with government assistance) include family agencies, child guidance clinics, and community centers. These agencies do not merely promote a group in a neutral way and then disengage from it; they influence the group at all stages of its development from conception to termination. A worker cannot effectively work with a group, therefore, without understanding, utilizing, and sometimes seeking to change agency conditions. Major issues related to this are how to involve the group and how to cope with the fact that the worker is an employee of the agency as well as a professional.

As a consequence, in this book we identify with what Hasenfeld calls "an organization practice model" and not a "clinical practice model."[1] The latter "focuses primarily (and often exclusively) on client-change agent relations and the purposeful use of these relations for change, with minimal attention given to the organization within which such relations exist or to the impact the organization has on the entire change process."[2] This chapter is devoted to helping the reader understand organizational effects on group work: Chapter 8 will present related change strategies.

The current range of group work activities and their relationship to the sponsoring agencies will be more meaningful if the history of group work is understood. This history is an exciting one in which group workers struggled to develop their ideas and to overcome opposition to them. An understanding of history should also help the reader see why the models described in the previous chapter were created, as well as the controversies surrounding them.

Group Work History

In discussing the history of group work, we must describe events that occurred before the phrase *group work* was even used. This is because important developments took place that would later be labeled "group work," and the individuals involved in these would later call themselves "group workers." This history, then, can be divided into five periods: the emergence of group work (1861 to 1927); the clarification of the method (1928 to 1946); the diffusion of practice (1947 to 1963); the move to the generic (1964 to 1979); and the revitalization of group work (1979 and after).

The Emergence of Group Work: 1861 to 1927

Developments in American society during this period that gave the greatest impetus to group services were the emergence of the United States and other countries as industrial societies, the shift of large populations from rural to urban settings to support such industrialization, and the immigrations from Europe, Mexico, and Asia. This led to the entrapment of people in communities that were overcrowded, unhealthy, and deteriorating. Many of these people were also hindered from improving their occupational status and felt powerless to change these conditions. These factors stimulated the creation of organizations to ameliorate these circumstances through progressive social reform activities.

One of the first agencies to respond to these problems through group services was the Young Men's Christian Association, organized in the United States in 1851 "to improve the spiritual condition of young men in the drapery and trades"; this developed into the broader objective of improving the "mental, social and physical condition of all young men of good moral character."[3]

The Young Women's Christian Association was founded in the United States fifteen years later. In the years after that, many additional organizations with similar orientations emerged, such as the Girl's Friendly Society of the United States (1877) and the Boys' Clubs of America (1906). According to one writer, these organizations "looked to the face-to-face group to restore opportunities for the good life taken from people by the speed and ruthlessness of post-Civil War industrialization."[4]

A more vigorous reform thrust, however, was provided by the introduction of the settlement house into the United States, inspired by similar institutions developed in England. Stanton Coit, after a visit to Toynbee Hall in London, established the Neighborhood Guild on the lower east side of New York in 1886. The settlement idea spread rapidly, and in 1891 there were six settlements in the United States; by 1900 there were more than four hundred.

The idea behind the settlements was that people interested in the problems of the poor could understand them better by participating in their community life. Settlements sought to create a variety of programs to ameliorate the specific problems of their communities. Thus settlements sponsored such diverse activities as kindergartens and preschool sessions, adult education, leisure time and cultural arts group, social action committees, and neighborhood councils—all group-oriented activities. Settlements, in contrast to many other social services that emphasized adjustment to the social order, had a social change focus. Their workers sought changes in social conditions as a way of attaining their objectives.

Group workers have tended to glorify the settlement movement and to forget the important principle that institutions are products of their times, and statements about institutions by contemporaries will suffer from this. The settlements were no exception, and a recent historical account by Berman-Rossi and Miller points out that the settlements had an "uneasy, ambivalent relation with and virtual neglect of service to African-Americans during their early years."[5] This was despite the strong tradition of mutual aid among blacks.

Berman-Rossi and Miller further state that

> *This historic "truth" appears to be that the "preferred" groups served by the settlements were the European immigrants, not African-American migrants. Europeans were apparently thought to be better able to identify with and be influenced by the cultural and social ideals of the settlements, their leadership, and their "settlers." The goal of assimilation was apparently intended for European-Americans only. This, indeed, is an unsettling irony to contemplate and rationalize. In the main, African-Americans were not sought or encouraged to use settlement services, particularly settlements where whites were ubiquitously present.[6]*

These authors extensively examined the historical literature and soundly conclude that this situation was clearly a product of racism. At the time the social work pioneers were creating settlements, blacks were being segregated in the same cities as the settlements, and these pioneers did little to confront this. Berman-Rossi and Miller cite, for example, the work of Philpott,[7] who demonstrated that settlements accepted the 1929 drive for restrictive covenants. Several settlement leaders such as Woods even justified such segregation.[8]

Nevertheless, black citizens were motivated by the same forces as those affecting other citizens to organize neighborhood services. Berman-Rossi and Miller offer a number of examples of this, such as the Institutional Church and Social Settlement, Trinity Mission, and the Negro Fellowship League, but all of these efforts suffered severely from lack of funds. [9]

The work of authors such as Berman-Rossi and Miller is important in reminding us that while we have much to be proud of in the history of group work, there are also many limitations and errors in judgment to examine. Such information not only helps us understand how our legacy may affect our current efforts, but also provides us with reason to approach our future with humility and a great deal of self-reflection.

Closely related to the development of the YMCA and YWCA and the settlements was the emergence of the Jewish Community Centers and the Young Men's and Women's Hebrew Associations. These organizations had philosophies similar to those of the Ys. A difference, however, was that they were often sponsored by the more affluent western European Jews who, having come to this country before eastern European Jews, used these associations to "Americanize" the latter group.[10]

During this period, there was a lack of professional identification among workers in these various agencies, who were referred to by their settings such as Y or scout leaders or settlement workers. While people from a number of professions such as education, psychology, sociology, and social work discussed with each other how to utilize groups, there was no agreement regarding a professional auspice.

Within social work itself, beyond those people who worked with groups, there was little appreciation of the value of group experience. However, Mary Richmond, one of the pioneers in the development of casework practice, began, in her later works, to emphasize a broad conception of social work practice and in 1920 wrote of the importance of "small group psychology."[11]

One writer who influenced these early workers was Mary P. Follett, a political scientist. In her book *The New State* Follett states that she thought solutions to social problems would emerge from the creation of groups in neighborhoods and around social interests.[12] Another thinker important to these workers was John Dewey, who developed the idea of progressive education. According to one view of the period, the social group work method "was an application of the principles of progressive education to small informal groups in leisure time settings."[13]

Group work, at first, was closely associated with community development concepts, and, in fact, the origins of community organization method and its citizens participation focus cannot be distinguished from the beginnings of group work. Another influential writer was Eduard C. Lindeman, who was interested in the fostering of community groups, also, and their role in a functioning democracy.[14]

Although these ideas and programs were developed in an atmosphere of excitement among reformers, educators, and social workers involved in them, it was not until the end of this period that a course in group work was introduced into a school of social work. The first course was taught by Mildred Chadsey at Western Reserve University in 1923. This began a long and productive period of that schools's commitment to the development of group work. Virtually all of the pioneers among group-oriented social workers either taught at Western Reserve or were closely associated with its faculty.

We chose 1927 to mark the end of this period of group work history because by then it was clear that a new approach had emerged. Evidence for this was that Western Reserve University, in that year, significantly increased its group services curriculum. Many agencies committed their resources to group activities, and people such as Kaiser, Newstetter, and Williamson drew upon these experiences to conceptualize a theory of practice.

Clarification of the Method: 1928 to 1946

The further development of group work from 1928 until the end of World War II was affected by two major cataclysms at the beginning and ending of this period: the depression and the war. The depression posed a new challenge to social reformers who believed that their earlier efforts had contributed to progress toward a humanitarian society. Social workers now were forced to question the validity of adjusting people to the existing social order. This gave impetus to group workers who saw groups as a vehicle for promoting social change. It is not surprising, therefore, that these years were productive for group work.

First, this increased awareness of the importance of group services was associated with an enhanced professional identity. Gertrude Wilson relates an interesting anecdote associated with this process. In 1927 Wilbur Newstetter of Western Reserve University and Walter Pettit of the New York School for Social Work (now Columbia University School of Social Work) were traveling together on a long train ride to the National Conference of Social Work. Newstetter could only describe the group work project at Western Reserve that had just begun, as he did not know what to call it. "Pettit said that it sounded to him as if the project would demonstrate the delivery of social services through groups and that at his school they call the delivery of social services to individuals *casework*; why not call this Western Reserve project *group work*."[15] Wilson explains that the phrase "group work" had been used before this time, in a programmatic sense, in religious education and adult education contexts. Newstetter was innovative in using "group work" to designate a social work method.

During the 1930s and 1940s, group work continued to be practiced primarily in the Ys, settlements, Jewish Centers, and scouts. It was a productive and peaceful phase of development in these agencies as they strove to meet the needs of people affected by depression and then war. Controversy, when it existed, was found between some professionals and educators as they struggled with the creation of a practice theory and a professional identity for group workers.

The creation of a *social work* identity for group workers posed a challenge. People interested in group work, such as Coyle, Kaiser, Wilson, and Newstetter, were closely related to social work; but it took several years for their efforts to take organizational form. The years 1935 and 1936 were important in this respect. In 1935 the National Conference of Social Work agreed to institute a section on group work, and a number of important papers were delivered at the 1935 meeting.[16] Group workers were also active on another organizational front. The National Association for the Study of Group Work was formed in 1936, and provided an organizational form for group workers to further their practice interests.

As group work pioneers advanced their ideas through social work channels, major conflicts appeared. One speaker at the 1935 National Conference saw group work as a "social mechanism perfectly competent people utilize to achieve their own ends."[17] He saw social workers' use of groups as an adaptation of something broader and more basic than simply a social work method. At the same time, caseworkers took issue, not with group work philosophy, but with the seriousness of group work as an enterprise. Wilson explains that group workers were described stereotypically as people who "play with children" or "run dances."[18]

Nevertheless, by 1937 ten schools of social work offered courses in group work. Others rejected this type of education because of its ties to recreation. Within the next two years, nevertheless, the number of schools offering group work education grew to seventeen. Six more schools taught about group work but did not provide an appropriate field experience.[19]

Coincident with these organizational activities was the development of group work practice theory. The audience for this was expanded when the National Association for the Study of Group Work established a publication in 1939—*The Group—in Education,*

Recreation, Social Work. A number of texts were also written in the 1930s that still continue to have an influence.

We consider this period of clarification of the method to have ended in 1946 because by then group workers had consolidated their existence as practitioners of an established method. They had formed the American Association of Group Workers, produced a consensus document on professional standards, and expanded their activities into new settings. This latter development was an important component of the next period as the influence of group work continued to grow.

The Diffusion of Practice: 1947 to 1963

As a result of the depression and the war, the idea of large-scale government involvement in programs and services led to the expansion of social work practice. On the other hand, the state of foreign affairs, particularly the cold war with the Soviet Union, was associated with fears of an "internal communist menace." The accusation that reformers were "subversive" impeded the social reform spirit of the previous period. Since many group workers were associated with the spirit of social reform, this period affected their endeavors.

These decades of the 1940s and 1950s, therefore, were not ones in which group workers sought to attain social change, but were ones in which they endeavored to clarify and expand group work practice theory and the movement of that practice into new settings. The connection of group work with social action was muted. An example is provided by the comparison of two discussions of social action printed during this era. The first, written by Grace Coyle in 1948, describes a situation in which a group of young people planned a lobbying strategy for Fair Employment Practice legislation.[21] Five years later, Alan Klein, in his discussion of social action, gave an example of a member of a group expelled by the police from a park. Through subsequent visits to the police station, the group was helped to develop a closer relationship with the police.[22] This latter type of accommodation to society was typical of the 1950s and contrasted with Coyle's illustration.

At the beginning of this period, ambiguity existed as to whether group work was a social work or an educational specialization. A crucial consensus was reached at the meeting of the National Conference on Social Work in 1946 in support of Grace Coyle's conclusion that "group work as a method falls within the larger scope of social work *as a method.*"[23] Coyle came to this conclusion through her analysis of the common concerns of caseworkers, group workers, and community organizers. This consensus led to the formation of the American Association of Group Workers (AAGW) as a professional membership organization, with membership based on the possession of professional training.

In this organizational environment, theoretical developments received great encouragement; many influential books were published, and *The Group*, now under AAGW sponsorship, continued to play an important role.[24] With this type of progress, it was inevitable that group workers would bring their skills to the performance of new tasks in new settings.

While the predominant employment of group workers continued to be in settlements, Ys, and youth organizations, demonstrations of the group technique were conducted in psychiatric services, hospitals, family agencies, correctional institutions, and schools. This was enhanced by the use of groups for the treatment of World War II veterans with psychiatric problems,[25] with reported beneficial effects. Support for many of these experiments with group work was provided by government funds as well as by the National Association of Social Workers.[26]

The entry of group workers into rehabilitation settings, nevertheless, led to considerable debate during the 1950s. Writers such as Robert Vinter argued that the preponderance of group workers in community agencies was a "retreat from the profession's historic mission of service to those most in need."[27] On the other hand, some group workers saw this shift as withdrawal from social action responsibilities.[28] Others also feared that the preventive function of group work would be lost.

A factor that created dilemmas for group workers was the idea that the social work method could be viewed in a generic sense. The "generic" idea was paralleled and enhanced by the 1962 decision of the National Association of Social Workers to eliminate "sections" devoted to separate methods such as group work. The next phase of group work history found many writers as well as group workers seeking to conceptualize social work as a single method.

The Move to the Generic Method: 1964 to 1979

The events in the society that affected the development of group work in the 1960s and 1970s were the War on Poverty and the Civil Rights Movement. Both led to pressures on social workers to see problems from new, often more sociological, perspectives and to seek ways to solve such problems that were not restricted by the traditional dogmas.

Thus the government was committed to funding experiments with new solutions to delinquency, poverty, and mental illness. In conceiving of such experiments, professionals were influenced by the Civil Rights struggles to consider comprehensive interventions. In addition, data from the evaluation of previously utilized interventions led to serious concern about their effectiveness. Thus one idea that emerged was that a combination of these methods would be more effective than only one.

Developments in group work practice theory during the 1947 to 1963 period facilitated the development of a generic approach. Because group work was increasingly practiced in psychiatric, medical, child welfare, correctional, and other "special" settings, the needs of group members were now similar to those of casework clients. Approaches to group work evolved in practice that utilized concepts familiar to caseworkers. For example, Robert Vinter, in his writings in the 1950s, prescribed the development of treatment goals for individuals served in groups and indicated these should be related to individual diagnoses. He saw the group as a means for achieving such treatment goals rather than as an end in itself. Writers such as Fritz Redl and Gisela Konopka also wrote about group work utilizing psychoanalytic concepts also employed by caseworkers.[29]

These trends in group work practice also led to the recognition that there were now schools of group work practice, namely, the ones described in the preceding chapter. Some of these schools were compatible with the generic practice idea, but writers associated with other schools feared that the essence of group work would be lost in a generic approach.

The latter writers' fears were not unfounded. Very few schools of social work retained separate group work sequences (a few of the exceptions were the Boston University School of Social Work and the University of Connecticut School of Social Work). Some schools offered a course in group work, more often that not as an elective that few students chose.

Presumably, since Council of Social Work Education requirements mandated educating students about groups, the schools included group work content in "generic" practice courses. Doubts were expressed by group workers as to how much content on groups was, in fact, offered and how competent the faculty were with regard to such content. This was doubly true if these faculty had not studied or practiced group work.

Groups were still being conducted in many agencies. The only conclusion many group workers were able to reach was that there was an assumption that one could conduct a group with no specialized training. This was not an assumption these workers could support.

The current controversies that surround group work stem from the historical events just described. Those who maintain that the group as an entity has a vital role in a democracy and should be nurtured by social workers are the heirs of the tradition of Follet and Lindeman, who wrote at a time when democracy was seen as threatened by rapid industrialization, war, and economic depression. Others more likely to emphasize the group as a means to individual change are in the tradition of Redl and Slavson, who were allied with psychology and psychiatry. The development of group work as therapy began during the individually oriented years of the 1920s[30] and continued in the 1950s when an ideology of individual rather than social responsibility for one's problems was strong.

The Revitalization of Group Work: 1979 and After

During the 1960s and 1970s, when major efforts were underway to integrate direct practice methods in social work, little attention was paid to the development of group work theory and to the quality and quantity of practice with groups in agencies. Nevertheless, there was growing concern regarding this inattention among practitioners and teachers who remained committed to work with groups. Several important steps were taken by such individuals to reaffirm the importance of work with groups *within* the arena of direct practice and the necessity of continuing to develop the theoretical base for work with groups.

One such step was the creation of the journal *Social Work with Groups* under the creative and capable editorship of Catherine Papell of Adelphi University and Beulah Rothman, first of Adelphi and then of Barry University.[31] This journal is not only devoted to articles for direct service practitioners but also to those involved with group issues in the agency and the community. It filled a gap left when *The Group* ceased publication under the mistaken assumption that the more general journals in social work could provide sufficient coverage of group-related developments.

Another important step occurred when people concerned about group work assembled during the 1978 Annual Program Meeting of the Council on Social Work Education. They created the Committee for the Advancement of Social Work with Groups, now the International Association for the Advancement of Social Work with Groups (a membership organization). The initial activity of the committee was to sponsor the first Annual Symposium on Social Work with Groups, held in Cleveland, Ohio, in October 1979. This location was chosen in recognition of the role played by Grace Coyle in the creation of contemporary group work practice and her association with Case Western Reserve University in Cleveland. The opening session of the symposium, in which Gisela Konopka, Mary Louise Somers, Margaret Hartford, James Garland, and William Schwartz were participants, was devoted to a panel discussion of the contributions of Grace Coyle. Over four hundred individuals attended, double the expectation of the symposium organizers. Many excellent presentations on all aspects of practice were offered, and the atmosphere of the meetings resembled a long-postponed reunion with old friends.

The symposium has become an annual event, with over one hundred presentations each year devoted to all aspects of work with groups. These offerings have been finding their way into all social work publications and have enriched all of direct practice. The conferences are sponsored by local planning groups, whose geographical spread attests to the international nature of this reemphasis on groups. Sponsorship has come from such areas as Arlington, Texas, Hartford, Toronto, Detroit, Chicago, and Los Angeles. People attending these meetings have come from all continents.

These events have undoubtedly affected education as well as practice in social work. Schools have reexamined their group offerings, and practitioners have sought postgraduate education in group work. Other activities have emerged, such as an annual symposium on empirical group work practice and the creation of local group work associations.

This is truly an exciting time for people interested in work with groups. We anticipate that the above activities, as well as many we do not have space to cite, will lead to a vigorous growth period for group practice.

In conclusion, when the social climate breeds concerns for society's democratic functioning, the role of the worker as facilitator of group process is favored, as in the 1930s when Grace Coyle's work was influential and in the 1960s when Schwartz's ideas influenced group workers profoundly. In contrast, in the more conservative atmosphere of the 1950s, group work was defined by one writer as "the systematic ways in which the worker affects social and group process to achieve specified objectives," and group process in social work groups was defined as "group process when consciously affected by the worker toward specified ends."[32]

In the later 1970s, when movements for social change were in abeyance, behavior modification approaches were of considerable interest, and a leading theorist on social work with groups wrote that "treatment planning involves choosing from a number of highly specific procedures that have been demonstrated to be related to achieving behavioral change goals."[33] The intent here is not to criticize these ideas but to place them in the social and historical contexts conducive to their development.

The 1980s, while representing a conservative political climate, was a period in which social workers sought to maintain social commitments despite the prevailing political atmosphere. The reaffirmation of group work, with its historical investment in individual empowerment and social change, was part of this professional mission.

The 1990s brought some new challenges to group workers, including the move toward *managed care* in health care. Use of group services for treatment purposes is likely to be supported by the individual's health plan. The administrators of the plan determine what institutions may be reimbursed for services and what problems may be treated under this reimbursement. Time limits are set and reports of progress in attaining goals are required.

All social work services, including group services, are affected by this arrangement. On the one hand, group services might benefit if they are viewed as economical. On the other hand, health provider organizations will determine which group services are eligible for reimbursement. The long-term impact of these institutional changes on group work is still unclear, although it is likely that short-term, highly structured group forms will be favored.

A tension exists between group workers who see themselves as altering behavior versus those who have the vision of a facilitating group process. As Perry London points out so well, ". . . means are being found, in all the crafts and sciences of man, society, and life, that will soon make possible precise control over much of people's individual actions, thoughts, emotions, moods and wills."[34] Both practitioners and philosophers have speculated on the possibility that such a development can be halted because of the threat posed to liberty. London, however, is pessimistic: "It is plain to anyone who troubles to look that once the potential for a particular technological development is clear, the actual technology follows, sometimes sooner, sometimes later, but without fail."[35] London's inevitable conclusion is, "The future, already upon us, must be controlled."[36]

As far as group work is concerned, group workers considered themselves as facilitators of group process before the emergence of technologies of behavior control. Some workers, now, with the creation of behavioral techniques, seek to implement group work procedures with immediate and potent effects. In this respect, group workers join the ranks of teachers, psychologists, and producers of the mass media, who can be divided into those who maintain a facilitative and educational stance versus those who seek to attain predetermined goals by the most expeditious means possible.

Now that we have examined the evolution of group work theories and practice settings, we shall analyze in detail the way settings currently affect practice. This discussion, as we stated earlier, should help the practitioner see ways of using agency conditions as well as, on occasion, seeking to change them.

Agency Conditions That Affect Group Work

Why Agencies Establish Groups

To supply a foundation for the worker's evaluation of agency conditions that affect group services, we will first list and discuss such conditions. We will then describe the current range of group work activities in terms of a classification of types of agency purposes.

Example: The X Family Agency decided to offer a "drop-in-group" to help mothers with young children discuss concerns around child rearing. Baby-sitting services were also provided while they attended the group.

Example: The Planned Parenthood Clinic offered "rap sessions" for teens concerned about sexuality and sexual behaviors.

Agencies always have a reason for allocating staff time to group work services, as the above examples imply. Sometimes these reasons are explicit and embodied in formal proposals or descriptions of services. Thus an agency may state that it supports groups to enhance the classroom behavior of school children or to assist previously hospitalized psychotic patients cope with a return to the community. At other times, there is no specific statement about the group work program, and one must refer to the overall program descriptions of the agency to infer agency purposes for groups. There also can be "hidden" purposes such as the transfer of clients from individual treatment caseloads because their workers no longer wish to work with them. Purposes may also be stated in very general terms, such as "helping children adjust better to institutional conditions," or they may be specific, such as "helping unwed mothers decide whether or not to place their children for adoption after delivery."

The agency purposes for the group will have a strong influence on group processes throughout the life of the group and will influence who is referred to the group, how the member is prepared (or not prepared) for the group, what kinds of group activities are reinforced, and how the agency is likely to respond to requests from the group and its worker.

An example of the way purpose is influential is that of a group of ten- and eleven-year-olds meeting in a community center. The agency composed the group from children referred from the local public school because of complaints about their classroom behavior. The agency had contacted the youths and their families, explained the *purposes* of the group, and inquired as to the youths' interest in participation.

When the youngsters got together, they asked if they could take trips. They were informed that this was not the *purpose* of the group, as the workers had explained prior to the group's first meeting. A trip might be taken, however, to reward the group for working out the details of how the group's meetings would be used to accomplish its *purposes*. The agency had equipped a room with some school supplies so the youngsters might, at some point, simulate their school room. The worker had asked for this resource because of the *purpose* of the group.

Group workers have the responsibility, before the beginning of a group, to help the agency consider purposes that can be accomplished through groups. Some purposes should not be implemented, such as attempting to cause members to accept agency injustices. Other purposes may be unethical, such as manipulating members to accept goals they might otherwise reject. The worker should also help the agency evaluate how its purposes are being achieved through groups so unfeasible ones might be modified. Workers should make clear to members what the group's purposes are and should help members to negotiate with the agency regarding these purposes either through the worker or directly.[37]

How Members Are Referred to or Recruited for the Groups

Example: In a psychiatric clinic, a worker asked other workers to refer socially isolated young adults to him, as he planned to start a group to help such persons make friends.

Example: In a child and family service agency, a policy was announced that all unmarried, pregnant women seeking help with decisions about adoption would be offered membership in a group established for that purpose. Those who expressed concern about group participation or who had other reasons for not being included in a group would be offered individual service.

Example: In a residential treatment center, a group worker offered to hold weekly meetings with the youths living in Cottage D.

These examples illustrate several ways people may be secured for group work services. The agency usually establishes recruitment procedures that have substantial influence on the future of the group, including agency intake itself, and when this process eliminates or recruits clients of specified ages, ethnic groups, social statuses, or with certain problems, the range of group services is predetermined. Subsequent to agency intake, the way clients are recruited for groups varies; for example, people may be offered individual services first and then may be referred to groups by "caseworkers." This may be before or after individual services have begun. Alternatively, group work may be presented as an option when individuals enter the agency.

When the agency stresses individual services, Hasenfeld hypothesizes that group work services will be considered marginal and group work practice ". . . confronts the problem of formulating a common basis for clients to interact as a group."[38] Thus the worker and clients will spend substantial energy identifying and maintaining the rationale for the group's existence.

In some cases, the agency interacts primarily with all its clients on a group basis as, for example, in residential institutions, where the group workers will often be in competition with other people who also transact with groups, such as teachers, nurses, and custodial personnel. This can blur the particular functions to be served by the group work experience.

When enrollment for groups is decided at the point of agency intake, who decides and how this is decided are important. One of the major influences a worker has on group events is through the composition of the group (see p. 54), and this depends on a sufficiently diverse pool of potential members. The composition procedures the workers utilize can be better implemented when they are part of decision making for services rather than when they are "political" and must depend on the beliefs of staff to whom the clients have been assigned and who must relinquish them.

Another major dimension of the intake process of concern to group workers is whether agency services as well as group work services are voluntary or compulsory. Again, according to Hasenfeld, in the latter case "the group is likely to develop apathy, self-aggression, frustration, and inability to adapt to free situations, which could undermine any treatment objective."[39]

For example, group services are offered frequently in prisons and psychiatric treatment facilities, where group members are pressured to attend. Much time is then spent by the worker discussing member reactions to determine if a basis for working together can be developed. (This process of identifying such a basis—the development of a contract—is discussed in Chapter 4; a more extensive discussion of issues in working with involuntary clients is presented in Chapter 13).

The way each member experiences entering the agency and then the group is important. As Yalom demonstrates, members will be more committed to the group and will interact more with each other if prepared individually for the group.[40] This procedure, however, takes time prior to the first meeting of the group, and the agency must facilitate this.

The ability of the worker to affect these intake events is a function of his or her status in the agency, an issue which we turn to now.

What Are the Status and Role of the Group Workers in the Agency?

Example: John's job assignment included work with individuals, families, and groups. He was seen as a professional equal by the other social workers in the Community Mental Health Center.

Example: Alice was a group worker in a residential treatment center. When the caseworkers at the agency saw her, they always jokingly asked her where her whistle was to call the children to activities.

Example: Bill was one of a staff of workers in a large settlement house. All of the workers spent most of their time either working with groups or supervising people who did.

The way the agency defines the job of the group workers and the location of this person in the agency hierarchy will impact the group. If the major technology in the agency is one-to-one treatment, a separate cadre of workers usually offers group services, and initial assignments of cases are made to caseworkers; the activities of the group worker are then likely to be seen as relatively unimportant. Members of groups often perceive the low status of their worker and react accordingly, even to the extent of rejecting group services.

The status of group workers can vary beyond the division of labor between work with individuals and work with groups. People with expertise and interest in work with groups may or may not be represented in the administration of the agency. On the other hand, group workers might be either supervised by people defined as caseworkers or else segregated into a separate unit. Even though this pattern may become less dominant as social work practice becomes more generic, it will be found in a number of agencies. The impact of such arrangements is less power for the worker to secure resources for the group, to influence the pattern of referrals to the group, and to have his or her ideas considered in agency determination of group purposes.

The resolution of this issue is affected by whether group workers define their method as unique amidst the methods of casework and community organization, or whether work with groups is seen as a skill developed by all workers. In the former case, it is important that group workers have as much power as other practitioners to influence policy, particularly policy on how services are offered. In the latter case, people who work with groups will, by definition, have as much power as any other worker. As indicated earlier, we prefer to conceive of group work as part of a range of skills to be developed by most workers.

Which Resources Do Agencies Allocate to the Group?

Example: The Child Guidance Clinic rented the gymnasium of a nearby YMCA for the use of an adolescent group.

Example: The family agency furnished one of its rooms with comfortable sofas and arm chairs for use as a group therapy room.

Example: The probation service established a small budget for refreshments at group meetings.

Group activities are enhanced if the worker has space, equipment, consultation, and other resources available. With the possible exception of play therapy and other treatment modalities for use with children, there is more of a tradition regarding the use of material objects and space in group work than in other social work approaches. This is because of the use group workers have made of a variety of program media to provide new experiences for members. Group workers have often required suitable space to engage, for example, in games with children or to help adults feel that this is a different experience from a class or committee meeting. Group members in residential situations may want to visit places outside of the institution as part of their learning experiences, which leads to such costs as transportation and worker time beyond the "therapeutic hour." All of these contingencies require agencies to consider the costs involved in group sessions. Group workers, in helping agencies establish such services, should be forthright in making this known to agency administration.

How Targets for Change Are Selected by Agencies

Example: A school system defined the targets of its school social work program as those classroom behaviors that would enhance learning. Family and peer relationship problems were not to be dealt with. Workers were expected to refer such situations to other agencies.

Example: The Child Guidance Clinic, because of the psychiatric orientation of its administrator, the focus of its consulting psychiatrist, and the material asked for on agency recording forms, oriented its efforts to parent-child, parent-peer, and child-authority transactions. Little attention was paid to job or community resource issues also of concern to clients.

As illustrated by these examples, agency conditions may predispose a worker to select some aspects of client-agency-environment transactions rather than others as targets for change. This is related to our proposition that the targets of social work intervention are created by the interactions of people and their situations. This is similar to the contention of many family therapists that "problems" in families are defined by the family in ways based on the family's systemic requirements.[41]

The workers have a number of options as to how to approach this issue of the agency's preferred targets. One way is to describe agency definitions of problems to clients, who may then choose to seek services elsewhere. On the other hand, some clients may wish, often with the help of the worker, to change the agency's orientation so that attention is given to the clients' targets. When the agency's and clients' preferred targets coincide, either fortuitously or from negotiation, it is more likely that necessary resources for the group and the worker will be forthcoming. The worker, then, will not be caught in a conflict between member and agency desires that can be immobilizing for all concerned.

What Effect Agencies Have on Groups' Social and Physical Environment

Example: In the Child Guidance Clinic, the agency assigned the social relations group, a group formed to help socially isolated teenagers, to one of the agency's club rooms. The group was given a set of drawers to keep records of how members were performing "social tasks" and a bulletin board to post clippings and quotations selected by members.

Example: A community center assigned several workers to "reach out" to teenage gangs in the area. When one of these groups decided to come to the agency for meetings and activities, the agency assigned one hour a week in the gym for the group's exclusive use.

Again, according to Hasenfeld, "the capacity of the group to develop well-defined boundaries and identity is partly determined by its ability to establish and shape it own 'territory' according to its needs."[42] The same writer also states that "development of the group requires a space that provides some insulation from the environment and protection from excessive external disturbances."[43] As we shall see in Chapter 4, a *sine qua non* for the effectiveness of the group to help its members is the attraction it holds for them, that is, its cohesiveness. An often neglected factor in enhancing this is the environment the agency offers the group. This includes the physical setting for the group meeting as well as the following:

1. The ways that other people in the agency, in addition to the group worker, interact with group members. These people include other clients, receptionists, other professional staff, secretaries, and maintenance workers.

2. The decor of the agency. Whether the agency looks orderly and maintained is often interpreted by members as showing the esteem with which clients are held; also relevant is the meaning to the members of visible objects in terms of their culture. For example, one agency placed pictures of its benefactors in its rooms and these were mostly Caucasians. The largely black clientele did not feel the agency valued them until important people in black history were also honored by having their pictures prominently displayed.

3. The "social" aspects of the agency. Workers should attempt to see the agency through the eyes of the group members, who will usually be willing to share their perceptions when asked. The "social" environment of the agency includes the degree to which the staff members function as a team, understand and support one another, and display high morale. The workers cannot ignore these variables any more than they can ignore internal actions in the group.

How Agencies Interact with Groups' Indigenous Leaders

Example: In Agency A, the director sent a letter to the group asking it to nominate from among its members an advisory committee on group services.

Example: In Agency B, the worker notified the group that the type of services received by the group were to be discontinued by the agency. Several group members sought out the agency director to discuss this decision but were told by her receptionist that she would not be available for an appointment for several weeks.

People tend to emerge in groups who have greater influence over group processes than others, who function as spokespersons for the group, or who are authorized by other group members to represent the group in external affairs. Agency definitions of client's status will affect these individuals. In some group work situations, however, members conceive of themselves as recipients of a service and do not expect to be involved in any processes with the agency after they have joined the group. This is most often true of those voluntarily seeking help with personal problems in psychiatric outpatient facilities.

In other cases, group members perceive themselves as constituents rather than as clients, in the traditional sense of the word, and *do* expect to be consulted by the agency and involved in its affairs. This is usually true in community centers. In yet another type of agency, clients may feel alienated and powerless in relationship to social institutions (for example, welfare agencies or prisons). The noninvolvement of these persons in the agencies offering them group experiences is more evidence of their powerlessness. In these cases, such involvement may be therapeutic in itself.

An asset of the group experience is the group members' awareness that they may share similar concerns. Out of this springs the possibility of joint action which creates even more power for members. Some agencies may seek to reinforce this possibility, while others may fear the consequences of group pressures and may act to inhibit them.

This issue of involvement of group members in extragroup processes is related, also, to how much control the agency has over clients. The agencies with the most control are those in which the client is institutionalized, such as mental hospitals, residential treatment centers, and prisons. Substantial control is also exercised by agencies given legal legitimation for control, such as probation and psychiatric aftercare programs. The least control is, of course, exercised by agencies in which the client is there voluntarily (a community center) or where the client may be performing a service for the agency (adoptive parents of hard-to-place children).

Group members are often least involved in those agencies with the greatest degree of control over them. The control issue will affect the way members exercise options related to group program, create indigenous leadership, respond to worker decisions, and participate in selecting group goals and targets.

What Are Agencies' Attitudes to Service Ideologies and Technologies?

Example: An institution for adolescents was committed to the use of positive peer culture (PPC). Staff received training in this approach, and referral agencies were informed of this emphasis. As soon as youths were admitted, other group members explained the way the PPC group was conducted.

Example: The Child Guidance Clinic was directed by a psychoanalytically oriented psychiatrist. Workers were hired based on their knowledge of this theory. At case conferences, clients were assessed in terms of ego functioning. Group experiences were recommended when seen as enhancing such functioning.

Most agencies prefer particular theories, ideologies, and techniques. These are manifested in the way services are defined, people are interviewed for staff positions, assumptions are made about intake, consultants are recruited, and agency record forms are conceived. Such preferences govern the way workers are expected to act in groups.

Agency clarity regarding preferred treatment approaches can be supportive of workers and group members, as the workers will know what is expected of them and will receive rewards for meeting these expectations. Clients will know what the available service is. In some instances, clients may even be informed of the effects and effectiveness of the approach through research evidence or case example.

Problems can arise when approaches to group work are utilized that are either ineffective, inappropriate, or not desired by workers, clients, or both. Under these mandatory circumstances, short of leaving the agency, workers can do the following: seek to hire staff trained in appropriate technologies; or, together with group members, creatively develop new group procedures.

The involvement of group members in the choice of service technologies presupposes that they have some knowledge of such matters. We believe that this information ought to be made routinely available and that workers should find ways of explaining the nature of the services offered to group members.

How Intraorganizational Relationships Affect Groups

Example: The worker for a young boys' treatment group in the Community Mental Health Program was told by his supervisor that the group had been too noisy and rambunctious in recent meetings. The supervisor thought the worker should exercise firmer controls. The worker, in turn, lectured the boys at the next meeting about their behavior.

Example: The school staff morale was low because a recent millage election had failed and many services were to be cut. The worker, in the next few meetings of the group, was lethargic, did not pursue new topics of importance to the members, and was not empathic with the members.

Hasenfeld raises an important, yet subtle, issue when he states that "a process of 'isomorphism' occurs in which worker-group relations come to reflect the same structural properties of worker relations with staff members in the agency."[44] This phenomenon occurs because other agency personnel, particularly those in authority, provide models for the worker. Agency conditions affect the worker's emotional state, also, and set norms for what is and is not rewarded. Workers have several options in regard to this issue:

1. When problems arise in the group, the workers should analyze whether they parallel agencywide situations.
2. The worker can then consider whether action should be initiated at an agency or group level or both.
3. The worker, as agency concerns are discussed at a staff level, can consider their effect at a group level.
4. At times the worker can "buffer" the group from agency conditions by acting in ways that are at variance with these conditions. For example, workers should consult with group members on decisions even if they are not, themselves, consulted by administrators.
5. At times it becomes necessary to inform members about agency conditions that lead to undesirable consequences for the group; the members may then seek to initiate changes in such conditions, sometimes in concert with the group worker; they may try to isolate themselves from the effects of the conditions; or they may decide that the conditions are really not a problem for them or may even be constructive.

Thus far in this chapter we have outlined selected agency conditions that may affect group work practice. We believe all of these are relevant to group work in any agency but also that agencies with certain types of functions are likely to approach these in ways that differ from agencies with other functions. Some of these ways enhance group services; others hinder them. We shall now turn to an analysis of agency "types."

A Typology of Agency Purposes

To facilitate this analysis as well as to illustrate the possible range of group work activities, we have developed a classification of agency purposes. To us, the phrase "agency purpose" means either the purpose the agency fulfills for the society, for the clientele, or both. Sometimes the agency purposes are directed toward societal objectives that are not, at least initially, sought by clients (for example, prisons). At other times, the purposes are mutual (a job training agency established to reduce unemployment for clients who wish jobs). In presenting this classification, we draw attention to several considerations:

1. It is rare, if not impossible, to find an agency whose services represent only one purpose. Thus all agencies have several purposes, but many are likely to emphasize some more than others.
2. An issue for any agency is the extent to which it has clarified for itself, if not for its clientele or the general public, what its purposes are.
3. When an agency seeks to fulfill a purpose, some of its activities may conflict with other activities because the agency has conflicting purposes. An example of this was found in a school program. Schools are society's way of socializing youngsters into roles by imparting skills, as well as society's way of ensuring that behavior follows societal norms. Sometimes these two functions conflict, as when a youngster seeks a future role (for example, social radical) that some teachers believe is inconsistent with their value of maintaining the system.

Vinter[45] and Hasenfeld[46] describe the two major purposes of agencies as socialization and resocialization of the client. The former category involves helping persons viewed as "normal" and who are progressing from one status to another. Examples of this are assisting adolescents to assume adult responsibilities, middle-aged persons to plan for retirement, and school children to make better use of their learning environment. The latter category, resocialization, refers to helping people viewed as not experiencing "normal" phases of development or role transitions. Such people are often labeled "deviant," and therefore experience conflict with others. Working with inmates of prisons and mental hospitals and some clients of mental health programs is an example of the resocialization category.

Subpurposes

Upon further consideration of these two categories, socialization and resocialization, we concluded that each category should be further subdivided. Under the heading of "socialization," one subpurpose is to help individuals having difficulty deciding on socialization goals. We have termed this subpurpose *identity development*. One example of a client who required this type of service was a woman trying to raise her level of consciousness of emerging and changing women's roles so she could pursue them in a personally more satisfying way; another was a gay person who also sought to identify and follow newly emerging norms; and another was an adolescent confronted with the changing and conflicting patterns for youth. It is interesting that in our discussion of this categorization with practitioners, they noted that almost all agencies have to deal with the problem of identity development to some degree; that is, clients frequently seek to understand and relate themselves to changing and conflicting norms. This may, therefore, be a highly significant phenomenon in our culture that always affects agency services.

Once people have decided on socialization goals and values, the next logical step is to achieve their goals. We have termed this subpurpose *skill attainment*. This type of helping recognizes that many people—citizens, employees, students, parents, and adults—need help meeting role requirements.

In considering the category of resocialization, we also recognized two subpurposes. The first refers to people who have not yet determined that they wish to fulfill a nondeviant, socially acceptable role. Because society establishes institutions such as courts to bring about resocialization, we have termed this subpurpose *social control*. Relevant to this is the issue of whether or not or to what degree social work as a profession is an instrument of social control. It is evident, however, that social workers frequently are employed in agencies with social control functions.

In a process similar to socialization, some clients who become group members do accept or come to accept resocialization goals. The purpose of helping such people is called *rehabilitation*; the people helped in this manner include many clients of outpatient psychiatric facilities, aftercare programs, and treatment-oriented correctional programs.

In the remainder of this chapter, we shall describe the kinds of agencies and groups that seek to fulfill each of these subpurposes. Longer examples are provided in Chapters 11–14. Again, the reader is reminded that there is no assumption that agencies fall into only one category. At any given moment, however, a worker should be able to identify which purpose an agency, a program, a group, or a group session is fulfilling. This framework, then, is a means to describe the range of group work activities so that later we can describe the different ways workers should act in relationship to the purposes appropriate to the situation.

Identity Development

Example: Nine women in their twenties met in a "Young Mothers' Club" in a community center. They had all been recently married and had either a young child or were pregnant. All had worked to supplement their family's income, most at occupations such as secretary, salesperson, or waitress. They came together, originally, as a social club because several had gone to school or worked together. In the process of informal discussions, they discovered that they were all experiencing similar problems. These included the kinds of expectations their husbands held of them that denied them the equality they expected in their marriages. On the other hand, many did believe that mothers had more responsibilities than fathers for childrearing, and they were uncertain how this related to the issue of equality. They asked each other for help in resolving some of these concerns and, when the Community Center was told of this, it offered them the services of a group worker.

In the first few meetings, the worker helped these young women describe to each other how these issues were manifested in their own families. At times, they were embarrassed to describe some of their experiences, but the worker helped them through discussing norms of confidentiality and through sharing some details of her own life. The worker also used value clarification exercises to help the members decide what each believed most about her rights in her marriage. When it became apparent that most of the members had trouble explaining their beliefs to their husbands, the worker introduced some role plays to help them be more assertive. The worker also helped them plan a joint meeting with their husbands to discuss the roles of each partner in a marriage.

Similar types of experiences to help members identify conflicting norms to which they are exposed are now offered in a number of agencies. Examples of organizations that have arisen to respond to these needs include teen "rap centers" associated with community mental health agencies and planned parenthood clinics, women's and minority groups' consciousness-raising organizations, and many counseling programs associated with universities. In addition, private organizations and institutions (some for profit) have formed to make this type of service available to the large number of people who desire it. Such clients are generally self-referred and highly motivated to participate, although they may not always be clear about the group experience they seek.

Several aspects of group work service focused on identity development are illustrated by the example of the "Young Mothers' Group." The group was formed around people who experienced similar normative problems. Because they quickly recognized that they were dealing with parallel issues, they were able to support yet confront one another. They had somewhat different ideas about the resolution of value conflicts affecting young women today and, therefore, could help each other to examine alternative solutions. These characteristics made a group rather than an individual counseling experience a particularly valid one.

Skill Attainment

Example: A high school was aware that a number of black students were motivated to complete their high school program but had various handicaps: (1) poor preparation, as they had been educated in less adequate grammar schools than other students; (2) insufficient support from families, as many had only one parent; and (3) hostility from school personnel who labeled them unmotivated and incompetent and failed to give them the help they needed.

One of several programs the school used to reverse this cycle of failure was group work on a voluntary basis; such individuals were invited to join a group conducted weekly by a social worker. In the first meetings, the students helped each other choose short-term goals for themselves. These included regular completion of homework assignments, better quality of work as attested to by higher grades, and decisions regarding future employment and education. The members then each decided on "tasks" to help them reach their goals. Each member's goals were discussed by the entire group, and suggestions were made as to appropriate tasks. For example, a young woman whose goal was better grades on tests chose as her tasks to study two hours a day after school and to complete two homework assignments during this period.

Members used their discussions at meetings to help each other accomplish their tasks. The student who wanted to improve grades spoke about interruptions from her family and friends while she was studying. The group members suggested how she could respond to these interruptions, and she practiced their ideas in role plays at group meetings.

Organizations that emphasize skill attainment include schools, settlement houses, family life and sex education agencies, nursery and preschool programs for children, and senior citizens' centers. The emphasis in this type of helping is not on giving up old attitudes, values, and behavior, but on anticipatory socialization and building on already-present knowledge and skills.

Adult clients who use these agencies tend to come voluntarily. Although children are required to participate in some programs, there is an overall assumption that client motivation is high and resistance to learning low. The focus of service is on career development's providing as many opportunities for learning as possible. Ideally, agency rules are open and flexible, and there is opportunity for democratic decision making.

The preceding example of a skill attainment group illustrates that such groups usually consist of members who seek similar socialization goals and are striving to overcome similar barriers to such achievement. Members will therefore, be prone to identify strongly with and give support to each other. The approach used in the example of picking tasks is only one of several that may be used. Such procedures, however, tend to focus on specific goals and means to attain them.

It is also common in socialization-oriented groups to discover barriers in the environment to such socialization (in this case the attitudes of teachers). As we shall see later, workers tend to focus on member behaviors rather than on environmental conditions, thus leading members into activities in which their desires will be frustrated. Socialization-oriented groups should draw on the long tradition of strong socialization in community center and settlement house work with such groups.

Social Control

Example: Group meetings were required of adolescent boys committed to the Training School. One such group consisted of ten boys ages fifteen to seventeen. They had been sent to the institution for such offenses as repeated theft and destruction of property. In the second group meeting, the members sat in postures that showed their boredom and resentment. A few boys looked fearful. As the worker waited until all boys had arrived to begin the meeting, those present complained about the institution and about being required to attend the group. The worker began the discussion by empathizing with the boys' feelings. After a short period, however, he confronted the members with the statement that their complaints were "going nowhere" and that perhaps they could figure out something they could do to help themselves. In the discussion, he also commented that their difficulty in knowing what to do in tough situations may have landed them in the Training School. Many of the boys ridiculed this idea and said it was another example of the kind of preaching they always heard. One boy, however, did not join in this discussion, and yet the worker knew he was respected by the others. The worker sought to draw him out by commenting that maybe he saw things a little differently.

The social control purpose illustrated here is employed in an organization because society, usually through legislative and judicial processes, has sanctioned the agency to limit deviant behavior. Organizations that emphasize social control purposes include mental hospitals, residential treatment institutions, training schools for the delinquent and the developmentally disabled, drug centers, child guidance clinics, and community mental health facilities.

Behavioral change is central to social control goals for clients, that is, the diminution or elimination of behavior that led to the client's trouble with society. Service to clients is often involuntary, as the agency's control over its clientele is relatively high. The development of new and more functional modes of performance to replace the dysfunctional behavior should be, but is not always, a focus of the agency's program. The rules of these organizations tend to be authoritarian and coercive, especially in closed settings, and clients are allowed relatively little option on a number of issues.

Clients recruited to social control organizations often resist change and rebel against the agency itself. This is sometimes fostered by the rigidity of agency rules and sanctions as well as by peer group pressure to engage in aggressive behavior. Thus the initial motivation for change among such clients may be low or even nonexistent. Further, it is usually necessary to deal with peer group resistance to change by seeking to change the norms and values of the group.

A major issue for the professional is the potential conflict between the social control purpose of the agency and the professional commitment to self-determination for clients. However the worker resolves the issue, it must be with honesty so that members know the limits of their situation as well as the worker's personal stands. Members must receive recognition for their desire to confront agency policies together and with support, to do this in a constructive manner; moreover, the agency must be helped to respond with understanding and flexibility.

Group treatment in these settings can be very effective because previous group forces often have molded the individual's norms, values, and behaviors. The opportunity afforded to individuals to change their behavior with the support of a benign group situation is invaluable.

The illustration beginning this section shows many of these issues—for example, the understandable resistance of the group members to the compulsory features of the situation. The worker empathizes with these feelings and yet does not deny the agency's power and its use to attain agency objectives. The worker uses confrontation more often than in other settings to point out the members' behavior and its possible effects. In this way the worker presents, nonetheless, the concept that the members have choices to make. Even though the worker may favor some choices over others, he or she employs the value of self-determination so the members ultimately are responsible for their own decisions.

Rehabilitation

Example: A psychiatric outpatient clinic has established a group of seven men and women who voluntarily came to the clinic. One was a man who had had a succession of relationships with women in which the woman had broken off with him for reasons he did not understand; another was a man who expressed a great deal of anxiety about starting relationships with either men or women; a third was a woman fired from a number of jobs with the charge she did not get along with co-workers; and others were a woman and man in the processes of divorce from their respective spouses who expressed strong feelings of loss and sadness around this. All of these people had an interest in being members of a group conducted by a social worker on the staff. As part of the intake process into the group, the worker had explained to them that their problems appeared to be related to how they interacted with others and that in a group they could learn about, get feedback on, and modify such transactions.

At early meetings, the members elaborated on the problems just described. In the way they presented their problems, some of the reasons for their difficulties could be seen. For instance, the man with the succession of lovers backed off from discussions in the group as soon as another member expressed too much "caring." The woman fired from her job asked intimate questions of other group members and tended to ridicule their answers. Gradually, with the help of the worker, the members began to point out these kinds of patterns to each other. Some then began to try out other ways of responding in the group.

When rehabilitation is the primary purpose, the focus in the group is on the development of new values, knowledge, and skills to replace outdated or dysfunctional ones. While the client is, or is likely to be, in trouble in his or her environment, there has not necessarily been a major violation of social norms with subsequent legal sanctions. While there may be considerable environmental pressure on clients to do something about their situation, they usually seek help voluntarily because of personal discomfort. Organizations serving these populations generally allow clients many more opportunities for choice than when social control functions are being exercised. An exception to this analysis is when inmates of correctional programs move voluntarily toward seeking rehabilitation. Under these circumstances, clients rarely resist change, and their motivation to learn alternative roles is often high. They may find change difficult, however, because of previous, even lifelong, patterns. The worker's efforts are directed at building on the motivation already present and increasing the client's comfort with this process. The peer group is used to increase client motivation by reinforcing individual change efforts. This type of group is also useful because clients' resocialization problems are intimately connected with the relationship patterns they enact in group situations and which simulate life outside the group.

Groups that function as instruments of social control often become rehabilitation groups. This occurs when group members identify a common ground between their needs and interests and those of the agency. Such a transition demands, however, that the agency be benign, have a therapeutic orientation, and be prepared to negotiate a common ground with groups and group members.

Other organizations that emphasize rehabilitation purposes as part of resocialization include sheltered workshops and similar skill development programs for the physically handicapped and the developmentally disabled, retraining programs for the unemployed, family service agencies, psychiatric clinics, medical social work departments, and family life education programs.

The preceding example illustrates how members in groups not only talk about their relationships but actually enact these behaviors *because* the group *is* a social situation. Members find that people in the group remind them of people outside. Members can also stereotype each other and hinder change as well as enhance it, which poses a problem to the group and worker. Thus a wide range of learning possibilities occurs in a rehabilitation group as members understand not only how to experiment with change but how to respond to people who seek to hinder it. This is especially true in experiences of resocialization as opposed to socialization, as new behaviors must replace old ones.

Because the group is, as stated, a social situation, members will also behave in socially conventional ways; they will resist commenting on each other's behaviors or revealing their own thoughts and feelings. As the previous example indicates, it takes considerable worker skill to help the members of such groups make good use of the group for change, even when motivation is present; this is because the possibility is ever present that members will reinforce existing behaviors rather than new ones.

Summary

This chapter began with a discussion of the importance of agency conditions in relation to group work practice—conditions that have evolved over more than half a century. An understanding of this provides many insights into the current group work situation; therefore, an extensive offering of group work history was presented.

Following the section on group work history, the specific organizational conditions that can either enhance or hinder the group work experience were described. These conditions include purposes assigned to the group, the selection of members, the status of the group workers, and the agency allocation of resources to the group. A number of additional organizational conditions were also described.

The final section of the chapter included a discussion of the range of group services based on a topology of such purposes. This topology subdivides purposes into socialization (further split into identity development and skill attainment) and resocialization (further split into social control and rehabilitation). Throughout this book, we shall use this set of categories to clarify existing variations in group work practice.

Exercise: Assessing an Agency's Effort on Group Work

The following questionnaire can help the reader assess the impact of agency conditions on group work services:

Purposes

1. What do agency documents state are the purposes of the agency?
2. What group purposes are compatible with agency purposes?
3. What types of clients are likely to come to the agency in view of its purposes? How will this affect group composition?
4. What will members perceive is expected of them in the light of agency purposes?
5. How will agency purposes affect activities of the group and the content of group deliberations?

Agency Referral Procedures

1. Are members recruited for or referred to groups before, during, or after agency intake?
2. Which agency staff are responsible for referral? How are people who work with groups in the agency involved in this process?
3. Is some service of the agency (for example, one-to-one casework) actually the preferred or predominant one?
4. Does the agency interact with its clients predominantly on a group, one-to-one, or family basis?
5. Is members' attendance at group meetings voluntary or compulsory?
6. How are potential members approached and prepared for the group?

7. What are the effects of this approach and preparation on (a) members' perceptions of the group, (b) members' attitudes toward the group, (c) the kinds of people likely to be referred to the group?

Status of the Group Worker

1. Does the group worker only work with groups? If not, what are his or her other tasks?
2. Are social workers who work with groups or who are highly knowledgeable about group work represented in supervisory and administrative positions to the same degree as social workers who are not?
3. What is the effect of the group worker's status on recruitment of group members, power to make decisions on ways of serving the group, and ability to secure resources for the group?

Resources Allocated by the Agency to the Group

1. What kind of room (that is, location, size, equipment) has the agency assigned to the group? To what other uses is it put? Is it regularly assigned? Are the group members allowed to alter the room in any way (for example, by putting up posters, shifting equipment)?
2. What kind of equipment is the group likely to require? Will it be readily available?
3. Will the group be likely to require other material resources (for example, transportation), and will the agency provide these?
4. Will the group require other human resources (for example, consultation), and will the agency provide these?
5. What are the effects of points 1–4 on group activities, morale, and climate?

Targets for Change Selected by the Agency

1. Does the agency perceive its groups as primarily directed at changing the members? If so, is this conceived of as changes in self-understanding, attitudes, knowledge, and/or behavior?
2. Does the agency perceive its group as seeking changes in the agency itself and/or in the environment outside the agency?
3. What are the effects of points 1 and 2 on the activities of the group and on the attitudes of the members to the group?

Interaction of the Group with the Agency and Staff

1. With which staff members, in relation to the group worker, are members of the group likely to interact? What will be the nature and effect of this interaction on the member and on the group?
2. How is the agency decorated and how well is it maintained? What will be the effect of this on the group?

Interactions of the Agency with the Group's Indigenous Leaders

1. Are group members involved in any way in agency decision making?
2. What are the effects of this involvement or lack of involvement on the group?

Agency's Preferred Service Technology

1. Does the agency have a preferred theory or approach to work with groups and/or individuals? What is it? How is it explained to members? What is the effect on the members?
2. How do the agency and the worker interact around preferred approaches (for example, consultation, training)?
3. Is the preferred approach consistent with approaches used in other services (for example, one-to-one, family, child care, custodial)? What is the effect on the group of this consistency or inconsistency?

Intraorganizational Relationships

1. How does the group worker interact with staff peers and administrators? How does this affect him or her? How does this ultimately affect the group?
2. What is the morale of the staff? How does this affect the group?

Endnotes

1. Yeheskel Hansenfeld, "Organizational Factors in Service to Groups," in *Individual Change Through Small Groups,* eds. Martin Sundel, Paul H. Glaser Rosemary Sarri, and Robert Vinter (New York: Free Press, 1985): 294

2. Ibid.

3. Gertrude Wilson, "From Practice to Theory: A Personalized History," in *Theories of Social Work with Groups,* eds. Robert Roberts and Helen Northen (New York: Columbia University Press, 1976): 6.

4. William Schwartz, "Social Group Work: The Interactionist Approach," in *Encyclopedia of Social Work* (New York: National Association of Social Workers, 1971): 1253.

5. Toby Berman-Rossi and Irving Miller, "African-Americans and the Settlements during the late Nineteenth and Early Twentieth Centuries," in *Social Work with Groups* 17(3) (1994): 78.

6. Ibid.

7. T.L. Philpott, *The Slum and the Ghetto: Immigrants, Blacks, and Reformers in Chicago, 1880–1930* (Belmont: Wadsworth Publishing Co., 1991).

8. Berman-Rossi, Toby and Miller, Ivan *African-Americans and the Settlements*: 85–86.

9. Ibid.: 88.

10. For a discussion of this, see Irving Howe, *World of Our Fathers* (New York: Simon & Schuster, 1976): 230.

11. Mary Richmond, "Some Next Steps in Social Treatment," *Proceedings of the National Conference of Social Work* (Chicago: University of Chicago Press, 1920): 256.

12. Mary Parker Follett, *The New State* (New York: Longman, 1926).

13. John Dewey, *How We Think* (Lexington, Mass.: Heath, 1933).

14. Harry Lawrence, "The Origins of Social Group Work" (unpublished manuscript, p. 13), quoted in Scott Briar, "Social Casework and Social Group Work: Historical Foundations," in *Encyclopedia of Social Work*: 1241.

15. Wilson, "From Practice to Theory,": 18.

16. These include Coyle's classic presentation of a philosophy for group work entitles "Group Work and

Social Change," Grace L. Coyle, *Group Experience and Democratic Values* (New York: Women's Press, 1947); and Newstetter's clarification of semantic and conceptual issues: W.I. Newstetter, "What is Social Group Work?" in *Proceedings of the National Conference of Social Work* (Chicago: University of Chicago Press, 1935), pp. 291–99. Coyle in her presentation stressed the dual function of group work to transmit cultural values to individuals while helping people to transform these values through democratic processes. Newstetter identified group work as a "field," a "process," and a "set of techniques."

17. Schwartz, *Encyclopedia of Social Work:* 1254.

18. Wilson, "From Practice to Theory,": 25.

19. Ibid.: 18.

20. For example, Grace Coyle, *Studies in Group Behavior* (New York: Harper & Row Pub., 1937); Clara A. Kaiser, *The Group Records of Four Clubs* (Cleveland: Western Reserve University, 1930); S.R. Slavson, *Creative Group Education* (New York: Association Press, 1937); and Margaretta Williamson, *The Social Worker in Group Work* (New York: Harper & Row, Pub., 1929).

21. Grace Coyle, *Group Work with American Youth* (New York: Harper & Row, Pub., 1948).

22. Alan Klein, *Society, Democracy and the Group* (New York: Morrow, 1953).

23. Harleigh B. Trecker, ed., *Group Work: Foundations and Frontiers* (New York: Whiteside, Inc., 1955): 340.

24. For example, Gertrude Wilson and Gladys Ryland, *Social Group Work Practice* (Boston: Houghton-Mifflin, 1949); Harleigh B. Trecker, *Social Group Work* (New York: Women's Press, 1948); Grace Coyle, *Group Experience and Democratic Values;* Gisela Konopka, *Therapeutic Group Work with Children* (Minneapolis: University of Minnesota Press, 1949); and a few years later Helen Phillips, *Essentials of Social Group Work Skill* (New York: Association Press, 1957).

25. Wilson, "From Practice to Theory,": 32–33

26. *Use of Groups in the Psychiatric Setting* (New York: National Association of Social Workers, 1960).

27. Robert D. Vinter, "Group Work: Perspectives and Prospects," in *Social Work with Groups* (New York: National Association of Social Workers, 1959): 128–49.

28. Wilson, "From Practice to Theory,": 33.

29. Konopka, *Therapeutic Group Work*; Fritz Redl, "The Therapeutic Ingredients in the Group Work Program in a Residential Treatment Center for Children," in *Group Work in the Psychiatric Setting*, ed. Harleigh Trecker (N.Y.: Whiteside, Inc., and Morrow, 1956): 43–46.

30. See, for example, T. Burrow, "The Basis for Group Analysis," *British Journal of Medical Psychology* 8, Pt. 3 (November 1928): 198–206.

31. The current editors are Roselle Kurland of Hunter College School of Social Work and Andrew Malekoff, a practitioner.

32. Marjorie Murphy, *The Social Group Work Method in Social Work Education* (New York: Council on Social Work Education, 1959): 312.

33. Sheldon Rose, *Group Therapy: A Behavioral Approach* (Englewood Cliffs, N.J.: Prentice Hall, 1977): 9.

34. Perry London, *Behavior Control* (New York: Harper & Row, Pub., 1971): 4.

35. Ibid.: 7.

36. Ibid.: 21.

37. For example, see Rose, *Group Therapy*.

38. Hasenfeld, "Organizational Factors,": 299.

39. Ibid.

40. Irvin D. Yalom, *The Theory and Practice of Group Psychotherapy,* 3rd ed. (New York: Basic Books, 1975): 294.

41. James Framo, "Symptoms from a Family Transactional Viewpoint," In *Progress in Group and Family Therapy,* eds. Clifford Sager and Helen Kaplan (New York Brunner/Mazel, 1972): 271–308.

42. Hansenfeld, "Organizational Factors,": 305.

43. Ibid.

44. Hasenfeld, "Organizational Factors,": 303.

45. Robert D. Vinter, "Analysis of Treatment Organizations," *Social Work* 8 (1963): 3–15.

46. Hasenfeld, "Organizational Factors,": 296.

Chapter *3*

The Pregroup Phase

In the first two chapters, we provided information on what group work is, how approaches to it vary, and how these approaches emerged historically. Chapters 3 and 4 contain a detailed presentation of the principles and procedures that guide practice with groups. These are activities in which the worker is engaged prior to the first meeting of the group (this chapter) and during the first phase of group development, group formation (Chapter 4).

The worker should perform a number of tasks before the first group meeting to make group experience more likely to succeed. In addition, research shows that the way these activities are performed will affect how rapidly and effectively the group moves toward its goals. The reader should remember, however, that unpredicted events can always occur, as many group workers' diaries will attest. Sometimes even the most carefully laid plans must be cast aside. The intent of preplanning is not to eliminate uncertainty about group events, but to reduce it.

One of the first tasks of the worker is to conceptualize the purpose of the group, at least in a general sense. As stated in Chapter 2, agencies often have purposes for sponsoring particular groups, and the worker must consider these or risk losing agency support. Sometimes agencies wish to relate their purposes to a needs assessment of clients, and we shall suggest means for accomplishing this. The reason for conceptualizing purpose before attempting other pregroup tasks is the relationship of purpose to other decisions such as group composition and size.

Because purpose is so closely allied to composition, we shall treat this topic next and shall discuss how to compose a group so that the selection of members will support the group's purposes. A topic that shall also be considered in relationship to composition is whether a group experience is appropriate for the individual concerned.

Another major topic we shall discuss is how to prepare members for the group. This is often done in one or more sessions before the group begins. The worker seeks to understand the problems or concerns that prompted the individuals to enter the agency and subsequently to contemplate a group experience. We shall describe ways in which the worker prepares other staff members to welcome the group as well as how the worker establishes physical conditions conducive to the group's beginning.

Group Purposes

By *group purposes*, we mean the specific reasons for which the group was established, usually expressed as the type of goals the group will try to help its members attain. Group purposes may be conceived in different ways by the worker and the members; even each member may have a different perception of the purposes of the group. Thus group purposes affect and are affected by decisions on group composition, group program, worker interventions, number of meetings planned, and even choice of a worker for the group. An example should help to clarify these statements about group purposes.

Example: A welfare department formed a group composed of parents of high school students. The agency's reason (*agency purpose*) for establishing the group was to provide support to their children to remain in school. To compose a group for this purpose, the agency asked workers to refer to the group worker those parents who had expressed concern about this issue (*composition related to purpose*). Agency purpose thus became worker's purpose. The agency wanted the members to have the opportunity to describe their situation in detail. A small group—about five members—was decided on (*size related to purpose*). The worker believed that parents gathering for this purpose would want to focus on the issue quickly and learn how to deal with it. Thus eight group meetings should be sufficient (*number of meetings related to purpose*).

When the group members were told about the group, several expressed opinion, privately, that the agency's "real" purpose was to check on how they were spending their welfare grant (*member's perception of purpose*). The worker anticipated that this might be what they thought and thus planned to discuss group purpose thoroughly at the first meeting.

At the first meeting, one member indicated a desire to be a member of a group that would help in making friends; the worker responded that perhaps another group could be formed for this purpose (*member's purpose*). The members, by the end of the first meeting, agreed that they had problems with keeping their youngsters in school and that they wanted to be in a group established for this reason (*members' consensus on purpose*). In planning for the second meeting, they also decided that the purpose of that meeting would be to report on the difficulties their children had told them they were experiencing in school (*short-term purpose*).

The reason for distinguishing among worker purpose, member purpose, consensus among members on purpose, and short-term and long-term purposes is that a logical relationship surrounding these phenomena must exist for the group to progress smoothly toward its goals. If members and workers have different conceptions of group purpose, they are unlikely to find it easy to work cooperatively; similarly, if members do not agree on purpose, they are also unlikely to agree on group goals or activities; if short-term purposes do not relate to the long-term ones, the group will not be able to build on its experiences to create significant accomplishments.

As reasons for discrepancies among purposes are discovered, these may suggest that purposes originally decided for the group should be changed. This is more valid than the idea that the members should forgo ideas they have about the group's purpose. While modifications in group purposes can and do occur, the process is time consuming and creates potential for severe conflict. Much of this can be obviated by careful planning about group purposes prior to first meetings, which is what we shall now address.

Needs Assessment

One way of establishing purposes that will lead to viable groups is through assessing the needs of people who are, or might be, served by the agency. The following is a sample of a series of items developed for a family agency. Such questions can be raised in an interview, a questionnaire, or with other professionals who refer people to groups.

Group Needs Assessment Questionnaire: We plan to start a group to help people with a variety of concerns they may have, such as relationships with family and friends, and job situations. It will help us set up groups of interest if you will answer the following questions. If you wish to be notified about a group of interest to you, a place is provided for you to sign your name.

1. Please indicate your interest in being in a group:
   _____ very interested
   _____ somewhat interested
   _____ not interested at all
2. Please check any areas you might like to discuss in a group:
   _____ relationship to husband/wife
   _____ relationship to person with whom you live (specify relationship) _____
   _____ relationship to friends
   _____ job concerns
   _____ feelings of discomfort (sadness, fears, worrying)
   _____ concerns about your future (job, schooling)
   _____ concerns about making an important decision (where you will live; going to school; leaving school or home)
3. Have you been in a group to discuss personal concerns?
   _____ yes   _____ no
4. If yes to question 3, what did you think of the experience?
5. Which of the following describes what you are like in groups? Check as many as apply.
   _____ I talk a lot.
   _____ I seldom say anything.
   _____ I make acquaintances easily.
   _____ It takes me a long time to get to know others.
   _____ My feelings get hurt easily.
   _____ I easily tell personal things about myself.
   _____ It is very hard for me to tell personal things about myself.
   _____ I think I have a good idea ow what others think of me.
   _____ I like to stay on the subject.
   _____ I have little influence on others.
   _____ I can influence others a great deal.

At times, workers have little influence over the composition of the group, which makes it difficult or impossible prior to the first meeting to determine the purpose of the group. This is true when there are very few referrals to the group, when the group is already established (youth gangs), or when the group has been created for other purposes (cottage groups in a residential treatment center). In these cases, the question is reversed: Instead of "Given a purpose, how shall the group be composed?" the worker asks "Given group composition, what purposes can be achieved?" The worker can still, however, use items such as those in the needs assessment instrument to help the group determine a purpose consistent with the purpose of the agency.

Organizational Functions and Group Purpose

To help the reader understand the range of purposes, we present some examples in relationship to each of the types of organizational functions described in the preceding chapter. In examining this list, remember that groups may also be composed of members with different needs; thus a group, on occasion, may serve several purposes.

Identity Development Purposes
1. To decide what type of sexual life style is consistent with each member's current identity as well as future aspirations.
2. To select the kinds of roles in marriage that conform to each member's values and desires regarding marriage.
3. To clarify the meaning of masculinity (femininity) and what this implies for each member's behavior, life style, and crucial decisions such as marriage, child-rearing, and occupation.
4. To determine how to integrate the values of one's ethnic culture with one's personal aspirations.

Skill Attainment Purposes
1. To learn how to fulfill the role of a parent.
2. To learn how to succeed in school by changing personal behavior and/or by changing school policies that may impede personal progress.
3. To learn the social skills necessary to function in adolescent (young adult, adult) situations.
4. For foster parents to learn to become better substitute parents.

Social Control Purposes
1. For individuals on parole to choose legitimate careers.
2. For a student in primary school to learn cooperative rather than disruptive classroom behaviors.
3. For a patient in a mental hospital to cease behaviors that are disruptive of hospital routines and/or aversive to other patients.

Rehabilitation Purposes

1. For mental patients who have been socially isolated due to unacceptable or bizarre behavior, to learn behaviors appropriate to the social roles they desire.
2. For child-abusing parents to learn to discipline their children in nonabusive ways.
3. For obese persons to learn eating habits that will lead to lower food intake and weight loss.

Group Composition

In situations where the purpose of the group is determined before it is created, the next step is to select the members. Some workers will have a large pool of people from whom to choose and will be able to consider many factors in this choice; in other situations, few prospective members are available, and the worker may even conclude that a selection from this limited set of people cannot possibly lead to a viable group.

The worker, in considering group composition principles, must be aware that there are many unknowns regarding the combination of member characteristics that will produce optimal groups. Also, there are many forces that affect group outcomes (for example, techniques employed by the worker, available resources in the agency), so the worker should pay attention to composition without becoming obsessed by it. As Yalom states, "Time and energy spent on delicately casting and balancing a group is not justified given our current state of knowledge; the therapist does better to invest that time and energy in careful selection of patients for group therapy and in their pre-therapy preparation."[1] Nevertheless, we do not advocate inattention to group composition, and we shall now discuss some major considerations for accomplishing this task. We also include an exercise at the end of this chapter so readers may experience the applications of the principles of composition.

Purpose and Group Composition

The central issue workers should consider in composition is the purpose of the group. Some purposes cannot be addressed in groups composed in certain ways, while for other purposes composition may be less crucial. Some examples of compositional issues related to the major categories of group purposes are now given.

Identity Development. A group in which members seek to determine or change their values should have members whose values are different enough to provide a range of ideas. One group for women seeking to clarify their female roles provided many models for the members because it included women who were career oriented, home oriented, or sought to combine both. The group also included women who were militant in their pursuit of their objectives as well as women who were not.

Skill Attainment. In situations where groups help members learn the skills to attain some role, it is best for members to have similar aspirations. Thus a group of adolescents seeking to attain school success provided a good deal of reinforcement to each other. Skill attainment groups are also facilitated if, in addition to sharing objectives, each member possesses knowledge and skills related to these objectives. Members can thus help one another overcome personal as well as social obstacles to fulfill their roles.

Social Control.   A group whose members hold similar values about an antisocial behavior can provide reinforcement to maintain that behavior. Dissimilarity in this regard is often sought. An important principle can be demonstrated here, namely, that when composition cannot be varied (as is often true in institutions serving offenders), new approaches to intervention must be developed. Thus in fairly homogeneous social-control-oriented groups, workers use confrontive approaches and encourage members to confront each other regarding their attitudes and behaviors. A compositional technique to secure some heterogeneity in these groups is to "seed" them with former members of other groups who have already begun the process of normative change.

Rehabilitation.   As in skill attainment groups, similarity of resocialization objectives is sought so members can help one another in that process. An example is that of a group of clients in a halfway house who had been previously diagnosed as schizophrenic and are now in the process of job training.

Ethnicity and Gender

There are many characteristics for the worker to evaluate when composing groups—age, social class, skills, and how the individual is likely to act in the group. Two variables, always crucial are the individual's gender and ethnicity. Under typical circumstances, it may not matter from which European country one's ancestors came, but it does matter whether one is a member of an economically or socially oppressed group such as blacks, Asians and Pacific Islanders, Latinos, or Native Americans.[2]

A general principle is not to compose a group in which a person(s) by virtue of such ethnicity or gender, represent(s) a small minority of one or two within the group. Under those circumstances the person(s) may experience little in common with other members. In addition, other members often see such individuals as representatives of their "group" rather than as individuals. The only woman or black in a group is often asked what all women or blacks think or feel. This is certainly an inappropriate and impossible burden.

At times it is appropriate and necessary to compose a group entirely of one gender or ethnic origin to resolve identity issues or to provide social support. Thus men's and women's consciousness-raising groups are increasingly being created, and groups have been conducted with members of ethnic groups, often children or adolescents, to assist in the process of socialization.[3]

When identity and socialization are not the main purposes for forming the group, workers will often compose groups with members from several ethnic backgrounds. Aside from avoiding "token" memberships, there are additional principles to consider. Davis, in an important review of these with regard to blacks, draws a number of conclusions.[4] He notes that in one report, black members at first questioned the legitimacy of an all-black treatment group, but this concern gradually dissipated. At times, blacks have questioned the competency of their black worker.

The proportion of blacks to whites within a group is also discussed by Davis. He explains that this topic is made more complex because blacks and whites interpret the meaning of proportions differently. Davis states:

> *Blacks, it appears, prefer groups that are 50 percent black and 50 percent white—numerical equality. Whites, on the other hand, appear to prefer groups that are approximately 20 percent black and 80 percent white, societal ratios of blacks and whites. Needless to say, the preferences of both groups cannot be simultaneously met. This difference in preference for racial balance has the potential to lead to member dissatisfaction, discomfort, and withdrawal (p. 102).*

Davis theorizes that whites "because of their customary numerical dominance, feel themselves to be psychologically in the minority, or outnumbered, if blacks are present in numbers greater than their societal proportions (p. 102). He also notes that race is apt to be a more salient issue in intimate situations and that intimacy varies with group size and purpose.

Davis bases his propositions about racial composition on his own carefully conducted research. Similar studies should be conducted as to how ethnic composition situations other than black-white are experienced by the members. Short of that, we have to rely on the experiences of practitioners. Chu and Sue,[5] in their discussion of how composition affects Asian-Americans, describe how these members tend to react differently from others in a group.

> *In a group of very verbose, articulate and aggressive non-Asians, the Asian member may be hesitant to speak up. In a confrontation, which inevitably happens at some point in a long-term group, the Asian may not know what to say, not being used to such interaction (p. 30).*

Chu and Sue conclude, therefore, that in at least the first stages of group experience, Asian-Americans should be grouped together. They assert that "Such a group can sense one another's communication and thus be more empathetic. Equal participation by Asians would also facilitate the development of leadership skills of some members within the group" (p. 30).

Ho[6] goes even further in recommending that members of Asian/Pacific-American ethnic groups of a particular nationality and geographic location should be grouped together because of commonalities in subculture and language necessary for good group progress.

In contrast, in a discussion of group work with Latinos, Acosta and Yamamoto[7] do not consider it necessary to separate people from different Latino backgrounds. They have experienced strong clashes between group members but believe this is due more to personality than variance in background.

Equally important in composition are gender issues. The worker must understand the processes likely to be created because a group is all of one gender, primarily of one gender, or about equally mixed. Martin and Shanahan, in a very thoughtful and comprehensive review of the relevant research, arrive at several conclusions.[8]

1. Even without interpersonal interaction (e.g., verbal exchanges) females are negatively "evaluated" in all-male groups and in groups in which they are tokens.
2. The quantity and content of verbal interaction in groups varies with sex composition of the group and by gender of the participant. For example, women talk less and are talked to less in mixed groups than in all-female groups; men in all-male groups tend to concentrate on competition and status topics while females in all-female groups focus on personal, home, and family topics. Both males and females are most likely to exhibit the greatest quantity of leader-like statements in same sex groups.
3. Females are perceived of less positively than males, even when equally influential.
4. "Solo" or "token" females in otherwise male groups tend to fare poorly.
5. The findings regarding women in all-female groups are inconsistent. Variations seem to be related to whether the study focused upon attraction to group, "growth" of members, inter-member influence, motivation for participation, or group effectiveness.

Martin and Shanahan make suggestions related to these effects. These include actions affirming the right of women to assume leadership and influential roles; ensuring that competence is equally rewarded in men and women; and ensuring balanced proportions of men and women in mixed groups. Additional issues, such as questioning the assumption that a division of labor and influence are undesirable features because they are found in men's groups, should be addressed in all-female groups so that women's groups can adopt these mechanisms when necessary.

In contrast to the many stresses with which women have to cope, men experience much that is valuable in mixed groups. Men are more likely to be "personal" and less competitive and disagreeable under these circumstances than when in all-male groups. Nevertheless, group leaders find that they have to discourage men from talking too much and from becoming overly competitive with one another in mixed groups.

Finally, in all-male groups the worker must help the men accept more intimacy and self-disclosure than they might otherwise adopt. They must similarly be helped to deal with too much competition and conflict.

The above principles have been generated from an examination of a variety of groups, yet there has been too limited an examination of gender issues in social work groups. We do not have good evidence as to whether some of these gender effects diminish over time, or about which approach to intervention is effective in changing stereotypical and undesirable reactions related to gender—reactions that limit the full development of the potential of group members. The preceding statements have to be taken, therefore, as hypotheses from which we may eventually create a sound approach to the role of group work in this aspect of human liberation.

Group Cohesiveness and Composition

For a group, certainly a voluntary one, to remain in existence, the members have to be motivated to attend, participate, and complete tasks. The concept that encompasses these variables is *cohesiveness*, usually defined as "the resultant of all the forces acting on all the members to remain in the group."[9]

Members can have many reasons to remain in a group, including attraction to other members, the worker, the goal, the activity, or the status associated with membership. Thibaut and Kelley have identified yet another variable, "the comparison level for alternatives," defined as "the standard that an individual uses to decide whether to remain in or to leave an interpersonal relationship."[10] This variable leads us to recognize that individuals not only choose to remain in groups because of what the group has to offer but because of how these offerings compare with other opportunities.

The cohesiveness of a group is analogous to the concept of *relationship* in one-to-one interactions. According to research findings, it is one of the most important forces accounting for the effectiveness of a group.[11] In reference to this, Yalom argues that if an individual experienced little sense of belonging or attraction to the group, even when measured early in the course of the sessions, there was little hope that he or she would benefit from the group and, in fact, a high likelihood that he or she would have a negative outcome.[12]

Although there are many bases of cohesiveness, the one most often studied as well as sought after is the attraction of members for each other. One way this attraction is enhanced is when members perceive each other as being similar. The worker can maximize cohesiveness, therefore, by composing groups of persons as similar as possible both on attributes (age, sex, race, socioeconomic status) and on behaviors (types of problems, skills in problem solving, interests in the same activities).

An issue that has troubled group workers is whether people will be reinforced for their dysfunctional ways of solving their problems if they are too similar in their behaviors. Many workers have argued that members should differ in their ways of coping. This will lead, presumably, to the kinds of constructive disagreements and tensions among members that will maintain interest in the group and stimulate members to consider new ideas and behaviors. Yalom has labeled this compositional model the "dissonance" one.[13]

Yalom concludes, based on his examination of both research and clinical experience, that there is no evidence that deliberately heterogeneously composed groups facilitate therapy,[14] and this has also been our experience. We, therefore, agree with Yalom's proposal that ". . . cohesiveness be our primary guideline in the composition of therapy groups."[15] This conclusion has been reached with the awareness that people differ considerably, and even the greatest efforts at matching will still produce an array of individuals with different experiences, ideas, and ways of responding to their environments.

Yalom asserts that cohesiveness should be emphasized in *therapy* groups. Thus he has a specific practice model in mind—one in which members are encouraged to remain in the group for a long period of time and treatment is accomplished through members' intensive examination of interpersonal processes in the group. Social workers often work with other kinds of groups. In these cases such an emphasis on homogeneity leading to cohesiveness may not be as necessary. Examples:

1. Groups formed for a specific short-term purpose such as preparation for discharge or orientation.[16]
2. Groups employing a structured format such as those for skills training.
3. Groups with a strong educational component such as parent training.

Deviance and Group Composition

Although we have stated that the worker should strive to select similar members when a cohesive group is sought, this is often not possible. The question then arises as to how dissimilar members can be. The danger is that a member significantly different from others will be perceived as undesirable or, in sociological terms, deviant by the other members. When the difference is based on some attribute such as age or race, the members may avoid communicating with this person, thus creating a group isolate. When the difference is based on a behavior such as topics discussed, personal disclosure, or social skills, the members may become critical of the individual and then scapegoat the person, who will then develop negative feelings toward the group, avoid its influences, and eventually drop out. In some cases, the member will try instead to modify his or her behavior so as to become more acceptable to others in the group, but the risk still remains that such a person will become alienated from the group.

The worker must, therefore, avoid introducing someone who differs in a way that group members consider salient to their interests. What constitutes such a salience must often be anticipated by the group worker based on experience with the population in question. For example, athletic skill may be an important consideration in an adolescent but not in an adult group; religious attitudes in a group to discuss child-rearing but not in one to discuss employment; and types of sexual experience in a marital counseling group but not in a preparation-for-retirement one.

There are several things the worker can do when group composition likely will lead to creating a deviant member. One is to enroll another member who is either similar to the person in question or who is somewhere in the "middle," thus creating a continuum of member characteristics. This continuum then avoids the extreme differences in attributes or behaviors between one person and the rest.

In some situations the worker may wish to constructively use a member's differences. One example was that of a friendship group of adolescent boys in a community center. The worker asked them to accept a boy with cerebral palsy as a group member. After much discussion, this was accomplished. Some months later, when this boy had become well integrated into the group, another member mentioned that the boys would never again use the word "spastic" to ridicule someone.

One device used to compose groups and avoid creating a group isolate or deviant is to rate each member on a series of scales. Each scale represents an attribute or behavior deemed significant by the worker.[17] This graphic device, as illustrated in Table 3.1, makes it easy to identify this type of undesirable situation. We have used such data to examine each attribute or behavior to identify individuals who are "extreme" on that variable. Other variables are then examined to see if that person is also extreme with regard to these. If not, we assume that these other conditions will provide the bases for the commonality necessary for interpersonal attraction and group cohesiveness. When an individual is placed at an extreme on several scales in relationship to other group members, it is best to introduce others who are similar in some ways to seek another group for him or her.

In our illustration (Table 3.1), Dick is older than the other boys; he is also verbally aggressive, engages in frequent physical fights, and is less interested in the group. His main area of identification is likely to be his race. On the other hand, he might serve as a

TABLE 3.1   Composition of an Adolescent Boys' Group

Name	Age	Race	Degree of Verbal Aggressiveness	Presenting Problem	Interest in Group
Sam	14	Black	Low	Severe conflict with teachers	Moderate
Bill	15	Black	Moderate	Theft from school	Moderate
Frank	15	White	Moderate	Runaway from family	Low
Carl	13	White	Moderate	Poor peer relations	High
Dick	17	Black	High	Frequent physical fights	Low

model for the younger, particularly black members, in ways that are problematic. In this situation, the worker introduced two additional members to the group: another black 17-year-old who had been a runaway from his family, and a 14-year-old white youth who had been involved in thefts—this latter member was not very aggressive, verbally or physically. The modified group composition, therefore, avoids the likely creation of an antisocial leader (Dick). It also avoids the equally likely creation of an isolate (Carl).

Program Activity and Group Composition

In most group situations, the major activity is group discussion, and verbal and cognitive approaches to treatment predominate. In group work, even before the advent of encounter and other groups that use nonverbal exercises, various activities were used to achieve group purposes, including games, crafts, music, and dance. While many of these "programs" are chosen by groups after the group has been formed, the likelihood of their selection can often be predicted.

When the media likely to be used are anticipated, group composition is influenced. If discussion is to be employed, verbal skills must be assessed. Similarly, if the members are likely to communicate through drama, art, or athletics, the interest and level of skill in these must be rated.

Assessing Members in Relationship to Group Composition

The preceding discussion of factors to consider in composing groups is based on the idea that aspects of a person's behavior can be predicted. This is a difficult task because a person's behavior is determined both by personal characteristics and by the forces present in a situation.[18] For this reason, the best indicator of a person's behavior in a group is his or her actions to a similar group situation.[19] Some group-serving agencies, to secure this kind of information, have set up "waiting list" groups or diagnostic groups.

Another possibility, suggested by Yalom, is an interpersonally oriented initial interview.[20] In this procedure, the worker assesses to what degree the clients can comment on the interpersonal process going on between them and the worker and how they assess and respond to the therapist's views of them. Also examined in such an interview is information about the clients' relationships with peers as well as the kinds of roles they have assumed in groups.

Various psychological instruments have been used to select members for groups, but probably the best known is Schutz's FIRO-B (Fundamental Interpersonal Relations Orientation) scales.[21] Schutz based his instrument on the proposition that everyone seeks to relate to others to satisfy three needs: *affection, control, and inclusion. Affection* pertains to close personal relationships, *control* to power over others, and *inclusion* to being with others. Everyone according to Schutz, can be described as to the degree with which each of these is expressed and whether it is manifested toward others as well as expected from them.

One social work writer, William Shalinsky, utilized Schutz's scales to study the effects of different kinds of composition in children's groups. Shalinsky created some groups that were compatible and some that were not. Compatibility was defined as groupings consisting of people "similar to others in [their] total amount of expressed and wanted behavior in the need area of affection."[22] This researcher found that members of compatible groups liked each other more, found their group more attractive, and were even more cooperative. Also, compatible groups engaged in competitive tasks won significantly more often than incompatible ones.

The implication of Shalinsky's findings are that these interpersonal traits should be considered in composing groups and that homogeneity should be sought in this regard. This is also consistent with Yalom's emphasis on seeking cohesiveness in therapy groups and basing this on such measures as those devised by Shalinsky.

Selection of Worker or Co-Worker

When one views the small group as a system, then the group worker is as much a part of the system as the members, albeit with a different role. Therefore, compositional dynamics are created as much by the worker's characteristics as by the members'. If the worker is the only male or female or black or white in the group, reactions will be the same as toward any group member with a characteristic that differs from others.

It is important, consequently, to consider the characteristics of the worker as carefully as those of the members. The worker's characteristics can, for example, be used to "solve" some compositional problems such as "supplementing" the number of members who share some attribute. Thus a mixed group of men and women, in which the number of referrals of women is small, might be offset with the appointment of a female worker.

Another question is whether there should be more than one worker assigned to the group, as in the co-worker situation. This device is sometimes used when the worker interested in facilitating the group differs from members in some important respect such as gender or ethnicity, and when it is important to provide a worker similar to members in these respects.

Usually there are reasons when workers desire to work in pairs other than composition. In work with multiple person systems such as groups and families, this is a controversial topic. Some writers and practitioners strongly support co-worker models because they believe that the two workers can bring different skills to the group; check each other's distortions about what is occurring in the group; constructively divide leadership roles such as those of task and social emotional facilitation; and model the ways that people can support each other and resolve differences. If the two workers are of different sexes, they can help members deal with some family dynamics such as those related to "mother" and "father."

Others seriously question the co-worker model. They think it often provides an example of conflict rather than cooperation and that members become sidetracked from dealing with their own issues as they become interested in the interactions between the workers.

In our own experience, we have frequently found a co-worker model useful but not essential. On the other hand, we have observed it to be destructive when dysfunctional patterns emerge between the workers. This often happens when one worker operates as a more powerful figure than the other and this is associated with such attributes as race or gender—that is, the male worker dominates the female or the white worker dominates the nonwhite. This situation is often found when a male psychiatrist and female social worker or a white fully trained worker and a nonwhite paraprofessional join together.

Under any circumstance, co-workers must examine their own interactions throughout the life of the group. They must be sensitive to such patterns as the dominance of one over the other, the creation of coalitions between one worker and a group member, the assumption of less-wanted activities by one worker such as cleaning up the meeting room after sessions, and so forth. This requires regular conferences between co-workers. Some workers have held such sessions in the presence of group members as a way of modeling the use of feedback to resolve differences between each other.[23]

Selection of Candidates for Groups

The process of composing groups consists of two stages: the first is to ascertain whether a group experience is an appropriate one at all; the second is to compose groups of people who are appropriate referrals to *any* group as well as to the one planned. In this respect, we assume that both group and one-to-one helping are equally valid for a large proportion of people served by social work agencies.

Family Treatment.   Probably the most important decisional issue is whether family treatment or other family involvement is required. Only after family approaches are rejected should a worker consider whether casework or group work should be employed. It is, of course, possible to have a group composed of several families.[24] The decision to involve the family should be based on the following assessment:

1. Is the problem maintained by processes operating in the family as a system?
2. How will the family respond to changes the individual may choose to make, and will these responses support or retard such changes?
3. Does the individual wish to involve the family, and is the family amenable to such involvement?

If the family interaction maintains the problem, or if the family opposes changes the individual chooses to make, effective helping requires the worker to involve other family members. Individual and group approaches should only be the worker's choice when these family considerations are lacking or minimal or when the client has rejected family involvement.

Client Preference.   Another consideration is whether the potential group member wishes to be in a group. Clients usually come to agencies with expectations regarding the kinds of services they will receive and, often, this is for one-to-one help. The client's choice of individual, group, or family services should be an informed one based on information regarding different forms of interpersonal helping and what they are like. To impart such knowledge of group work, agencies have presented films, tapes, or even "comic books" that portray what happens in the agency's groups.

A group experience may be desirable for some clients but is rejected because of some aspect of their situation. One example is a concern regarding confidentiality. In some cases, this problem is very "real" in that some information regarding clients might be harmful to them if publicized. On the other hand, all groups develop norms regarding confidentiality, and breaches of this are almost nonexistent. Most clients with such concerns are reassured by discussion of this issue prior to the group and during the first meetings.

Research Findings. A modest amount of research has been conducted to determine how group treatment compares in effectiveness with individual treatment. Toseland and Siporin reviewed this research and reported that group treatment was found to be more effective than individual treatment in 25 percent of the studies reviewed, and that individual treatment was not found more effective than group in any of the studies. As one might expect, group work was found to be efficient.[25] This review, however, did not locate any clear findings as to the types of problems for which group work was the most effective approach. Toseland and his colleagues, however, found in subsequent work that group work is likely to be more effective than individual for increasing social support and less effective for intense interpersonal problems.[26]

Yalom offers an extensive discussion of therapy group member selection that does draw on research findings.[27] The problem of generalizing from his discussion is that it is based almost entirely on research and experience from either adult therapy groups or encounter groups. Group workers often work with children's, short-term, and nonverbal activity groups, to name a few, where Yalom's conclusions may not hold.

For example, Yalom cites the "clinical consensus" that the following people are poor candidates for outpatient intensive group therapy: (1) brain-damaged, (2) paranoid, (3) extremely narcissistic, (4) hypochondriacal, (5) suicidal, (6) addicted to drugs or alcohol, (7) acutely psychotic, or (8) sociopathic.[28] Group workers have worked with brain-damaged people; crisis groups have included suicidal people; groups patterned after Alcoholics Anonymous have been used with alcoholics; and confrontive group technologies such as Synanon games and guided group interaction have been used with people labeled sociopathic. At least anecdotal reports suggest some success with these populations through group methods other than traditional psychotherapy.

Yalom, while referring to groups that do not represent the full range of group work activities, took an imaginative approach to the issue of selecting appropriate members for groups. Since it is difficult to determine for whom groups are best suited, he examined, instead, the kinds of people who dropped out of therapy groups after twelve or fewer meetings.[29] Obviously, if people terminate early from a group, they are unlikely to have benefited from it. In the absence, therefore, of a replication of this study with social work groups, Yalom's findings should be considered in selecting members for such groups. The reasons, according to Yalom, for such premature termination were as follows:

1. External Factors

These included conflicts between attending meetings and other events. Yalom implies the conflict may be a rationalization based on resistance to the group. Also, some people who present this kind of resistance to group attendance may be experiencing a crisis and wishing to secure help on an immediate one-to-one basis.

2. Group Deviancy

People viewed by themselves and others in the group as different in attributes relevant to the group are likely to be harmed rather than helped through the group process. As Yalom states, "There is experimental evidence, then, that the group deviant derives less satisfaction from the group, experiences anxiety, is less valued by the group, is less prone to be influenced or benefited by the group, is more likely to be harmed by the group, and is far more prone than nondeviants to terminate membership."[30] Here Yalom is describing people who are deviant in therapy groups because of their attitudes and behaviors, such as their strong use of denial and projection, their lack of interest in the intrapsychic, and their tendency to blame physical and health factors for their difficulties. From our group work experience, we conclude, also, that the worker's inability to find a group for a person in which other members have some similar attributes militates against offering group service to that person.

3. Problems of Intimacy

The people Yalom included in this category were those who manifested schizoid withdrawal, too rapid and intense self-disclosure, great fear of self-disclosure, and "unrealistic demands for instant intimacy."[31] Yalom recognizes that there is a paradox in the concept of problems with intimacy, as these are the reasons people are often referred to groups. The implication here is that some people are capable of working on these in group situations while others are overwhelmed in one way or another by the stimuli experienced in groups.

We remind the reader that Yalom is describing member problems with intimacy evoked in groups whose major focus is on the examination of relationship patterns. People with some severe intimacy problems have been helped with relationship issues in social work groups such as those where the programmatic emphasis is on activities requiring less verbal exchange and fewer demands for disclosure. Groups in mental health settings have utilized art, dramatics, and even games, which have helped shape social interaction behaviors and desensitize people whose fears led to inappropriate behaviors regarding disclosure and intimacy. A subsequent experience may then appropriately be in a verbally oriented therapy group.

4. Fear of Emotional Contagion

This category of group dropouts includes people who "reported that they had been extremely adversely affected by hearing the problems of the other group members."[32] Yalom believes that such people may gradually be desensitized to this. In many groups in which the process is structured, such individuals may have less cause for anxiety as to how they will be affected by the behaviors and problems of others.

When Yalom's list of categories of group dropouts is reviewed, the variable that seems the most pervasive for referral to any group is the likelihood that the person will find others to whom he or she can relate and who will reciprocate the desire for a relationship. In addition, expressions of difficulty in attending meetings, if not resolved, often indicate strong resistance to the group and militate against such a referral.

Yalom discusses "inclusion criteria" as those characteristics that most point to group therapy. He concludes that any person not excluded for the reasons just listed can profit from group therapy. In one study, he found that those people who profited the most were those who were most attracted to the group and were introspective.[33] In another study specifically devoted to outcomes of encounter groups, the set of predictors of good outcomes included being valued by other members, desiring personal change, viewing oneself as deficient in understanding one's feelings, and having high expectations of the group.[34]

One problem with these studies is that they do not distinguish between those who benefited from group therapy and those who benefited from other group approaches. Another problem is that the findings may be confounded by therapist expectations that motivated, verbal, socially assertive persons will succeed in therapy. This also points to the strong need for research regarding the ways the many different types of groups conducted by social group workers are likely to affect their members.

Preparing for Groups

Once candidates for the group have been selected, and prior to the first group meeting, the worker will accomplish a series of tasks. These tasks include preparing the individuals for the group, determining the optimum size of the group, and arranging the physical setting. Other people in the agency must also be prepared for the group so they can support the arrangements made. Finally, Schwartz suggests the worker engage in a process of "tuning in" prior to the group session.[35] Careful attention to these details will do much to ensure the success of the group.

Preparing Members for the Group

The idea that members prepared for the group experience are more likely to benefit from it is receiving increased support. This has led to efforts to specify such systems of preparation sufficiently so they can be tested. Northen, for example, recommends that the worker help the potential group member explore reactions to group placement and at the same time become acquainted with the worker. This, she asserts, will lead to a reduction in pregroup anxiety and confusion.[36]

Goldstein, Heller, and Sechrest present the following hypothesis: "Giving patients prior information about the nature of psychotherapy, the theories underlying it, and the techniques to be used will facilitate progress in psychotherapy."[37] Based on this type of prediction, investigations have been conducted as to the effects of explanations given to clients in a "role induction" interview. In one study conducted as early as 1964, patients told how to behave in therapy rated higher on attendance, relationships, and other therapy-related behaviors, as well as on outcome measures, than those not receiving such instruction.[38] Based on this finding, Goldstein and co-workers suggest that any such preparation present a theory relevant to the disorder, a rationale for the treatment, and a description of the treatment to follow.[39] Yalom developed and tested a procedure for preparation for clients for groups that conforms to the preceding criteria.[40] In this approach, he includes the following information, which he tailors to the individual being interviewed:

1. All who enter psychotherapy have problems in relationships with others.
2. The therapy group is a place for "honest interpersonal exploration" but this will not be easy.
3. There will be a "carryover" from the working out of relationships in the group to relationships outside the group.
4. To accomplish this carryover, group members must be honest and direct with their feelings at the moment.
5. "Stumbling blocks," such as feeling discouraged in early meetings, will occur and members should not follow an inclination to leave during this period.
6. Treatment is gradual and long.

In addition, Yalom tells members about the history of group therapy as well as the results of current outcome studies. They are also alerted to the issue of confidentiality. Finally, members are informed that if they develop relationships with other members outside the group, they should discuss this with the group.

In a test of this procedure with sixty people waiting for group psychotherapy, members of "prepared" groups had more faith in therapy and engaged in more group interaction than those in "unprepared" groups. This piece of research presents strong evidence for such preparation.

The task now is to develop analogous systems of preparation for the different types of groups served by group workers. One important step in this direction is the work of Diane Meadow.[41] She investigated the effects of pregroup preparation on time-limited groups led by M.S.W.'s practicing in community-based, family-oriented agencies. In the experimental groups, members were prepared by discussing their expectations of the group, their perceptions of how to use the group, their reasons for joining the group (including any skepticism), their understanding of the referral to the group, their reservations about the experience (which they were assured were typical), their past experiences with groups, and the role of the group worker.

Meadow's findings were that members of the experimental groups, if they dropped out, were more likely than control group members to discuss this decision with the worker; members of the experimental groups also were less likely to miss meetings than those in control groups, although this was not statistically significant. In addition, experimental group members were more likely than the controls to feel a greater sense of responsibility to the group and/or the group leader. They also had a clearer understanding of group purpose. Significant differences were not found between the experimental and control groups with reference to a number of group processes, but it is conceivable that as more work is done in preparing members for groups and examining group outcomes, these might also be affected.

Group Size

The size of the group should be determined by group purpose. The worker should also understand the kinds of processes that occur in groups of varying sizes. Small groups, such as those of about four to eight members, demand and produce more intimacy than larger groups. Such small groups are likely to bring pressure on members to participate. Larger groups, on the other hand, allow members to withdraw from active participation. The tendency in such groups is for polarization, with some members talking a great deal while others seldom speak.

Writers on verbally oriented group psychotherapy have recommended that such groups have about seven members. This allows for a sufficient number to carry on the group when inevitable absences occur. Members have sufficient time to focus on their own issues, and withdrawal from participation and intermember hostility are quickly noted and discussed.

Usually children's groups should be of a smaller size. In general, children are unlikely to postpone attention to their concerns for any length of time. In addition, if there is any likelihood of destructive or aggressive behavior, the group will be small enough for the worker to respond to this while remaining in control of the overall group situation. The same may be true of adolescent groups. On the other hand sometimes adolescents want the comfort of withdrawing from a demand for participation, which can be accomplished in larger groups.

In large groups it is possible to employ some devices to produce greater intimacy. These include extending the length of meetings so more members have time to receive group attention and dividing the group into subgroups, or even pairs, for discussion of issues, receipt of feedback, and reinforcement.

The following are some propositions relating group size to group purpose. Groups devoted to helping members clarify their values can be large if similar sets of values are examined; otherwise such groups should be small. Skill attainment groups in which members face similar barriers to achieving socialization goals may be large, otherwise small. Social control groups, if large, may undesirably allow members to avoid confrontation usually employed in such groups. On the other hand, some individuals may be "turned off" by too early confrontation and also may profit from observing other people able to deal constructively with such confrontation in a large group. Rehabilitation groups often require attention to the conflicts each member experiences and therefore should be small. People who are fearful of disclosure, however, might initially benefit from a large group in which models for such behavior are available.

Preparing the Physical and Social Setting

Often neglected but important details in group beginnings are the selection of the group's meeting place and the preparation of other staff for the impact of the group. If possible, the group should have a permanent room. This facilitates the group members' sense of group identity and permanence. The room should have pictures or other symbols that indicate the agency's receptivity to the group. These might include pictures of scenes pleasurable to the members or of people with whom members might identify. Occasionally, abstract art is used as a way of eliciting members' projections.

Bruno Bettelheim, for example, has presented the epitome of thoughtfulness regarding a rationale for the selection of decoration and objects in a therapeutic setting.[42] He discusses in great detail the objects in his agency's (a residential treatment center for children) reception room—the "living room." These include an antique crib, which communicates the belief that an infant's early experiences are important; a wall hanging showing a fairy tale; some furnishings suitable for adults and some for children; and an elaborately carved "throne," which easily supports a variety of images or fantasies.

The size of the room should also be planned with reference to the purposes and activities of the group. Too large a space can give members the illusion that the group has no boundaries. Yet one worker "made do" in such a situation by structuring a fence of chairs across the width of a large room. This helped to set some limits for a large group of hyperactive children, otherwise likely to fan out beyond the worker's control. Too small a space, on the other hand, can cause anxiety in a group whose members are fearful of being prematurely forced into intimacy.

It has become a stereotype that a group worker arranges chairs into a circle at all meetings. Yet this face-to-face contact promotes more interaction than other arrangements. The distance between chairs can also be varied, although members will usually move chairs into positions in which they are comfortable, this will help the worker assess the structure of interpersonal relationships. Groups with problems with interpersonal contact can, however, sit around a table as a sort of barrier.

The objects in the room will also suggest activities to the members (for example, chalk and blackboard, games, sports equipment). For group therapy situations, either comfortable chairs or large cushions on a carpeted floor communicate the idea that informal interaction is anticipated.

Other staff members should be aware of the beginning of the group. The receptionist should appear knowledgeable; attending a first meeting is anxiety-provoking enough without confusion beginning literally at the door of the agency. Members should be shown to the meeting room on arrival. The worker should be present early because the way members arrive and the timing of arrival will also disclose much about their attitudes to the group.

When other staff direct members to the room, their knowing about the group further communicates the agency's receptivity to the service. Staff, particularly those who have made referrals, will be asked questions by prospective members and, therefore, should be given information about the purpose, schedule, and location of the group meetings.

Part of the preparation for the first group meeting is the preparation of the worker himself or herself. We all experience feelings and thoughts about beginnings—whether the experience will be what we anticipate, whether we will be able to cope with events, whether we will be liked by others, whether we will like them, whether the group will be a success. Some workers handle these concerns by overstructuring first meetings; others deny these feelings and present a facade to members; still others openly admit to members that they, like the members, have concerns about the beginning of the group but that together they can work to share and resolve these. Whatever the preferred style of beginning, the worker should be aware of what his or her style is, what it is a response to, and how it affects the members as they cope with a new experience.

Tuning In

We agree with Schwartz that, in addition to being aware of their own styles of beginning, workers should prepare for sessions by "tuning in." Schwartz defines this as responding to the question: "How can I prepare myself to enter (or reenter, if we are past the first meeting) the group's life process so that I can begin the work as soon as possible?"[43] Schwartz suggests that a way to do this is to use one's "prior knowledge to anticipate clues that will be thrown up so quickly, and in such disguised ways, that the worker will miss them unless he is somehow 'tuned' to their frequency."[44] This involves contemplating the themes the members are likely to bring up, responses they are likely to have to agency purposes, ways they are likely to view the workers, and activities they are likely to anticipate. While workers may anticipate these things, they must be able to find out what members actually think. Schwartz sees "tuning in" as a preparation for listening, not a substitute for it. He continues his analysis:

> *I will be learning the language of hidden meanings, hidden agendas, so that I, the worker, will become a more sensitive instrument for decoding these messages and signals. I should become better prepared to understand the connections that will be implicit in the interaction, the connections between ideas and experience, ideas and their accompanying feeling.*[45]

Workers are sometimes concerned about their ability to "tune in" because their experiences have been different from those of group members. He states, with respect to this, that

> *It is important to remember that the inability to call up the exact life experience of the unmarried mother, the aged client, the young delinquent, is not necessarily a final deterrent to the worker trying to tune in. What he does is to call forth those elements of his own history that correspond most closely to what he is about to see before him. Thus, he has experienced rejection, as the unmarried mother is experiencing social punishment; he knows what it is like to disobey and be afraid and defiant, as is the young delinquent.*[46]

An example of this is a worker who was preparing for his first meeting with a group of patients in a hospital for people suffering from severe forms of alcoholism. He remembered from his previous meetings with these patients that they were feeling a great deal of ambivalence. On the one hand, they desperately wanted to solve their alcohol problems and thought they needed help. On the other hand, they often denied their problems and their need of help. They were also anxious about whether they could hold on to their marriages, their jobs, and their other relationships. He anticipated they would talk about their jobs and relationships and would also be struggling with whether they defined themselves as alcoholic. He anticipated that some of the members would be hostile, others withdrawn, and some even outwardly compliant.

He thought about his own anxieties in meeting with these clients. While he did not see himself as having any alcohol or drug problems, he remembered his own conflicts around overeating.

At the first meeting, some of the anticipated themes did emerge. In addition, the members discussed whether the staff could really accept them. One member said this was the best thing that ever happened to him. The worker, in view of his tuning in, considered the possibility that this member was trying to ensure that the worker was on his side and was an ally in obtaining what he wanted from the staff. The worker told this member that he could understand his hopes about the group, but that he also wanted to know what the members feared from it.

Type of Group

Prior to beginning the group, the worker will also anticipate the group's overall *format.* The alternatives include whether the group will be short-term or long-term; whether all members will be expected to begin and end at the same time (open-ended versus closed-ended groups); and whether the activities of the meetings will be predetermined or evolve from the immediate interaction among the members and the worker (structured and unstructured groups). We shall now discuss some of the criteria workers use in making these decisions.

We think of groups as short-term if, by plan, they meet for two or three months or less. Long-term groups meet for more than six months. We conceive of a "grey area" (groups that meet from three to six months) to incorporate some characteristics of each type. We find that most groups conducted by social workers, in view of client motivation and resources, are short-term. This is likely to coincide with the idea of many clients that they are applying for or accepting services to resolve particular problems. We also find that some group members who continue in a group long after the original reason for joining the group has been resolved may either develop a dependency upon the group as a substitute for other social interactions or may even create problems in order to justify remaining in the group.

We recommend time-limited groups for most agency and client situations; however, there are several exceptions. One is that of the client not likely to function without continued support. An example of this is the long-term client suffering from a serious mental illness who is living in the community. Even in this case, however, we hope that a range of self-help support groups will be made available when a professionally led group is no longer contributing substantially to the client's progress.

Another exception is long-term group therapy for people with severe disorders such as *borderline personality.* We recognize that psychiatric opinion is often in favor of individual therapy for such people. We, nevertheless, have seen some of these clients make progress in skillfully conducted groups that provide support, opportunities to develop social skills, feedback on relationship patterns, and considerable empathy.

We believe that groups with members who begin and end together have an advantage in terms of trust among members, knowledge members attain of each other, and the level of cohesiveness the group develops. Nevertheless, it is seldom feasible to form such groups. For example, social workers conduct groups in inpatient settings where patients are admitted daily and often remain for a few weeks or less. Another situation is when members enter a group, contract to work on a specific problem or problems, and terminate when their goals are attained. This group may consist of some members who are developing goals, some who are working on attaining them, and some who are terminating.

We have observed many open-ended groups and are strongly convinced that they "work." The main issue for the worker is to help members make use of their current interactions with others in the group in two crucial ways: (1) to gain support and feedback regarding their identification of and work toward attaining individual goals and (2) to examine their "here-and-now" experiences in the group as a means of identifying and assessing their problems in functioning with others.[47]

With reference to "structured" and "unstructured" groups, we believe that a continuum exists and may range from a minimum of interaction among members in some groups conducted primarily for imparting information, to a maximum in some psychotherapy groups in which workers and members react to processes as they emerge. We believe that the more structured end of the continuum should be used when the purpose of the group is primarily to help members acquire a very specific skill such as in communication, problem solving, assertiveness, or parenting training. The less structured end should be used when members are being helped to identify problems, to become aware of or to modify their characteristic ways of interacting with others, or to apply some of the skills they have acquired through more structured phases of the group.

Summary

In this chapter, we have presented a rationale for preparing for the group and have discussed its various aspects. Preplanning includes determining group purpose, deciding which persons can be helped in a group, determining the size and composition of the group, selecting and preparing the physical setting, "tuning in," and determining the group's format.

Group Composition Exercise

Goals

1. To learn to apply the principles of group composition.
2. To identify the steps involved in a group composition procedure.
3. To learn how to evaluate the adequacy of one's group composition procedure by assessing whether initial group processes are the ones intended by the way the group was composed.

Procedure

1. Prior to the exercise, trainees read about and discuss the principles of group composition described in this chapter.
2. Trainees (preferably about twenty, but the exercise can be done with sixteen) fill out the accompanying Assessment Form. This simulates a needs assessment and group referral process.

3. The instructor divides the group in half, and the halves exchange Assessment Forms. The two halves created in this way are instructed to compose a group consisting of about five persons from the other half. (If the halves are too small, they can supplement each other to form the group.) This task is to be completed by utilizing the principles of group composition the trainees have discussed. The group may secure additional information to accomplish this task through delegating someone to go to the other half to arrange for a private "interview" with one or another prospective member.

There are two alternatives for the next step in the exercise:

a. Each half reports on the group it has composed and the rationale for believing it to be viable. The entire class discusses the issues this raises.
b. After composing a group, the trainees predict how the group is likely to begin (that is, topics likely to be discussed, initial exploration of commonalities, purposes which emerge, subgroupings). One or two members volunteer to be group workers and actually conduct a minisession (about twenty minutes) of the group. The trainees then present their rationale for composing the group, their predictions, and the initial group outcomes. The entire class discusses the issues posed by this.

Questions for Discussion

1. How was the initial purpose for the group determined?
2. How were individual reasons for wishing to be in a group related to group purpose?
3. What types of attributes were considered and why were they considered?
4. What types of member behaviors were considered and why were they considered?
5. How was motivation to be in a group considered?
6. How did the "workers" plan to begin the group in light of the way it was composed? Did this plan involve some mechanism for dealing with some deficits in the composition (too great heterogeneity; insufficient basis for interpersonal attraction)?

Group Composition Assessment Form

Name _____

Sex _____   Age Group _____ 20–25 _____ 26–30 _____ over 30

Briefly describe a question, concern, or issue you would like to discuss in a group, if none, write NONE.

How active are you in groups?
_____ talk a great deal   _____ talk little
_____ talk somewhat   _____ say nothing or almost nothing

What are some of your hobbies or interests?

How do you feel about being in a group composed as part of this class?

_____ very interested   _____ somewhat opposed

_____ somewhat interested   _____ very opposed

_____ neutral

Notes for Group Composition Rater

"Tuning-In" Exercise

This exercise can be used in conjunction with the "Group Composition Exercise" or as distinct from it. If the former, the participants in the exercise can respond to the exercise in terms of the group they have created. If the latter, the participants can respond in terms of a group of clients they would like to work with or actually plan on serving.

Procedure

1. Describe the purpose the agency has in forming the group.
2. List the individuals likely to attend the first meeting and briefly describe them in terms of their demographic characteristics (age, gender, ethnicity, and so forth) as well as the reasons they may have for coming to the group.
3. Consider the answers to the following questions:

   a. What issues are the members likely to bring up?
   b. What feelings are the members likely to have about coming to this group?
   c. What do you think the members will perceive as the attitudes of significant others in their lives who will know they are attending the group?
   d. What are the members likely to think are the factors that contribute to their difficulties?
   e. What are some feelings members are likely to have about the problems they experience?

4. How do you as the group worker think and feel with respect to the possible thoughts and feelings of potential group members?
5. How will you check out whether your "hunches" about members' thoughts and feelings are correct?
6. How do you anticipate being helpful to the members during the meeting in light of your answers to the above questions?

Endnotes

1. Irvin D. Yalom, *The Theory and Practice of Group Psychotherapy*, 4th ed. (New York: Basic Books, 1995): 265.

2. For an extended discussion on this topic, see Larry E. Davis and Enola R. Proctor, *Race, Gender,* and Class: Guidelines for Practice with Individuals, Families, and Groups* (Englewood Cliffs: Prentice Hall, 1989): 89–117.

3. For example, see E.D. Edwards, M.E. Edwards, G.M. Dianes, and F. Eddy, "Enhancing Self-Concept and

Identification with 'Indianness' of American Indian Girls," *Social Work with Groups I* (1978), pp. 209–18; K. Hynes and J. Werbin, "Group Psychotherapy for Spanish Speaking Women," *Psychiatric Annals VII* (1977): 622–27.

4. L.E. Davis, "Essential Components of Group Work with Black Americans," *Social Work with Groups VII* (1984): 97–109.

5. J. Chu and S. Sue, "Asian/Pacific-Americans and Group Practice," *Social Work with Groups VII* (1984), pp. 23–36.

6. M.K. Ho, "Social Group Work with Asian/Pacific-Americans," *Social Work with Groups VII* (1984): 49–61.

7. F.X. Acosta and J. Yamamoto, "The Utility of Group Work Practice for Hispanic Americans," *Social Work with Groups VII* (1984): 63–73.

8. P.Y. Martin and K.A. Shanahan, "Transcending the Effects of Sex Composition in Small Groups," *Social Work with Groups VII* (1983): 19–32; also see Davis and Proctor, *Race, Gender, and Class:* 221–50.

9. L. Festinger, "Informal Social Communication," *Psychological Review* LVII (1950): 274.

10. J.W. Thibaut and H.H. Kelly, *The Social Psychology of Groups* (New York: John Wiley, 1959): 15.

11. Yalom, *Group Psychotherapy:* 47–68.

12. Ibid.: 67.

13. Ibid.: 261.

14. Ibid.

15. Ibid.: 263.

16. Recent discussions of this type of group include I.D. Yalom, *Inpatient Group Psychotherapy* (New York: Basic Books, 1983); and J.H. Schopler and M.J. Galinsky, "Meeting Practice Needs: Conceptualizing the Open-ended Group," *Social Work with Groups VII* (Summer 1984): 3–21.

17. For more details on this procedure, see Harvey J. Bertcher and Frank Maple, "Elements and Issues in Group Composition," in *Individual Change Through Small Groups*, eds. Martin Sundel, Paul Glasser, Rosemary Sarri, and Robert Vinter (New York: Free Press, 1985): 180–202.

18. For a discussion of the point, see Marvin E. Shaw, *Group Dynamics: The Psychology of Small Group Behavior*, 3rd ed. (New York: McGraw-Hill, 1981): 191-201.

19. A. Goldstein, K. Heller, and L. Sechrest, *Psychotherapy and the Psychology of Behavior Change* (New York: John Wiley, 1966): 329.

20. Ibid.: 257–58.

21. William C. Schutz, *Firo: A Three Dimensional Theory of Interpersonal Orientations* (New York: Holt, Reinhart & Winston, 1958).

22. William I. Shalinsky, "The Effects of Group Composition on Aspects of Group Functioning" (unpublished doctoral dissertation, Western Reserve University, 1967).

23. A comprehensive discussion of co-worker issues is provided in a special journal issue devoted to this topic. See *Social Work with Groups III* (1980).

24. H. Laqueur, H. Laburt, and G. Morong, "Multiple Family Therapy: Further Developments," *International Journal of Social Psychiatry* (1964) Congress Issue: 70–80.

25. Roland Toseland and Max Siporin, "When to Recommend Group Treatment: A Review of the Clinical and Research Literature," *International Journal of Group Psychotherapy* 36(2) (1986): 171–201.

26. R. Toseland, C. Rossiter, T. Peak, and G. Smith, "Comparative Effectiveness of Individual and Group Interventions to Support Family Caregivers," *Social Work*, 35(3) (1990): 209–19.

27. Yalom, *Group Psychotherapy*, pp. 217–43.

28. Ibid.: 219.

29. Ibid.: 221–25.

30. Ibid.: 228.

31. Ibid.: 231.

32. Ibid.: 233.

33. Ibid.: 235–37.

34. Morton A. Lieberman, Irvin Yalom, and M. Miles, *Encounter Groups: First Facts* (New York: Basic Books, 1973): 315–55.

35. William Schwartz, "Social Work with Groups: The Search for a Method", in *Social Work: The Collected Writings of William Schwartz*, ed. Toby Berman-Rossi (Itasca, Ill.: Peacock, 1994): 134–46.

36. Helen Northen, *Social Work with Groups* (New York: Columbia University Press, 1969): 108.

37. Goldstein, Heller, and Sechrest, *Psychotherapy:* 245.

38. R. Hoehn-Saric and others, "Systematic Preparation of Patients for Psychotherapy: Effects on Therapy Behavior and Outcome," *Journal of Psychiatry Research, II* (1964): 267–81.

39. Goldstein, Heller, and Sechrest, *Psychotherapy:* 250.

40. Yalom, *Group Psychotherapy:* 278–92.

41. Diane Meadow, "Connecting Theory and Practice: The Effect of Pregroup Preparation on Individual and Group Behavior," No Date (Mimeographed).

42. Bruno Bettelheim, *A Home for the Heart* (New York: Knopf, 1974): 104–58.

43. Schwartz, *Social Work with Groups:* 134.

44. Ibid.: 135.

45. Ibid.: 143.

46. Ibid.: 144.

47. See Yalom, *Inpatient Group Psychotherapy*, for an extensive discussion of how to work with such groups.

Chapter *4*

Beginning a Group

In this chapter we shall describe the processes that occur in groups during their beginning phases and the activities of group workers to facilitate these processes. Group workers seek to understand the processes of group beginnings for several reasons.

1. All groups go through formation phases, and the workers who understand these will not be overly concerned by inevitable events in the group. Rather, they will understand these as efforts of group members to cope with determining group purposes, selecting activities to achieve these purposes, and learning to trust and cooperate with each other.[1]
2. The worker can learn to differentiate between fairly typical patterns and those that require the worker and members to take special measures to save the group from inertia or destruction.

As we indicated in Chapter 3, the worker must learn to integrate knowledge of phases of group development with stages of the group work process. Chapter 4 seeks to enhance this integration with reference to group beginnings.

In the first part of the chapter, we present the process of group formation as it may occur in any group. Following this general discussion of group formation, we present the tasks the worker must undertake to accomplish the group purpose. These tasks include assisting the members to decide on group purposes that will help them to achieve their goals as well as group rules that will govern behavior. Both the members and the worker will have to gather information to choose effective ways of accomplishing the group's goals. Usually, when the group is thought of as "treatment," this information gathering is conceived of as an *assessment*.

A number of issues regarding member emotions in beginning phases must also be understood. Members are often ambivalent because they are attracted to the group while also experiencing some anxiety about investing in it. The members will have feelings about the worker with which they must learn to cope.

We conclude the chapter with a discussion of how to resolve atypical formation difficulties. A group exercise based on enhancing one's understanding of group formation is also included.

Process of Group Formation

In the first meetings of groups, particularly those in which members have not known each other, there is little sharing of personal, intimate reactions and experiences. Rather, members will interact based on fairly superficial attributes or experiences. For example, members will comment on the similarities and differences of places they have lived, and they will talk primarily with people similar in obvious ways such as age, race, and sex. Members may also seek out others in the group with common interests in sports, politics, religion, or leisure activities.

In his discussion of group beginnings, Yalom notes that in groups defined as offering therapy, symptom description is a favorite early issue, along with previous experiences, medications, and the like.[2] He sees this "stereotyped" activity as one way of coping with the anxiety posed by beginnings.

Decisions on Group Purpose

In the process of becoming acquainted, members must determine group purpose(s). This may be simple, as when a group has been formed around some highly specific issue such as enhancing assertiveness or parenting. Members in these circumstances have joined the group to learn specific social skills or discipline techniques. The determination of group purpose may, however, be a more complex one when members have additional, alternative, or even covert reasons for joining the group.

One example of a covert reason for joining a group was that of a member of an assertiveness group who had hoped to make friends; another example was a woman in a parent education group who sought encouragement to find employment outside her home. Another person joined a job placement group to recruit people for a social action project to promote a public service career program.

A thorough discussion of purposes in a group's formation period leads, in most circumstances, to a choice of group purpose that has the strongest commitment of all members. In some instances, however, individual issues that will broaden or change group purposes do not surface until the group progresses to the subsequent phase and activities to accomplish group purposes are determined. Problems that arise in choosing activities often result from lack of commitment to the group purpose by some or all members.

In some groups, the initial statement of purpose is vague, as in "enhancing interpersonal relationships." Such groups must further discuss and clarify purpose as a basis for decisions regarding group activities.

Assessment in Groups

Usually, in concert with determining purposes, members will find it necessary to gather various kinds of information. This activity can help members specify group purposes in detail as they list problems that concern them individually or as a group. Such information gathering will also include securing details about individual or group problems. In groups devoted to achieving specific individual treatment goals, members will obtain data related to the causes of and solutions to individual behavior problems, thus forming an assessment of the member's individual behavior problems. In addition to or instead of a member-oriented assessment, data gathering may focus on analyzing other systems such as the schools, communities, or work places of members' families.

A number of useful guidelines exist for assessing individuals, groups, and larger systems, such as those provided by Siporin, Compton and Galaway, and Rose.[3] These frameworks can be used in individual, family, or group work. In all these contexts, workers and clients should base their actions on an analysis of the systems relevant to the problem at hand.

Assessments of the problems of group members will employ the same concepts and theories as those used with individuals. There is no consensus in social work, however, regarding a theoretical framework for assessment, and group workers will use behavioral, ego psychological, role, or other theoretical systems in the same manner as other social workers. Group workers can draw upon the members, however, in the assessment process in several ways: first, members can be trained to participate in assessments of each other; second, behavior in the group provides direct evidence regarding the member's interpersonal behavior that is not available through individual ways of helping.

Members, with or without a common conceptual framework, are likely to ask each other questions and to contribute information about their problems. Because of similarities in problems, cultures, and life experiences, members may have more insight into each other's difficulties than the worker has. This is a major advantage of the group context. In addition, members can be taught to utilize established frameworks for assessment.

One example of a framework successfully taught to members of treatment groups is behavioral assessment.[4] One applicable form of behavioral assessment involves explaining to members that behavior is *caused* by its antecedents and consequences.

There are two types of antecedents and consequences: overt and covert. Overt ones occur in the environment; covert ones occur in the thoughts and feelings of the individual. A study of *antecedents* includes an examination of the thoughts and feelings of the person before the behavior occurs, the place where it occurs, who was present at the time, and what these people were doing. *Consequences* is a less technical expression than *reinforcement* and *punishment* but refers to both terms as well as to the likelihood that specified behaviors will be met with pleasurable or aversive responses, or none at all.

Members have been taught to recognize antecedents and consequences through explanation of these terms followed by examples and role plays, which are analyzed in this manner. Because of the members' familiarity with each other's circumstances, the group is an effective place to perform a behavioral assessment.

The group, because it represents a small society in its own right, also provides direct information about the causes of member behaviors. The workers and members observe each other reacting to stress, nurturance, ambiguity, and other interpersonal circumstances. This use of the group for assessment purposes can be enhanced in several ways.

One method is role playing. Members can set up simulations of environmental situations or can replay intragroup ones. The members comment on these events, utilizing the variety of data provided. A member can even observe while another member plays his or her role and thus gain objectivity regarding the circumstances.

A second assessment device is provided by activities. The worker can introduce crafts, dramatics, and games, to name a few, and through these media enable members to express their concerns and display responses to a variety of situations.[5]

A third device, usually referred to as the "fishbowl," requires part of the group to observe and give feedback to another part of the group. This procedure provides excellent training for members in the understanding of behavior. The observing subgroup, or even single members asked to observe the group, can be supplied with simple questionnaires or rating instruments to support this activity.

Determination of Norms

The formation period of the group is crucial in relationship to norm development. The norms that social workers seek to instill in groups are derived from the values of social work stated in Chapter 1, but are more specific indications of how members expect each other to behave. Glassman and Kates, in a book on this subject, have done an excellent job of specifying the norms that are consistent with the humanistic orientation of most group workers.[6] The following draws substantially from their description of such norms.

In relationship to the value regarding the inherent worth of the individual, the norm that workers specify is for members to value the sanctity and rights of every other member. The worker helps this norm develop by emphasizing the value of each member's contribution to the work and direction of the group, and by recognizing that members come from different cultures and backgrounds.

For the value of members assuming responsibility for one another, the worker specifies the norm that members should find ways to experience caring for one another. The worker facilitates this by helping members explore their feelings for one another and by matching this to a criterion of caring. Related to this value is the norm that members should seek ways of cooperating rather than competing with one another. The worker helps by identifying situations of noncooperation and by supporting the sharing of resources and the emerging of experiences through which members can work together.

Another value in group work is the right to be accepted unconditionally and, therefore, the right to be included in experiences that meet one's needs. A group norm that relates to this is that all members have an equal right to belong to the group. Clearly, all groups must have boundaries that define membership, but the worker insists that these be carefully determined, after which the individual's membership in the group is secure. This kind of security has extraordinary curative potential for the members.

Definitions of membership must be based on the needs of individuals and not on arbitrary ethnic, racial, class, or other stereotypes. Based upon this, the group will not seek to exclude "difficult" members. As Glassman and Kates state elsewhere, "It is a group that may choose to struggle with such a member and to develop fuller ways of coping with that individual, [that strengthens] itself as a collective."[7] The worker will often model this and struggle to accept and interact with difficult members. At times, members must be excluded for their own protection, but this step is taken only after careful consideration of the alternatives and with due recognition of the threat to their security.

The worth of every human being emphasizes the norm that "Everyone takes part and is helped to take part."[8] This leads the worker to encourage members with low participation rates and to subdue those who "overparticipate."

The value placed upon self-determination has many implications for group norms, relating both to the self-determination of the individuals and the self-determination of the group-as-a-whole. In supporting this norm, the worker will help the group examine power issues relevant to how group decisions affect the group itself and its individual members.

This norm relates to the topic of democracy in the group. Some groups will function with all of the democratic procedures that have been developed, such as those in *Robert's Rules of Order*.[9] Members in some other groups are unable to feel secure without a great degree of worker control, as in groups where members suffer from a psychosis, are very young, or have very limited mental abilities. The principle must be that workers help groups develop as much democratic decision making as possible. Anything short of this must be justified to the members and to others in a position to safeguard their rights (such as the client's rights officer created in many settings, the client's relatives, and sometimes the client's attorneys). Even in the latter instances, the worker will always try to help members move to a greater level of participation in decision making.

Glassman and Kates also state the value that "The worker is accountable to the group."[10] This norm is implemented by encouraging members to ask questions about the worker's actions and to evaluate the worker periodically.

Other values cited by Glassman and Kates are the right to freedom of speech and expression, the belief that difference is enriching, and freedom of choice regarding whether to change or not. We believe that these are as important as the ones previously quoted, and in some sense may be an amplification of these values.

Although the worker seeks to instill values and norms while the group is being formed, a discussion of values and norms continues throughout its life. One of the most potent aspects of group process, as the group becomes more cohesive, is the pressure that emerges for conformity to norms. When this is therapeutic, by helping members achieve a personal goal of self-control, it is a valuable phenomenon. Otherwise the group can be a destructive experience, which the worker should make known to the group. An excellent discussion of such negatives that can emerge in groups is provided by Galinsky and Schopler.[11]

Emotional Reactions to Group Formation

An emotional issue present in group beginnings is the conflict between being attracted to the group and simultaneously experiencing anxiety about the group.[12] This constitutes a form of approach-avoidance conflict for the members. The attraction to the group is attested to at least in voluntary groups by the members' presence. Members come because they hope the group will help them attain their objectives. They may also look forward to the gratification of interacting with other members and/or with the worker. On the other hand, members often have apprehensions about the group. Will it help them to achieve their purposes, or will it restrain them? Will other members be hostile, unaccepting, or unlikable? Will the costs of achieving goals be too great? Will the members find some familiar and comfortable position in the group?

If the group, in its first meetings, appears more on the positive side compared to other ways members might satisfy their wants, the members will remain and invest themselves in it. If the group, in the same period, is seen negatively, several members will discontinue, which may destroy the group.

The worker should comment on these ambivalent feelings since this may help sustain the members through difficulties usually present in group beginnings. This action should have an empathic quality and may also enhance member-worker relationships. In addition, an empathic response invites the members to work on their feelings about the group's beginning and to cope with fears about the group. This type of discussion may also help members approach formation issues in a more relaxed manner.

In the beginning of groups, as well as at other crucial times in their existence, members sometimes develop a tradition of a "round." This involves members, in turn, sharing their feelings at that moment. Since shared feelings often relate to common group themes, this procedure helps prepare the way for discussion.

Relationship of Group Worker to Members

Members, in an emotional sense, place the workers in a central position because of their presumed expertise and responsibility for the group. The members address a large proportion of their communications to the worker and may appear dependent on that person for solutions to individual and group problems. According to at least one writer, this early dependence on the group worker is the need for an omnipotent, omniscient, omnicaring parent.[13]

Too much dependence can be confronted at an appropriate stage in the development of the group. In the beginning, however, even though the worker risks dependence, he or she should nurture a relationship with each member. At the most elementary level, this includes addressing each member by name. To accentuate this expression of interest, the worker should seek occasions to single out each member for a comment, question, or encouraging remark. The worker also often takes responsibility for opening the group meeting. This shows a readiness to take a share of responsibility for the group, even when the worker's plan and philosophy calls for the group's eventual assumption of responsibility for itself.

Research has demonstrated that the outcome of helping processes are strongly related to the degree to which the worker demonstrates three types of behaviors—empathy, genuineness, and warmth.[14] While much of the research on these variables has been done in the one-to-one counseling situation, some substantiation of their potency in group situations is available.[15]

Empathy

Empathy refers to the accuracy of the worker's feedback regarding the members' feelings. Accuracy includes not only the feeling but the context in which the feeling was aroused. Some techniques, such as the exact repetition of members' statements, are often aversive to many people who view this as mocking. The worker must, therefore, choose a sincere and natural way of paraphrasing members' feelings. An example of a worker's empathic response to a member's statement that "I was frightened when I went home and found my wife had gone out," was "It was a scary feeling for you when you got back from work and found your wife wasn't home." The member continued, "That's right and I didn't know what to do."

An important experience in a group is for members to offer and receive empathic responses from each other. This also enhances the cohesiveness of the group. The worker increases the likelihood that members will be empathic with each other by the model he or she presents. In addition, the worker explains the value of empathy and trains members to make empathic responses to each other. This training can be done through calling attention to his or her own responses, role playing of empathic responses, or giving feedback to members when they naturally interact in this way.

The frequency of empathic responses in a group can be increased by having a member or observer count them. If the group believes this too low, an increase can become a group goal, and the group can reward itself for achieving it. This type of self-monitoring is usually done in early stages of groups or when members are concerned about the group atmosphere.

Genuineness

Genuineness consists of the honesty and openness of the worker with the members. To be genuine the worker must have a substantial amount of self-awareness, otherwise he or she may unknowingly behave in inconsistent or covert ways. Genuine behavior will be devoid of contradictions in various aspects of the worker's behavior. The worker who is genuine, for example, will not deny being angry with members at times. Similarly, when the worker feels warmly towards members, he or she will be free to say so. The worker will also engage in appropriate self-disclosure. While evidence exists of the value of the worker's revealing aspects of his or her own experiences to model openness for members and provide useful data, a great deal of judgment must be exercised regarding when and how much disclosure should take place.[16]

In an extensive discussion of worker self-disclosure in groups, Weiner[17] points out that when members can observe the worker interact with other members, it represents a degree of disclosure. In addition, members can help each other deal with their reactions to worker disclosures.

Another aspect of genuineness is the willingness of the worker to provide feedback to members regarding perceptions of *their* behavior. The worker who withholds personal reactions to individuals in the group, as well as to the group itself, will not be evaluated by the members as having been honest with them. The worker must use judgment as to the way such reactions are shared and whether they reflect his or her biases in ways destructive to the members. Some examples of workers' reactions are given to illustrate this point.

Example: A worker told a group of young adults with socialization problems that they were wasting *their* time when they avoided discussions of their relationships to each other.

Example: A worker for a group of parents who sought better ways of raising their children pointed out to them the amount of time they spent complaining about their children rather than seeking better ways of responding in difficult encounters with them. The worker said they were doing some of the kinds of things they complained about their children doing.

At the same time, the worker must help the members behave more genuinely to each other. The following is an example of this.

Example: When Robert turned his back on Sam as the members were discussing Sam's problem, the worker pointed this out to him (helping Robert to be aware of the contradictory messages he presents to Sam). The worker then encouraged Robert to discuss what about Sam was upsetting him (helping Robert to engage in appropriate self-disclosure). In this discussion, the worker also supported Robert in telling Sam that whenever he (Robert) tried to help Sam, he (Sam) also turned away (helping Robert present his perceptions of Sam honestly to Sam).

Warmth

Warmth, usually referred to as nonpossessive warmth, is somewhat harder to show than empathy and genuineness because much of its expression is in the form of feelings. As Schulman points out, "Several characteristics are included in the concept of warmth—equal worth, absence of blame, nondefensiveness, and closeness."[18] A rating scale Schulman uses divides warmth, for this reason, into two dimensions: positive regard and respect.[19]

Positive regard is the degree to which the worker shows interest in the group members and concern for his or her welfare. It also includes the acceptance, by the worker, of the members' freedom to be themselves. This does not preclude the worker's expectation that the members will seek to realize their fullest capacities.

Respect, on the other hand, is reflected in the way the worker appreciates the members' efforts. Even when they fail at these efforts or behave unpleasantly to others, the worker recognizes that the members are trying to cope with difficult situations.

Example: When Mary reported to the group that she failed her examination, she was in tears as the worker placed her arm on Mary's shoulder. At this, Mary, even while crying, angrily attacked her teacher as a "mean old bitch." The worker, while her arm was still around Mary, said she could see Mary felt this way because of her past experiences. The worker also asked Mary how the group could help her. Mary said she knew that Sue had had a "run in" with the same teacher and she asked Sue how she had handled it. The worker, in this way, helped Mary secure expressions of warmth from other group members.

The worker's race and gender will have many effects on the relationships that emerge, at least initially, between the worker and the members. Members may prefer a worker similar to themselves because they believe such a worker will understand them better and identify with their concerns.

Some members may prefer a worker different in some way because they fear that a worker may judge their behavior as others in their group do. For example, some Catholic members worried that a Catholic worker would judge them negatively because they had been divorced. In another group, Jewish members feared that a Jewish worker would criticize them for failing to restrict themselves to eating only Kosher foods. In still another group, a black member feared that a black worker would criticize her for dating a white man.

In some groups, the race or gender of the worker may be of special relevance. A group for women dealing with the trauma of rape wanted nothing to do with a male worker and made this very clear (the agency had no intention of assigning a man to this group). On the other hand, a group for men who had abused women was assigned both a man and a woman worker, as the agency thought men needed feedback from a woman regarding their statements about significant women in their lives.

In any case, we strongly recommend that workers explore the feelings of the members about the worker's ethnicity and gender. Some workers have told us that this is unnecessary or inappropriate in the beginning stage of group work. We disagree with this. Even if members are not ready to deal with this issue, the worker has declared a willingness to discuss this topic in detail when appropriate.

Relationships among Members

Members' feelings toward one another, if primarily positive, will be the major reason they return to the group. The trust they develop in one another will also be the major determinant of their ability to help one another with personal difficulties or with tasks.

Seeking Similarities

The worker seeks to develop relationships among the members by helping them discover similarities in their life experiences, their difficulties, and their ways of responding to situations. This is initiated by encouraging members to tell about themselves, while seeing to it that a few members do not monopolize the first sessions, thus causing other members to lose interest in the group. One relevant question could be how they came to join the group. In a child guidance clinic, children in a group used small dolls to describe their family composition; in a group of handicapped people undergoing physical and occupational rehabilitation, members described the rehabilitation programs in which they had participated.

In some groups where the intent is for the group to continue for a long period and complex interactional patterns are likely to be discussed, the worker may draw attention to more subtle similarities. In a group served by an outpatient psychiatric clinic, one member spoke of his difficulties in setting out for the group meeting that evening; another spoke of problems in starting school; and a third talked of how difficult it had been in the beginning of her marriage. The worker pointed out the common theme of feelings about difficult beginnings.

Talking to Each Other

One major issue in first meetings is that members tend to talk to the worker rather than to each other. This may be inevitable when the worker offers information to orient members. On the other hand, members must be encouraged to talk to each other, and in the group's beginning this should be raised as an issue. The worker can draw attention to this in several ways: first, by redirecting questions, placed to him or her, back to group members;

second, by directly pointing out the value of members helping each other; third, by identifying commonalities among the members. The worker may also choose to raise the issue of overdependency on the worker for discussion.

Reducing Distortions

Members should be helped to separate perceptions of each other from realities. While this process continues over the life of the group, it is important to begin early. Some workers accelerate the process by asking members to select a member who reminds them of someone. Members then discuss this either in pairs or with the whole group. A less direct form of this exercise is to ask members in rotation to focus on one member at a time and associate colors, animals, and so forth with that member. This experience is then discussed and can lead to an awareness of the emotions and meanings members project onto each other.

During these kinds of early processes, the worker should be aware that closeness among members, or for that matter among any persons, is not easy to attain and may be particularly difficult for the people served by social workers. The worker should acknowledge this as empathically as possible.

Careful Listening

One technique to facilitate closeness is to enhance the way members listen to each other. Some of the approaches mentioned in this chapter are likely to encourage such careful listening. Thus identifying one's fantasies about other members helps one be more attentive to the actual rather than imagined statements of the other people. Being sensitive to common concerns also has this effect. One technique directly related to this issue is to help members be aware of times when they are not listening, and out of this awareness to commit themselves to practice listening.

For training in listening, some workers use the exercise of asking members, for a limited period, to repeat the previous comment before continuing on with their own. Another is for members to rotate the role of "summarizer." The group will then be asked to turn to the "summarizer" whenever it wishes to examine its recent process.

When the members who have failed to listen are confronted by the worker, they can be asked to talk about feelings they had at such times. Members, particularly children being taught group discussion skills, can be rewarded with tokens by other group members when such other members feel understood.

Group Structure during Formation

Another task of the worker in the beginning of a group is to enable the group to have the kinds of structures conducive to further group development. Group structures consist of the patterns of relationships among members. We shall deal here with group structure issues relevant to group beginnings; in the next chapter, we shall elaborate on structural issues occurring in groups at later stages.

Types of Structures

Some of the major group structures are the following:

1. Communications structure: who speaks to whom about what and under what circumstances.[20]
2. Sociometric structure: who likes or dislikes whom in the group. (These emotional patterns contribute to the creation of subgroups. Groups are often subdivided into cliques of members who interact with each other more frequently than they do with others outside of the subgroup.)[21]
3. Power structure: who influences whom in the group and in what manner.[22]
4. Leadership structure: who contributes most to the determination and accomplishment of group tasks, as well as who contributes most to reducing tensions, enhancing group cohesiveness, and securing compliance with formal and informal rules.[23]
5. Role structure: who occupies formally recognized positions such as chairpersons, secretaries, and so forth, who fills positions created by group activities (for example, pitcher, expert in sewing), and who fulfills categories growing out of even more informal group interactions (for example, mediator, clown, rebel).[24]

Structural Changes

The worker should examine each of the structures just listed in terms of their effects on group beginnings. The communications structure should become one in which the maximum number of members participate and in which members respond to each other. Rose, for example, suggests devices to measure communication patterns,[25] including simple tallies of the number of times each member talks. We have also used a form of recording (Figure 4.1) that captures who is spoken to as well as who speaks. Rose also uses behavioral approaches to change these patterns, such as the person on the speaker's right reinforcing low-frequency speakers with tokens and restraining high-frequency speakers with a hand on their shoulder.

Sociometric structures early in the group's life are not likely to be defined rigidly. The exception may be when members have some definite cleavages determined by race, age, or sex. The worker's role is to use activities or encourage participation so members have as much contact as possible with those who differ from themselves. These activities may include games, discussions in dyads or triads, and role plays that require various types of subgroups for execution.

Similarly, some members may appear to have more power than other members by virtue of their expertise, control over resources (for example, a car, sports equipment), ability to punish (for example, use of sarcasm), or ability to inflict physical harm. The worker strives to help members to use power to attain treatment goals without interfering with other members' attainment of goals.

Some individuals who experience themselves as relatively powerless should be helped to gain a share of influence in the group. This can be done through helping them to assume useful roles in the group, coaching them to be more assertive in the group, and supporting their contributions during group meetings.

Person Spoken To

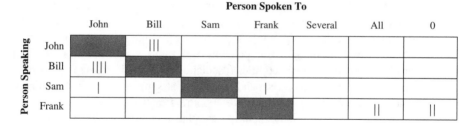

	John	Bill	Sam	Frank	Several	All	0
John	▓	|||					
Bill	||||	▓					
Sam				▓				
Frank				▓		||	||

(row labels grouped under vertical heading **Person Speaking**; Sam row: | under John, | under Bill, shaded Sam, | under Frank)

FIGURE 4.1   Communication Structure Rating Form

In reference to leadership structure, Sarri and Galinsky have pointed out that the beginning phase is characterized by "leadership roles played by the more assertive and aggressive individuals."[26] This may be functional at the early stage in group development, but the group must have the flexibility, as purposes and tasks are clarified, to allow inputs from other people. The worker, consequently, should try to keep the leadership structure fluid by emphasizing temporary assignments to group tasks and rotation of any influential positions.

Finally, in regard to role structure, the worker must examine how all of the roles just described are performed. When members have joined the group to solve problems through discussion, the group is unlikely to choose "officers" in any formal sense. On the other hand, in identity development and skill attainment group situations, the members' assumption of group leadership positions may be an important experience. In groups with formal leadership roles, the worker in the group formation stage helps the members determine the nature of such positions, the ways in which members will be chosen to fill them, and the attributes that members should possess to be chosen for positions.

A broader issue, in terms of role structure, is how to fill positions created by group activities. For example, when the group utilizes role play, members should be selected for the roles consistent with their goals. Similarly, in a game, members may have different tasks, and the worker should try to match people to positions in constructive ways.

During the process of group formation, the worker will utilize the role structure of the group to help members become committed to the group and to deal with ambivalence about the group. The worker can also use role assignments to obtain information about the problems of members. The following are a few examples of this use of role structure.

Example: In the second meeting of a parents' group, the worker suggested that the members take turns summarizing the discussion taking place. The worker thought it would help members to think about and take more responsibility for the problem-solving activity of the group.

Example: In the third meeting of a group of ten-year-old boys with problems following school rules, the worker introduced a game in which the group was divided into two teams. He asked a boy who had been rebellious against rules to be the scorekeeper. The worker was interested in seeing how this boy handled rules when he had some responsibility for their execution.

The worker watches to see what kinds of informal positions members enter through various transactions among themselves. Some of these will be conducive to the further development of the group, while some will not. Some members will function as tension relievers through humor (group "clowns"), through compromise (group "diplomats"), or through promoting social activities ("social directors"). The group will turn to these individuals when such needs arise, and the ability of some members to function in this way is beneficial to the group and should be supported by the worker.

On the other hand, some members are placed in positions likely to be harmful to themselves or the group. This includes scapegoats and *overactive deviants*—a term used by Bales to describe people who are verbally active yet do not contribute positively to resolving task or social-emotional issues.[27] The worker should quickly identify the emergence of these phenomena so their causes can be assessed and coped with.

In regard to scapegoating and deviance, the worker should try to prevent some members from becoming locked into such roles in early meetings, as it is difficult to remove a "deviant" label once it has been affixed. It is even possible that such members will either be pushed out of the group or will leave voluntarily. These issues are complex and often difficult to manage. We shall, therefore, discuss management of deviance in group situations in more detail in later chapters devoted to middle phases of the group's evolution.

In early stages, one activity of the worker with regard to such issues as scapegoating is to promote the group norm that members should take responsibility for their actions toward each other and should seek to help one another. This means that members should be confronted with the consequences of their behavior.

The worker should also initiate a group norm that the group will *examine* how it responds to deviant member. Each members should, in this way, take responsibility for his or her role in this process.

Individual and Group Goals

Research evidence is strong that clarity of goals elicits actions to achieve these goals, and clarity regarding such intended actions helps to secure their enactment.[28] While this principle is sound, there are many ways that workers and members can select goals and the means to achieve them.

Frequently, members in the early meetings are not ready to select and agree on goals stated in specific terms. In these cases, the worker should attempt to secure agreement that one of the "goals" of early interactions is to identify and agree on individual and group goals. According to Croxton, this is often "no more than agreement to try out the process."[29] This can include an agreement to attend a few meetings, explore whether goals that can be met through the group experience exist, and sample the types of activities and interactions that will occur in the group.

The group worker considers several orders of goals. This is a complex matter because individual and group goals must be related to each other. Individual goals are the changes the members would like to achieve in themselves, their situations, or both, as a result of participation in the group; group goals are the changes the group agrees to seek to achieve in its members, itself, or its environment as a result of the group activity. An example of an individual goal is a desire to act more assertively with fellow students. The same group chose the group goal that all of the members should act more assertively in their social situations. This group of high school students chose another group goal: to change school conditions that punished assertive behavior.

Our approach to group work [30] is oriented toward describing goals as specifically and as early as possible. We characterize a well-formulated goal statement as including a specific description of the behavior desired in oneself or others, the conditions under which the behavior will occur, and the criterion of successful performance. Rose gives an example of such a goal statement: "By the end of treatment, George will carry on conversation with his friends while maintaining eye contact with them at least 50 percent of the time."[31] This statement meets the requirements of a goal statement as it specifies the behavior (carrying on a conversation while maintaining eye contact), the circumstances (with friends), and the criterion of successful performance (50 percent of the time).

Other group work approaches place less emphasis on specific individual goals as an outcome of the group work experience. These tend to see this goal-oriented approach as false to their view of reality that individuals continuously modify their aspirations on the basis of current experience. Adherents of that view argue that too much of a future orientation prevents the fullest and finest involvement in and acquisition of benefits from contemporary ("here-and-now") events. Some emphasis on future outcomes is necessary in any approach. Schwartz, for example, speaks of "valued outcomes" during different phases of the group's work.[32]

Our view incorporates both positions and conforms to our perception of how people cope effectively with their situations. People often seek to fulfill their wants through a choice of future goals selected by thoughtful appraisal of personal and social realities. In pursuing such goals, however, a great deal may be learned about their realities; as a result, these goals may need to be altered. The group work process, therefore, can operate both with a goal orientation and a withdrawal of commitment to such goals when they are determined to be inappropriate, unattainable, or no longer relevant because of the changing situation.

The Group Work Contract

The idea of a group work contract draws on ethical as well as research considerations. The ethical issue is that the dimensions of the group work experience are agreed to by the group members and not imposed on them by the worker. These include goals, means of achieving goals, and actions to maintain the group, such as helping other members, attending meetings, and paying fees. The research considerations relate to the finding, noted in the discussion of goals, that clarity of goals, as well as the means of attaining them, enhances the effectiveness of the group experience.

Contracts in group work are of five types:

1. Between the group-as-a-whole and the agency.
2. Between the group and the worker.
3. Between a group member and the worker.
4. Between one member and another.
5. Between a member and the group.

The term *contract* has been used to describe an actual written document signed by the separate parties; it has also been used to describe verbal agreements that are specific as to the terms; finally it has been used to describe agreements that are not as formalized as the former types but are acknowledged as operative by the group members and the worker.

We believe all of these contracts to be valid under different circumstances. Schwartz, for example, refers to a contract between the group-as-a-whole and the agency when he states that the worker asks both to "reach some consensus about the members' needs and the agency's stake in offering the service." He seems, however, to be addressing the group-worker contracts when he writes of a "contracting phase" in which a consensus is sought on "purposes, roles, and procedures." Finally, Schwartz sees the worker monitoring the terms of the contract and asking the group and agency to "renegotiate" when this becomes necessary.[33]

Garvin and Glasser in their discussion of contract refer to an agreement between the members and the worker regarding the problems to be dealt with by each individual and the means that will be employed to attain these ends.[34] Neither Garvin and Glasser's nor Schwartz's conceptions refer to written documents and, in fact, Garvin and Glasser specifically write that "the group work contract, in contrast to the legal contract, is not a fixed document; rather it is a process with many subtle components." Modifications, therefore, can occur from session to session or "even during a given interaction."[35]

Sheldon Rose, in contrast, favors a written instrument. An example he presents includes commitments of the member regarding fees, attendance, punctuality, completion of homework assignments, attention during meetings, and participation in research. The workers commit themselves to the time of meetings, the clarification of member problems, the facilitation of members' use of resources, the provision of effective procedures, respect for confidentiality, and the refund of fees under specified circumstances.[36]

At times workers will become even more specific about aspects of the contract. These include goal statements, procedures to be used, reasons for believing in the procedures' effectiveness (for example, research studies,) and potential "side effects" (possible negative effects of participation in the group).

Member-to-member contracts are often used in phases of the group that occur after formation when members attempt to attain individual goals. These contracts are commitments of members to reward other members for an activity or the completion of a task. One such procedure, for example, is for two nonverbal members to agree to reward each other with money they have put into a common pool if a specified increase in group participation takes place. This type of reinforcement can also take place with the group-as-a-whole giving a reward for the accomplishments of members.

Problems in Group Beginnings

The preceding material may appear to suggest that beginnings of groups are easy. Actually, beginnings are always somewhat difficult because of the risks people think they are taking in entering any new enterprise. For some people, however, their mistrust of others and their fears of the unknown are so great that the worker must put forth great efforts to accomplish the tasks associated with formation.

One such situation occurs when the members are highly resistant in the beginning. This resistance can be manifested in refusal to participate verbally, in direct expressions of hostility, or in indirect expressions such as disagreeing, insincerely, with the purposes of the group. The worker, in these circumstances, does not deny the reality of what is happening; the worker rather, poses it as a problem for solution.[37]

Above all, however, the worker does not make the mistake of thinking the group can move ahead before this kind of resistance is diminished. Workers must not convey, on the other hand, that they are paralyzed by expressions of resistance, for this can communicate that "something dreadful" exists that justifies all the self-protection the members can muster. Workers use a variety of program tools to help overcome the difficulties experienced in group beginnings. These include "ice-breakers" such as games in which members have to guess "who they are" with reference to names pinned to the back of their clothes. Or, members interview each other in pairs and take turns introducing each other. Under some circumstances, to reinforce coming to the first meeting, workers will offer something to eat as soon as members arrive.

At times, the worker can diminish initial resistance by reducing members' anxiety. Ways of doing this include relaxation training[38] as well as introducing fun activities. Direct discussions of feelings can also be promoted. Finally, the relaxing way the worker handles the stresses of beginning the group is also important.

Another problem that can confront the group worker is the group that seems to remain too long in its formation phase. Such a group will continue to argue about, question, or frequently shift its goals; the same members do not attend consecutive meetings, and group cohesiveness remains low. This state may result from agency conditions such as those prevailing in some residential settings where persons do not remain very long. It may also result from group composition factors, incorrectly chosen group purposes, a truncated process of negotiating group goals, or a group norm of resistance to the agency or worker. When formation is prolonged, all of these as well as other possible contributing factors should be examined so that barriers to the further development of the group may be removed.

It is possible, also, that a group that never goes beyond formation can also be intentionally established. Some groups formed to provide a moderate amount of support to people leaving a program fall into this category. Some very short-term groups (five sessions or less) may move quickly beyond formation if they are carefully composed and have clear yet modest objectives.

Other groups may continue with frequent additions or departures of members. Schopler and Galinsky indicate that there is a wide range of groups of this type to be found in general and psychiatric hospitals, social service departments, mental health centers, family service agencies, drug and alcohol rehabilitation centers, residential treatment facilities, nursing and maternity homes, and prisons.[39]

These groups, according to Schopler and Galinsky, meet a great variety of needs such as immediate availability of service, prompt offering and obtaining of information, and screening for other services. They state more specific purposes:

> *The specific purposes identified in open-ended groups can be categorized as: (1) helping clients cope with transitions and crises; (2) providing other types of short- and long-term therapy; (3) offering support to clients with common problems; (4) assessing or screening clients; (5) orienting and educating clients; (6) training and supervising staff and students; and (7) facilitating outreach efforts.*[40]

Schopler and Galinsky summarize several reports regarding the impact of a new member on group development in such groups. New members appear to have the least impact during the formation stage itself since the group is still forming. During the "power and control stage" when conflict is high, a new member might heighten the conflict. Several writers agree that during a "differentiation" stage, when members are seeking to develop a greater balance between interdependence and autonomy, there may be a resentment of new members.[41] From this discussion, it can be seen that contrary to some views, such open-ended groups are not locked into perpetual formation. Intimacy and interaction do increase as members become familiar with group norms even with an ever-changing membership.

A distinguishing feature of many of these groups is the focus of their work on the "present." This leads to rapidly developed decisions and attachments to the group. According to Schopler and Galinsky, the group also "profits from the constant reminders of reality and the broader frame of reference offered by new members."[42] Adopting a positive view of such groups, they state that

> *Every session involves preparation or "tuning in" to the particular demands of change. New members may need to be introduced or departing members may need to deal with separation; and, the work of the group must go on. Since change may be an almost constant phenomenon, the leader must help the group establish mechanisms for dealing with turnover, adapt a leadership style appropriate to the group's development, and create a supportive environment.[43]*

Summary

In this chapter we reviewed the events that occur in a group during its formation phase. This includes deciding on group purposes, formulating individual and group goals, gathering information necessary to achieve these purposes and goals, and determining norms. During this phase, the worker helps the members with emotional reactions to beginnings as well as with relationships among themselves and with the worker. The latter relationship is enhanced by the worker's empathy, genuineness, and nonpossessive warmth. The worker is aided in facilitating the group's development by an understanding of structures and processes as they occur when the group is forming. A contract is often developed between the worker and group as well as among the members as to expectations of each other. Problems can occur in formation that will affect group development. These were also discussed.

Group Formation Exercise

Goals

1. To understand group tasks during the group formation stage.
2. To identify ways of helping a group accomplish formation tasks.
3. To learn to assess the degree to which the group has accomplished group formation.

Procedure

1. Prior to the exercise, trainees read about and discuss the principles of group formation described in this chapter.
2. Five trainees are asked to volunteer to form a group, which will hold a short meeting in the center of the class. An interest in a common topic is desirable (for example, how group members will apply this course to their work; finding better housing; dealing with "burnout").
3. Members of the group are centered in the front of the class and instructed to act as if they were having a first meeting of a group related to the issue selected in step 2. No group worker is present.
4. After about 10–15 minutes, the group discussion is suspended. The accompanying Group Formation Assessment Form is utilized to discuss how well the group is handling the tasks of formation. Ways of helping the group with formation tasks are also discussed. (Depending on time, the trainer may choose to emphasize some but not all items on the form.)
5. Another member of the class (or two members if co-workers are desired) is asked to volunteer to be a group worker to help the group in ways suggested in step 4.
6. After 10–15 minutes of the group meeting with a group worker, the group stops and the class, utilizing the Group Formation Assessment Form, discusses further progress in group formation and the role of the worker in this.

Group Formation Assessment Form

Group Purposes

1. For each member, use the following table to indicate the member's purpose for being in the group and the degree of relationship to the stated purpose of the group.

Member's Name	Member's Purpose	Relationship to Stated Purpose*

* Code: A for highly related; B for moderately related; C for slightly related or not related at all.

2. Which of the following should a worker do in light of 1?

_____ Because purposes are clear and a consensus exists, plan activities related to purpose.

_____ Because there is a dissent on purpose, renegotiate either purpose or composition.

_____ Purposes of members in relationship to group purposes are not yet clear; continue discussing purpose.

_____ Other (specify) _____

Gathering Relevant Information

3. Has the group decided on the type of information it needs to plan activities to accomplish purpose?

_____ yes   _____ no

Specify the type of information to be sought.

4. Has the group decided how it will secure this information? Specify how the group will secure this information.

5. What should a worker do to initiate or enhance the collection of information? (More than one of these activities can be listed.)

_____ Suggest the type and source of information.

_____ Instruct the group about an individual assessment procedure (behavioral analysis; transactional analysis; kinds of motivation, capacity, opportunity, and so on.).

_____ Instruct the group about an environmental assessment procedure.

_____ Other (specify) _____

Determination of Norms

6. Check which norms are relevant and rate the degree of agreement.

	Relevant		
	Yes	No	Agreement*
Confidentiality			
Attendance			
Honesty with each other			
Help each other			
Other (specify)			

* Code: A for all or most; B for some; C for few or none.

7. What should the worker do in light of step 6?

_____ Ask for discussion of norm.

_____ State his or her position on norm.

_____ Other (specify) _____

Emotional Reactions to Group Formation

8. Rate the percentage of members who are strongly experiencing the emotion and indicate how the worker might respond to this.

Emotion	Percentage Strongly Experiencing	Suggested Worker Response*
Attraction to group		
Fear		
Anger		
Mixed attraction to & rejection of group		
Other (specify)		

* Code: A for discussion of emotion; B for utilization of relaxation procedure; C for offering of self or others as models; D for other (specify).

Relationship to Group Worker

9. Which of the following characterizes the reaction of some members to the worker? Indicate how the worker should respond to this.

Reaction of Some Member to Worker	Suggestions for Worker Response
Dependency	
Anger	
Liking	
Fear	
Rejection	
No visible reaction	

10. How do members seem to be reacting to the gender and ethnicity of the worker?

Relationship among Members

11. Have members sought and found similarities among one another?

12. For a five-minute interval, evaluate the pattern of member and worker communications by writing "m" each time a person speaks and "w" each time the worker speaks (for example, w m m w m m m m).

How would you characterize the member communication pattern in the group?

_____ Primarily member to member

_____ About evenly mixed between members talking to each other and to the worker

_____ Members talk primarily to worker

13. How frequently are expressions of warmth or caring expressed by a member to a member?

_____ Frequently

_____ Occasionally

_____ Seldom

_____ Never

Goals

14. Have any members stated goals for themselves? (specify)

15. Has the group set any goals for itself? (specify)

Emergence of Group Structures

16. Which members seek to exert the most influence? Is that helpful or harmful to others?

17. Do members volunteer for tasks? What is the effect of this or other member roles on group development?

18. Are any members seen as deviant by other members? What is the effect on the member(s) in question?

Contract

19. What kinds of agreements have been reached on the following procedures and processes? (specify)

Attendance _____

_____

Punctuality _____

_____

Participation _____

_____

Helping each other _____

_____

Helping specific others in group _____

_____

Expectations of worker _____

_____

Expectations of agency _____

_____

Endnotes

1. Our discussion of group formation draws on such portrayals of group development as Rosemary C. Sarri, and Maeda Galinsky, "A Conceptual Framework for Group Development," in *Individual Change Through Small Groups*, eds. Martin Sundel, Paul Glasser, Rosemary Sarri, and Robert Vinter (New York: Free Press, 1985): 70–86; James A. Garland, Hubert E. Jones, and Ralph Kolodny, "A Model for Stages of Development in Social Work Groups," in *Explorations in Group Work*, ed. Saul Bernstein (Boston: Boston University School of Social Work, 1965), pp. 12–13; and Irvin D. Yalom, *The Theory and Practice of Group Psychotherapy*, 4th ed. (New York: Basic Books, 1995): 299–332.

2. Yalom, *Group Psychotherapy*: 297.

3. Max Siporin, *Introduction to Social Work Practice* (New York: Macmillan, 1975): 219–50; Beulah Compton and Burt Galaway, *Social Work Processes*, 5th ed. Pacific Grove, Calif; Brooks/Cole Publishing Co., 1994): 346–94; and Sheldon D. Rose, *Group Therapy: A Behavioral Approach* (Englewood Cliffs, N.J.: Prentice Hall, 1977): 25–40.

4. For examples of the way this is taught in groups, see Rose, *Group Therapy:* 95–102.

5. Sallie R. Churchill, "Social Group Work: A Diagnostic Tool in Child Guidance," *American Journal of Orthopsychiatry* 35 (April 1965): 581–88.

6. Urania Glassman and Len Kates, *Group Work: A Humanistic Approach* (Newbury Park, Calif.: Sage Publications, 1990.)

7. Urania Glassman and Len Kates, "The Technical Development of the Democratic-Humanistic Norms of the Social Work Group," Adelphi University School of Social Work, No Date (mimeographed).

8. Ibid.: 16.

9. H. Robert, *Robert's Rules of Order* (Glenview, Ill.: Scott Foresman and Co., 1970).

10. Glassman and Kates, "The Technical Development of the Democratic-Humanistic Norms,": 21.

11. M. Galinsky and J. Schopler, "Warning: Groups May be Dangerous," *Social Work* 22 (1977): 89–94.

12. Garland, Jones, and Kolodny, in *Explorations in Group Work*: 21.

13. See Yalom, *Group Psychotherapy*, Chapter 7.

14. Morris B. Parloff, Irene Elkin Waskow, and Barry E. Wolfe, "Research on Therapist Variables in Relationship to Process and Outcome," in *Handbook of Psychotherapy and Behavior Change: An Empirical Analysis*, 2nd ed., eds. Sol L. Garfield and Allen E. Bergin (New York: John Wiley, 1978): 242–52.

15. C.B. Truax, R.R. Carkhuff, and I. Rodman, Jr., "Relationships Between Therapist Offered Conditions and Patient Change in Group Psychotherapy," *Journal of Clinical Psychology* XXI (1965): 327–29; C.B. Truax, J. Wittmer, and D.G. Wargo, "Effects of the Therapeutic Conditions of Accurate Empathy, Nonpossessive Warmth, and Genuineness on Hospitalized Mental Patients During Group Therapy," *Journal of Clinical Psychology* XXVII (1971): 137–42.

16. See Parloff, Waskow, and Wolfe, in *Handbook of Psychotherapy*: 242–52.

17. M.F. Weiner, *Therapist Disclosure: The Use of Self in Psychotherapy* (Boston: Butterworths, 1978): 128–51.

18. Eveline D. Schulman, *Intervention in Human Services*, 2nd ed. (St. Louis: C.V. Mosby, 1978): 225.

19. Ibid.: 231.

20. Margaret E. Hartford, *Groups in Social Work: Applications of Small Group Theory and Research to Social Work Practice* (New York: Columbia University Press, 1972): 218–27.

21. Ibid.: 196.

22. Ibid.: 261–69.

23. Ibid.: 264–67.

24. Ibid.: 216–18.

25. Rose, *Group Therapy:* 133–40.

26. Sarri and Galinsky, in *Individual Change*: 74.

27. Robert F. Bales, "Task Roles and Social Roles in Problem Solving Groups," in *Readings in Social Psychology*, 3rd ed., eds. Eleanor E. Maccoby, Theodore M. Newcomb, and Eugene L. Hartley (New York: Holt, Rinehart & Winston, 1958): 427–46.

28. Janice H. Schopler, Maeda Galinsky, and Mark Alicke, "Goals in Social Group Work Practice: Formulation, Implementation, and Evaluation," in *Individual Change Through Small Groups*, eds. Sundel, Glasser, Sarri, and Vinter (New York: Free Press, 1985): 140–58.

29. Tom A. Croxton, "The Therapeutic Contract in Social Treatment," in *Individual Change Through Small Groups*, eds. Sundel, Glasser, Sarri, and Vinter (New York: Free Press, 1985): 172.

30. Robert D. Vinter, "The Essential Components of Social Work Practice," in *Individual Change Through Small Groups*, eds. Sundel, Glasser, Sarri, and Vinter (New York: Free Press, 1985): 15–17.

31. Rose, *Group Therapy*: 76.

32. William Schwartz, "Social Group Work: The Interactionist Approach," in *Encyclopedia of Social Work* II (New York: National Association of Social Workers, 1971): 1260.

33. Ibid.: 1260.

34. Charles D. Garvin and Paul H. Glasser, "Social Group Work: The Preventive and Rehabilitative Approach," *Individual Change Through Small Groups*, eds. Sundel, Glasser, Sarri, and Vinter (New York: Free Press, 1985): 38.

35. Ibid.

36. Rose, *Group Therapy*: 23.

37. For an excellent discussion of formation problems in social control situations and how to respond to them, see Ronald H. Rooney, *Strategies for Work with Involuntary Clients* (New York: Columbia University Press, 1992): 179–94.

38. Douglas A. Bernstein and Thomas D. Borkovec, *Progressive Relaxation Training: A Manual for the Helping Professions* (Champaign, Ill.: Research Press, 1973).

39. J.H. Schopler and M.J. Galinsky, "Meeting Practice Needs: Conceptualizing the Open-Ended Group," *Social Work with Groups* 7 (1984): 3–21.

40. Ibid.: 5.

41. Ibid.: 8–9.

42. Ibid.: 11.

43. Ibid.: 12.

Chapter 5

Achieving Group Purposes through Changes in Group Conditions

In the previous chapter, we considered how the worker interacts with individuals and the group-as-a-whole during the group's formation period. In this and the next three chapters, we shall consider how the worker assesses and works with the group, its members, and the environment during the "middle" phases of the group's life as well as with so-called "therapeutic factors." We shall assume, therefore, that we are presenting material relevant to both a group and its members who have determined their purposes and selected their initial goals. The members have developed some attraction to each other as well as sufficient cohesiveness, so they are motivated to choose and pursue activities to attain group and individual goals. The group has also developed an initial structure and some group rules regarding procedures.

Actions of the Group Worker

Group work writers generally assert that the value of group experience, as contrasted with one-to-one helping, centers on the ways group conditions can help members attain their goals. As we discussed earlier, some workers seek to bring this about by specifying such benefits specifically and uniquely for each individual. Others seek the creation of a group which, by virtue of circumstances such as norms of honesty, broad participation, and democratic decision making, is assumed to be beneficial to members.

In any case, the worker will interact with individual members, several members, the entire group, and people and institutions outside the group to help create desired group conditions. All of these entities interact and affect one another. A worker, consequently, to achieve changes in the group-as-a-whole, may initiate this change process through transactions with any one or more of these four components, and, in fact, different workers may achieve the same needs with different approaches. Whether one of these types of transactions is more appropriate or effective than the others has not been established. The "practice wisdom" is undoubtedly that it depends on the circumstances. The group worker must be able, therefore, to employ skills relevant to interacting with members, subgroups, groups, and group environments. In any group the worker is likely to do all of these. Sometimes this is a planned sequence such as in the following example.

Example: The group worker sought a volunteer from the group to describe a problem she was having in social relationships. Agnes volunteered and the worker asked her to describe an example (*interaction with an individual*).

Agnes later agreed to role play a family situation about which she was concerned. The worker and Agnes secured several volunteers to role play Agnes's family, and she helped them set up the role play (*interaction with a subgroup*).

After the role play, the worker asked the group to give feedback to Agnes on her handling of the situation (*interaction with the entire group*).

The worker, at Agnes's request, agreed to interview her husband to help him deal with his concerns about her participation in the group (*interaction with person outside the group on behalf of a group member*).

At other times, the worker interacts first with one of the various systems related to a member's concern and then makes decisions about subsequent interactions based on the flow of events. This is seen in the next example.

Example: The worker discussed with the boys in the group home the destructive events that took place on "Devil's Night." Several of the boys had thrown eggs at an elderly man on the street near the home (*interaction with entire group*). Jim denied any part in the affair, although the other boys said he had been with them. The worker asked Jim what his feelings would be if his participation in something like this were known (*interaction with individual*). Jim said that Bill always tried to put him on the spot, and the worker encouraged Jim and Bill to discuss this (*interaction with subgroup*). The worker also told the group about his discussion with the man who had been assaulted when he had come to the home to complain (*interaction with person outside the group*).

The worker is aware that talking with one or several members in the group will affect the other members. This can affect their own problem solving as well as their interactions with each other. During a group meeting, in a sense, it is impossible to interact with only some members. Nevertheless, the worker may, at times, have a compelling reason to single out a member. The effect on other members may or may not be a major consideration.

At other times, when the worker speaks to some members, he or she may desire an effect on other members. Still again, when effects on other members are anticipated and undesirable, the worker will refrain from individual attention. Similarly, when workers intervene in processes of the group-as-a-whole, they must consider how the process affects each individual member. Sometimes this is predictable. At other times, the effects of group processes on members are not known until they have occurred. Then the worker must quickly decide what to do next. An example of this occurred when a worker with a group of youngsters in a residential treatment center participated in a discussion of feelings about holidays. He did not realize that two of the members had been very depressed a few weeks previously on Thanksgiving because their parents had not visited them. When the discussion began, these two members became emotionally withdrawn. The worker asked them about this behavior and learned about their parents. The worker expressed his understanding of their feelings, thus shifting his attention from the group-as-a-whole to the individual members.

As the preceding shows, it is impossible to affect one level of the individual-group-environment set without affecting all levels. Workers, nevertheless, frequently focus their attention on one level or another. Even though in practice the worker recognizes the interrelatedness of such parts, we shall consider separately in this and the following three chapters how the worker might use one or another system when the target is the group, the individual, or the environment. In this chapter, we shall focus on the group.

This way of approaching the activities of the worker is similar to that of Pincus and Minahan, who distinguish between action and target systems.[1] *Action systems* are those with which the worker directly interacts; *target systems* are those to be changed as a result of these interactions. These two systems can, of course, coincide, such as when the worker helps the group (*action system*) change its methods of problem solving (*target system*). These two systems can be different, as when the worker helps the group (*action system*) plan a strategy for changing an agency rule (*target system*).

When the target system is the group, the worker should involve the members in deciding what aspects of the group need to be changed and how this should be brought about. We believe that the following is a logical way of dealing with this situation:

1. Help the group identify a problem in its functioning. This can often be accomplished by asking members whether they think there is something standing in the way of the group's accomplishing its purposes.
2. Help the group assess which group conditions serve to maintain the group problem. A typology of group conditions will be presented shortly.
3. Help the group measure the group condition using some of the approaches described throughout this book, and in Chapter 9 in particular.
4. Help the group choose a way of modifying the group condition. The first decision is whether the action system used to promote this change will be a member, a subgroup, the group-as-a-whole, or some person or system outside of the group. The second decision involves the specific strategy to be utilized with the action system, which will be described throughout this chapter. We shall then summarize this material with a table in which we suggest linkages between the group-level problem and the choice of action system and strategy to ameliorate it.
5. Help the group evaluate the effectiveness of the approach it has chosen to modify a group condition. This can be done by using the measure selected at step 3.
6. If the outcome is less than satisfactory, help the group return to step 4 and seek to change group conditions by using another approach.

Assessment of Group Conditions

The worker will continuously assess the conditions that exist in the group and help the members modify the conditions that impede the attainment of individual and group goals.

By *group conditions*, we mean some phenomenon characteristic of the group, either a way the members are acting, thinking, or feeling, or a situation present in the particular group.

Admittedly, this assessment is a complex task, and beginning group workers can feel overwhelmed by a discussion of group conditions. Eventually they will understand these conditions so well that they will be able to identify and focus on them quickly. Our classification of group conditions follows:

1. Stage of group development
2. Group structure
3. Group process
4. Group culture
5. Group resources
6. Extragroup transactions
7. Group boundaries
8. Group climate

We shall now describe each of these conditions more fully so the reader may identify them when working with a group. We shall then identify ways in which the worker can help the members have an impact on conditions present in their group.

Middle Phases of Group Development

In the preceding chapter, we described the formation phase of group development. At this point we shall focus on "middle" phases. Most authorities agree that during this period group members' energies are invested in initiating and carrying out activities related to their purposes.[2] While doing this, members develop new or more complex structures related to leadership and group tasks. They also develop processes for goal attainment such as how to approach problem solving, how to deal with differences of opinion, and how to respond to members who represent a minority on issues. By this time groups have also developed some spoken or unspoken rules (norms) regarding such behaviors as attendance and behavior at meetings.

After an initial period of considerable agreement, however, groups usually enter into a period of conflict. Garland, Jones, and Kolodny refer to this as a "power and control" phase, while Sarri and Galinsky term it a "revision" phase.[3] At this time, leadership (either indigenous or that of the worker) is challenged, and goals and activities are questioned. This is due to the larger number of members who now feel free to express their sentiments, as well as to a reaction against the initial leadership often held by the more aggressive individuals. Early experiences with pursuing goals may also produce new information or disclose unknown barriers that require new procedures, leadership, and so forth.

During this phase the worker must be supportive when cohesiveness declines because of anxiety-producing conflict in the group. It is hoped that the worker and the members will be able to resolve conflicts to lead to leadership patterns and reformulated goals to which members are even more committed than before. The experience of resolving conflicts can also lead to a feeling of closeness among members as well as a conviction that conflicts can be constructively coped with in the group.

After "revision" phases, the group resumes its activities with even more cohesiveness, commitment to goals, and appropriateness of structure. The members, however, with increased feelings of closeness to each other may stress their commonalities rather than their differences. This can lead to a degree of dependency not as conducive to pursuing individual goals as might be desirable. The worker should then support efforts of members to stress their individuality as well as commonality, thus creating a phase referred to by Garland and his colleagues as "differentiation."[4] In this phase, members reinforce each other's uniqueness.

During these middle phase processes, the worker examines specific group conditions to determine if they enhance or hinder goal-directed activities. We shall turn, therefore, to a closer description of such group conditions as they emerge in the group's middle phases.

Group Structures

In the previous chapter, concepts frequently used to characterize group structures were defined and illustrated for the period of group formation. In this chapter we shall use the same concepts to describe group conditions during middle phases.

Communications Structure.   During the formation period, members tend to direct many of their remarks to the worker. By the middle phases, the members have developed more familiarity with each other and should have developed a commitment to helping one another. For these reasons, communication among members increases and between members and the worker decreases. Patterns of communication emerge that are characteristic of the way members communicate in their life situations; and these may also have contributed to the problems that led to their seeking group services.

These patterns include dominating discussion, talking primarily to the worker, or withdrawing from interaction. Such patterns may vary with the content of the discussion; some members will only talk about certain topics to selected members. This can relate to a desire to secure reinforcement for behavior, a perceived similarity of the other member to a significant figure in one's history, or a wish to evoke a particular emotional response. Members may be willing to participate in discussions on some topics but not others. The worker should try to identify communication issues such as these. Depending on the relationship of the members' communication patterns to the members' problems, the worker will seek to help the members change such patterns. Ways to do this will be described later in this chapter.

Sociometric Structure.   The worker should assess the nature of the subgroups formed in the group. This can be done by observing who chooses to interact with whom, who comes or leaves meetings with whom, and the expressions of caring and affection exchanged among members. The sociometric questionnaire is not a device generally used by the worker to ask members about feelings of closeness within the group. Members consider such questionnaires threatening, and fear of being excluded or rejected can cause anxieties. A sociometric analysis can usually be achieved through observation.

Some of the problems in middle phases of groups that are illuminated through sociometric analysis include the existence of dyads in which members reinforce each other's problematic behaviors, subgroups that compete with each other in destructive ways for control of the group, isolate members who may become scapegoats, and intermember conflicts that reduce the overall cohesiveness of the group.

Power Structure.   In the middle phases of the group, various members often seek to have more influence on group decisions and processes than they possessed in the beginning. This can be desirable if members use this influence to make the group responsive to them and also to help one another. At times, this is not the case, and members challenge the authority of the worker in destructive ways or seek to manipulate other members in directions contrary to such members' goals. These actions may represent the uses of power outside of the group that have created the problems for which the members seek help.

Other kinds of power issues are members' attempts to coerce others into deviant activity; worker's inability to limit behavior destructive to individuals or even the whole group; and outsiders' (teacher, parents, spouse) use of power over the group members in a negative way.

Therefore, the worker analyzes the sources of power (stemming from expertise, control over resources, ability to punish, function as a role model) possessed by the worker, the members, and the people outside the group. The ways power must be used to help accomplish individual and group tasks is determined. When detrimental uses of power exist, the worker must seek to change these.

Role Structure.   A role consideration during middle phases of the group is whether the members possess the skills to carry out their responsibilities during this period. If there is a formal leadership structure, members may not be able to perform leadership functions because of behavioral deficits related to leadership. In any group when problem solving occurs, members should be able to give and ask for information and suggestions. If not, the worker will have to train members in such skills.

In later phases of the group, also, members might become locked into dysfunctional roles. The "clown" may wish to behave more seriously, the "mediator" to take sides, and passive people to function assertively. The worker, being cognizant of roles created out of group interactions, will attend to those that impede either the attainment of individual goals or the creation of an effective group. In any case, the middle phase of the group should provide many opportunities for members to experiment with new roles and to consider employing these outside of the group in their natural systems.

Group Processes

As commonly defined, "process" is a continuous action, operation, or series of changes taking place in a definite manner. A group continuously changes over time, and the nature of these changes constitutes *group process.*[5] Group process is a more difficult concept to grasp than group structure, perhaps because it is easier to think about a phenomenon as if it were unchanging. Also, group workers have often thought of process as one or another single aspect of the range of variables that change in groups. When Yalom defines process as the relationship implications of interpersonal transactions (a very important *aspect* of process), he is discussing a process component, but not the only one.[6]

For this reason, in another discussion we defined process as "changes that take place in group conditions."[7] Again, as with group structure, we must recognize that changes are in *the group as an entity* and that their subdivision is only for analytical purposes. In fact, there are many valid ways for workers and members to examine their group's *process:* one important way is to consider some dimension of process, such as stages of problem solving. Another is to examine the specific sequence of events in a group session to investigate some pattern, causal event, or consequence of the sequence.

We have conceptualized a classification of dimensions of group process that we believe incorporates all of the sequences of events that might occur in the group. As shown in Table 5.1, these dimensions are the (1) goal-oriented *activities* of the group, and the (2) quality of the *interactions* among the members. The former largely corresponds to the goal attainment and the latter to the group maintenance functions referred to in the small group literature.[8]

We have further subdivided these two dimensions of process into those that occur at the *overt* levels and those that occur at the *covert* levels. Overt refers to observable events, as in the actions and communications of group members. Covert refers to the feelings and thoughts of members as these are reported by them and as these relate to activities and interactions.

Our definitions of these dimensions of group process follow. Goal determination (1) consists of all of the actions of members as they seek to determine group goals. Goal pursuit (2) consists of everything members do to attain these goals. The covert goal-oriented activity is the evolution of agreed-upon values (3) related to the group's goals and the ways the group acts to attain them.

Role differentiation (4) refers to the evolution of the group's role structure. Such a structure consists of the perceptions and expectations of members regarding how each will behave because of his or her position in the group. Communication-interaction (5) refers to the messages members send one another as they define and enact their roles. Conflict resolution-behavior control (6) refers to the interactions that occur among members as they seek to perpetuate the group through controlling tension-inducing behavior. The covert interaction-oriented activity is that of emotions (7) including caring as well as hostile affects members experience toward one another.

Because it is highly important for workers to identify the dimensions of group process that may be causing problems to members, we shall describe each dimension in more detail. Later in the chapter, we shall describe ways workers and members may work together to modify such problematic situations.

1. Goal Determination.   This dimension of process occurs as members interact to determine the desired end-state to be achieved by the group. This interaction often takes place in stages related to short- and long-range goals. Thus a long-range group goal of helping

TABLE 5.1   Aspects of Group Process

	Goal-Oriented Activities	Quality of Interactions
OVERT	1. Goal determination	4. Role differentiation
	2. Goal pursuit	5. Communication-interaction
		6. Conflict resolution and behavior control
COVERT	3. Values and norms	7. Emotions

members to develop social skills might be coupled with short-range goals of learning how to approach others, carry on conversations, and act assertively.

An example of the process of goal determination is a discussion of the kinds of personal difficulties to be worked on in the group. This discussion includes whether the group would seek to change some aspects of the members' environments or how the members were able to cope with those environments.

2. Goal Pursuit. McGrath has generated a comprehensive typology of the activities in which groups can engage to attain their goals.[9] His presentation is very useful in summarizing all of the major research efforts related to each activity. We believe it would be a useful intellectual effort for a group work theoretician to develop practice principles derived from McGrath's work. This cannot be done within the limits of this book, but it will be valuable for practitioners to consider the following list of the activities identified by McGrath when they help groups to choose ways to pursue goals.

McGrath indicates four types of activities that he calls *tasks*. Each task is subdivided into two subtasks.[10]

Generating Tasks

Planning Tasks: Generating plans as to how the group will undertake some activity.

Creativity Tasks: Generating ideas as in "brainstorming."

Choosing Tasks

Intellective Tasks: Solving problems in which there exists an answer whose "correctness" will be clearly evident.

Decision-Making Tasks: Solving problems about which some ambiguity exists as to how members will agree upon the "correctness" of the answer.

Negotiating Tasks

Cognitive-Conflict Tasks: Resolving conflicts of viewpoints, that is, members do not agree as to how the issue to be resolved is to be understood or evaluated.

Mixed-Motive Tasks: Members have a conflict of interests, that is, gains may be made by some members at the expense of others.

Executing Tasks

Contests/Battles: Activities in which members are pitted against one another as in competitive sports.

Performances: Psychomotor tasks performed against objective or absolute standards of excellence such as in executing a painting or a dance step.

In traditional group work terminology, the activities undertaken by the group to achieve its goals are termed *programs*. Analytic methods for planning and assessing programs have not been extensively dealt with, however, in the group work literature. An important contribution to this need is the work of Vinter.[11] We shall discuss his work later in this chapter, as well as a range of ways in which program (task) is used in group work to modify group conditions.

A type of task, referred to in McGrath's typology as "choosing," is often referred to by group workers simply as *problem solving*.[12] We shall discuss this process in more detail later in this chapter.

The goal pursuit dimension of process usually involves several of the tasks defined by McGrath. For example, a group session began in a prison with members discussing how, when seeking employment, they could overcome the stigma of having been in jail. Several members indicated they wished, instead, to discuss a complaint they had against a guard. Several minutes were spent determining which issue would be discussed that day (negotiating task, probably a mixed-motive type). The majority was in favor of discussing the employment-related topic, and this was the one they pursued.

This discussion began with sharing information about actual job-seeking experiences. Questions were raised as to the availability of jobs and the resources to help ex-offenders. Several members were able to supply enough information to satisfy the others (intellective task). Several suggestions were made for ways to find jobs. These were evaluated and members helped each other to determine which suggestions to implement (decision-making task).

During this discussion, it was evident that the men were apprehensive about talking with potential employers. A script was created (creativity task) from some of the ideas offered during the discussion. Various members used the script to role play both the applicants and the employers (performance task). After each role play, members gave feedback to each other regarding how each had handled the "interview"; they also suggested to each other how to improve their interviewing behavior.

3. Values and Norms.   In the preceding chapter, we described the norms the worker helps the group develop to attain goals within the value framework accepted by most group workers. Group norms, however, continue to develop and change throughout the life of the group. We discuss norms as the covert level of the activity dimension of group process because they strongly influence the members' choice of goals as well as how they will be pursued. Admittedly, norms influence interactions, but this ultimately refers back to which interactions are required for the group to accomplish its purposes.

The norms the group members focus upon are related to the developmental phase of the group. During the revision phase, when conflict is often heightened, social control mechanisms are developed further and deviation from norms are more pronounced. Pressures toward uniformity and consensus are clearly apparent.

In the revision phase, the group's norms may also change. The revision stage is likely to be ending when the group develops a stronger consensus regarding its norms as well as sanctions related to them. In later phases of group life, norms become even more clearly enunciated, and deviation will certainly be noted.

4. Role Differentiation.   This dimension of process involves a change from (1) an undifferentiated condition to one in which roles are clearly defined or (2) a change in the group from the presence of one set of roles to another. The latter occurs when a group undertakes a new project that requires interactions not needed previously.

Role differentiation also becomes more elaborate as the group develops. In the formation stage, for example, leadership roles are often unclear, shifting, and likely to be assumed by the more aggressive members. During the revision phase, the leadership of these individuals is likely to be challenged. In later stages, the identity of members who most frequently play task and social-emotional leadership roles is much clearer and more likely to be accepted.

In group treatment situations, members go through a role differentiation process when they clarify and assume the role of "client"; and when they demonstrate helping behaviors toward each other, the group becomes a mutual-aid system. This process also is evident as workers help members assume roles in activities to further the members' attainment of their treatment goals.

5. Communication-Interaction.   This process dimension refers to communications among members with regard to existing or emerging differentiation of roles. It fulfills the function of helping members coordinate their roles with each other. We referred earlier to a communications structure of "who speaks to whom about what." The process dimension involves how the pattern of communication evolves and shifts as both the group and its members develop.

During group formation, the communication-interaction process occurs as members seek out their commonalities. In the next stages, members communicate with each other in ways that are necessary for them to develop and carry out their tasks. When conflicts arise, members are likely to interact intensively and frequently to reduce the related stress.

Maintenance of the group requires that members test how far they can trust each other before sharing sensitive information. In this process, members will express emotions regarding role assignments and will react to each other's emotional expression. This may include expressions of fear or anger regarding the role of the worker as well as of other members.

Some examples of communication-interaction are questions addressed to workers to determine their expertise, attitudes, and expectations; questions members direct to other members about expectations they hold for each other; and statements members make about how they hope other members will help them. We shall discuss in the chapter devoted to individual change a type of intervention into communication process called *process commentary*. This intervention can have major effects upon the way all group members communicate with one another as well as upon the competence of each individual to interact with others.

6. Conflict Resolution and Behavior Control.   Some of the processes that relate to this dimension are (1) struggles for power among members, (2) struggles for power between members and the group worker, and (3) efforts to control behavior that deviates from group norms. None of these events are intrinsically good or bad, and the worker's judgments regarding them will depend on the purposes and goals of the group. For example, some power struggles can occur between those members who are committed to the goals of the group and those who are not.

At other times, power conflicts may be provoked by some members who have problems in finding a role in the group. In a group of adolescents, for example, an influential member supported the goal of "making it" in school. Another member sought the recognition of others in the group and thought the only way he could do this was to rebel against the idea that it is desirable to secure additional education. The worker helped the members understand this process so that they could choose alternative means of gaining status consistent with the group's purpose to support educational attainment.

When the behavior control process is directed at a member who is violating a norm, several stages are often observed. Members are likely to first draw attention to the deviant behavior, after which they will increase their communications to that person. If the deviant behavior does not cease, the members will gradually withdraw their attention from the deviant individual and may then seek to avoid or even to eject him or her from the group. In view of the group and individual goals in the specific situation, the worker may support either the group or the individual but usually will prohibit expelling the individual. Workers will strive to limit any excessive sanction imposed by the group. Groups can become punitive in the pursuit of their legitimate ends and, in this way, defeat them (the proverbial means-ends question).

7. Emotions.   This aspect of process refers to changes in the positive and negative feelings members have about each other as well as the group. Members, as we indicated in the previous chapter, will usually enter the group with mixed feelings about the group and with few feelings about other members except those they knew. There can be an immediate emotional reaction to others in the group if members see others as similar to people not in the group. In therapy group situations, workers will often help members state their first impressions as a way of helping them to recognize the ways they distort the "here and now."

During the revision phase of the group, members will tend to polarize their feelings as they show support for those with whom they agree and act negatively toward those with whom they are in conflict. A resolution of the conflict, typical of this phase, will often lead to warm feelings toward those previously disliked.

Some of the emotions members experience may have erotic overtones, and the worker can help the members feel safe with these, whether directed at the worker or at other members. As sexuality is an inevitable part of life, so it is of group experience.

Group Culture

The group's culture consists of the ways members believe they should behave, think, or feel. These views sometimes stem from the group members' ethnic, religious, or other cultural backgrounds. When we find a group beginning a meeting, for example, with a prayer or other ritual, this is frequently because the members are accustomed to doing this in other groups. The worker is well advised, therefore, to learn as much as possible about the members' cultural backgrounds.

In addition, groups will develop rituals that grow out of the group experience, particularly if they become cohesive. In a similar vein, members may come to hold common views about their social realities. This phenomenon will further add to the attraction members feel toward their group.

In social work groups, shared views may be problematic; for example, members may believe in the superiority of certain social classes, or races, or of one sex over another. They may believe it is not possible to succeed in life, or they may reinforce in each other dysfunctional attributions about the causes of their problems. On the other hand, such shared attributions may enhance the achievement of the members' goals; for example, members may come to accept the value of analyzing the antecedents and consequences of their behaviors, or they may adopt the view that all human beings are potent and capable of modifying their destinies.

Whitaker and Lieberman[13] have developed a model of group therapy based upon the way members evolve a view of group conditions in similar ways. These authors conceptualize group events as embodying a *group focal conflict* between a wish that they term a *disturbing motive* and an associated fear that they term a *reactive motive*. These wishes and fears come to be held by many or most of the members as they associate with and influence each other's views.

An example of a focal group conflict occurred in a group of adolescent girls who *wished* to discuss some of their questions about sexual behavior (disturbing motive). They feared that this discussion would cause them to be rejected by the worker (reactive motive). The conflict between this wish and this fear led the girls to attack the worker "before she can attack us." This behavior is a "solution" to the conflict that will not help the girls reach their goal. The worker, therefore, sought to help them understand their views, how they emerged, and the consequences of holding such views. This process resulted in the girls being able to satisfy their wishes for a meaningful discussion.

Group Resources

To exist, groups require many resources. One that often comes to mind is the physical setting for the group, such as the type of room (or outdoor space), the size of the room, and the equipment and furniture. Program supplies such as sports, craft, music, or other equipment are needed resources, too. Since group members may wish to serve refreshments, these are sometimes required. Other supplies may be sought for use as rewards in a behavioral reinforcement program.

In addition to material resources, members may require human ones such as experts who bring knowledge or skills not possessed by the group worker. These may be speakers on health issues, teachers of program skills, group process observers, or individuals who have the power to bring about environmental changes sought by the members.

Many events within the group are dictated by the presence or absence of resources and must be assessed by the worker in terms of the purposes of the group. Some groups cannot attain their goals at all if a particular resource is not supplied, but this is a rare event. A very positive consequence often results when the members, with the help of the worker, struggle successfully (or even unsuccessfully) to secure a resource. The lesson learned in the former case relates to resourcefulness in the face of scarcity. The lesson in the latter one is how to survive without a needed resource—something that is a frequent challenge to the people served by group workers.

Extragroup Transactions

Groups served by group workers do not exist in isolation but may interact with other groups in the agency, the agency as an entity, and with groups and institutions outside of the agency as well as the families of the members. These interactions include the following types of activities:

The group has a joint event with another system.

The group asks for support from another system.

Another system makes a demand or request of the group for resources, support, or compliance.

The group (or its representative) cooperates with other systems to attain mutual benefits.

Members receive treatment from other systems in addition to the group, and these systems interact with one or more members of the group.

The worker will assess these transactions to evaluate their impact on the group. The worker, as we shall describe in this chapter and the succeeding ones that discuss environmental change, will mediate between the group and other systems, will advocate for the group, or will help the group members to become more competent in dealing with the environment.

Group Boundaries

The group members frequently have to make or respond to decisions about the addition and deletion of members. These decisions may be made by the group-as-a-whole, by individual members, by the worker, or by the agency. This issue of who is in the group is defined as one of boundaries. At times the boundary of the group can be a rigid one in which members take every step they can to prevent an old member from leaving or a new one from joining. At other times, the boundary may be a very loose one in which it is difficult to tell who is a member and who is not, and little attention is paid to this issue.

The kinds of issues that arise in groups around boundaries are illustrated by the following questions: Should a person who has missed a number of meetings, violated an important group norm, or resigned be considered a member? Can people join the group for a short period? Does a person become a member immediately or is there a probationary period?

The worker seeks to understand the way the group members define boundaries by observing their reactions when individuals enter or leave the group, miss meetings, or express a desire to join the group. The very act of asking members questions about these events will impact the group's boundaries. In any case, the nature of the group's boundaries should be examined in light of the group's purposes. If strong cohesiveness is desired, for example, clear boundaries are usually important. On the other hand, the open-ended groups we described earlier required a much looser set of group boundaries.

Group Climate

It is frequently possible to identify the emotional climate present in a group at a specified time. The members may appear happy, energetic, depressed, apathetic, subdued, and so on. It is also possible to find different subgroups within the group displaying different emotions.

When several or all of the members exhibit the same emotion, it may be because they are reacting to a common event or because emotions experienced by some members are "contagious." These emotions can strongly affect how the group accomplishes its purposes. The worker will assess these emotional states by observing members' nonverbal expressions or by asking members directly about their feelings. A "projective" approach can be used by asking members to associate colors or adjectives to the group. In ways that we shall discuss later in this chapter, the worker will seek to impact the emotional character of the group.

The Modification of Group Conditions

The preceding discussion presents the way we assess group conditions. We shall now turn to the ways group workers *act* to influence or to facilitate the members' efforts to change such group conditions.

One way we categorize ways of changing group conditions is by the action system utilized. The worker can affect group conditions by interacting with (1) one member (in front of others or privately), (2) several members, (3) the entire group, or (4) people outside the group. This decision is often made as a result of group discussion. We shall describe various approaches used to modify group conditions, then relate these approaches to the group conditions listed previously.

Modifying Group Conditions through Individuals

One way of influencing the group is for the worker to interact with one member. Single members can significantly affect group conditions when they (1) have tasks to perform for the group, (2) have considerable power in the group, or (3) fulfill critical functions in the group.

Some examples of the first category, *tasks to perform*, are members who arrange for group activities, secure resources for the group (information, equipment), or fulfill roles such as observer, chairperson, secretary, or referee. The allocation of the tasks constitutes part of the structure of the group. The worker usually is active in decisions as to who will fulfill these roles. The worker, when necessary, will facilitate the way the members perform these roles, thus contributing to goal attainment.

One way the worker facilitates role performance is by "coaching" the member. This term is analogous to coaching in athletics: the worker gives support to such members as well as feedback on their effectiveness and "tips" on how to do the job.

The worker may use behavior modification techniques to help members with their roles, such as offering to tell or to show the member how to perform the role (modeling); the worker can also reinforce the member for his or her actions. Members may be anxious about the way they are carrying out group responsibilities, and the worker can help the members to reduce some of their tension through relaxation techniques.[14]

In the second circumstance, when the member fulfills a leadership function for the group (for example, chairperson or committee member), in addition to the preceding techniques, the worker can also provide leadership training. This consists of sessions with some or all of the members on such leadership skills as moderating a discussion or facilitating participation.[15]

At times the worker interacts with a member in relationship to the power structure of the group. This occurs most often when an imbalance of power hinders the effective functioning of the group. For example, some members may dominate group decision making and exclude others from this process. The worker can involve the entire group in an examination of this problem but may interact instead with the individuals concerned. For instance, the worker may empower some individuals through assertiveness training or by helping them assume power roles in the group.

At other times, the worker helps more powerful individuals to relinquish power or to use it sparingly in the interests of other members. This can be done by developing values of concern for one another as well as helping them see how domination of others can be destructive to themselves.

The third circumstance, when workers interact with individuals to modify group conditions, is when the individual's behavior maintains problematic group structures or processes. Such circumstances are maintained *both* by the behavior of the individual concerned and by the responses of other group members. A good example of this is a scapegoating process. Northen states, that the scapegoat symbolizes some of the attacking members problems with self-esteem, identity, and displaced anger.[16]

The worker responds to scapegoating situations by calling the member's attention to his or her own behavior and also the other group members' attention to the reasons for their response to it. Both "parties" should examine their contribution to the maintenance of a scapegoating situation. Shulman warns the worker against "preempting" this encounter between member and group as both attempt to cope with the scapegoating process.[17] The worker can do this by too rapid a defense of the scapegoat or condemnation of the other members. As the worker helps the group members take common responsibility for a scapegoating process, they may each then be supported in behaving differently.

Sometimes scapegoating is a dysfunctional response to a stress from outside the group, such as stigma placed on group membership. The worker will then help members redirect their efforts to cope directly with these sources of tension.

Modifying Group Conditions through Subgroups

Group conditions are also changed by the worker's interactions with subgroups. The following are some examples of occasions when attention to a subgroup is an appropriate way of changing a group condition.

A subgroup may form and sabotage the whole group by opposing group purposes or activities or by rebelling against the worker. The usual cause is that the subgroup members seek a "place in the group" and recognition of their uniqueness that they cannot find through acceptable behavior. This happens when relevant roles have been preempted by other members. Members of such a subgroup also want to influence the group, and they may even experience the worker as undercutting this.

Based on the worker's assessment of such issues, he or she can discuss legitimate desires for influence on the group with the subgroup members. The worker can also create useful roles for such subgroup members by helping them accomplish tasks for the group, thus attaining more influence in the group. Instead of responding to a tendency to "fight back," the worker looks for ways to "connect" with dissident subgroups and to demonstrate a concern for their wants.

Subgroups can be helped to take responsibility for planning activities for the whole group, gathering information for the group, and providing feedback to the group through observing other subgroups in a "fishbowl" format.

Members of a subgroup may be motivated to help the group change in desirable ways which, for some reason, the group is unable or unwilling to accomplish. Using a subsystem to change a larger system (and vice-versa) is important group work practice.

Modifying Group Conditions through the Whole Group

Workers can interact with the group-as-a-whole to help members change group conditions by impacting members' attributions, behaviors, tasks and activities, norms, ways of problem solving, and emotions. We shall discuss each of these in turn.

Altering Member Attributions.   The group members can become aware of group conditions and plan a different way of structuring the group, engaging in a process, and so forth. This can occur when workers help members examine group conditions and make a decision to change them. This usually occurs when members develop a new picture of the group by gathering data about some aspect of their group's operation. We shall discuss this type of data collection in Chapter 9. In addition to the types of quantitative measures discussed in Chapter 9, members can be taught a conceptual framework for understanding group phenomena. For example, Bion's concepts of basic assumption groups can be taught to members.[18]

A device used to motivate members to examine their attributions is to assign the group the responsibility of making important decisions affecting the members, such as granting "passes" to leave the residential institution.[19] Poor decisions can be rejected by staff or administration. The group is expected, however, to examine the processes that led to its decisions.

Another approach to help a group modify its conditions is what Yalom calls *Mass Group Process Commentary*.[20] He defines this as occurring when

> . . . *leaders choose to focus primarily or entirely on mass group phenomena. These leaders refer, in their statements, to "the group" or "we" or "all of us"; they attempt to clarify the relationship between "the group" as an entity and its primary task (the investigation of intermember—and I include the leader here—relationships), or between the "group" and one of its members, a subgroup, the leader, or some shared concerns.*[21]

Some examples of such comments made by the author in a group established to help members work on problems with intimacy in relationships are the following:

When Mary spoke recently of the pain she was recently experiencing, no one said anything.

When Bob returned to the group after a several-week absence, no member said anything to him about his absence.

When Sarah told a long story a few minutes ago, many of you yawned and Rick looked like he was sleeping. None of you said anything about your reactions to Sarah.

Yalom states it very well: "The purpose of a mass group interpretation is to remove some obstacle that has arisen to obstruct the progress of the entire group."[22] He gives as examples of such obstacles the existence of anxiety-laden issues and of antitherapeutic group norms. The commentary helps the group identify and select a means of overcoming the obstacle. In the example of Mary, above, the group members feared that talking about Mary's pain would reveal their own, which they felt unsafe in doing. Regarding Bob, the members felt angry at him and feared he would retaliate if they criticized him. Regarding Sarah, the members were also angry at her but feared she would be unable to handle their feelings if they expressed them.

Modifying Members' Behavior.   In the preceding section, we noted that group conditions can sometimes be changed through modifying one member's behavior. It is also possible to change the group by modifying the interpersonal behavior of many members through a single procedure. The following is a series of examples of how this has been done in groups.

Example: A group of boys had a low rate of participation in group discussions. When the worker gave each boy a peanut every time he spoke, the overall rate increased. Subsequently, to increase the number of conversations devoted to the group's purpose, peanuts were only awarded for that type of contribution. The boys, in this case, were not only affected by being given rewards but by observing the entire process and by vicariously experiencing each other's rewards. This type of procedure can be used to change any class of behavior in the group, such as statements about feelings and personal statements, and is an example of positive reinforcement.[23]

Example: As we stated earlier, Rose reported on changing a pattern in which some members talked too much and others too little. Low participants were reinforced by people on their right whenever they spoke, while high participants received a restraining hand on their shoulders whenever they spoke.[24] This is another example of positive reinforcement.

Example: Another example provided by Rose was of a group in which members spoke more frequently to the worker than they did to each other, thus limiting many of the ways they could help one another. This pattern was pointed out by an observer who recorded the sequence of member and worker contributions in a simple manner: L M L M M L M L. The group discussed this pattern and decided that the person sitting next to the worker would remind him of his behavior by holding a card up to him that read "pause."[25]

Example: One group, also reported by Rose, was composed of mothers. Their problem—frequent deviation from their planned agenda—was dealt with in the following manner:

> *. . . the trainer showed a video tape of a segment of the previous week's meeting. She pointed out how the off-task discussion prevented the members from achieving the agreed upon goals. However, she noted that social contact with each other was an important part of coming to the group. She wondered how the members could meet both aims—the achievement of the task goals and the satisfaction of*

informal discussion. One member suggested that they plan to stay a few minutes longer after the formal session to discuss their children. The trainer agreed to increase the break between the first and second hours to 15 minutes. The group members then tried to define task-oriented discussion. They decided that it referred to any verbal contribution related to the agenda item being handled at any given point in time. If it was not related, it was off-task. One member agreed to review the tapes with the trainer to monitor the off-task behavior. They then decided that each person would remind her buddy if she were off-task. The trainer suggested that if the agenda items were finished early, the meeting could be ended early, which would give them more time for socializing.[26]

Example: A final behavioral technique, also reported by Rose, was used in a group where members made too many critical and unpleasant remarks to one another. Each time members felt abused, they placed a white poker chip in a large can in the center of the group; a red chip signified a feeling of reinforcement. This simple procedure immediately modified the type of comments made and led to more reinforcing responses.[27]

Utilizing Tasks and Activities.   One of the most creative contributions group workers bring to their work is activities. This is based on their understanding of the effects of program activities on both group conditions and member goal attainment. Virtually every group work text describes the use of media such as crafts, games, dramatics, cooking, nature study, and dance. One of the earliest and best of these efforts is the classic work of Wilson and Ryland. The authors describe each of these media in great detail and how they can be used to enhance the purposes of group work.[28] Another classic on this subject is by Middleman.[29]

Along with these authors, we consider program activities to be more than simply another set of techniques for enhancing group experience. Through such activities, individuals can express their creativity, approach situations in a manner that generates new perspectives on themselves and their environments, communicate with others on more nonverbal levels, and develop new interests and talents. It is possible for people to reveal much to each other in group discussion, but it is also possible to conceal a great deal. When people engage in activities with each other, such as a game or a dramatic enactment, they "tell" a good deal about how they react to situations. They can also experiment with new ways of responding to such situations.

Program activities make it possible for group workers to be involved with many individuals who are not accessible to standard forms of group psychotherapy in which they are expected to *talk* to others about their problems. This includes children (group workers understood many of the ideas of "play therapy" before that term was ever used), adults who are relatively inarticulate, people of any age who are not motivated to approach problems verbally but seek help in interacting with others, and those who can benefit from social contacts but who are not ready to sustain such contacts without a good deal of structure and support.

We shall describe briefly some of the major activities used by group workers as well as a conceptual framework for assessing the way activities can be adapted to the needs of particular group members. Some of the most common activities employed by group workers are *games*. Games include those in which an element of competition is present (some board games, sports, "low-organized" games such as "tag"); those in which there is no "winner" (games that elicit some response such as a series of cards that are drawn from a deck with "personal" questions—favorite food, music, and so forth); those that elicit some emotional reaction such as laughter or surprise (supplying words to fill in the blanks in a story without "hearing" the story until afterwards). Games can create many structural patterns in the group such as pairs, triads, leaders, and competitors.

Workers use games to "break the ice" in the beginning phases of a group, to promote more interactions, or to change existing interactional patterns. Games are used to generate immediate reactions to events such as winning, losing, cooperating, leading, or following. They are also used to alter the emotional climate of the group, to help members discharge tensions, or even to create situations in which members explore new ways to handle tensions.

Another activity workers or members may introduce is *arts or crafts*, where members may engage singly in drawing, making a ceramic object, or sewing a shirt. Or, they may participate cooperatively with a group to create a mural or construct something for all to use, such as a game.

Workers promote arts or crafts projects to help members communicate with one another in nonverbal ways, experience a sense of their own creativity or competence, or cooperate. These projects can also help members express emotions that are difficult to put into words but that can be conveyed through the use of color, through the way a medium is used (such as clay, finger paints, hammer and nails), or through abstract images.

Workers and members may also utilize *drama* activities—role plays, skits, improvisations, play readings, charades, as well as full dramatic productions.

Role plays have many different purposes: they may help a member prepare to use a behavior outside of the group (behavioral rehearsal); they may be used for diagnostic purposes in which the member demonstrates how he or she responds to a problem situation; they may be employed to help the member understand the reactions of others through "playing the part" of a "significant other"; they may be created so that some other members or the worker can model a behavior for a member; finally, they may facilitate decision making as the member experiments with different responses to a situation.

The other types of dramatic activities can fulfill the same functions as role plays but can also accomplish others. The drama may raise value or other questions that members may become motivated to think about and to discuss because of their involvement. Members may develop the ability to express emotions or act in ways they previously refrained from because they have "tried it out" in a "make believe" situation. The group may become more cohesive because the members have cooperated in a highly interactive activity.

Members in social work groups can also benefit from engaging in activities that draw upon *music*. These include singing, writing songs, playing musical instruments, and moving rhythmically through clapping and dancing. Some of the benefits of these activities are a feeling of unity by engaging in simultaneous actions, the release of emotions, the stimulation of happy feelings when the music is spirited, and the opportunity to lead or to follow others. Dance provides the additional benefit of helping participants express themselves through bodily movement in ways that transcend the verbal.

Members may also listen to music. By associating thoughts and feelings to what they hear, they often become aware of aspects of themselves and their experiences that were previously not accessible. Music can be combined with another medium, as when members are encouraged to paint abstractly while listening to music.

Another activity often used in groups is *cooking* and then eating what was prepared. Simple refreshments (such as coffee for adults and punch for children) may be served to help members relax or even to provide reinforcement for attendance and participation. Cooking elaborate refreshments, because of the meaning food has to people, will motivate members to cooperate with others in the group when no other activity is likely to initiate this. Thus food preparation frequently has been used with children and adolescents, the developmentally disabled, and low-functioning clients.

Food preparation has also been used to teach the skill of cooking in its own right. Low-income people have been taught how to prepare nutritious yet inexpensive and tasty dishes, and people with limited social skills have been taught how to entertain others through the medium of food.

At times, social work groups will take *trips* for a variety of purposes. Some low-functioning members travel to restaurants, stores, or places of amusement to learn behaviors appropriate to those places; other groups go to places that will expand knowledge or aspirations, such as a group of adolescents who traveled to a variety of workplaces as part of a discussion of careers.

The use of camping by group workers is almost legendary. The camping experience has often provided a crucial turning point for delinquents, people with limited social skills, and people with physical handicaps. The experiences of living together, sharing a full round of daily activities, overcoming hardships such as bad weather or getting lost when on a group hike, improvising necessities, and enjoying a campfire and stories on a starry night have come close to performing miracles with severely troubled members.

A final item in this list of activities is the use of *fantasy*. Members will sometimes be asked to imagine a specified type of event and, for those who wish, to share the experience afterwards. Small groups of members can also be asked to create a fantasy together. This kind of activity serves several purposes. When members are tense, they can be helped to relax by imagining a peaceful scene. When members appear to wish they were elsewhere, they can "leave" the meeting in fantasy and then "return," thus identifying some sources of resistance to group participation.

Another version of this activity is a "continuation" story in which each member does an "add on" to the events described by another member. This and other devices help members to express, albeit indirectly, wishes, concerns, and other aspects of their mental lives.

When the worker selects or helps the members select an activity, he or she must anticipate its effects on the group. Vinter has developed a way for workers to analyze programmatic components to make this possible.[30] A description of this framework follows, as well as an exercise at the end of the chapter, to enable the reader to develop proficiency in its use.

Vinter's analysis begins with the idea that all activities take place in a *physical field*. This "refers to the physical space and terrain, and the physical and social objects characteristic of each activity." Group workers learn to predict the positive and negative effects of items in the physical field. It does not take much experience, for example, to forecast what happens when a person of the other sex enters the meeting room of a group of adolescents. Group workers interacting with children, also, never forget such experiences as bringing a group of hyperactive boys into a room with lumps of clay on the table—the clay soon flies. A positive example is that of a worker who wished to stimulate a group of youths to consider occupational career issues and, therefore, placed a number of colorful career pamphlets in the meeting room.

All activities also consist of *constituent performances*, which are "behaviors that are essential to the activity and thus are required of participants." For example, a discussion requires members to listen to each other and to respond appropriately, and a baseball game requires participants to learn a set of rules and to follow them in accomplishing such actions as running bases, catching the ball, and batting.

Vinter states that the physical field and the constituent performances constitute the *activity-setting*. The activity-setting produces the *respondent behaviors*, which are "individual participant actions evoked by, but not essential to, participation in the activity." Thus, in a game, group members may cheer, express feelings of disappointment on losing, or embrace each other. These are respondent behaviors occurring through that activity. Group workers will choose or help the members choose activities that require constituent performances or elicit respondent behaviors relevant to the member's goals.

An example of this type of planning is a group worker who introduced a simple craft project into a group of developmentally disabled children. The project necessitated that the children learn some construction skills and cooperate with each other (constituent performances). The worker's conviction was that these skills would be useful to the children; cooperative behavior was also a treatment goal. In the process of accomplishing the activity, the members struck up conversations with one another (respondent behaviors), which also was consistent with the worker's goals of helping the members acquire social skills.

The worker planning an activity or predicting the effect of an activity on the group can utilize Vinter's scheme for assessment of the dimensions of activity-settings. These dimensions consist of six factors.

The first factor, the *prescriptiveness of the pattern of constituent performances*, denotes "the degree and range of rules or other guides for conduct." Thus baseball is more prescriptive than tag and painting a portrait that is an accurate likeness is more prescriptive than creating an abstract drawing.

The second factor, the *institutionalized controls governing participant activity*, consists of the "form and source or agent of controls that are exercised over participants during the activity." The control might be exerted by the group worker or by members of the group on each other or might stem from norms internalized by the members. A group discussion or project in which the rules or procedures are maintained by the worker through the use of rewards places the worker as the source of controls. In many activities chosen by the members and known to them, such as a basketball game selected by adolescents, the members will enforce the rules on each other and the group will be the source of controls. If the activity has been engaged in frequently by members, they are likely to have internalized the rules to such an extent that very little control is exerted actively by either the worker or other members.

The source of controls has great implications for the power structure of the group. Workers should be aware that activities that force them to exert most of the controls are likely to produce hostility toward the worker. Thus workers will choose or support activities, particularly in early stages of the group, that produce controls from within the group and even within each member. A worker, for example, who was planning a first meeting with a group of aggressive, hyperactive youngsters included a tag game they all knew. The game had the dual function of releasing energy and drawing on rules members were likely to follow without external pressure.

The *provision for physical movement*, the third factor, involves "the extent to which participants are required or permitted to move their bodies in the activity-setting." A discussion is obviously more restricted in movement than a ball game. Even within a discussion, however, members may have opportunities to move around or may be restrained from such movement. These physical movement options will have such effects on the members as allowing or limiting discharge of tension, encouraging or discouraging interactions, or increasing or decreasing the ability of the worker or the members to exert controls.

Fourth, the *competence required for performance*, is "the minimum level of ability required to participate in the activity." The level of ability is usually determined by the worker and/or the members and is not primarily a product of impersonal and remote decisions of "authorities." Thus the members of a group or the worker will decide whether a person is "good enough" to play ball or take part in discussions or join in a song.

Norms regarding competence will also have many effects on group conditions: they will determine whether a member is regarded as deviant because he or she is much more or much less competent than others; whether a member has much or little power because of degrees of expertise; and whether subgroups will form because of similarities and differences in competence for group activities.

Provision for participant interactiveness is the fifth factor. The definition of this dimension is "the way the activity-setting locates and engages participants so that interaction among them is required or provoked." A group discussion, for example, in which members direct most comments to the worker is less interactive than one in which members are reinforced for responding to each other. An art project involving a group mural is likely to be more interactive than an art project involving separate drawings. Thus this dimension has many implications for the kinds of group structures and processes that emerge.

The final dimension, the *reward structure*, consists of "the types of rewards available, their abundance or scarcity, and the manner in which they are distributed." Some aspects of the reward structure are easier to assess than others because a full assessment of rewards must include the intrinsic gratifications that members receive from participation (for example, feelings of worth, release of emotions) as well as the extrinsic ones such as tokens, food, or being a "winner." The importance of the reward structure is severalfold: whether members will enter the activity at all or stay with it; whether members will tolerate a large number of rules, a restriction in movement, or a demand to increase competence; and whether members will modify previously acquired structures or processes or are affected by the availability of rewards. Within limits, therefore, a change in any dimension can be enhanced by appropriate rewards.

Vinter's approach to analyzing program activities and their effects has been used to generate many hypotheses about differential use of programs. Vinter, himself, indicated the likely efforts on respondent behaviors of variations in each of the activity-setting dimensions.[31] For example, he predicted that high prescriptiveness is associated with high fatigue, high physical movement with aggressiveness, and scarcity of rewards with competitiveness.

Whitaker, utilizing Vinter's format, makes highly specific recommendations for programs that might meet the needs of various kinds of children as group members.[32] He utilizes the member variables of skill, motivation, and internal controls to define eight categories of children out of the various permutations possible for high or low ratings on these three attributes. Thus one child may have high skills, motivation, and control; another may be low on all three of these; a third may have high control but have low skill and motivation, and so on.

His example of the latter child who is low on skill and motivation but high on control is stated as follows: "This child is poorly motivated and unskilled but presents no great control problem. He is probably a shy, withdrawing youngster who feels rebuffed by his peers and has a very low self-image. He too needs immediate successes and uncomplicated games and projects. Lots of help and praise will enhance his development; the rest of the group could help in this respect."[33] Whitaker indicates the kinds of activity-setting dimensions each of these types of children will require. He selects "programs" such as swimming, finger painting, copper enameling, kickball, and Simon Says and rates them with regard to such dimensions. This then leads to specific prescriptions of such activities for each type of child.

Such an analysis has not been made for programs used primarily in adult groups, but Whitaker's approach could be extended in this way. This is an important area—one which could easily be researched and to which more attention should be paid. Even without research validation, however, the knowledge of how to analyze the dimensions of programs is very useful to practitioners.

Altering Group Norms.   Group conditions are, in part, maintained by group norms. These are beliefs about what such conditions ought to be. Group workers will use a number of approaches to help members alter their norms to modify group conditions.

One set of techniques for altering group norms is *value clarification exercises*, which can be used to help members identify and change their individual beliefs, as well as to alter beliefs collectively held by all or most group members and which serve, therefore, to maintain group conditions. Value clarification exercises usually help members become aware of values they hold in specified situations or on specified topics. The following are a few examples of such value clarification experiences.

Example: A Values Auction. In a value auction, members are given a set amount of play money. An "auction" is then held for such "values" as friendship, health, a guarantee of a good job, and a good marriage. Members keep an account of how much they bid on each of these items. On the bases of this, a discussion is held as to how and why values differ. Members discover others in the group who hold similar as well as different values, and they seek these people out to discuss how they wish to realize their values.

Example: Alligator River. The group worker reads the group a story about a woman who wishes to cross a river to meet her lover. She consulted one friend who refused to be involved. A boatman then agreed to take her across at the price of sexual relations. When she had thus crossed, her lover found out the "price she paid" and deserted her. She told another friend about this, and he did harm to the lover. The story thus ends. The members of the group are asked to rank these characters in terms of the most harmful and the most harmed individuals. Afterwards, members share and discuss their ratings. The exercise illuminates values associated with sex roles and loyalties. Members, as in the first example, seek others in the group for further clarification of similarities and differences on these issues.

Because group workers can come to have a great deal of emotional meaning to group members, statements of their own values can affect the values of group members. Workers can express their points of view on what constitutes respect, how human beings ought to treat one another, what constitutes a "good" society, or what are desirable norms on sexuality, economic honesty, or cheating on examinations. Workers will avoid stating their values when this will interfere with members' exploration of their own values or when worker statements will be regarded as "preachy." Another important set of norms has to do with openness among group members and the kinds of self-disclosure that should take place.

For many normative issues, the worker will be careful to indicate what his or her beliefs are and will state that members must examine and take responsibility for their own beliefs. Some workers take the position, in addition, that some beliefs are so essential to human dignity that the workers should present these vigorously and conclusively. These include, for example, nonuse of violence (for example, sexual assault) to achieve one's objectives.

Some values are relevant immediately to group processes, such as requiring full consensus on some issues and at least majority rule on others. The full consensus rule is employed when a decision could harm a member; an agreement not to discuss sensitive issues without full agreement in a group of anxious persons is an example of this. These kinds of decisional roles are included in what Vinter calls "operating and governing procedures." Such procedures can also include standardized ways of opening and closing meetings, expressing opinions on topics, serving refreshments, notifying the group about absences or tardiness, and so on. These procedures, then, are supported by group norms. They also provide members with a sense of structure which, for many, is associated with security. It also defines the group as different from others, which can also enhance the members' sense of the group as an entity with which they can identify.

Another norm related to group processes is that a member should not be pressured to give personal information or to take part in an exercise. The worker should assess the need for all of these kinds of norms as part of creating a safe group atmosphere.

The worker also has the responsibility to set limits in the group. This is more often required in some groups, such as children's groups, than in others. The worker, in these groups, may be required to restrain members from physically attacking one another or destroying property. Children may run in and out of the room disturbing other activities in the agency, or they may use obscene language which, at times, is anxiety provoking to themselves or others.

The worker faced with such behavior has several options. A statement regarding permissible behavior and group discussion and support of such rules will help to prevent some antisocial behavior. Additional prevention is possible when workers are aware of and respond to tensions that are building in groups before they reach the point where the members with the poorest controls begin to act aggressively. The major tool the worker will use is *program*, which can help to discharge tension or to control behavior because the rules intrinsic to the activity lead to rewards that are also part of it.

Fritz Redl and David Wineman have described techniques useful in group situations to control behavior.[34] These include "planned ignoring," "tension decontamination through humor," "direct appeal," "antiseptic bouncing," "physical restraint," and "permission and authoritative verbot."

Control issues can also be present in adult groups. They arise more frequently in groups of adults who are psychotic or seriously developmentally disabled. In any adult group in which interpersonal relationship issues are intensively examined, however, strong emotions may be aroused. Emotions such as crying or expressions of caring and affection are not usually inhibited by the worker, but aggressive expressions likely to lead to physical attack will be. In this latter case, in some encounter-type groups, members are encouraged to express physical competition in such controlled ways as arm wrestling.

Even minor physical encounters are controversial as a group therapeutic device, although some therapists have written favorably about personal issues that have been brought to awareness and dealt with in this manner.[35] The determining criteria should be that no physical or psychological harm is likely. This certainly places a heavy burden of proof on the worker.

Enhancing Group Problem Solving.   In most groups, much time is spent seeking solutions to problems through a rational and orderly discussion. Even though a problem-solving discussion is a type of group task (or what we have termed program activity), it is such an important component of group work that we provide a separate discussion of it. In social work groups, the problem discussed may involve a decision by one individual affecting himself or herself or may involve a decision by the group members affecting them all. The decision may also involve a problem common to several or all of the members. We recommend the following steps be taken by the group, with help from the worker, in any problem-solving process:[36]

1. The Problem Is Specified in Detail.   This specification includes the details of the problematic situation, such as who does what to whom, under what conditions, and with what response; how frequently this occurs; how much harm is done; and how motivated the person is to do something to ameliorate the problem.

2. The Group Members Determine Whether a Group Problem-Solving Process Should Occur.   The members must decide whether this problem takes precedence over others and how much group time to allocate to the process. The worker must motivate the members to invest themselves in the process, such as becoming involved in the problem specification process (by asking questions) or by seeing how problem solving is relevant to their own concerns. As Toseland and Rivas point out, the members must decide that the problem is legitimate and can be resolved successfully.[37]

3. The Group Members Are Oriented to Problem Solving.   If the group members have had little experience in systematic problem-solving, they should be taught its components by having information presented to them. Group members tend to jump from problem specification to solution without taking the necessary steps; they also tend to adopt the first solution presented. These "errors" can be avoided when members are made aware of the disadvantages of such actions.

4. Goals to Be Attained through Problem Solving Are Specified.   The members are helped to develop an idea of what the situation will be like when the problem is solved. This will help the members determine when the problem-solving process has been completed. Some problems may actually be resolved in part of a group session, while others may be discussed over a number of sessions. It may be possible to subdivide a problem and make it easier to resolve by developing a series of subgoals worked on in sequence. If the group establishes a time schedule for this, it will also help the member or members engage in required tasks.

5. Information Is Sought to Help the Group Members Generate Possible Solutions as Well As Evaluate Such Solutions. Such information includes what the member has done before, other data about the member's personality, the situation, and the resources available to carry out each solution. The worker will use techniques to help members generate solutions openly. One such technique is "brainstorming": a rule is agreed to that any and all ideas can be stated, with no criticism or discussion of any one until a sufficient list of ideas is generated. Another technique is to introduce an analogy that will help members view their problem in a new manner. An example of this in one group was a problem provided by a member who had been unsuccessful in a series of job interviews. The worker asked, "How is seeking a job like selling a new type of radio?" The members gave answers such as, "The radio must appear to be different and better than other radios," and "The purchasers must believe that they are receiving more for their money." The worker then asked how these principles might be used by the member in her job interviews. Toseland and Rivas refer to this type of approach as "lateral thinking," which they describe as follows:

> *Lateral thinking processes are particularly useful when vertical thinking processes have not yielded a creative solution. Lateral thinking helps to free ideas that have been blocked by stale, routine ways of conceptualizing a problem and its potential solutions. Instead of relying on an orderly, linear combination of facts, lateral thinking is characterized by the use of analogies, metaphors, similarities, contrasts, and paradoxes.*[38]

6. Alternative Solutions Are Evaluated. The criteria evaluated are what the benefits to the group member as well as others will be if the solution is chosen, and what negative consequences may result. In addition, the values of the member as well as of significant others should be considered.

7. One Alternative Is Chosen. In accomplishing this task, the members first review the alternatives so that they are clear to each one. This activity sometimes leads to a combination of several alternatives to maximize the benefits. The choice of an alternative should be based on such criteria as feasibility, length of time to enact, costs, benefits, impact on others, value considerations, long-term and short-term consequences, and the resources and other supports available. If the problem is that of a single member, he or she will make the final choice of alternatives. If the problem is one the group has identified, the group will have to decide what decisional rule (majority, consensus, two-thirds) to employ.

8. Planning the Details for Carrying Out the Chosen Alternative. Simply choosing an alternative is not sufficient. The member or members will usually need help in planning how and when to enact the alternative. This may involve role playing, rehearsing the action in words, anticipating the reaction of others, identifying barriers, planning how to evaluate the consequences of the action, and determining the future role of the group and its members with reference to the problem and its solution.

Altering Group Emotional States.   Other techniques for modifying group conditions through direct interactions with the group are directed at the emotions of group members. Some of these are employed when the group climate is tense because of the anxiety of all or many group members. Under these circumstances, workers may simply discuss the tension then explore its sources. An example from one group was a discussion of an untrue rumor that the agency would close.

Group workers, to reduce tensions also introduce procedures to enhance coping with an issue that all members face, such as the termination of the group. The worker's ability to model relaxation in the face of such stresses is useful in this process.

At other times, the worker will choose to deal with the group members' tension level through a relaxation procedure. This can range from encouraging members to be more conscious of their breathing to using a progressive relaxation exercise. The latter requires that the worker develop skills in the use of relaxation training. One way of providing this training involves, according to Rose, "The alternation of tension of the muscles in each large muscle group, with the release of that tension . . . "[39] The member must receive feedback on the appropriate actions, which Rose accomplishes through pairing the members, with one member being the coach and the other the relaxer. The coach can call the worker over when uncertainties as to the proper instruction arise. Rose cautions the worker to bring members out of a relaxation procedure gradually by slow movements of various body segments. He also warns that the procedure is not to be rushed and that part of several sessions should be used to learn the entire procedure. Members must also try, if possible, to practice relaxation outside of group sessions.[40]

Another technique for relaxation involves the use of fantasy. Each member is encouraged to imagine a peaceful scene. Some members have chosen listening to music or sitting by a slowly moving river. The members picture themselves at such scenes. Members are then gradually encouraged to "return" to the group.

Sometimes the emotional condition the worker seeks to alter is the lack of positive emotional expression among the members when members feel it but do not communicate it. Lange and Jakubowski describe an exercise they call "giving and receiving compliments" that helps to instill more skill in expressing and receiving this sentiment.[41] The exercise involves pointing out behavior that discourages compliments, such as denying their validity, or behavior that is a negative way of giving a compliment, such as depreciating one's self in the process. A demonstration and practice of brief, unqualified compliments follow. In the experiential part of the exercise, members stand in a circle, give a compliment to the person to their right, and receive an appropriate response. In a second "go round," each "giver" expresses to the receiver something he or she specifically *liked* about how the "receiver" responded to his or her compliment.

A host of other emotional conditions arise in groups and may be idiosyncratic to some members or widely shared. These include competitiveness, sadness, jealousy, and elation. The worker on occasion desires members to become more aware of these affects and to examine their affects on behavior. This can often be secured through process illumination, that is, asking members to discuss the implications of their communications to one another.

At other times workers will introduce an exercise to elicit already-present emotions. Thus a game might reveal some competitive feelings; an art project, feelings of elation or depression; and a discussion of positives members see in each other, feelings of jealousy.

Modifying Group Conditions through Influences from the Environment

The Agency.   In Chapter 2 we discussed the ways that the agency can affect group work. Several of these can be utilized by the worker who wishes to use the agency to change some internal condition of the group. The worker can do this either through making the agency's input more visible or by approaching others in the agency in an effort to *change* the organizational input.

One of the agency conditions that can be made more visible is the agency's purpose for the group. A group that avoids working on members' problems can be reminded of this purpose by the worker, or the agency can act, for instance, by asking the group to evaluate how well it is responding to its purposes.

The agency can also affect group conditions by referring more members to the group, thus modifying composition. Some of the occasions when the worker might ask the agency to do this are when the group is overloaded with antisocial members, when the group members lack expertise to carry out the group's purposes, or when some members have become isolated because of their differences.

The agency can also modify the group through the resources allocated to the group. The room in which the group meets can be changed to another more conducive to desired activities, and equipment can be supplied to the group for prescribed programs. Expertise, in addition to that of the worker, can also be made available. An example of this could be a speaker on contraception for an adolescent group, a "process observer" for a social skills group, and an expert on value clarification for a group of probationers.

The agency can also affect the group through interacting with indigenous leaders or other group members. Some agencies will form either a council of representatives of groups or will include members and other consumers of services on advisory committees or boards, where issues of importance to the agency will be reported to the group and discussed. This may affect the group's goals, activities, and values. An example of this was a discussion an agency had with such an advisory committee regarding the fact that the agency, a settlement house, was underused by the Chicano members of the community. Following this discussion, several of the youth groups in the agency sought out Chicanos and invited them to join their groups.

Agencies have a major effect on group conditions through their preferences for the techniques workers should use with groups. One agency, for example, wished to facilitate the use of behavior modification. It solicited items that could be offered to members in exchange for tokens, made various counting devices available for determining the frequency of behaviors, and issued brochures to members explaining a behavioral approach to group work. This had a major influence on the discussions and approaches utilized by these members.

Last, it is important to remember that groups are likely to interact with other staff and other clients of the agency. The agency, therefore, can use these actions purposefully to modify group conditions. Groups can be brought together in the agency when the interaction between them can prove beneficial; members of one group can visit another to describe to the host group how their own group dealt with selected issues; a few members from each of several groups can be brought together around a common issue and still return to their "own" group; and group members may receive one-to-one services from staff members other than their group worker.

In all of these examples of how an agency might affect conditions within the group, the group worker should have had a role in initiating the agency input or in approving it. The worker's subsequent role within the group then becomes a different one than when he or she sought the change by interventions within the group. The worker can become the person who helps the group members consider their response to the agency input. This places the worker in a mediating rather than directive role, which can be important in work with some resistant groups.

The Family.   Group conditions can be modified by other forces outside of the agency, which the worker may decide to utilize. The families of the group members are one important possibility. Workers who form groups for children in agencies such as child guidance clinics will usually meet with the parents, often in a group. Joint meetings can also be arranged between the parents' and children's groups. The parents can discuss such issues as how to reinforce the children's progress and commitment to their group and how to deal with issues that the children might bring home about their group. The parents can also encourage the children to raise their concerns in their own group.

Another example of the impact of relatives on a group was presented in a report of work done with a group of husbands who assaulted their wives.[42] The group consisted of some men who were ordered by the court to attend as well as some men who came voluntarily. The worker maintained contact with the local abused women's shelter that provided referrals. The worker networked with the abused women's network.

The Community.   Workers also seek to influence group conditions through the impact of other agencies in the community. For example, a group service agency formed groups of children referred by the local school because of difficulties they were having in the classroom. The worker set goals with each child concerning what the child hoped to achieve through group participation. In many cases this involved securing better classroom grades. The grading period, however, was too far off to provide the immediate reinforcement each child needed. The worker, therefore, secured agreements from the teachers to provide more immediate feedback and encouragement to the children.

Workers also seek the cooperation of indigenous community groups because of their impact on group conditions. Spergel, for example, presents an extended discussion of work with adolescent gangs.[43] An intrinsic part of his approach is the worker's activity with community groups because of their impact on the adolescents. This type of effort can include helping the group members find jobs, cope with the restrictions of probation, and learn new skills.

A very important part, also, of the environmental impact on the group relates to culture and ethnicity. One of the ways this is manifested, for example, is on the structuring of group meetings. In some cultures, group meetings begin and end with a prayer or a song. Quaker groups are accustomed to silent periods in which members reflect quietly before speaking. Some cultures have values regarding what may be addressed in public gatherings and what must be restricted to intrafamilial deliberations.

The worker can utilize knowledge of cultural inputs into the group in several other ways. A group's utilization of cultural forms can enhance its cohesiveness through the members' awareness of their common heritage. The worker can also help the larger cultural system interpret its values to group members. A case of the latter was when a worker suggested the group invite members of the Southern Christian Leadership Conference (SCLC) to speak about the SCLC and its goals for social change in reference to black people. This presentation provided inspiration to group members when they discussed their personal goals.

At times the worker will target cultural conditions that have negative impacts on group processes for change. In one ethnic community, there was little encouragement for higher education, yet many members of a group meeting in a community center wished to consider this career option. The worker held several meetings with parents and other community leaders to discuss and try to change their antipathy to education. She felt that only in this way might the youths in the group secure the support or at least acceptance they needed.

Employing the Model for Changing Group Conditions

At the beginning of the chapter, we presented a six-step model for working with the group's members to create a group conducive to their goal attainment. The model prescribes that when the worker and members identify a group level problem, they should determine the group condition that maintains the problem and then choose a means of altering that condition. We shall now offer examples of these relationships that we hope will help workers better understand how to make use of the ideas in this chapter.

Group Problem: Members Are Not Sufficiently Attracted to the Group.   Some of the group conditions related to this problem: the group may be at an early *stage of development* when members are ambivalent about membership; the *group climate* may be an angry or fearful one; or the *boundaries* of the group that define group membership might be unclear. Some of the approaches for change the worker might introduce are at the *group* level. The worker might introduce a *program* activity in which members deal with such formation issues as determining group purpose, developing relationships with other members, and expressing feelings about the group. The worker might initiate a *problem-solving* process in which the members select a solution to the group's lack of attractiveness. The worker might introduce an activity that will have an impact on climate if the problem is with group climate; or the worker might help the members find ways to relax if they are anxious about the group, or to ventilate their feelings if they are angry. If the relevant group condition is a boundary issue, the worker might intervene at the *environmental* level. This might involve negotiations with systems in the environment that affect the group's boundaries.

Group Problem: Members Think Group Is Not Helping Them to Achieve Their Goals.   Some conditions that contribute to this problem: the group might be in the formation *stage of development*; the aspect of *group process* that we have labeled *goal pursuit* may be faulty in that an inappropriate task has been chosen; or the group may lack *resources* to attain the goals chosen by the members. A *group level* intervention is often used to resolve this type of problem. The worker, if this is a stage of development issue, might move more quickly to help the members select the type of activities conducive to goal attainment, or the worker may remind the members that they have not yet clarified their group goals. If inappropriate activities have been chosen, the worker might employ the framework we referred to earlier in this chapter to help the group modify the current activity or to choose a new one altogether. If the group lacks resources, the worker may help them engage in *problem solving* to find a way to secure resources, or the worker may help them interact with institutions capable of providing these resources.

Group Problem: The Members Are in Conflict with or Hostile to One Another.   The group conditions that might contribute to this problem: a *group structure* in which the *power* component is dysfunctional; the group's *stage of development* in which power and control issues are foremost (revision phase); or the *group process* in which the group task promotes competitiveness among members. The worker might intervene at the *individual* level by helping a member assume the role of mediator between the conflicting members. The worker, alternatively, might act at the *subgroup* level by encouraging the conflicting members to talk to each other and resolve it while other members remain in the background. The worker might intervene at the group level by helping the members consider normative issues that underlie their conflicts, by helping the members engage in problem solving, or by discussing the stage of development issue with the members, if that is the source of the conflict. This last approach requires the worker to provide emotional support to the members as they cope with inevitable leadership and power shifts within the group.

Group Problem: Some Members Oppose the Agency Purposes That Led to the Agency's Creation or Sponsorship of the Group.   The conditions that might contribute to this problem: the group might be in the formation *stage of development;* its *extragroup transactions* with other groups that have an impact on member attitudes might be problematic; or the group's culture might incorporate values in opposition to those of the agency. If the problem is related to group formation, the worker will likely intervene at the *group* level by helping the members consider their purposes and how they may or may not relate to agency purposes. If the problem relates to the impact of other systems, the worker might act at the *environmental* level by mediating between the group and such environmental systems as the agency, the members' families, or the members' peers. If the group's culture creates tension between it and the agency, the worker might also intervene at the *environmental* level by mediating between the group and the agency. The worker might alternatively intervene at the *group* level by helping the members consider how their norms might be hindering the attainment of their goals.

While we cannot list all the problems that workers and members encounter in their groups, we can indicate some typical problems related to each of the group conditions we have described. We indicate these in Table 5.2, along with some of the change strategies we have found useful for each problem. The reader should note that we have referred to specific types of processes in this table.

The contents of this chapter illustrate how practitioners should help groups resolve their problems. We urge readers to develop ways of recording and communicating to others

TABLE 5.2   Group Problems and Suggested Change Strategies

Group Condition	Typical Problems Associated with Condition	Change Strategies
Group development	Group members confused over purpose; members challenge indigenous or worker-initiated leadership; members protest the scheduled ending of the group; confusion over who the members actually are	Group process comments that illuminate group's stage of development; group problem solving
Group structure	Friendship cliques emerge that are antagonistic to one another; one member dominates others; necessary information communicated to only some members although required by all; some members overloaded with work	Mass group process comments; utilize tasks and activities that introduce new group structures
Group-environment processes; extra-group transactions	Group members in conflict with members of other groups; group does not have access to necessary resources; space for meetings is inadequate or inappropriate	Worker mediates between group and environment; advocates for group in environment
Process of interpersonal attraction	Some members avoided by others; members demand the attention of one member in ways that are dysfunctional to that member	Worker mediates among members; worker makes group process comments; worker helps build interpersonal skills
Process of group socialization	Members leave the group complaining they never understood what was expected of them	Worker helps group clarify group purpose and expectations of members; worker helps members clarify individual goals
Process of conformity to group norms	Members imitate the behavior of a member in ways harmful to themselves; members fail to observe group rules	Group process comments; help group clarify norms; help group determine consequences of failure to observe norms that are therapeutically appropriate
Power and leadership processes	Group accomplishes little or some members control the group in ways that prevent attainment of group purposes	Worker employs appropriate group leadership techniques or helps members learn group leadership skills; group problem solving
Performance processes	Members do not adequately carry out assigned tasks	Utilize tasks and activities that build skills; help members learn skills
Group decision-making processes	Group members cannot agree on how to solve group problems	Educate the members regarding effective problem-solving processes

(Continued.)

TABLE 5.2   *Continued.*

Group Condition	Typical Problems Associated with Condition	Change Strategies
Group culture	Members do not understand each other's expectations and roles that they have learned from their cultures; members make racist and sexist comments	Make mass group process comments that help members explore diversity and create new group traditions that are culturally acceptable; confront sexism and racism in the group in ways that help members identify how they use a position of privilege they have acquired in society as well as how they can cope with oppression
Group climate	Members appear anxious or depressed	Facilitate expression of feelings; help members identify the conditions that have led to their feelings; help members cope with these conditions; help members learn relaxation responses as required

how they have assessed group problems and worked with groups to resolve them. The field of group practice will become more effective as its practitioners use a common framework to evaluate their practice and disseminate their findings.

Summary

In this chapter we presented a model for facilitating the development of groups to help members accomplish their purposes, and described a set of variables for assessing group conditions relevant to this. These variables were group development, group structure, group process, group culture, group resources, extragroup transactions, group boundaries, and group climate. We subsequently described how workers can intervene to help the members modify such group conditions. These interventions can occur with individuals, subgroups, the group-as-a-whole, or systems in the environment.

Workers help members as individuals modify group conditions through performing tasks for the group, utilizing power in a responsible manner, and examining the critical functions they fulfill for the group. They help subgroups modify group conditions by using their influence constructively or by performing tasks for the group.

Workers intervene with the group-as-a-whole by impacting members' attributions, behaviors, tasks and activities, norms, ways of problem solving, and emotions. They can intervene in the environment by making environmental inputs more visible, by changing some aspect of the agency, by interacting with members' families, by treating some aspect of the community as an action system, and by focusing on some aspect of the members' ethnicity and culture.

In the next chapter, we continue this discussion of group conditions as these relate to "curative" forces in groups.

Group Development Exercise

Goals

1. To be able to identify the stage of development of the group.
2. To understand the means of helping a group achieve group conditions conducive to accomplishing group purposes.

Procedure

1. Prior to the exercise, trainees read about and discuss the nature of group conditions during its middle phases and the means for modifying such group conditions.
2. One of the problems in experiential learning around middle phases is that role plays and simulations, however characterized, are "new experiences" and that participants usually respond in ways appropriate to formation process. The accompanying observation questions should be used with a genuine middle phase. Several options are available to the trainee to accomplish this.

   a. Have observers respond to a discussion in the classroom itself, as the group. This can be the discussion called for in step (1).
   b. Have a student bring in a tape of an actual group that has completed the process of formation.
   c. Have a group of students, for whatever purpose, agree early in the course to meet several times outside of the class and to hold a "later" meeting in a "fishbowl" format in the class. This can be a brief meeting (about fifteen minutes).
   d. Have the trainees "as a last resort" attempt to role play a group in its middle phases. The best way to do this is to have a class member describe to the role players the behaviors at a meeting of a group he or she has participated in that was in its middle phases. The players try to simulate that meeting.

Assessment of Phase

1. Is the group, "in fact," post formation? (The answer is probably "yes" if several of the following items are present.)

   _____ Group is more invested in carrying out an activity (including discussion) than in deciding what activities are relevant. If an activity or discussion topic is picked, this occurs easily and with considerable consensus.

   _____ If there is disagreement about choosing or carrying out the activity, there exists considerable consensus among at least one set of group members, and this is opposed by another subgroup or a member or members. (This may be true in a so-called "revision" or "power and control" phase.)

_____ References are made to agreed-upon group norms or rules.

_____ Members talk as much or more to each other than they do to group worker.

_____ A pattern exists as to who talks to whom, where persons sit, who has most influence, and who carries out which tasks.

_____ Group purposes and/or goals are clear.

Group Structure Observation

2. Using a "sociogram" format, [for example,] sketch who seems to be most attracted to whom. Is this conducive to attaining group goals?
3. Who appears to have the most influence on members? Is this conducive to attaining group goals?

Group Process Observation

Select some comments members made to others in the meeting.

4. What implications did these comments have for the relationship among the members concerned?
5. What kinds of discussion, if any, took place regarding the relationship implications of these interactions?
6. What was the impact of the discussion referred to in Question 5 on the achievement of group goals?

For any problem-solving discussion(s) during the session, use the following scale.

7. By the end of the problem-solving discussion, what was the status of the problem?

    _____ Completely resolved: all aspects of the situation were decided on to the complete satisfaction of the group [and the member(s) concerned] so that no further work was necessary in this area.

    _____ There has been movement toward resolution, but the group [and member(s) concerned] could have moved further toward resolution given the time and resources available.

    _____ No change took place toward resolving the problem, yet the problem was not worsened in the process.

    _____ There has been movement away from resolution during this episode in that greater verbal differences were produced and/or more "friction" occurred.

    _____ The movement was completely away from the problem in that the issue was abandoned due either to frustration or to the immediate attraction of an alternate issue.

8. Did a member or members speak or act substantially differently from most others in the group? How did other members respond to this? After a group response, did the member change his or her "deviant" behavior?

Shared Attribution Observation

9. Indicate an example in which the members appeared to agree on the "causes" of a situation. Did this shared perception of cause facilitate or hinder the group's achieving its goal?

Worker's Efforts to Change Structures, Processes, or Attribution

Choose one of the preceding group conditions the worker sought to modify.

10. Which of the following ways characterized the worker's intervention to change the group condition:

Modifying group conditions through individuals

_____ Assigning an individual a task

_____ Assigning an individual a role

_____ Coaching or training an individual

_____ Reinforcing an individual

_____ Modifying the influence of an individual

_____ Other (specify)

Modifying group conditions through subgroups

_____ Modifying the influence of a subgroup

_____ Assigning the subgroup a task

_____ Helping a subgroup study its process

_____ Other (specify)

Modifying good conditions through interacting with the group-as-a-whole

_____ Altering member cognitions of these group conditions

_____ Modifying the behavior of many members

_____ Using program (task, activity)

_____ Altering norms

_____ Offering mass group process comments

_____ Other (specify)

Modifying group conditions through the environment

_____ Using agency purpose for group

_____ Securing change in agency allocation of resources

_____ Establishing or changing linkage between some group members and external people or systems

_____ Changing interactions between group or group members and people or systems outside of agency

_____ Using norms and traditions coming from a reference group of the members (for example, ethnic groups)

_____ Other (specify)

Program Exercise

(Adapted from an exercise originally developed by Harvey Bertcher for classroom use.)

Goals

1. To be able to analyze a "program" in terms of its physical field, constituent performances, respondent behaviors, and activity dimensions.
2. To be able to plan a modification in the activity dimensions of a "program" to better attain the group's purposes.

Procedures

1. Prior to the exercise, trainees read about and discuss ways of analyzing a "program."
2. Trainees are divided into three groups. Each group is assigned one of the accompanying program problems. The group will follow the instructions for choosing, role playing, and analyzing a "program" to solve the problem.
3. After completion of the entire exercise, trainees can discuss program problems from their own practice as a way of learning more about this approach to programming.

The Program Problems

Group A.   The Mental Health Association has decided to sponsor the formation of a social club for ex-psychiatric hospital patients, and has employed you part-time to direct its activities. The club's purpose is to assist members with reality problems such as finding employment, developing friendships, and becoming involved in community activities with people who are not ex-patients, rather than to treat their psychological problems. You have had three meetings with the group and are still having trouble helping the members interact. You have to use a game for this purpose.

1. Select one game and *demonstrate* your use of it with such a group. (Read the General Instructions before proceeding.)

Group B.   You have been assigned to work with a group in one ward of a psychiatric hospital. Most of the patients on this ward have been in the hospital for several years and are extremely withdrawn. While a long-range goal is to help patients improve sufficiently so that they can leave the hospital, you are primarily concerned at this time with getting them to communicate with one another—something they generally avoid. Since several of the members seem to enjoy music, you have decided to introduce a *musical activity*.

2. Select a musical activity and demonstrate your use of it with such a group. (Read the General Instructions before proceeding.)

Group C.   You are working with a group of college students having difficulty focusing on their reason for attending the group, which is that they are having difficulties in interpersonal relationships. You have decided that an exercise involving *fantasy* might help them face the reason they have joined the group. The group is meeting in the Counseling Services of the University.

3. Select an activity involving fantasy and *demonstrate* your use of it with such a group. (Read the General Instructions before proceeding.)

General Instructions—All Groups

You will be expected to present an analysis of the activity or task you have been assigned with regard to the following, using Vinter's "Program" paper as a guide:

1. Identify

    a. The physical field
    b. The constituent performance
    c. The respondent behaviors

2. Rate the activity according to Vinter's six "activity-setting dimensions."
3. Select a particular respondent behavior you might like to have seen increased or decreased. Indicate which of the activity's dimensions can be altered or decreased. Indicate which of the activity's dimensions can be altered to secure the desired change. Also indicate how this alteration would affect all of the other dimensions. (Obviously, this will be based on the respondent behaviors observed in class during your presentation.)

Endnotes

1. Allen Pincus and Anne Minahan, *Social Work Practice: Model and Method* (Itasca, Ill.: F.E. Peacock, 1973).

2. Our discussion of group development draws upon such authors as Rosemary C. Sarri, and Maeda Galinsky, "A Conceptual Framework for Group Development," in *Individual Change Through Small Groups*, eds. Martin Sundel, Paul Glasser, Rosemary Sarri, and Robert Vinter (New York: Free Press, 1985), pp. 70–86; James A. Garland, Hubert E. Jones, and Ralph Kolodny, "A Model for Stages of Development in Social Work Groups," in *Explorations in Group Work*, ed. Saul Bernstein (Boston: Boston University School of Social Work, 1965): 113; and Irvin D. Yalom, *The Theory and Practice of Group Psychotherapy*, 4th ed. (New York: Basic Books, 1995): 293–369.

3. Garland, Jones, and Kolodny, in *Explorations in Group Work*: 30–34; Sarri, and Galinsky, in *Individual Change*: 76.

4. Garland, Jones, and Kolodny, in *Explorations in Group Work*: 37–41.

5. For an extended discussion of group process, see Charles D. Garvin, "Group Process: Usage and Uses in Social Work Practice," in *Individual Change Through Small Groups*, 2nd ed., eds. Martin Sundel,

Paul Glasser, Rosemary Sarri, and Robert Vinter (New York: Free Press, 1985): 203–25.

6. Irving D. Yalom, *The Theory and Practice of Group Psychotherapy*, 4th ed. (New York: Basic Books, 1995): 131.

7. Garvin, "Group Process,": 203.

8. Robert F. Bales, "Task Roles and Social-Emotional Roles in Problem-Solving Groups," in *Readings in Social Psychology*, 3rd ed., eds. E.E. Maccoby, T.M. Newcomb, and E.T. Hartley (New York: Holt, Rinehart and Winston, 1958): 437–47.

9. Joseph E. McGrath, *Groups: Interaction and Performance* (Englewood Cliffs, N.J.: Prentice Hall, 1984).

10. Ibid.: 62.

11. Robert D. Vinter, "Program Activities: An Analysis of Their Effects on Participant Behavior," in *Individual Change Through Small Groups*, eds. Martin Sundel, Paul Glasser, Rosemary Sarri, and Robert Vinter (New York: Free Press, 1985): 226–36.

12. For a presentation of the extensive research on problem solving, see Harold H. Kelley, and John W. Thibaut, "Group Problem Solving," in *The Handbook of Social Psychology*, 2nd ed., eds. Gardner Lindzey and Elliot Aronson, (Reading, Mass.: Addison-Wesley, 1969), IV: 1–101.

13. Dorothy S. Whitaker and Morton A. Lieberman, *Psychotherapy Through the Group Process* (New York: Lieber-Atherton, Inc., 1964).

14. Douglas A. Bernstein and Thomas D. Borkovec, *Progressive Relaxation Training: A Manual for the Helping Professions* (Champaign, Ill.: Research Press, 1973).

15. Harvey Bertcher, *Group Participation Techniques for Leaders and Members*, 2nd ed. (Thousand Oaks, Calif.: Sage Publications, Inc., 1994).

16. Helen Northen, *Social Work With Groups*, 2nd ed. (New York: Columbia University Press, 1988): 246.

17. Lawrence Shulman, "Scapegoats, Group Workers, and Preemptive Intervention," *Social Work* XII (2) (1967): 37–43.

18. W.R. Bion, *Experiences in Groups* (New York: Basic Books, 1959).

19. See George W. Fairweather, ed., *Social Psychology in Treating Mental Illness: An Experimental Approach* (New York: John Wiley, 1964).

20. Irvin D. Yalom, *The Theory and Practice of Group Psychotherapy*, 4th ed. (New York: Basic Books, 1995): 177.

21. Ibid.

22. Ibid.: 178. Emphasis in the original.

23. For an extensive discussion of such procedures, see Rose, *Group Therapy*: 86–102.

24. Ibid.: 137.

25. Ibid.: 139.

26. Ibid.: 141.

27. Ibid.: 142.

28. Gertrude Wilson and Gladys Ryland, *Social Group Work Practice* (Boston: Houghton-Mifflin, 1949).

29. Ruth Middleman, *The Non-Verbal Method in Working with Groups* (New York: Association Press, 1968).

30. Vinter, *Individual Change:* 226–36.

31. Ibid.: 239–41.

32. James K. Whitaker, "Program Activities: Their Selection and Use in a Therapeutic Milieu," in *Individual Change Through Small Groups*, eds. Martin Sundel, Paul Glasser, Rosemary Sarri, and Robert Vinter (New York: Free Press, 1985): 237–50.

33. Ibid.: 241.

34. Fritz Redl and David Wineman, *Controls From Within* (New York: Free Press, 1956): 153–45.

35. William C. Schutz, *Here Comes Everybody* (New York: Harper & Row, Pub., 1971).

36. The following discussion draws heavily from Charles Garvin and Brett Seabury, *Interpersonal Practice in Social Work: Processes and Procedures* (Englewood Cliffs, N.J.: Prentice Hall, 1984): 244–46.

37. Ronald W. Toseland and Robert F. Rivas, *An Introduction to Group Work Practice,* 2nd ed. (New York: Allyn & Bacon, 1995): 319.

38. Ibid.: 323.

39. Rose, *Group Therapy:* 121.

40. Ibid.: 122.

41. Arthur J. Lange and Patricia Jakubowski, *Responsible Assertive Behavior* (Champaign, Ill.: Research Press, 1976): 74–76.

42. Joseph Beninati, Pilot Project For Male Batterers. *Social Work with Groups* 12(2) (1989): 63–74.

43. Irving Spergel, *Street Gang Work: Theory and Practice* (Reading, Mass.: Addison-Wesley, 1966).

Chapter 6

Enhancing the Member's Use of Therapeutic Factors in Groups

The Concept of Therapeutic Factors

The ability of group workers to enhance the ways groups help their members achieve individual goals was strengthened by the identification of "therapeutic factors" that emerge in group psychotherapy. A great deal of the initial work on this topic was done by Yalom,[1] and most of his now-classic work on group psychotherapy is organized around these factors.

While many additional studies of these factors have been conducted, a very important contribution was made by Bloch and Crouch. They examined virtually all of the research as well as conceptualizations of therapeutic factors conducted prior to the time of their investigation. They reported their work in a book published in 1985, in which they discuss each factor in detail in terms of the theoretical issues relevant to the factor as well as the empirical research on the factor.[2] Bloch and Crouch built upon the work of Yalom and of several other authors.[3]

Yalom developed his list of curative factors from an analysis of his own experiences and ideas as to the identifiable elements that might account for the impact of the group on its members. He also consulted many colleagues in this effort and created instruments to secure information from group members as to how important they thought each factor was in the gains they achieved in the group. He created a list that differs somewhat from that of Bloch and Crouch, which is used in this chapter.

Based upon their review, Bloch and Crouch defined a therapeutic factor: "An element of group therapy that contributes to improvement in a patient's condition and is a function of the actions of the group therapist, the other group members, and the patient himself."[4]

They distinguish therapeutic factors from conditions for change and from techniques, the latter being what the worker does to enhance the operation of a therapeutic factor.

Since 1985, many investigations have been conducted of therapeutic factors in groups utilizing similar frameworks to those of Yalom and Bloch and Crouch. This research, conducted in many countries, has involved diverse groups. A few examples are AA and Al-Anon groups,[5] long-term inpatient groups,[6] adolescent psychodrama groups,[7] self-help groups,[8] children from chemically dependent families,[9] and incest survivor groups.[10] Each of these, as well as many other studies we have located, demonstrate that there are relationships between the presence of these factors and desired group outcomes. A complex issue, however, is that different factors seem to be important in different groups. This research, therefore, has to be regarded as preliminary to the creation of propositions about which factors workers should seek to maximize in which groups. We, consequently, use our discussion here to inform the practitioners of the existence of these factors so they can examine how they operate in their own group and with what outcomes. We are convinced that they do capture much of the essence of how members can benefit from groups.

In this chapter, we shall discuss each factor, how the therapeutic factors appear in groups conducted by social workers, and how social workers can enhance the functioning of these factors.

Categories of Therapeutic Factors

There are several reasons for the differences between the lists of therapeutic factors created by Yalom and by Bloch and Crouch. The latter were interested in developing a more theoretically neutral set of variables than that developed by Yalom. They, consequently, omitted his category of "corrective recapitulation of the primary family group" as they saw it as highly related to Yalom's theoretical stance. They omitted "existential factors" for the same reason. These factors deal with the significance group members attach to their experiences as they deal with such philosophical issues as mortality, the meaning of life events, and our ultimate separateness from one another. Bloch and Crouch saw the conclusions people draw about these issues as more the result of group therapy than an essential part of the process.

Bloch and Crouch added an item which, while Yalom deals with it, he does not include it in his list of therapeutic factors: self disclosure. Bloch and Crouch believe that learning to present information about one's self in a group situation is an essential part of the process. Table 6.1 presents a comparison of the two lists.

The Use of Therapeutic Factors in Group Work

Most of the factors operate in all therapeutic settings, whether individual, family, or group. Of special interest to us here is the unique contribution of the group setting to the factor. The group processes associated with the factor, consequently, will be the focus of our attention.

**TABLE 6.1   Therapeutic Factors in Groups: A Comparison
of Yalom and Bloch and Crouch**[*]

Yalom	Bloch and Crouch
Instillation of hope	Instillation of hope
Universality	Universality
Imparting of information	Guidance
Altruism	Altruism
Corrective recapitulation of the primary family group	
Development of socializing techniques	Learning from interpersonal action
Imitative behavior	Vicarious learning
Interpersonal learning	Insight
Group cohesiveness	Acceptance
Catharsis	Catharsis
Existential factors	
	Self-disclosure

[*]When the two conceptualizations are parallel (use the same terms or mean the same thing), we have placed the terms in adjoining cells.

Instillation of Hope

Bloch and Crouch define this factor as occurring as "the patient gains a sense of optimism about his progress or potential for progress through his actual experiences in the therapy group."[11] The unique aspect of the group experience with respect to this factor is that it flows not only from the worker but from other group members.

A major source of hope in groups is that the member can observe other members in similar circumstances make progress. The issue with respect to hope is not how the members are achieving their gains (this is another factor) but that it is possible for them to achieve. The member also observes others who may be more optimistic about the outcomes of their efforts than she or he is. Finally, the member will observe that other members do achieve changes in themselves and others.

A problem in one-to-one helping is that a worker may express unrealistic hope and the client knows this. In our experience, this is less likely to occur in groups, as members are likely to recognize the dangers of holding out false hopes to each other. The worker, however, should point out in appropriate circumstances that offering unrealistic hope is unhelpful.

While most of the therapeutic factors have been investigated empirically, hope is one of the exceptions. The only studies that bore on the value of this factor were those in which members were asked to rate the importance of the factors. The instillation of hope was not rated the most nor the least important but was placed a little below the middle rank.[12] Nevertheless, we agree with many other writers that the instillation of hope is important in motivating members to invest in the group.

The worker can help instill hope in the following ways:

1. When a member is pessimistic about outcomes, the worker can ask others to talk about how they coped with feelings of pessimism.
2. When a member makes progress, the worker can point this out to other members struggling with analogous issues. This must be said in a way that does not imply

criticism of the member who has not yet achieved the goal. The worker might say that when the member is ready, she or he will accomplish the same thing.

3. Members can be invited to encourage others in the group, and the worker might suggest this as a group norm.

A number of subtle issues underlie the worker's decision to instill hope. Some members may relish the attention they receive when they express their feelings of hopelessness, and this should be dealt with through group process discussions. Some members express a lack of hope when they suffer from a clinical depression. The worker's response to this will be governed by her or his approach to helping people cope with depression, a topic beyond the scope of this volume.

An example of instillation of hope took place in a group of unemployed people. A member had applied for several jobs but had not been offered any of them. She said she was about to give up hope that she would ever get off public assistance. Several other members indicated, in response to the worker's questions, that they had felt the same way at times but had vowed to keep trying. One said he wanted to work on the way he handled job interviews. Another said she thought that some people discriminated in the hiring of blacks and that the group should do something about this. Most members commented that it was important that they keep each other's spirits up, as they relied on each other when the going was rough.

Universality

This factor occurs when members have similar concerns and feelings. The members, consequently, feel less isolated as they cope with their problems. Many social work clients with problems such as alcoholism, mental illness, and criminality are likely to feel stigmatized, and a feeling of universality can help reduce their feelings of rejection. Bloch and Crouch point out that this is a predominant factor in self-help groups.[13]

The factor of universality has not been examined empirically beyond studies in which members rated the importance to them of each factor. Universality, like hope, was placed in the middle range in the rankings.

The worker can help members develop a sense of universality in the following ways:

1. In the formation phase of the group, as members become acquainted with one another, the worker can emphasize their common histories and problems as these become evident.
2. As members engage in self-disclosure as the group continues, the worker should continue to point out similarities in problems and experiences among the members.
3. The worker can reinforce a sense of universality by asking members to identify other members whom they perceive as sharing feelings and experiences.

Some members will deny that anyone else in the group can understand their "unique" experiences. This might be a resistance to change with which the worker can work. This requires the worker to help the member understand how she or he is resisting change, the kinds of feelings that evoke resistance (such as fear of change), and how such resistance creates a barrier to relationships with other group members. The worker should time this approach with member readiness to deal with such an interpretive approach.

Guidance

This factor includes the provision of information and advice to group members from the worker and from other members. The role of guidance has been underestimated in group therapy because of the impact of psychoanalytic theory. This theory focused on the necessity of helping the member identify and overcome internal resistances and distortions, and guidance was seen as interfering with this process.

Guidance plays a bigger role in many groups conducted by social workers or to which they refer members. Many social work groups are established to provide information to members, such as groups for parents, cancer patients, people about to be released from institutions, and potential foster parents. Many members of these groups have had experiences that enable them to provide information to others in the group that even the worker does not possess.

There has been little research on the role of guidance in groups, which Bloch and Crouch attribute to the low opinion practitioners hold of it.[14] They located, however, research carefully conducted by Flowers involving sex offenders.[15] The experimental groups were offered different types of advice such as simple direct advice, suggested alternatives, and detailed instructions. The latter types of advice were found to be the most effective.

Self-help groups offer opportunities for members to secure advice from others who face similar situations. Hurvitz discovered that the popularity of these groups is, in part, related to this factor.[16] It seems likely, nevertheless, that the value of guidance depends greatly on the type of group and the theoretical approach being used in it. Even self-help groups will differ as to the kinds of guidance that will benefit their members.

The following principles should be utilized with guidance in groups:

1. The members should indicate a desire to receive guidance. Members may wish to secure information from their own sources.
2. The worker should determine what kind of information is lacking among group members. The worker should avoid presenting information members already possess, although some members can provide information to others who lack it.
3. Good teaching techniques should be utilized in imparting information, such as providing no more information than members can absorb and utilizing visual aids and handouts when these are more effective than transmitting information orally. Workers should elicit questions and find some ways of reinforcing the retention of the information such as helping members instruct others. Many workers create workbooks in which members can take notes and which prompt the members to use the information in appropriate ways.

An example of guidance took place in a group for parents whose adult children had recently been diagnosed with schizophrenia. Several sessions were devoted to imparting information about the following:

1. Current knowledge about the causes of schizophrenia.
2. Current knowledge about the types of treatment and their expected effects.

3. Information on the medications to treat schizophrenia.
4. The steps toward recovery typical of people with this disorder.
5. The ways family members can help.
6. The resources that may be called upon, especially in crises.

The above example is similar to the work of Anderson and her colleagues. They report excellent success with this model in helping family members cope with someone in the family who has this disease, thereby helping that person enhance his or her functioning in the community.[17]

Altruism

This factor is defined as the members' feelings about and views of themselves due to the help they offer other members. As Bloch and Crouch state,

> *Altruism operates when the patient: offers support, reassurance, suggestions, or comments to help other group members; shares similar problems with the purpose of helping other members; feels a sense of being needed and helpful; can forget about himself in favor of another member; and recognizes that he wants to do something for a fellow member.[18]*
>
> *This factor is unique to group work as compared to individual work, although it occurs for somewhat different reasons in family work as part of the responsibility family members have for one another. It represents an important value to foster in society, namely, that we have responsibilities for each other. It also reflects the long-standing value placed upon mutual aid by social workers with groups.*

We have experienced in virtually every group with which we have worked that members receive much support for their own worth when they recognize how much their caring and helping is valued by other group members. Many group members have been devalued so often that their self-esteem is very low. It is a profound realization that they can help others in the group and that the other members care for them.

The research on this factor has mainly been performed on self-help groups. These investigations list it as a major component of the self-help experience. Helping others is expected of the member of a self-help group.[19] In 12-step organizations such as Alcoholics Anonymous, the twelfth step specifically charges the individual to do this, as is shown in the following quote: "Having had a spiritual awakening as a result of these steps, we tried to carry this message to alcoholics and to practice these principles in all our affairs."

The following actions can help to develop altruism in the group:

1. The worker can state the idea that the function of group work is to help the members help one another. The members should be helped to discuss this and to accept it as a group norm.
2. The worker should point out occasions when members have helped each other and can encourage the members to thank one another when they value their contributions.

3. The worker should reinforce members' recognition of the value of the help and caring they offer one another.

An example of this occurred in a group in a residential treatment center for adolescents who had been in trouble with the law. One group member had run away from the institution and returned home. The worker, with the permission of the runaway youth, asked the members if they would like to meet with the youth in his home. They appeared elated and proceeded to plan the trip to miss the maximum amount of school. The trip took on the character of an outing to the city, as it would take several hours and require a meal on the way. The worker said that the member they would visit would simply think that they were looking for an outing that had little to do with him. After much discussion, the members decided to go during a weekend, when they were not in school. They also agreed to do a specified amount of work to earn the money for gas and food. That way, when the missing youth asked why they came, they could truthfully answer, "Because we care for you, we earned the money to come and came on our own time!"

Learning from Interpersonal Action

Bloch and Crouch define this factor as "the attempt to relate constructively and adaptively within the group, either by imitating some behavior or responding to other group members."[20] This process occurs when members seek to clarify their relationships to other group members and to experiment with new, and hopefully more adaptive, ways of relating to other members.

This factor is seen by most group work and group therapy writers as one of the main benefits of the group experience. The well-functioning group is invariably described as a safe place for members to become aware of their interpersonal behaviors and to try out new ways of handling interpersonal situations. Despite this, Bloch and Crouch point out, not many empirical examinations of this process have been done. They were only able to locate two studies, by Land and by Kaye, that linked this factor to outcomes, and both studies suffered from methodological or conceptual problems.[21] This appears to be another example of the major gaps in the research related to group work, especially gaps in empirical examinations of group processes and how these relate to outcomes.

We suggest the following actions, however, for group workers who wish to enhance the members' learning from their interpersonal behavior in the group:

1. Help the members become aware of their actions toward others in the group by making process comments. These are described in Chapter 7.
2. Help members tell each other how they perceive the actions of others in the group.
3. Help members consider and choose among alternative ways of behaving in the group. Support them as they try out these new ways of behaving. Help the member obtain feedback from other group members regarding her or his new efforts.

An example of this process took place in a group of men and women who joined the group to improve the ways they dealt with relationships. Sam sought to help Mark by offering him much advice on how to deal with his brother. The worker asked Mark to tell Sam how he experienced this. Mark said he felt intimidated by Sam's suggestions and didn't think Sam understood his situation well enough to make these suggestions. He also wondered whether Sam had his own reasons for wanting him to follow this advice. Sam responded that he thought this was true and that he wanted to draw others out rather than impose his ideas upon them. The worker encouraged Sam to try this out next. Sam responded by asking Mark to tell the group some more things about his relationship with his brother.

Vicarious Learning

Groups offer their members many opportunities to learn new behaviors by observing how other members act. This observation can be either of their behavior in the group or of descriptions members give of their behavior outside of the group. Bloch and Crouch descrⁱᵇₑ this:

> *We thus regard the basis of vicarious learning as the patient exⁱ ₑencing something of value for himself through the observation of other group members including the therapist. It operates when a patient benefits by observing the therapy experience of another patient; identifies with a co-member to the extent that he himself gains from the co-member's therapy experience; recognizes some positive aspect of the behavior of the therapist, or of other patients, to imitate; or finds models in the positive behavior of other group members, including the therapist, towards which he can strive.*[22]

The opportunity to learn to behave differently by observing and enacting the behavior of others is a main feature of cognitive-behavioral approaches to practice, and much research has been conducted in groups that demonstrates the efficacy of this method.[23] Much of this research compared groups in which members had the opportunity to view models with groups in which the major activity was discussion; the former was invariably more effective. Despite this, we are convinced that members observe the behavior of others in groups and learn from this. Whether this variable is a more or less powerful one than others still remains to be demonstrated across the full spectrum of social work groups.

The worker who wishes to enhance the ways members utilize models can do the following:

1. When members ask for suggestions on how to deal with a situation, they can be asked if they ever observed someone handle the situation the way they wished they could. They can also be asked if they think anyone in the group has acted in this way. The member can then describe what he or she observed in the member chosen as a model.
2. Members with ideas on how others in the group can deal with a situation can be asked to role play their idea rather than simply describe it (although description can also lead to imitation on the part of others).
3. When workers observe that group members are acting in ways helpful to others, the members' attention can be drawn to this behavior.

An example of vicarious learning took place in a group of young adults who joined the group to improve their social skills. Ann indicated that she really didn't know how to start a conversation with classmates when she wished to get to know them better. The worker asked the group members to suggest ways to initiate a conversation. As members provided suggestions, she listed them on the blackboard. After about five suggestions, the worker asked if someone would demonstrate how they would act in these ways; Jack volunteered. Carol volunteered to be the person he wanted to get to know. The role play proceeded as planned. Afterwards, the worker asked the group members what they liked about how Jack had made Carol's acquaintance.

Insight

"Insight" in psychotherapy often has a meaning derived from psychoanalytic theory relating to such concepts as the unconscious. We do not intend this word to be understood in this way but join Bloch and Crouch in defining insight as when "the patient learns something important about himself."[24] This learning may encompass the members' awareness of how they behave, of how they view themselves, of the attributions they make about the causes of their behavior, of how others view them, and of new ways of viewing the reasons for their problems.

A major debate has taken place for many years among psychotherapists as to whether insight is a necessary condition for change. It is quite clear that for such problems as phobias, this understanding is not required for change. Increasingly, however, the role of cognitions in maintaining other problems is being recognized.[25]

The work of Meichenbaum and his colleagues is often cited in this respect.[26] These investigators compared four treatments: insight, desensitization, combined, and placebo. The result of the experiment was that insight and desensitization groups had the best, and equal, outcomes. The combined group did not do as well, and the placebo group did the worst.

Research has also been done on "feedback," as this is often utilized to promote insight in groups. Bloch and Crouch examined several studies on feedback and concluded that people prefer and are likely to benefit more from positive than from negative feedback as they discover their assets and strengths; they also benefit more from feedback on their behavior than on their emotions. Negative feedback is sometimes best accepted when written down and given anonymously by the therapist. Negative feedback is most effective when it precedes positive feedback in groups in which trust has become well established, but this is not true in new groups.[27]

Workers who desire to help members develop these kinds of insight can utilize some of the same approaches we listed above for helping members learn from interpersonal action. In fact, these factors often go together as members gain insight and try out new behaviors in the group. Specifically, however, the worker might do the following to enhance processes related to insight.

1. Foster a norm in the group that members are expected to provide feedback to one another, with members taking responsibility for emphasizing positive as well as negative feedback and for assessing whether the feedback will be helpful. Negative feedback is not likely to be helpful when the member giving it has negative feelings toward the recipient.

2. The worker may explain his or her ideas as to the relationship among events in the members' lives, and help members do likewise. These should be viewed as hypotheses rather than as facts; it is ultimately up to the individual to determine which hypotheses are valid. These alternative attributions can help the members consider changes in how they think and act.

An example of the process of promoting insight took place in a group of adolescents in foster care. They were discussing how they were replaced at the instigation of the foster parents. Dick said he was sure he had been replaced because he could not learn how to act toward adults. Several members pointed out to Dick the things he had done that were appropriate ways of relating to foster parents. Greg told him that many foster parents simply don't like to take teenagers and that they are afraid of them.

Al, however, pointed out that Dick had refused to do chores, saying he wasn't a servant. Al explained that family members all had to do chores, and Dick seemed to be refusing to "join" the family. Dick said that these ideas all seemed to be true, and that he had better start thinking differently if he hoped to get a foster parent to "take him on."

Acceptance

The concept of "acceptance" is closely related to the social psychological concept of group cohesiveness, which we defined in Chapter 3 as a product of all the forces acting on the members to remain in the group. We join Bloch and Crouch, however, in using the term "acceptance" when we are concerned with therapeutic factors because this term better reflects the members' sense of valuing the group, identifying with it, and feeling accepted by and important to other members.

There are a variety of therapeutic consequences of acceptance. Many members of social work groups have felt isolated and rejected in many of their social situations, perhaps from being defined as mentally ill, criminal, alcoholic, or deviant in other ways. The social work group is often one of the few places where these members do not experience such rejection but instead feel valued. This can give them a new sense of their own worth and an appreciation of their ability to contribute to the welfare of others. In these circumstances they are likely to accept the norms of the group and to work hard to accomplish the group's purposes as well as their own.

Several studies are cited by Bloch and Crouch to demonstrate the relationship between acceptance (cohesiveness) and desirable outcomes.[28] While all of these studies had methodological limitations, the relationship between client outcome and acceptance or cohesiveness was found in each. Several more recent studies have also shown a positive relationship between cohesiveness and group therapy outcomes.[29]

Workers can take a number of actions to enhance acceptance in groups, as follows:

1. When members spontaneously mention their regard for each other or for the group, the worker should reinforce this expression.
2. The worker should explain to the members how the value they place on their relationship with each other affects the benefits they attain from the group.

3. The worker should enhance the cohesiveness of the group by promoting enjoyable program activities when appropriate; by enhancing the status of the group in the larger environment; by helping members value group purposes; and by reinforcing the bond among the members.

An example of a worker enhancing acceptance in a group took place in a group of single parents learning to cope with their family stresses. Fran commented that the group was one of the best things that had happened to her. Her family would have nothing to do with her, and she had been deserted by her husband. The worker pointed out that they were "all in the same boat," so they could identify with each other and knew a lot about what the others were going through. Sue said she agreed with this. She also thought that Fran had come a long way, as Sue remembered when Fran questioned whether she really belonged in the group. The worker said it was understandable that people who found it hard to get accepted elsewhere would believe that they finally had found a place where caring for each other could be so strong.

Catharsis

Some writers include in the concept of catharsis both the release of emotions and the thoughts that previously had been repressed. We agree with Bloch and Crouch, however, that these are two different processes and that expression of thoughts should be covered by another term.[30] These authors define catharsis as follows:

> *As emotional release, i.e. ventilation of feelings, leading to relief, within the group, either of past or here-and-now material. These feelings include anger, affection, sorrow, and grief which have been previously difficult or impossible to discharge.*[31]

Research on the effects of catharsis in groups necessarily is related to which emotion is expressed, and Bloch and Crouch cite some examples without coming to firm conclusions as to what the research shows.[32] In our experience, different processes occur when the expression is anger, sadness, anxiety, or guilt—to mention a few emotions that might occur during group sessions. It is difficult to assess the effect of emotional expression without considering the type of emotion, the reaction of other group members, the subsequent events in the group, and whether the emotion is still strong at the end of the group session or has diminished. Thus research on this topic is difficult to design.

Nevertheless, we believe that the expression of emotion in relationship to what members say helps the members feel fully invested in the issues under discussion. If the feelings have been repressed, their expression can bring relief, especially if this expression is integrated with the members' understanding of the situations related to the emotions.

Another issue is whether the member experiences some resolution about the emotion so that she or he does not leave the session substantially sadder, more anxious, or more depressed. This circumstance might lead a member who is distressed after a session to require crisis intervention. It is possible, and not desirable, to induce a great deal of intense emotional expression in groups when the processes of group contagion are strong and the worker is charismatic. The experienced and responsible therapist guards against this and helps members cope with strong emotions when these are expressed in groups.

The following are some practice principles regarding catharsis:

1. Workers should establish a group norm that expressing feelings is an accepted and even desirable behavior in the group.
2. Workers should inquire about feelings when a member blandly discusses a highly charged situation. This does not mean a member must "name" a feeling when what the member feels is clear to him or her and other members.
3. The member should be helped to discuss the situation that evoked the feelings and the related feelings, if possible, until the member demonstrates coping with the feelings.
4. Workers can use techniques described in the preceding chapter to help members relax in coping with feelings, especially anxiety.

An example of catharsis took place in a group whose purpose was to help members deal with losses such as the death of family members. At one meeting, there were two new members who had recently lost spouses. Sarah asked them how they were doing. Beatrice said she wasn't doing too well. During and after the funeral, many friends came to see her, but this had largely stopped. Her friends seemed uncomfortable when she wanted to speak about her dead husband. Several even said to her it was about time she "buried the dead." Sometimes she felt like crying, although she knew this made other people uncomfortable. Brian said he understood, as this was what had happened to him. He added that the group all understood her need to talk about her husband and to continue to mourn him. The worker asked her how she felt right then, and she said she felt relieved, but she began to cry softly into her handkerchief. A member gently placed her hand on Beatrice's arm.

Self-Disclosure

This factor is defined as the member telling other members personal things about herself or himself. This intimate information is not easily divulged to people with whom one does not have a trusting relationship. A special category of self-disclosure is information about how the member thinks and feels about the group and its members.

We do not in any way imply that the member must be driven to reveal things that he or she is not ready to reveal or that are not pertinent to work in the group. We see self-disclosure as a gradual process in which the member consciously makes decisions regarding what to reveal in relationship to current issues in the group. The process involves the evolution of trust in other group members, the development of self-understanding, and an awareness of what is important to reveal at any given moment.

Self-disclosure has been examined empirically in many studies. Much of this research utilizes the Jourard self-disclosure questionnaire.[33] In this instrument, the respondents indicate the degree to which they talked about each of sixty topics to significant others. The items are weighted by whether the disclosure has been general or detailed.

Studies have been conducted to determine the relationship between self-disclosure and other variables, although most of the research has sought to identify the relationship between self-disclosure and cohesiveness. This relationship is demonstrated by the research, although the investigation reported by Slavin found a relationship between here-and-now disclosure but not there-and-then disclosure and cohesiveness.[34] A relationship has also been found between self-disclosure of a member and liking for that member.[35]

Finally, Bloch and Crouch cite several studies that examined the relationship between self-disclosure and outcomes. These studies show that the impact of self-disclosure on therapeutic outcome is a complex question. The studies to which they refer showed a positive relationship between self-disclosure and outcomes for hospitalized psychiatric patients but not for delinquents. Another study did not show this relationship for long-term hospitalized mental patients. Yet another study showed a relationship between self-disclosure and the development of insight.[36]

When workers wish to increase the amount of self-disclosure, they should do the following:

1. Point out the times members make abstract statements as opposed to more personal ones and discuss the reasons for and implications of this.
2. When a member makes a self-disclosing statement, acknowledge it. If it appears that this self-disclosure makes that member or others uncomfortable, discuss this and remove the reasons for the discomfort.
3. If it appears that the self-disclosure will make the member or others uncomfortable and this is unlikely to be resolved within the session, limit the amount of self-disclosure in that session.

The following example of a worker relating herself to self-disclosure issues took place in a group for adults working on problems with close relationships. Bob, in response to Sally's statement that she was lonely on weekends, stated that people are often lonely on weekends because of the progression of their lives over a week and the anticipation of a similar progression in the week ahead. Sally seemed confused by this response. Alex then joined in and said that he often was sad on weekends when he thought of unfilled wishes. The worker commented that the group members seemed to be discussing things on a very abstract level that day. She wondered if this were because Sally's problem had touched a chord in the rest of them that they found it difficult to deal with. Bob said this was true and that he also found weekends difficult because he began to think of living another week without his ex-wife, from whom he had recently been divorced. Alex said that his sadness was related to his fears that some group members might be leaving. The worker later wrote in her progress notes that her comment seemed to lead back to appropriate self-disclosures and touched upon some members' fears as to how they would feel if they made self-disclosing statements.

Summary

In this chapter, the nature of therapeutic factors in group work was discussed. A list of therapeutic factors was presented, including instillation of hope, universality, guidance, altruism, learning from interpersonal action, vicarious learning, insight, acceptance, catharsis, and self-disclosure. The nature of each of these factors was discussed as well as evidence as to its effects in groups. Means for enhancing the operation of the factor were presented.

Each section of the chapter concluded with a practice example from a social work group related to the factor.

Therapeutic Factor Exercise

Goals

1. To identify occasions for strengthening the operation of therapeutic factors in groups.
2. To identify the skills used by workers to strengthen therapeutic factors.

Procedure

1. Prior to the exercise, trainees read about and discuss the therapeutic factors discussed in this chapter.
2. Five trainees are asked to volunteer to form an individual change group, which will hold a short meeting in the center of the class.
3. The five volunteers meet briefly to pick the type of group they will role play, the topic of the meeting, and what their respective roles should be. One should function as group worker.
4. While the volunteers are fulfilling the task described in (3), the rest of the class is divided into 9 groups and each group is assigned to represent one of the therapeutic factors.
5. The group role play is enacted. During the enactment, each observing group makes notes on the following:

   a. Note any example of the therapeutic factor assigned to your subgroup; describe.
   b. Were there occasions when the worker should have enhanced the operation of your therapeutic factor? Describe.
   c. How did the worker (or should the worker have) strengthen the operation of your therapeutic factor?

6. After the role play, each subgroup prepares a brief report on its observations and thoughts.
7. The subgroups report to the entire class, which discusses the reports.

Endnotes

1. Irvin D. Yalom, *The Theory and Practice of Group Psychotherapy, 4th ed.* (New York: Basic Books, 1995).
2. Sidney Bloch and Eric Crouch, *Therapeutic Factors in Group Psychotherapy* (New York: Oxford University Press, 1985).
3. R. Corsini and B. Rosenberg, "Mechanisms of Group Psychotherapy: Processes and Dynamics," *Journal of Abnormal and Social Psychology*, 51 (1955): 406–11; W.F. Hill, "Further Considerations of Therapeutic Mechanisms in Group Therapy," *Small Group Behavior* 6 (1975): 421–29; B. Berzon, C. Pious, and R. Farson, "The Therapeutic Event in Group Psychotherapy: A Study of Subjective Reports by Group Members," *Journal of Individual Psychology* 19 (1963): 204–12.

4. Bloch and Crouch, *Therapeutic Factors:* 4.

5. Adam Mickiewicz, "Therapeutic Factors in AA and Al-Anon Groups," *Polish Psychological Bulletin* 25 (1) (1994): 59–73.

6. Volker Tschuschke and Robert R. Dies, "Intensive Analysis of Therapeutic Factors and Outcome in Long-Term Inpatient Groups," *International Journal of Group Psychotherapy* 44(2) (1994): 185–208.

7. Haluk Ozbay, Erol Koka, Emine Ozturk, and Serpil Gungor, "Therapeutic Factors in an Adolescent Psychodrama Group," *Journal of Group Psychotherapy, Psychodrama, and Sociometry* 46 (1) (1993): 3–11.

8. Richard A. Heil, "A Comparative Analysis of Therapeutic Factors in Self-Help Groups," *Dissertation Abstracts International* 53 (8B) (1993): 4373–374.

9. Renate Rohde, "The Group as an Effective Medium for Working with Children of Chemically Dependent Families," *Journal for Specialists in Group Work* 18 (4) (1993): 182–88.

10. Inese Wheeler, Kathleen O'Malley, Michael Waldo, and James Murphy, "Participant's Perception of Therapeutic Factors in Groups for Incest Survivors," *Journal for Specialists in Group Work.* 17 (2) (1992): 89–95.

11. Bloch and Crouch, *Therapeutic Factors:* 199–200.

12. Ibid.: 205–41.

13. Ibid.: 189–90.

14. Ibid.: 174.

15. J.V. Flowers, "The Differential Outcome Effects of Simple Advice, Alternatives, and Instructions in Group Psychotherapy," *International Journal of Group Psychotherapy* 29 (1979): 305–16.

16. N. Hurvitz, "Peer Self-Help Psychotherapy Groups and their Implication for Psychotherapy," *Psychotherapy: Theory, Research, and Practice* 7 (1970): 41–9.

17. Carol M. Anderson, *Schizophrenia and the Family: A Practitioner's Guide to Psychoeducation and Management* (New York: Guilford Press, 1986).

18. Bloch and Crouch, *Therapeutic Factors:* 192.

19. M. Killilea, "Mutual Help Organizations: Interpretations in the Literature," in *Support Systems and Mutual Help: Multidisciplinary Explorations*, eds. G. Caplan and M. Killilea (New York: Grune and Stratton, 1976); P. Antze, "The Role of Ideologies in

Peer Psychotherapy Organizations: Some Theoretical Considerations and Three Case Studies," *Journal of Applied Behavioral Science* 12 (1976): 323–46.

20. Bloch and Crouch, *Therapeutic Factors:* 70.

21. E.C. Land, "A Comparison of Patient Improvement Resulting from Two Therapeutic Techniques," *Dissertation Abstracts* 25 (1964): 628–29; J.D. Kaye, "Group Interaction and Interpersonal Learning," *Small Group Behavior* 4(1973): 424–48.

22. Bloch and Crouch, *Therapeutic Factors:* 195.

23. I. Falloon, "Interpersonal Variables in Behavioral Group Therapy," *British Journal of Medical Psychology* 54 (1981), pp. 133–41; I. Falloon, P. Lindley, R. McDonald, et al, "Social Skills Training of Out-Patient Groups," *British Journal of Psychiatry* 131 (1977), pp. 599–609; Sheldon D. Rose, "Putting the Group Into Cognitive-Behavioral Treatment," *Social Work with Groups* 13 (3) (1990), pp. 71–83; Jeffrey A. Kelly, "Group Social Skills Training," *Behavior Therapist* 8 (5) (1985), pp. 93–95; Sherry B. Borgers and Randy W. Koenig, "Uses and Effects of Modeling by the Therapist in Group Therapy," *Journal for Specialists in Group Work* 8 (3) (1983): 133–38.

24. Bloch and Crouch, *Therapeutic Factors:* 28.

25. Ibid.: 41.

26. D.H. Meichenbaum, J.B. Gilmore, and A.L. Fedoravicius, "Group Insight Versus Group Desensitization in Treating Speech Anxiety," *Journal of Consulting and Clinical Psychology* 36 (1971): 420–21.

27. Bloch and Crouch, *Therapeutic Factors:* 41–62.

28. F.T. Kapp, G. Gleser, A. Brissenden, et al, "Group Participation and Self Perceived Personality Change," *Journal of Nervous and Mental Disease* 139 (1964), pp. 255–65; I.D. Yalom, P.S. Houts, S.M. Zimerberg, et al, "Prediction of Improvement in Group Therapy," *Archives of General Psychiatry* 17 (1967), pp. 159–68; B.J. Weiss, "The Development of Cohesiveness In Marathon Growth Groups," *Dissertation Abstracts International* 32 (1972): 6065B.

29. Volker Tschuschke and Robert R. Dies, "Intensive Analysis of Therapeutic Factors and Outcome in Long Term Inpatient Groups," *International Journal of Group Psychotherapy* 44 (2) (1994), pp. 185–208; John V. Flowers, Curtis D. Booraem, and Karen A. Hartman, "Client Improvement on Higher and Lower Intensity Problems as a Function

of Group Cohesiveness," *Psychotherapy: Theory, Research, and Practice* 18 (2) (1981): 246–51.

30. The term is "self-disclosure," the last in the set of factors discussed in this chapter.

31. Bloch and Crouch, *Therapeutic Factors:* 162.

32. Ibid.: 163–67.

33. S. Jourard, *The Transparent Self.* (New York: Van Nostrand, 1971).

34. Bloch and Crouch, *Therapeutic Factors:* 133–34; Roberta L. Slavin, "The Significance of Here-and-Now Disclosure in Promoting Cohesion in Group Psychotherapy," 50th Annual Conference of the American Group Psychotherapy Association, *Group* 17 (3) (1993): 143–50.

35. M.H. Kahn and K.E. Rudestam, "The Relationship Between Liking and Perceived Self-Disclosure in Small Groups," *Journal of Psychology* 78 (1971): 81–85; R.G. Weigel, N. Dinges, R. Dyer et al, "Perceived Self-Disclosure, Mental Health, and Who is Liked in Group Treatment," *Journal of Counseling Psychology* 19 (1972): 47–52.

36. Bloch and Crouch, *Therapeutic Factors:* 151–55.

C h a p t e r 7

Achieving Individual Change through Groups

Some group workers may assume that creating a set of desirable conditions in a group will benefit all or most members. There is no strong evidence to support this proposition that conditions such as democratic processes, maximum participation, norms of self-disclosure, or any combination of such group events will help members achieve their goals. These conditions may be sought by members and may even be necessary to achieve individual change, but they are not sufficient. This chapter will consider a variety of approaches and procedures that may be required, in addition to creating a supportive group, for members to attain their goals. An application of these approaches is included through an individual change exercise at the end of the chapter.

In a broad sense, many individuals who seek help from group participation do so to accomplish one or more of the following types of goals:

1. To improve one's ability to create and sustain intimate relationships.
2. To improve one's ability, in an intimate relationship, to maintain an appropriate level of separateness. This allows the individual to take responsibility for his or her own actions, to fulfill his or her needs, and to act in a manner consistent with his or her values.
3. To acquire skills in social interactions such as initiating relationships, communicating effectively, resolving conflicts, working cooperatively, and giving and receiving feedback from others.
4. To learn to cope with the stress of changing roles associated with new phases in life or into other types of social roles such as divorcee, widower, employee, or parent, and to be able to give and receive support from others in this process.
5. To solve specific problems by utilizing the experiences of others as well as by learning more effective means of problem solving.
6. To change oppressive social situations by joining others who also seek such change and who agree to work together to accomplish this.
7. To develop new interests and skills in social activities.

In achieving these goals, members will at times interact with the worker, with a few members (a subgroup), with all members, and with others in the environment. The worker may also interact with individuals in the environment on behalf of the members. The process of changing one's self and one's social situation will involve the members' awareness of themselves and others, their understanding of how and why things occur, and their feelings, attitudes, and behaviors.

Throughout the members' experiences in the group, they can benefit from increasing their awareness of how their methods of interacting with other group members may parallel their problems in interacting with people in the environment outside of the group. Particularly in groups viewed as "treatment" focused, this awareness will frequently be facilitated through a method known as "process commentary" in which members give and receive feedback on the way they experience intragroup interactions. We shall describe this later in the chapter. Members will use the information to experiment with new ways of relating to others, first in the group and later in the environment.

As the above discussion implies, we shall present ways of facilitating individual change through worker intervention at various systematic levels, namely, the one-to-one (often in the presence of other group members), the group, and the outside-of-group environment. These interventions should be based on an assessment of the problems of members and individualized goals and plans.

Even though we are presenting the change process in an orderly manner, it is often less orderly in the actual group situation. Individual, subgroup, and whole group processes occur simultaneously or in rapid succession, and the worker is certainly not in the position of controlling all of this even if he or she wishes to do so.

Our intent, therefore, is to present the worker with a way of identifying individual change potential in the situation and being able to act with self-awareness of what he or she is seeking to accomplish and through what means. The group situation is always one where many events occur, each with the possibility of being used by individuals to create change. No one group aspect is the *only* source of change, and workers should not be dismayed by missed opportunities. There is always another one around the proverbial corner. The experienced worker, consequently, will see the vast array of possibilities, which we will illustrate in the material that follows.

One-to-One Interactions

A central issue for some group workers is whether there should even be any significant one-to-one interaction between the worker and an individual member. Some group workers believe that this can undermine the mutual aid contract that members should help one another and that they should receive what they need through participation in group processes. We believe that this is an extreme position based more on ideology than research.

In contrast, we believe that the decision to help a member through a one-to-one transaction or through affecting a group process that, in turn, will benefit the member is to be decided through an examination of the specific situation. The following criteria should be used to decide on this issue:

1. Is the group ready to act in ways that will benefit the member? The group may be preoccupied with initial organizational tasks; the number of members requiring individual attention at a particular meeting may be too great; the group may have a nontherapeutic attitude toward the member, as in the case of members seen as deviant. In these situations, the worker will often interact directly with the member.

2. Is the member's problem such a crisis that a lack of immediate help will have serious consequences? The worker can try to change some of the group conditions mentioned in criterion 1 if the member can wait for help. The worker, therefore, is frequently in the position of weighing the costs of waiting until the group is ready to help against the costs of "jumping in" instead of relying on the group. Such an issue can be discussed with some groups as a way of helping the group become more aware of the changes it should make in itself to be more helpful to members. Such a discussion may even help the group move more quickly to help members.

3. Will there be negative consequences, in the long run, for members helped on a one-to-one basis? We are all familiar with the "teacher's pet" phenomenon. This is only one of several negative consequences of giving attention to only one person in a group. The members may become hostile to the person the worker helps the most or, in contrast, may join in helping this person to such a degree that he or she is permanently labeled as needy and maintained always in a dependent position in the group.

4. Will there be negative consequences, in the long run, for the group when the worker helps members on a one-to-one basis? As described in the preceding chapter, the rationale for group work is that the group does provide resources not available in one-to-one approaches. The objective of the worker, therefore, should be to help the group help the members and, whenever possible, to strengthen the group's commitment to this. One-to-one helping by group workers should be used but not as the preferred mode. Too frequent use of it will create the expectation that the only or major help to individuals is from the worker, a perception that often exists early in the group's life and can be hard to overcome. Group workers have always been highly critical of practitioners who establish communication structures in which members speak primarily to the worker rather than to each other, and this has been disparaged as "casework in the group."

5. Will the group's help to one member harm other members? A member may have a problem that, if dealt within or by the group, may harm another member. An example of this occurred in a group of patients in a mental hospital. A member had a great deal of anxiety about sexual fantasies. The worker believed that the group's discussion of sexual problems would provoke anxiety in other members that they could not handle at that time. He, therefore, offered to talk with the member outside of the group.

6. Are there legitimate reasons for one-to-one confidentiality? A member's presentation of an issue may require the member to reveal information to the group that violates commitments made to others. On the other hand, members do illegitimately confide in the worker rather than the group. Their desire may be to occupy a special position vis-a-vis the worker, or they may be avoiding efforts to develop more trust between themselves and other members. These latter problems will be discussed with the member in terms of the implicit or covert intent of the member so that appropriate solutions may be found.

7. Which form of help—individual or group—will be the most potent for solving the problem? In most cases, when the group is prepared to consider the problem, the influence of other members will be greater than the influence of the worker alone. Exceptions may be when the group has a great deal of dissension or conflict regarding the ends sought by the member (and the member is made insecure by this),when the group has little or no expertise or experience with the issue, or when the member is an isolate in the group. Thus, when an analysis of all other factors is not conclusive for the worker's decision as to how to help, the most effective and efficient approach should be used. Even in the examples just given, however, if the situation is not an emergency, the worker may rely on the group's processes. Helping the member in areas in which the group lacks knowledge may lead to all members acquiring more information. Seeking to help an isolate may lead to less isolation for the individual.

After considering the preceding criteria, the worker must still decide whether an interaction with the member should take place outside of the group meeting or in the presence of other group members. When interaction takes place other than in group sessions, workers will employ the same techniques as those used in individual sessions. These include problem-solving approaches, interpretation, confrontation, support, and offering advice. All group workers must be skillful in individual interviewing and must be able to engage effectively in this activity during intake periods, in an auxiliary way after the group is formed, and for follow-up and transfer of learning purposes after the group has terminated.

Several of the preceding criteria are also relevant to the choice of talking with the member either during or after a meeting: the first when there is no time to deal with a crisis issue during a meeting, the fifth when the discussion will harm another, and the sixth when confidentiality is essential. These are the main reasons for extra group sessions with individuals. The other criteria suggest reasons for employing group processes or worker-member communications *during* a meeting.

In addition to these criteria, there are some additional considerations for a one-to-one session outside of a meeting. The worker must consider whether the one-to-one session afterward will diminish the member's investment in the group: this should be discussed with the member. The worker should also assume that the member may make reference to the session, and even its content, to other group members publicly and privately, which will affect group processes.

An example of the latter was a discussion by a worker when a member approached her after the meeting of a group formed to help socially isolated adolescents. The worker held this discussion because the member was anxious about an invitation to a party before the next group meeting. At the meeting, the member told of his party experience and of the suggestions the worker had made. Because the other members envied the social success of their peer, they deprecated the worker's suggestions as well as the value of the member's experience. The worker recognized the necessity of discussing this response with the members.

Another consideration is that the member's concern may involve relationships with other group members. In this case, the worker should postpone the discussion until all relevant members are present. At the very least, it may be necessary to report the content of the discussion to the other members because they may resent that the worker discussed material relevant to them when they were absent.

When workers talk with one member during a group meeting, they use all of the techniques social workers employ when working with a single client. The difference is that the worker must consider the effect of the technique when others are "listening in"; this may cause the intervention to have a different impact on the member in question than when it is used privately. In addition, the intervention may affect members in addition to the one at whom it is directed. Although this is not a book devoted to one-on-one helping, we shall briefly describe the major types of one-to-one interventions used by group workers.

Changing Thoughts and Beliefs. Members may make irrational statements that lead to negative judgments of themselves. Here are some of these: one must be loved or respected by everyone; it is easier to avoid responsibilities than to face them; one must be extraordinarily competent in order to achieve; and, one will find it impossible to control one's emotions. Ellis and Harper have developed a set of techniques workers use to help members modify such statements.[1] These include teaching them the importance of identifying and modifying such beliefs, pointing out such beliefs when they are explicitly or implicitly expressed, and suggesting alternative and more rational beliefs to members.

Enhancing Awareness. One technique for enhancing member awareness of themselves or others is *confrontation.* This takes the form of a firm statement to the member about the feeling, thought, or behavior he or she is blocking from awareness. Because the individual often blocks perceptions in this manner (not to do so may be uncomfortable), the confrontation may lead to anxiety or anger, and the worker has to be prepared to respond to such feelings. The worker is most able to do this if he or she has a relationship with the client. The confrontation is then viewed as helpful rather than hostile. The member must be secure enough with the worker and with other group members to reflect on the implications of the information presented through the confrontation without becoming defensive.

Another technique for enhancing member awareness is *interpretation.* As we use the term, an interpretation is a process rather than a single statement of the worker whereby the member becomes aware of the relationship between two sets of events. An example of such awareness occurred when a member discovered that she was reacting toward another group member (one set of events) in the same dependent manner she had used with her sister (another set of events). The process begins when the member becomes aware of one set of events, then the other, and finally the connection between the two. This usually happens through an extended period of time during which the member reflects on each series of events and the possible relationships between them.

A third technique for enhancing member awareness is to alter the members' *attributions.* These consist of the beliefs members have about the nature and causes of events from within themselves and from their environments. Workers will modify such attributions by stating their own beliefs and their reasons for them. This is sometimes referred to as "reframing." An example occurred in a group situation when one member accused another of expressing too much criticism of him. The worker pointed out that this was one way the critical member expressed her caring. This prompted a fruitful discussion of better ways of expressing caring.

Offering Reinforcement. Workers can help members sustain a desirable behavior by rewarding the member. This reward acts as reinforcement if the result is, in fact, that the member continues to behave in the way desired. Reinforcement can be the following: verbal, as in praise; physical, as in a touch on the arm; or material, as in a "token" that can be exchanged for something of value. Another behavioral technique involves the use of an aversive act to decrease a behavior. In view of social work ethics, the worker's most frequently used aversive act is to express disapproval or criticism.

Offering a Model.   Workers also help members learn desirable behaviors by modeling them. The worker may do this implicitly by talking softly when a member is shouting; explicitly when asking a member to observe the worker as he or she "plays a role" that the client must enact; or verbally as the worker describes how an act may be performed.

Helping with Feelings.   One thing workers do to help members with their feelings is to encourage their expression. Another way is to help the member relax. This can be done by training all members in progressive muscle relaxations[2], then encouraging a member to use this procedure when he or she is tense. An individual can also be instructed to take a series of deep breaths to reduce tension.

Modifying Attitudes.   The worker will help members modify attitudes that are barriers to their attaining their goals or using the aid available from the group. Workers can suggest reasons members should change their attitude. They can also urge the members to act in some way that is inconsistent with their attitudes. An example of the former is a member who held negative attitudes toward blacks. The worker offered the member evidence that his beliefs were faulty. An example of the latter occurred when the worker urged the member to share a personal experience with a black member of the group, even though he believed that the black member would not understand the experience.

Utilizing Role Assignments.   In group situations, a worker has an additional tool for affecting members' behaviors that is not easily used in one-to-one situations—the opportunity to affect the roles that the member assumes in group activities. A worker can ask a member to chair a committee, distribute refreshments, play first base, become "it" in a tag game, or lead a discussion. All of these assignments offer the opportunity to learn new behaviors, change the views others have of one's self, express new feelings, and see things from a different perspective.

When the worker communicates with an individual during a group session, the effect on others must be assessed. For purposes of analysis, this can be sequentially divided into events prior to, during, and subsequent to the worker's action.

Prior to such one-to-one encounters in a group, the worker considers the following:

1. Are other members likely to act with similar intent to the worker's? If not, can they be helped to do so?
2. Should the entire group be asked to discuss the issue?
3. Does the member in question prefer the worker to help, other members to help, or no one to interfere?
4. Will the worker's action facilitate or hinder subsequent helping behavior by others in the group?

5. How will the worker's action affect other group conditions such as group cohesiveness, group norms, or group attributions?

During the worker's interaction with a single member, he or she observes the immediate effects on other members. Some of these effects may be as follows:

1. Other members observe the worker's intent and join in to support it by imitating the worker's actions, agreeing with them, or praising them.
2. Other members react negatively to the worker's actions and seek to sabotage them by disagreement and ridicule.
3. The worker's actions initiate a group process in which the actions, their intent, or their content are discussed or reacted to in some other way. For example, in a group of 10- and 11-year-old boys, some members reacted to the worker's discussions with a boy about the quality of his work by adding that the important thing was not whether anyone else thought your work was good but how you felt about it yourself. As the boys worked on their project, they continued to discuss times when work of their own, which they liked, had been criticized by others.

After the worker interacts with a member, he or she observes the subsequent and longer-term effects on others. These can include the following:

1. Members continue efforts to help the member initially helped by the worker.
2. Members utilize the worker as a model and seek to help others in ways demonstrated by the worker.
3. Members withdraw from or react to the member in negative ways.
4. Members become more dependent on the worker for help.
5. The worker's words and actions affect group norms, group structures, group processes, or group attributions.

Example: In a group of ten- and eleven-year-old boys in a child guidance clinic, the activity at one session included a project in which the boys worked on decorative plaques to take home. Jim, who was of low status in the group, complained that he did not have the skill. The worker said that he would teach him to do the things he did not know how to do. The worker also expressed his understanding that Jim was worried about how his plaque would look (*helping with feelings*). As Jim worked on his plaque, Bob made some critical remarks about it. The worker reminded Bob about the group's rule that when a boy said something about another, it should be with an effort to be helpful (*modifying attitudes*). A little later on, Jim appeared discouraged about his work, even though it was clearly as good as that of the other boys. The worker reminded Jim of discussions they had had about how heavily Jim criticized himself and the reasons for this (*changing thoughts and beliefs*). Toward the end of the session, Bill said that he did not know how to apply shellac, so the worker asked Jim to show him, as Jim had done this very well (*utilizing role assignments*).

In each of these interventions, the worker could have turned to the group. He did not primarily because he thought the group was not ready and the consequences of inaction might be costly for the boys. The worker planned, as the group continued, to help the group members take these kinds of responsibilities for each other.

Group Interventions on Behalf of Individuals

In the previous chapter, we described ways the worker modifies group conditions to create a group beneficial to all members as well as a group conducive to facilitating individual goal attainment. At this point, we shall describe how the worker intervenes in group processes to benefit *specific individuals*.

Factors Affecting Use of Group

Time.　In this discussion of enhancing individual change through group processes, we elaborate on several factors affecting the worker's intervention plan. The first of these is the time frame, that is, whether the worker asks the group to allocate substantial time to a member, or whether the attention paid to the member by the group is brief. The second is the specific approach used in the group to help the individual (for example, problem solving, role allocation, feedback). The third is the intent of the group's attention to the member, whether it is to help the member understand himself or herself or the situation, set personal goals, change some aspect of self or situation, or evaluate and maintain a change. With regard to each of these issues, we shall discuss the worker's actions and the criteria for employing them.

An issue, when the group is focusing on a member, is how much time the group will invest. The range can be from briefly commenting on a member's problem or behavior to devoting an entire meeting to it. Brief comments on a member's behavior by other group members are appropriate under several circumstances. One is when the group has a good understanding of the goals of a member and how the member hopes to achieve them. Such brief attention is then for giving praise or feedback, or even for confronting the member with some aspect of behavior. The following is an example from a weight-reduction group.

Example:　When members reported on their progress the preceding week, one member said that she had attended a dinner party and had not asked for second helpings; she was praised by several members. Another member briefly illustrated how she had refused an offer of food; but, in this case, it was pointed out to her that she did not sound very convincing. Another member told of her effort to find a job but she was confronted with the fact that, in her reports, she avoided telling of her efforts to diet. The worker had previously discussed with the group the usefulness of these types of comments.

Brief comments by group members to one another do not present as many issues for the group worker as spending most or all of a meeting on the problem of one member. Obviously, under those circumstances, the worker must seriously consider how this attention will affect other members. If their concerns are similar, they will not grow impatient or uninterested, and they may learn vicariously. In any case, a group should not be expected to use its time in this way during group formation except under crisis conditions for one member. When members have developed concern for one another and have learned that each person's needs for group attention will be met, such use of a meeting will be more acceptable.

Size.　The size of the group will be a major factor in how much time a group can comfortably give a member. A small group of five to seven members will usually be willing to spend time in this way because in a few meetings all who desire this experience can receive it. Members of a larger group will frequently not be willing to devote an entire meeting to one member but may focus on one member's problems if several persons receive such help at each meeting. This type of group usually has two-hour or two and one-half-hour sessions. It is possible, in larger groups, to subdivide the group into pairs to give feedback to all or most members.

Theoretical Issues.   Opinions about focusing extensively on one member differ greatly. Yalom, for example, in his emphasis on group process, has the group focus on relationships among members rather than on one member as such.[3] Members who seek to spend much time on their "story" are described in Yalom's chapter on problem patients as "monopolists."[4]

Several approaches do focus on individuals. In one gestalt technique, the "hot seat," the worker directs attention to one individual, often asking that person to take roles representing parts of self, significant individuals, or people and objects in a dream.[5] The rest of the group remains passive during this procedure unless called on to give the member feedback or to provide the person with an opportunity to experience some emotion or thought by repeating it to others. Several people, but not everyone, may take the hot seat at a session. The exception is a marathon session, often lasting six to eight hours, in which each person is likely to "work" in this way.

In gestalt groups also—and increasingly in any group—members may do a "round." The procedure is for members, usually in rotation, to speak for a few minutes about their current thoughts and feelings. This may be used at the opening of a meeting, when the meeting has reached some impasse or plateau, and at its end. Members are not expected to react to each other's statements; however, content that emerges may be used either for "hot seat" work or for general group discussion, and new and important material is often uncovered in this way.

Another example of focusing on one individual is from positive peer culture groups for delinquent adolescents. Members will declare problems they have had since the last session using agreed-upon terms to characterize such problems. Members then state whether or not they wish to be "awarded the meeting." The group decides this based on a consensus as to who most needs help that day.[6]

Many group workers will not use the gestalt and positive peer culture approaches because of their emphasis on one individual's receiving help for a sustained period and, in traditional gestalt groups, more from the worker than from other members. The emphasis in group work is on helping members help one another through group discussions and other activities. In the latter, one member may, in view of the circumstances, become the focus of attention for most or all of a meeting, but this is not standard practice.

We agree with this group work norm and do not recommend, as a group work procedure, the standard "hot seat" technique or even an award of an entire meeting to a member. These remove attention from the current interactions among members and what is learned from these. Nevertheless, there are occasions when only such sustained attention can affect strong yet maladaptive defenses, and workers and members can allocate their meeting time in these situations accordingly.

More research should be done on such issues. The effects of sustained attention to one member should be compared to briefer process comments to the same or other members. The immediate and long-range effects of such interventions should be examined in terms of the actual behavior in question, the group cohesiveness, the individual's attitude to the group, and the ways the individual is perceived by others.

An important distinction is whether the group's change strategy is *active* or *passive*. By "active" we mean that the group, with intent and planning, participates in the change effort; for example, the members of one group agreed to praise Don for assertive behaviors. By "passive" we recognize that a group may modify the behavior of a member without intentionally seeking to do so; for example, Don observed assertive behaviors of other group members and sought to emulate them. The passive effects are very important and powerful and constitute one of the main reasons for referring people to groups. Other reasons are opportunities to imitate other members, to learn vicariously from the efforts of others, to identify with group norms, and to behave in such a way as to secure status in the group. Nevertheless, these influences are more nebulous than the active, so we shall give the latter the most attention.

Active forces that the worker helps the group to mobilize are used to (1) change the perceptions, cognition, affects, and actions, and (2) facilitate the problem solving of the member. These efforts take place through interactional processes between the member and the group and through the ways the member's role is structured by the group. The worker's role in each of these efforts will now be described.

Techniques for Changing Individual Perceptions

One of the best-established propositions about groups is that they are influential in modifying a member's perception of reality.[7] This principle, of course, can work in opposite ways: either to move the individual's perceptions closer to "reality" or away from it. Nevertheless, the idea of reliability rests on the argument that when several people see the same thing, it is more likely to be so than when only one person sees it. The group worker operates on this principle in several ways: When there is some question as to the accuracy of the member's views, the worker will ask others to offer their perceptions of the member's behavior as well as of other people's actions toward the member.

Example: A group of socially inadequate young adults had recently gone to a restaurant. A member was convinced she had been singled out by the waitress for poor service. She attributed this to her lack of attractiveness. The other group members, when asked by the worker, had all noticed that the waitress was very busy and that she had not given any of the members enough attention.

Techniques for Changing Individual Cognitions

Members' problems are often related to what they think and perceive about their situations. One crucial type of cognition is attributions, namely, what members believe about the causes of their behavior or that of others.[8] Attributions are important because people will strive to change circumstances they believe cause their difficulties. Some are likely to attribute their difficulties to the environment, others to themselves, and still others to both.

The group can affect attributions in several ways. As Strong states in reference to clients in general, "If the client believes his behavior is due to a specific circumstance, event, or person, showing him a consistent pattern of similar actions over a wide spectrum of other persons or events would free the act for stable personal attribution." When the opposite occurs and the individual in some inappropriate way attributes something to self, "information that suggests he responds in that way only to a particular individual or circumstance, or that he has never behaved that way before or since, leads to external or circumstantial attribution."[9]

The process of determining attributions, as described by Strong, is common in groups. Members can observe one another's behavior and provide feedback to each other. The worker can use this feedback to help each member choose suitable change targets, whether internally, in the environment, or both.

When the behavior has occurred in many circumstances and is pointed out to the member, the member is likely to attribute negative outcomes to self. The member is then likely to seek to change his or her behavior to secure better outcomes in those situations. When the behavior, on the other hand, as pointed out in the group, typically occurs only in one situation, the member is likely to attribute problematic outcomes to that situation and will try to change the situation.

Example: In a group of adult parolees, one member complained that his employer did not listen to "his side" of an argument. The worker asked the group if they recalled other similar complaints from this member. Several members pointed out that he had made such complaints about his wife and even about other members of the group. The member then moved to a personal attribution of the causes of the problem and was open to the worker's observation that it may have had something to do with how he presented his "side."

Example: In contrast, in a group composed of couples working on marital problems, a wife stated that she believed her problem was that she was not as intelligent or articulate as her husband. The members pointed out to her the many occasions in the group when she made well-stated and insightful comments. This led to a change in her attributions in the direction of considering her husband's attitude to her rather than her sense of personal inadequacy. She and her husband became more open to considering the sexist roots of their troubles rather than to blaming them on the wife.

One major technique used in treatment groups to enhance members' understanding of the effects of their behavior on others is *process commentary.* Workers introduce this intervention by directing the members' attention to an interaction that had just occurred in the group. This is often referred to as a "here and now" focus. This is a powerful technique because the members cannot easily disguise the behavior they had demonstrated in full view of all the others. This type of reflection in the group ultimately helps members resolve problems outside of the group because of the relationship that is likely to exist between actions and reactions in both places. Members also learn from this experience how to examine interactions in situations of which they are a part, outside of the group. Because of the awareness promoted by a process discussion, the member will experiment with ways of interacting with others that are more likely to meet his or her needs.

Workers may draw attention to processes by questions such as the following:

How did you feel when X said that to you?

What did you think Y was saying?

What did X remind you of when she/he said that?

Why did X attack Y?

Why was X attacked when he said that?

Why are you not saying anything now?

Why did you laugh when X said that?

Each time I said something tonight, you disagreed with me.

Even though you argue with me, you always sit next to me.

Techniques for Changing Individual Affects

This section should more appropriately be labeled "expressing affects" as, aside from learning to be relaxed in some situations, members learn to be more aware of and expressive of their feelings from group interaction. This can be facilitated by the worker in several ways, including asking the members to provide information to the individual as to the kind of emotion he or she communicates, verbally and nonverbally.

Example: In a group of recently divorced people, one member, Jack, denied that he was angry when another member criticized him. Several members then told him that he had said this with clenched teeth, loudly, and while "jabbing his finger" at the group. Jack smiled and said, "I guess I have a hard time admitting what I feel."

A technique the worker can use to help members express feelings is to set up practice opportunities in the group.

Example: Sarah, a member of an assertiveness group, said that she had difficulty letting people know that she felt good about them or what they did. The worker asked her to pick out another member who had done something that she liked and to tell her about it. Sarah told Jane she liked the way she accepted the ideas of others without becoming defensive. The worker asked Jane to give Sarah feedback on Sarah's compliment. Jane said that Sarah acted sincerely and warmly when she said this.

Techniques for Changing Individual Actions

Members can directly affect each other's actions, thoughts, perceptions, and feelings. As discussed in this book, members, by plan, can increase or decrease behaviors by applying reinforcement principles. This can be in the form of a reward for desirable actions or an aversive stimulus for undesirable ones. The reward can be verbal (for example, praise) or nonverbal (for example, tokens, candy, money). The aversive stimulus can also be in either form. The verbal one can range from extended criticism to a simple "no." The nonverbal one can include a token whose color is designated as "criticism" (red for criticism, blue for reward) or can consist of taking back tokens already awarded. In any of these cases, the worker will help the member contract with some or all of the other members to provide these stimuli.

Example: In a group of school-age boys in a child guidance clinic, Bob frequently hit other boys in the group when he felt angry with them. He indicated that he wanted to decrease this behavior and instead tell the other boy what was bothering him. A contract was established, with all in agreement, that Bob would receive a token each time he initiated a conversation about his feelings and would relinquish one each time he threatened to or actually hit another. The tokens were exchangeable for items in the group's "store."

Members can also influence each other's behavior by various forms of modeling. A verbal form of modeling is for one member to describe to another how he or she could act in a given circumstance. The member can try this out either through a role play in the group, with appropriate coaching and feedback, or in the real-life situation. In the latter case, the member will report back to the group.

A behavioral form of modeling involves one member demonstrating to another how the latter might act in a specified situation. As with verbal modeling, the member can rehearse the behavior in the group, execute it in the environment, or both.

A "trial-and-error" approach can also be used when the members do not offer behavioral suggestions or when the member does not want them. The member tries out a behavior in a role play or describes a potential behavior, then other members join the member in evaluating the effects of the behavior.

In all these ways of affecting an individual's behavior, the group is analogous to a rich "smorgasbord." Members usually possess a great variety of experience among them, which each can draw on to broaden behavioral options and to become more socially adequate and effective.

Techniques for Helping Individuals Solve Problems

The ways just described in which the group can help the members are, in a sense, forms of problem solving where changes are sought to solve problems. As indicated in the previous chapter, we use the term *problem solving* to mean the rational and cognitive process of identifying, evaluating, choosing, and implementing a solution from among a range of alternatives. Problem solving can be used to determine a course of action for the group, a solution to a problem affecting several members, or a solution to the problem of one member.

Subject to the considerations regarding the amount of time consumed by one member, the group may agree to engage in a process of finding a solution to one member's problem. A major difference between this and problem solving in respect to a group problem is in whose hands the final decision rests. In the former case, the decision ultimately is made either under a consensus or a majority rule. In the latter, since it is the individual's "life," he or she must be the final arbiter. This can be frustrating to the group if the individual rejects the solution the other members support. This is not likely to happen, however, when the individual is part of the process of problem solving rather than a bystander. When it does occur, it may be an example of a game transactional analysts call "yes, but," in which the individual invites suggestions then finds a basis for rejecting each suggestion.

Under the right circumstances, a group problem-solving process related to a member's problem can be a valuable experience for the member and can employ all of the procedures previously discussed in this chapter. The member's perception of what the problem is can become clearer when various members describe the problem as they see it or ask the member questions about it. Sometimes members, even more than the worker, can help assess the problem because of their similar problems, ages, social backgrounds, environmental circumstances, and so on.

Similarly, the members will use their life experience to help the individual evaluate solutions to the problem. Again, they may know better than the worker which suggestions are feasible in terms of both the capacities of the member and the responses of the environment. When the individual, with the help of the group, has determined a course of action, the members can reinforce the member's behavior as well as engage in further problem solving as new problems arise.

Techniques for Structuring the Member's Role

The preceding group procedures are all based on the idea that the members may affect each other through direct interactions among themselves. In addition, the group, as facilitated by the worker, can seek to change a member through assigning the member particular roles in the group. The expectations of the member as he or she seeks to perform the role are then instrumental in producing the changes the member desires. The worker can, with the concurrence of the group, make such role assignments, or the group can, with the help of the worker, make its own decisions.

One set of roles about which the group makes decisions is "officers," in groups that are structured in this way. Whatever role is being considered, the group should be helped by the worker to assess the needs of both the group and its members considered for various positions.

Example: A group of teenagers meeting in a community center, selected as its treasurer, a boy who felt he was not accepted by the others because he was the only Chicano. The boys said they wanted to show Carlos that they liked him and wanted him to feel part of the group. The worker had been active in helping the boys and Carlos discuss how they felt about their cultural differences, and the decision was an outcome of this discussion.

Some roles are specific to particular activities. Thus there are playing positions in a baseball game, "teacher" of a song, "designer" of an art project, and "creator" of a fantasy to be acted out by the group. Those who perform these roles will have their behavior affected by that performance. No "cook book" exists regarding this use of roles, but even beginning workers, out of their own experience, can analyze such positional effects. These effects include following sets of rules, expressing repressed aspects of one's self, developing skills, learning to control impulsive behavior, and changing self-image.

A third set of roles grows out of the interactions among members. These roles are very informal, sometimes to the degree that they exist but are not recognized. These roles may sometimes harm the member, as in the group scapegoat or deviant. Others can be constructive, if consistent with the individual's goals, as in the group "mediator," "tension breaker," or "most objective" of the group members.

The existence of such "interactive" roles can be identified by the worker when one member is consistently called on by the group to perform the same task or to be the recipient of either negative or positive emotions. When the role benefits the member, the worker can reinforce the members for responding in the way they do. When the role is not beneficial, it usually takes many discussions with the member and the whole group to get the member "off the hook."

The worker can even create such roles. Thus, in a difficult situation for the group, the worker might say, "Let's see what Sue thinks about this. She's usually pretty sound in her ideas on this subject." Or, when the group needs tension release, the worker can turn to a member who has provided the appropriate light touch before, and even with a nod communicate this need.

Phases of Individual Change

Many changes individuals achieve through group participation take place in unplanned ways. We do not wish to minimize the sudden insight, the accidental discovery of a skill or an interest, or a leap that may take place in a member's sense of self. Nevertheless, many changes can and should result from a process moving through problem identification, assessment, goal determination, creation and implementation of a change plan, and assessment and stabilization of change. This sequence, in more or less orderly fashion, can take place through group experience as well as one-to-one counseling. The ways that groups, with the help of the worker, facilitate individual change are employed in all of these phases of change. Each, however, is more pertinent to some change tasks than others.

Problem identification can be enhanced through expansion of the member's perception of the situation. As previously described, this can be accomplished when other members share their perceptions of the member, particularly the member's behavior in the group. Assessment is affected by the member's attributions regarding the problem and are determined, in part, by the way the group helps the member identify the occasions when he or she behaves in specified ways. Goals are determined by the member in terms of what is realistic, given the member's capacities and the environmental opportunities. Other members' perceptions of these realities are useful. In addition, the individual must be aware of and be able to express his or her feelings about the problem and the individuals related to the problem—and the group, as we have shown, facilitates this.

The change plan, under some circumstances, is a matter of choosing the right change procedure. Depending on the nature of the problem, this may be a choice to change a perception, feeling, attribution, or action. The group can help the member do this in any of the ways described in this chapter. Under some circumstances, the change plan must be chosen from a range of alternatives whose appropriateness can only be determined as a result of a problem-solving process. The group can help the individual identify various actions, evaluate them on the basis of appropriateness and effectiveness, and choose one for application to the problem.

The group, subsequently, can help the member in various ways to implement the change plan. The members can rehearse various parts of the plan by either discussing or role playing their behaviors in the group. The members reinforce with praise, for example, the member's efforts. They can provide him or her with feedback on how well the plan is being carried out. They can suggest modifications of the plan to take new information into consideration. A buddy "system" can be employed in which the member calls others in the group for support when the group is not in session.

When the change involves the member acting differently, this new behavior must be stabilized and maintained in the member's actual environment. The group can help with this in the following ways:[10]

1. The group can afford the member a continuing opportunity to practice the behavior, so as to strengthen it.
2. The group can provide the member an opportunity to practice the behavior under a variety of circumstances. This principle also contributes to the member's ability to behave in the desired way. This variety can be provided by role playing the behavior as it may occur in many different circumstances. It can also be provided through the program of the group. For example, a group of adult mental patients in a halfway house were taken on weekly trips by the worker. The members had been learning effective ways of making requests. The trips were to a restaurant, a vocational training program, a department store, and a community center. With regard to each of these institutions, the members planned ways of expressing requests. The worker helped the group list how to make effective requests such as knowing what you want, describing what you want specifically, deciding what alternatives you will settle for, and so on. Members then evaluated each other's behavior on the trips in terms of these criteria.
3. The group can help the member think of "natural reinforcers." This means that some sort of gratification, reward, or support must be found in the member's environment to help maintain the change. Because members are likely to be familiar with each other's life circumstances, they are in good positions to suggest realistic natural reinforcers to each other. These may include encouragement from friends or family members or membership in a "support group." Members may have to learn how to ask for encouragement, which can also be practiced in the group.
4. It is difficult to think of an example of a change sought through group experience, either in one's self or others, that will continue without problems or "setbacks." The worker initiates a discussion of this for several reasons: Members will be less likely to become discouraged when this occurs; also, they can be prepared with coping strategies for at least some contingencies. The worker can help the members help each other, particularly around the latter issue. Members, again because of the frequent similarity in their circumstances, can predict some of the setbacks for each other. Some may have already struggled with these setbacks and can describe what they did and how this worked for them.

Rose gives a number of specific suggestions for dealing with setbacks:[11]

1. Members can be helped to create lists of what they can and cannot control in relationship to maintaining their progress. Members can then help each other work out plans for influencing those situations that can be modified. For others that cannot be influenced, the members can at least discuss ways of dealing with the resulting feelings of inadequacy and frustration.
2. Members can help each other create lists of potential resources, particularly social service agencies, together with notations on the types of services rendered and the way one applies for service. Members may discuss their previous experiences with these

resources so that members can approach them with concrete knowledge rather than with the general information provided in informational bulletins.

3. Members, with suggestions from the worker, can role play some situations where setbacks are likely to take place. Rose suggests that an element of surprise can be introduced by the workers from their knowledge of previous occasions for setback. Members will then give feedback to each other on how they coped with these unexpected occasions.

A generalized reason for setbacks stems from what Rose refers to as an "unsympathetic environment."[12] Anyone involved with groups oriented to the personal growth of their members has experienced the kind of almost utopian group atmosphere that can emerge. The group can be a place in which members are accepting and supportive and in which they can take risks through sharing personal experiences and experimenting with new behaviors. This leads to two types of stress. One is that others in the environment must adapt to changes that have taken place in the member, which can be a major source of setback. It is, in fact, the major argument for a "systems" perspective in which others are involved in one way or another in the change process rather than having to adapt to its "results." Another stress occurs when group members experience a "halo effect" in which they "expect" people outside the group to be as understanding and supportive as the group has been. Members should discuss this with each other so they can cope with the transition between group and environment; they may also seek to make their families, work places, and other environments more like the group, that is, more honest and supportive.

Environmental Interactions

In this chapter we have considered how people may be helped to change and to cope more effectively with their environments through the worker's one-to-one interactions with each member and through the worker's facilitation of the group's attention to members as individuals. Effective individual help may require, however, a third level of worker intervention: the worker's activity in the environment on behalf of individual members. In the next chapter, we shall elaborate on how individuals and groups attempt to change their environment. At this point we shall consider how and when the worker acts on *behalf of* members to change the environment to promote individual change.

The term "environment" is nonspecific. Operationally, in group work, the aspects of the environment targeted for change are likely to be the agency itself, the members' families, other social institutions (schools, welfare departments, and various social agencies), law enforcement and criminal justice agencies, and peer groups.

Examples of worker interventions in this category are a worker's actions to have the agency obtain a Big Brother for a member of a boys' group; a discussion with a child's parents as to how they can support the behavioral changes sought in the group; a conference with a probation officer to ask for reinforcement for a probationer's participation in the group; and a meeting with a public assistance worker to back a group member's appeal for additional funds because of the cost of attending the group.

The worker will target the environment as part of the plan to help the members attain their goals. Such plans almost always include modifying some aspect of one's self as well as of the environment. The worker will directly intervene in the member's environment under the following circumstances:

1. The environmental change is a prerequisite to individual change, and the member lacks the skill or power to accomplish the change. Workers will try to help members acquire such skill and power, which shall be discussed in the next chapter. Sometimes this is not possible within the time frame of the group, or the consequences of waiting until the member can acquire these resources may be too great. In the example in which the worker consulted with the member's parents, the member was a developmentally disabled youngster whose parents overprotected him. The member in this case would not be able to point this out to them until much more work was done both in the group and in other training environments.

2. The members should be fully apprised of the choice between changing their own environments or having the worker do so. Their wishes in this matter will be the main factor in the worker's decision. The worker, however, should seek to understand the members' reasons for this preference. Some members are too dependent and may seek, inappropriately, to have the worker act in their behalf outside the group as well as in. Equally inappropriate, other members may tell the worker to refrain from acting in their behalf in the environment. This may be due to a dysfunctional desire to avoid seeking any help from others; it may also be due to fears that the worker's actions will lead to punishment of the member.

3. When the members cannot act in their own behalf, the worker must determine that the appropriate agency of change is the worker and not the group. The group, as we shall see in the next chapter, can also take actions in the environment on behalf of individual members. This is most likely to be appropriate when the "environment" targeted is a large system such as the service agency itself or another institution or agency. The group may represent more power by virtue of its numbers, and therefore, may be more potent than the worker acting alone. The other members might also have had similar problems with the organization in question.

   On the other hand, the worker will be more likely to act alone with smaller systems such as the family and the peer group. In these cases, group action might be overwhelming. Confidentiality can also be a concern in these situations.

Example: In a group formed to help mothers receiving Aid to Families of Dependent Children grants, the members had concerns about helping their children achieve in school. One of the mothers was concerned with the rules of the school that made it impossible for her child to receive needed extra help. The entire group composed a petition and asked to meet with the principal as a way of changing the rule. Their reason was that several of their children had had trouble with the same rule in the past (*group takes action for change on behalf of individual*). The group was successful in having the rule changed. The son was reluctant to take advantage of the new rule, as he was embarrassed by the group's action. The worker met with him one-to-one to help him overcome this feeling. In this instance, the boy represented part of the "environment" of the mother in the group.

Worker's Roles

When the worker intervenes in the environment to change group member behavior, the worker takes on one of four roles, each role associated with specific techniques. We shall not give extensive detail on these roles here, as they are generic skills of all social workers, not only group workers, and they are dealt with extensively in most practice texts.[13] We shall, however, briefly describe them.

Advocate. The first worker role is *advocate.* The social work client is often in conflict with social institutions.[14] When workers function as advocates, they become partisans in such conflict. They will "argue, debate, bargain, negotiate, and manipulate the environment on behalf of the client."[15]

The role of advocate is appropriate in many circumstances to group workers. Examples of these include a group worker urging a judge to grant probation to a member of an adolescent group; pressuring a housing agency to grant a priority to a member of a group of welfare recipients; requesting a manpower training program to respond better to the career aspirations of a member of a rehabilitation group; and insisting that the agency reevaluate the basis for calculating the service fee that the worker believed was too high for a member of a therapy group.

Several cautions have been raised regarding fulfillment of the advocacy role. One is that some workers serve as the client's advocate when the client has not clearly agreed to this. The other is that the client may suffer retribution for having used the worker as an advocate. A consensus on this should clearly be sought as part of the member-worker contract.

Mediator. The second role is *mediator.* In this role the worker resolves disputes between members and others. This includes helping the parties negotiate and find common ground for their respective interests. The worker's techniques include facilitating, listening and communication, maintaining engagement, focusing on the issue at hand, persuading, and conciliating.

Examples of group workers using mediation include a worker mediating between some members of a women's group and their partners, between some members of a foster children's group and their foster parents, and between some members of a school group and their teachers.

The caution in fulfilling this role is to avoid taking sides inappropriately. The group members must not perceive the group worker as turning against them. The people in the environment must, on the other hand, also perceive the worker as empathizing with their feelings and concerns.

Broker. The third role is *broker.* In this role the worker helps members select social resources they require and then helps them use the necessary resources. The environmental change aspect of this is to help the environmental component provide information to the client and facilitate the client's entry. Worker techniques include gathering information, clarifying organizational requirements, communicating how intake procedures should change to meet the needs of particular clients, and securing support from the agency for the client's entry.

Some examples of this from group work include securing marital counseling for a member of a job training support group, tutoring for a member of a child guidance group, and medical care for a member of a group of older persons.

The caution for the worker is to be well enough acquainted with the community services to be sure that the referral is appropriate. The intake procedures of those agencies must also be familiar to the worker; frequently these are problematic to group members, which can lead to either an advocacy or a mediation role for the worker.

Conferee.   The final role is *conferee*. Middleman and Goldberg describe this role as fulfilled when "two or more persons consult together, compare opinions, deliberate, and devise actions to be taken after the conference."[16] Unlike the advocacy role, there is no assumption that the worker and client have determined in advance their expectations of the system in question. Rather, the assumption is that something is amiss in service to the client, and that this will be worked out in a collaborative way, usually involving the client. The primary skills in this activity are problem solving and enhancing communication. An example of this role was a meeting held with a member of a hospital group and her doctor.

Group workers who have assumed the role of conferee have been from agencies offering a variety of services to the group member, as well as from several agencies cooperating in offering a service to the group member and seeking a consensus on compatible ways of offering services.

The major caution here is for the worker to refrain from placing agency needs for conflict-free service ahead of client needs. Another concern is to prevent major decision making without client involvement.

Summary

This chapter has been devoted to presenting ways the group worker facilitates change in individual group members. The worker's activity can be with the member in question, the group, and the environment. The worker must decide which of these, singly or in combination, should be utilized for such facilitation. The complexity present in groups is that such decisions must be made in ways that consider the effects on other group members as individuals as well as on the group-as-a-whole. This is difficult, and often all the worker can do is to monitor such effects rather than to know and to consider them prior to an intervention.

The worker's activity on behalf of individuals can draw from many techniques, depending on whether the action system is the individual, the group, or people outside of the group. The special skills of the group worker, when interacting with individuals in the group, is related to knowledge of the effects on other individuals and how these will also affect the member in question. The group worker possesses skills in applying knowledge to the different ways groups can impact on individuals. Finally, the group worker, along with all social workers, must be skillful in affecting the environment on behalf of clients. These environmental techniques were summarized in terms of the roles of advocate, broker, mediator, and conferee.

Chapters 5, 6, and 7 have considered the activities of the worker when the target system is the group and the individual. In the next chapter, we shall consider the activities of the worker when the target system is the environment.

Individual Change through Groups Exercises

Exercise I

Objective

1. To identify group effects on individual behavior.

Procedure

1. Trainees read and discuss the section of Chapter 7 that represents group effects on individual behavior (pp. 162 to 163).
2. Trainees observe a group for fifteen to thirty minutes while taking notes of the effects on individual behavior utilizing the accompanying observation form.
3. The trainer leads a discussion drawing upon feedback from the Group Effects on Individual Members Observation Form.

Exercise II

Objective

1. To identify worker's efforts to facilitate change in a member.

Procedure

1. Trainees read and discuss the sections of Chapter 7 in which worker's actions to change members' behavior (through one-to-one, group, and extra group interventions) are presented (pp. 155 to 171).
2. Trainees observe a group (or read a group record).
3. Each trainee selects a behavior of a member in the group that the member wishes, or would be likely to wish, to change.
4. Trainees complete the accompanying Planning and Assessment Form.
5. The trainer leads a discussion based on this form.

Group Effects on Individual Members Observation Form

Select one member in the group and observe the following:
Name _____ Sex _____ Age _____

Passive Effects

In which of the following is this member like other members? Describe.

1. Style of dress (formal, informal).
2. Posture (erect, slumped).

3. Use of language (uses slang, repeats terms).
4. Expresses support of goal, value, or activity as stated by others.
5. Acts toward a member and to others in the group in similar ways.

Active Effects

Describe each of the following, including the effects on the member observed.

6. Do others tell this member how they expect him or her to perceive something?
7. Do others explain an event to this member and expect him or her to accept this?
8. Do members ask or tell this person how he or she feels or seek to change his or her affects?
9. Do members seek to reward or punish this person's behavior?
10. Do members seek to teach this person how to perform tasks?
11. Do members seek to help this person go through a problem-solving process in relation to his or her "own issue"?
12. Do members assign this person a "role"?
13. Do members seek to secure a commitment of this member to change himself or herself?

Individual Change Planning and Assessment Form

1. Describe the behavior of an individual in the group as *it occurs in a specific situation* and what the target of change might be.
2. Describe the behavior as it should occur at the end of a planned intervention.
3. To change this behavior, check any of the following worker (with member) interventions that would be likely to help achieve the change as described in 2.

    _____ Encourage/reinforce.

    _____ Relate to feelings.

    _____ Model behavior.

    _____ Describe a rule, policy, or value.

    _____ Warn of consequences of behavior.

    _____ Interpret behavior.

    _____ Give homework, task, behavioral assignment.

    _____ Orient and assign member to role.

4. Check any of the following worker (with group) interventions that would be likely to help achieve the change as described in 2.

    _____ Help the group discuss their perceptions of the nature of the member's behavior, or offer other forms of process commentary.

    _____ Help the group discuss their perceptions of the causes of the member's behavior.

    _____ Help the group discuss the member's feelings.

    _____ Help other members reward the member's behavior.

_____ Help other members criticize the member's behavior.

_____ Help other members model behavior for the member.

5. Check any of the following worker (with environment) roles that would be likely to help achieve the change as described in 2. (First indicate the person or system in the environment to be contacted.)

_____

_____ Broker

_____ Advocate

_____ Mediator

_____ Conferee

6. Which of the preceding approaches that you checked will be the most appropriate given the member's attitudes and capacities, member's gender and ethnicity, group conditions, and environmental realities?

Endnotes

1. A. Ellis and R.A. Harper, *A New Guide to Rational Living* (North Hollywood, Calif.: Wilshire, 1975).

2. See J. Fisher, *Effective Casework Practice: An Eclectic Approach* (New York: McGraw-Hill, 1978): 298–99.

3. Irving D. Yalom, *The Theory and Practice of Group Psychotherapy,* 4th ed. (New York: Basic Books, 1995): 17–23.

4. Ibid.: 369–74.

5. F.S. Perls, R.F. Hefferline, and P. Goodman, *Gestalt Therapy* (New York: Julian Press, 1965): 146–61.

6. Harry H. Vorrath and Larry K. Brendtro, *Positive Peer Culture* (Chicago: Aldine, 1974): 100–101.

7. M.A. Deutsch and A.B. Gerard, "A Study of Normative and Informational Social Influences upon Individual Judgment." *Journal of Abnormal and Social Psychology* 51 (1955): 629–36.

8. For some important clinical applications of attributional concepts, see S.R. Strong, and R.P. Matross, "A Study of Attribution Techniques in the Interview," *Office for Student Affairs Research Bulletin, University of Minnesota* 15, (2) (1974).

9. Stanley R. Strong, "Social Psychological Approach to Psychotherapy Research," in *Handbook of Psychotherapy and Behavior Change: An Empirical Analysis,* 2nd ed., eds. Sol L. Garfield and Allen E. Bergin (New York: John Wiley, 1978): 126.

10. This section draws on a similar discussion in Sheldon D. Rose, *Group Therapy: A Behavioral Approach* (Englewood Cliffs, N.J.: Prentice Hall, 1977): 154–63.

11. Ibid.: 158–59.

12. Ibid.: 159–60.

13. See Beulah R. Compton and Burt Galaway, *Social Work Processes* (Pacific Grove, Calif.: Brooks/Cole, 1994): 427–37.

14. Ibid.: 434.

15. Ibid.

16. Middleman and Goldberg, *Social Service Delivery*: 73.

Chapter *8*

Group Work and Environmental Change

Throughout this book we have asserted that all social work activity should be directed at understanding the impact on individuals of their own behavior, their environments, and the interactions between the two. Worker interventions can be directed, as required, at changes in any one of these. In this chapter, our focus shall be on occasions requiring changes in the environment and on ways of achieving these changes through group services. Such changes may be by the individual (often with the help of the group), by the group (on behalf of one or all members), or by the worker. The worker's activities in the environment were dealt with in the last chapter; the way workers help members change their own environments shall be presented now.

We shall begin with a discussion of the rationale for environmental change, followed by an analysis of how to assess and alter the "environment." Actual procedures for changing the environment as employed by members, by individuals, and by the group-as-a-whole shall comprise the final section of the chapter. An environmental change exercise follows the chapter.

Rationale for Environmental Change

Interaction with Environment

The proposition that the individual's behavior is a consequence of his or her interaction with the environment is the first reason for the group worker's attention to environmental change. Vinter has termed this type of analysis "an interactional view of deviance," which he clarifies as follows:

> *All behavior amenable to change is regarded as socially induced, acquired through learning and related processes; it is exhibited, evoked, or constrained within the context of specific social situations. The sources of behavior lie both within the individual (in terms of his enduring attributes and acquired capabilities) and within the*

social situation (in terms of opportunities, demands, and inducements). Behavior, moreover, is judged, encouraged or sanctioned by others within the person's immediate social situation. These actions between persons constitute a series of interactions which shape and sustain behavioral patterns. The judgments and responses of others must be regarded as crucial features of all behavioral patterns. Social definitions of deviance are necessarily relative, and those who define behavior as problematic often refer to specialized standards of conduct. In this view, therefore, the targets of intervention include not only the individual whose behavior is judged to be inadequate or deviant, but also the judgments and interactional responses of individuals and groups whom he contacts regularly or frequently at the time.[1]

The "interactional view of deviance," therefore, means that those environmental transactions and forces that maintain problems of group members must be identified and changed. At issue is the degree to which environmental forces that initially created such problems must be examined when they no longer exist.

Those who argue for some historical reconstruction believe that the members' understanding of such forces is necessary for individual change, particularly as they may be unable to free themselves from their memories of the past. Furthermore, an uncovering of the history and initial causes of problems may provide clues to forces that may be operating in the current situation. Those who oppose attention to history believe that this may obstruct a focus on current conditions when it is the current conditions that must be understood and changed; furthermore, behavior *can* be changed through modification in the current situation with little or no attention to historical causes.

Our position is the moderate one. We do not find that attention to history is always required, and such attention can obstruct efforts to change the contemporary situation. Nevertheless, the individual sometimes must be freed from "unfinished business" in the form of an obsession with the past; the past also provides clues to present patterns in functioning. The worker must help the members to assess, then, in the group how their reflections on the past are used.

Labeling Process

Another reason for attention to the environment is that, as Vinter also suggested in the preceding quotation, it is the environment that has "observed, evaluated, and officially labeled the behavior."[2] Changes in this evaluation and labeling process are often required for the group members to be able to function in desired ways.

Example: In a group of boys with problems in associating with peers, one member, John, fought a great deal with other children. The initial causes of his behavior stemmed from the abusive ways his parents had disciplined him. Currently, however, he is labeled as a "bad" boy by the neighbors, who keep their children away from him. He was also under the frequent scrutiny of the police, who had been contacted by a neighbor; the police often told John to "stay out of trouble," which led John to feel stigmatized and rejected. The worker concluded that it was necessary, consequently, to target the neighbors and the police for change.

Choosing New Environments and Transactions

A third reason for attention to the environment is that, as a solution to their problems, members may wish to function in new environments or in different ways in the environment. The environment may not provide opportunities for this, thus requiring an analysis of and change in environmental opportunity structures.[3]

Example: A deficient opportunity structure was observed relevant to group work in an elementary school. The group worker recognized that several members of the group needed tutoring to compensate for educational deficits. This service was not available, so the worker, joined with a group of parents to lobby for it.

Example: In a group of welfare recipients, most of the members were from black and Chicano groups. They experienced discrimination in employment from several of the employers in the area. In this case, necessary opportunity structures were closed to them because of racism. They decided, with the aid of the worker, to seek the help of a union to challenge this discrimination.

One issue raised by some workers is the appropriateness of any environmental targets at all. These workers argue that focusing on the environment can be a type of member "projection" and an abdication of personal responsibility for one's life. These workers, furthermore, are only willing to contract with members to facilitate individual change. We are strongly opposed to this position, as many of the problems brought by members to social work groups are maintained by dysfunctional environments and can only be solved by changes in those social conditions.

Furthermore, we have found that even when the member's behavior constitutes a major component of the problem, many members would not accept help if they were prematurely demanded to recognize this. A good example of this principle is found in a report of group work with husbands who physically abused their wives.[4] In the first sessions of the group, the men blamed their wives for "making them do it." After they had developed sufficient trust and cohesiveness, they were able to look at their responsibility for the violence in their marriages. In addition, when a member states that something is entirely the fault of other people or systems, the worker can ask, "What do you want to do about it?" This immediately prompts the members to examine their own behavior as well as others'.

Selection of Environmental Targets

Choosing the System

The first task confronting workers and members is the selection of those systems in which change is necessary for members to achieve their goals. The following are some examples of the major types of targets likely to be chosen.

Family Targets.   In a group of adolescents, the members discussed such issues as the rules established by their parents, the kinds of support they received in their families for achievement, and conflicts between their parents that were deflected onto them. They discussed strategies for helping their parents to change, including joint meetings with the parents.

Peer Targets.   A group of men preparing themselves for discharge from a prison discussed many ways that peers had influenced them, thus contributing to their lack of adjustment prior to committing their offenses. This included pressures to go to bars as well as to join in illegal activities. The men discussed ways of being more assertive in rejecting such pressures as well as, on occasion, seeking to change the behavior of friends with regard to such destructive acts.

Organizational Targets.   A group of youths in a residential treatment center discussed the rules of the institution. They believed that some of these rules were arbitrary and more for the convenience of the staff than for the benefit of the youths. This point of view was reinforced by thoughtful discussion in the group. The members explored ways in which they had input into agency rules. The youths also attended a local public high school. Their discussion of rules turned to the ways that the high school maintained discipline. The members thought that some of the methods for changing their agency's rules could also be used to change the high school's rules.

Societal Targets.   A group worker met with a group of welfare recipients enrolled in a program for training and employment. They learned that new legislation was being considered by Congress to restrict the amount of training the program could offer. The members resolved to contact the local welfare rights organization to see if they could do anything to oppose this legislation.

Choosing the "Level"

The second task for the group and the worker is to consider the "level" of the chosen environmental system that should be targeted. The levels include one individual within the system (for example, mother in the family, teacher in the school, co-worker in the factory); a set of people with similar roles in the system (for example, all teachers, both parents, all fellow employees); the entire system (for example, all members of the family, the entire school, the business or factory); or finally, the system's authority structure (for example, the board of directors of the agency).

The following criteria will help the worker and the group decide which level to target.[5]

1. The members must decide the degree to which the behavior of some individual external to the group is determined by idiosyncratic factors or organizational ones. For example, is the individual following "orders" or creating them? This is sometimes a difficult assessment to make because people can perform in ways condoned by the "system" but not within its official rules. Thus a teacher might discriminate against some group of students when this is unofficially supported by the school yet is not part of its "official rules."

   When the behavior of the individual is idiosyncratic, the member should seek to affect that individual's behavior. An exception to this is when the individual is intransigent; the member may then seek to have the larger organization exert influence on this person or remove him or her. Thus a teacher who was stubbornly prejudiced against members of a minority group was replaced after an appeal to school authorities.

2. The members should also assess the aspects of the external system most amenable to change. In some school situations, for example, the teacher concerned might be most responsive; in others it may be the principal, the teacher's union, or the superintendent. As a general rule, it may be easier to change an individual or a few individuals than the whole system, unless such individuals are acting in clear conformity with the rules and procedures of their organization.

When seeking to change a system, rather than a few individuals within it, consideration should be given to which aspect of the system to change. The reader can utilize the list of group dimensions we presented in Chapter 5 to analyze aspects of other systems also. These dimensions consisted of the system's stage of development, structure, process, culture, resources, extrasystem transactions, boundaries, and climate. Examples of some of these as targets of environmental change are the following:

1. *The culture of the system.* A youth group sought to change the school's ideas regarding what kind of content was acceptable in the school newspaper.
2. *The structure of the system.* Members of a group sought to change the channels of communication in a school system so that they would be permitted to express their grievances to the Board of Education without first consulting the principal; another group wanted to alter the decisional structure in a hospital by establishing an advisory group of patients; another wanted to modify the division of labor in a residential treatment center so that paraprofessional workers, with whom they felt secure, would be allowed to sponsor "support" groups.
3. *The allocation of resources in the system.* In a residential treatment center, some rooms appropriate for group meetings were reserved, even after school hours, for the use of the agency's school. The members of a group sought to change this allocation of space.

Strategies for Environmental Change

Before a specific strategy is chosen, a decision must be made as to whether the major instrument of change is the individual, the group, or the worker. Since the choice of the worker was described in the preceding chapter, the decision regarding individual or group shall be presented here. As we stated elsewhere, "Clients should be maximally involved in securing changes in the environments which affect them, so that ultimately they will be able to act on their own behalf without professional help."[6] Constraints on this are suggested by an evaluation of the following factors:

1. Member Motivation. The member must desire to act to attain environmental change. This desire will be a product of previous experiences with efforts to change the environment. Such experiences may have met with reinforcement either in terms of actual success or other rewards for having made the effort. On the other hand, the member may have experienced failure or may have been otherwise punished for such activity. The members may also have identified other reasons for anticipating their success or failure in modifying social conditions and situations, such as knowledge of the experiences of others and assessments of the actual situation.

2. Member Capacity.   The member's willingness to seek environmental change or the worker's judgment that this is appropriate will be related to the skills the member possesses. These skills, as we stated elsewhere, include the member's ability "to understand the intent of the change effort, perform the actions required, and withstand the anxiety and stress which may be engendered by the effort."[7] We concluded in that discussion that young children, psychotics, or some developmentally disabled individuals will not be able to contribute a great deal to environmental change, especially beyond the immediate social situation, but that public welfare recipients, inmates of correctional institutions, and parents of school children will have the capacity for such activity.

3. Other Criteria.   In our previous discussion of factors to be considered in selecting the agent for environmental change, we also listed the likely effectiveness of any strategy, the risks to which the group member will be exposed, the effect of the effort on such group conditions as cohesiveness and group structure, and its relationship to the members' goals.

Based on the preceding criteria, the individual and the group should consider whether the group will help the individual plan his or her own strategy for environmental change or whether the entire group will take action on behalf of one or more members. The following are some examples of such decisions.

Example: In a group of high school students experiencing school difficulties, a member complained about a teacher who did not give him adequate explanations when he asked questions. The member discussed with the group how to explain his needs to the teacher. He was helped to role play appropriate assertive responses that would make his needs known and would not be experienced by the teacher as an attack. In this case, an individual change effort was appropriate because it was likely to be effective, the client wished to take responsibility, and it was consistent with the members' goal to become more assertive with people in authority.

In the same group, several members concluded that they received less help from their teachers than other students because they were not considered "college material." In this case, the members planned to invite their teachers to a group meeting in which they would discuss their own ambitions and the role of a high school education in achieving these. The group meeting was deemed more appropriate than individual appeals because the worker and group believed this would be the most effective strategy. Also, the members were better able (*capacity*) to present their case collectively. They were not as highly motivated as the student in the previous case who acted as an individual, and they needed the group's reinforcement to present their case. Moreover, they were still acting on their own behalf, and this was a step toward developing motivation and capacity to act as an individual when necessary.

We shall now present the strategies that can be employed for environmental change.[8] Some of these are most appropriately used by individuals, others by the group. In any case, our assumption is that the choice of strategy should be a produce of group problem-solving activity.

One important consideration in selecting an environmental change strategy is the level of conflict induced when the system is being changed. In some cases, the environment can be changed in benign ways; that is, the environmental system may consider the change in its own best interests; in other cases, the environmental system is only amenable to change when forced to do so in ways that it regards as unpleasant or punitive. We propose that the best strategy is the least conflictual one that can attain the desired objective. This is usually the least costly in terms of energy and resources; it has the fewest side effects in terms of future retaliation; and it still permits an escalation of conflict when this is deemed necessary. Finally, the least conflictual approach is also viewed by observers as a just one. We shall, therefore, present and rank strategies in an ascending order of conflict.

A second consideration underlying any environmental change is that such efforts require the members to be *assertive*. Extensive literature exists on means of acquiring assertive behavior.[9] Such behavior is defined as acts that secure a person his or her rights without denying the rights of others. It is distinguished from *nonassertive* behavior, which fails to assert one's rights, and *aggressive* behavior, which attains one's rights while denying those of others. Assertiveness is related also to a philosophy that leads people to value themselves and to believe that they have the right to actualize themselves and to prevent others from infringing on this right.

Assertive responses can be increased through training. Such training, usually done in groups, begins with helping members understand and apply an assertive philosophy. Members then are taught the differences among assertive, nonassertive, and aggressive behaviors. Situations are subsequently identified in which members have not behaved assertively. With the facilitation of the worker, the members help each other identify the nonassertive or aggressive components of their responses and how these can be made assertive. Members practice such assertive responses through role playing with other members. The members try these responses out in the environment and report back to the group on the result. This may require further modification of member responses if the member's objectives have not been adequately achieved because the response was inadequately assertive. An escalation in the degree of conflict may also be justifiable when the member's rights are still denied.

Environmental Change Activities Solely for Individuals

Some environmental change activities can only be employed by the group members as individuals because they involve immediate ways of interacting with environments.

Avoidance.   In the avoidance approach, the member changes the environment *as it affects him or her* by staying away from it. An example of this is adolescents who avoid peers who elicit behavior that will get them into trouble. The group can help the youth find alternative peer groups as well as resist invitations to associate with the problematic group.

Alternate Reactions.   In employing alternate reactions, the member changes his or her own behavior without making any overt demand on the other person. This change, however, is presumed to lead to a change in the other. An example of this is a husband who resolves to respond to his wife's aggressive responses with assertive ones, although he had been aggressive before. He hopes that his wife will use his newly acquired behaviors as a model for her own behavior.

Manipulation of the Social and/or Physical Situation.   An example of manipulation occurred in a group meeting in a children's residential treatment center. A member of the group lived in a cottage with several bedrooms. The other boys in his room were older than he and tended to reinforce his dependence on others. With the help of the other group members, he resolved to ask for a change to a room with younger boys.

Environmental Change Activities Employed by Individuals and Groups

Interpretation.   One action that can be used either by members in their own interests or by the group on behalf of members is *interpretation;* that is, to explain to others the causes or consequences of either the member's behavior or their own. One example is a group that helped a member explain to the teacher that his sleepiness in class was due to his new medication to prevent seizures. In another youth group, the members decided to explain to an agency that assigning them the meeting room occupied by the nursery school program was leading to ridicule from other groups.

Education.   Another approach is *education,* as the actions of others may be due to incorrect or missing knowledge. A group of former prisoners, for example, discussed their difficulties in securing employment. They realized that many employers were unaware of the excellent work performance of rehabilitated offenders. The group drew up a fact book indicating research findings members would use to better inform themselves and prospective employers.

Evaluation.   Evaluation involves gathering information on the behavior of individuals or organizations. Such data may relate to either the extent of the behavior itself or its effects. A wife, for example, complained that her husband seldom showed her affection. The group suggested to her that she talk to her husband about keeping a chart of the frequency of this behavior. She later reported to the group that his demonstrations of affection increased when he became aware of their low frequency. In another group, the sponsoring agency decided to raise the fees for service, arguing that increased revenues were necessary but would not affect members' use of the agency. The group members discussed this and suggested that the agency keep a record of attendance and continuance. After three months, this information was compared to the experience during the three months prior to the new policy. The agency discovered that the members with lowest income began to use services less; this led the agency to reexamine the policy.

Use of Influentials.   The strategy of using influentials is one in which the member or the group asks a person with power to change a person or system. A group of patients in a hospital, for example, were concerned about some of the actions of the nursing staff. They had originally tried interpretative and educational approaches without success and now believed that an escalation of power was legitimate, even if this led to conflict. They invited the director of nursing to meet with them so they could convince her of the justice of their cause. They hoped she would use her influence to change the actions of the nurses. In another example, a college student in a group sponsored by the university's counseling services complained about unfair grading policies of an instructor. He had been helped previously by the group to explain the results of his policies to the instructor (*interpretation*). He had also urged the instructor to ask for feedback from the students on the policy (*evaluation*). Since neither approach was acceptable to the instructor, the student was helped by the group to plan how to present his case to the department chairperson.

Bargaining. Either the member or the group can use *bargaining* by doing something in exchange for a desired environmental modification. A group wanted a meeting room of its own. It agreed to clean out a room, now used for storage, if it was made available to the group. The woman in the previous illustration who did not receive the affection she wished from her husband considered offering to go with him to a movie in exchange for more attention.

Confrontation. The strategy of confrontation can lead to more conflict than the other strategies because it forces people to face how their behavior or attitudes are problematic and need change. This type of action can also be taken by the group. A member of an adolescent group was concerned that he was usually singled out for blame whenever the classroom became noisy or was disruptive. The group, many of whose members were in the same classroom, confirmed his perception that he was a scapegoat in that situation. The member was supported in his plan to tell the teacher to stop scapegoating him and to find a better way of affixing the blame. In another group of welfare recipients, several of the members had the same Assistance Payments Worker. This worker, they believed, was lax in submitting legitimate requests for more funds for his clients. The group members drew up a list of occasions when the worker had been negligent and submitted this to him. He was told that his actions would be reviewed in a month and that if better service were not received, charges against him would be filed with the director of the agency.

Mass Media. Groups will also resort, on occasion, to using the *mass media,* such as newspapers. Individuals in the group, as well as the group-as-a-whole, can submit documentation on injustice to the mass media. For this purpose members have used the "letters to the editor" column as well as contacts with feature reporters. Members of an adolescent group in a residential treatment center asked a reporter to investigate charges that the agency overlooked drug use in the agency and failed to protect suicidal members. This process induces great conflict with the agency because of the repercussions from legislators and other funding sources.

Resistance. The two most extreme strategies for change are *passive* and *active resistance.* Both intend to significantly disrupt the system at which they are directed. The former accomplishes this through noncooperation with key authorities. Members engaging in passive resistance will refuse to perform tasks or, in a more extreme way, will obstruct other activities by "sit-ins." People in groups that use this device have refused to do homework regarded as excessive or "make work" chores in residential centers or at places of employment. Members, operating singly, have been reluctant to use this strategy because they usually perceive themselves as powerless and likely to lose more than they gain when confronting the full power of social institutions. Nevertheless, constant frustration of legitimate demands often leaves few other choices.

Passive resistance must be part of a long-term, complex strategy with structures for maintaining such a strategy in the face of immediate retaliation. For example, a group of welfare mothers who "sat in" in a local welfare department to demand clothing allowances were arrested and jailed. The group was so demoralized that it was completely destroyed.

Admittedly, these forms of resistance are more often used when the group is viewed as part of a community organization effort. Nevertheless, with poor or otherwise oppressed people, it is difficult to separate the need for personal change from social change, as both are so interwoven and so necessary to improve their lot. Some agencies, such as the Mobilization for Youth program in New York in the 1960s, employed teams of treatment-oriented as well as community-oriented workers to work with individuals and groups.[10] This method of service, while at its peak in the 1960s, may have its day again.

Active resistance involves taking an action likely to be unpleasant or disruptive to a system. Actions that fall in this category are picketing and marching. More extreme forms include destroying property or depriving people, even temporarily, of their freedom. The more extreme forms are not considered by most social workers to be professionally acceptable.[11] Nevertheless, social workers should be cognizant of the extremely cruel conditions that have led some clients to engage in prison riots, university disruptions, or industrial actions. In these circumstances, attention should clearly be drawn also to the systems that are inhumane and self-seeking.

Whenever any escalation of conflict is contemplated, even short of active and passive resistance, group members must be helped to consider whether less conflictual strategies are likely to be effective. Some people, because of the kinds of neglect and abuse they have suffered in their lives, believe they are justified in responding in destructive ways. This type of characterological problem requires expert and sensitive handling by workers so that members will not persist in ultimately self-destructive responses. Some such members are found in groups meeting in correctional settings, where confronting this behavior is not easy because of the support the behavior may receive from other clients as well as the reality support it will encounter whenever injustices reoccur.

Environmental Change Activities Employed by Groups

The previous list is composed of strategies that may be used by individuals or groups; there are also two procedures that require a group to be executed.

Cooptation.   Cooptation involves the interaction of the people to be influenced with the group. This is accomplished so the group becomes a reference group for the person, helping to define his or her values and perceptions. An example of this is provided by Klein in his discussion of a youth group's efforts to cope with police officers who harassed the members when they used the local park. The member's strategy included inviting members of the police force to visit some of their meetings to become better acquainted with them and their activities.[12]

Alliance.   In the alliance strategy, the group joins with other groups to attain a common environmental change goal. Here is an example by Glasser and co-workers: "A psychiatric orderly consistently brings the ward patients to the dining room late. As a result they must eat hurriedly and sometimes do not get a full meal. Treatment group patients may enlist the support of the other groups on the ward or organize other patients into a larger group, to put pressure on the attendant to change his pattern."[13]

Summary

In accomplishing group work goals, the targets of change at any given time may be the individual, the group, or some aspect of the environment. This chapter was devoted to procedures used when the latter is the target. The instrument of such change can be the individual member, as influenced by the worker and/or the group, the group itself, or the worker. When the worker tries to change the member's environment, it is usually to affect some subsequent change in the member; therefore, we dealt with worker efforts to change the environment in the previous chapter.

This chapter presented a rationale for environmental change, followed by procedures to accomplish this by members acting alone, either by members as individuals or the group-as-a-whole, and finally by group action. Each procedure was defined, and examples from group work practice were provided.

Environmental Change Exercise

Goals

1. To identify occasions for environmental changes.
2. To discriminate among occasions when the members, the worker, or the members and worker together seek to change the environment.
3. To choose the appropriate strategy for environmental change.

Procedure

1. Prior to the exercise, trainees read about and discuss reasons for environmental change and strategies for accomplishing this.
2. Five trainees are asked to volunteer to form a group, which will hold a short meeting in front of the class. The topic of the meeting is to be "Concerns I have about learning to be a group worker." One member is chosen as worker for the group.
3. After the meeting, the entire training group or class uses the environmental change planning form as a means of analyzing the group meeting.

Environmental Change Planning Form

1. Briefly describe a problem one or more members have in attaining a goal.
2. Will a person or persons outside of the group hinder the member from attaining the goal? If so, describe.

3. Is this hindrance a product of one of the following? (check any that apply)

_____ stage of development of the system

_____ structure of the system

_____ process of the system

_____ culture

_____ extrasystem transactions

_____ system boundaries

_____ system climate

_____ the way the system allocates resources

4. Describe motivation of member(s) to seek changes in the environment through his or her own efforts.

5. Describe capacity of member(s) to seek changes in the environment.

6. What risks will the member(s) incur by seeking changes in the environment?

7. In view of 4, 5, and 6, should the member be helped to plan changes in the environment alone or with the help of the worker, or should the worker become the main instrument of change?

8. Which of the following change strategies will be used?

_____ avoidance

_____ alternative reactions

_____ manipulation of situation

_____ interpretation

_____ education

_____ evaluation

_____ use of influentials

_____ bargaining

_____ confrontation

_____ mass media

_____ passive resistance

9. Describe in detail the way the strategy will be used.

10. How will the effectiveness of the strategy be evaluated? (Trainees can consult Chapter 9, Evaluation of Group Work Practice, for help in answering this question.)

Endnotes

1. Robert D. Vinter, "An Approach to Group Work Practice," in *Individual Change Through Small Groups,* 2nd ed., eds. Martin Sundel, Paul Glasser, Rosemary Sarri, and Robert Vinter (New York: Free Press, 1985): 5–6.

2. Robert D. Vinter with Malda J. Galinsky, "Extragroup Relations and Approaches," in *Individual change Through Small Groups,* 2nd ed., eds. Martin Sundel, Paul Glassser, Rosemary Sarri, and Robert Vinter (New York: Free Press, 1985): 268.

3. A more extended discussion of the importance of opportunity structures is found in Richard A. Cloward, and Lloyd E. Ohlin, *Delinquency and Opportunity* (Glencoe, Ill.: Free Press, 1969).

4. Janet A. Geller, "Reaching the Battering Husband," *Social Work with Groups* I (Spring 1978): 27–38.

5. For a more extended discussion of organizational change in social work, see Edward J. Pawlak, "Organization Tinkering," in *Social Work Processes.* 5th ed., eds. Beulah Roberts Compton and Burt Galaway (Pacific Grove, Calif.: Brooks/Cole, 1994): 210–16.

6. Charles Garvin and others, "Group Work Intervention in the Social Environment," in *Individual Change Through Small Groups,* 2nd ed., eds. Martin Sundel, Paul Glasser, Rosemary Sarri, and Robert Vinter (New York: Free Press, 1985): 282. The discussion that follows draws extensively from this work.

7. Ibid.: 282.

8. These categories of environmental change activities are a modification of one presented in Garvin and others, in *Individual Change*: 286–92.

9. See, for example, Richard F. Rakos, *Assertive Behavior: Theory, Research, and Training* (London, New York: Routledge, 1991) .

10. For a case study of this combination of individual, group, and community services, see Francis P. Purcell and Harry Specht, "The House on Sixth Street," in *Social Work* 10, (4) (October 1965): 69–76.

11. For an extended discussion of the ethical issues involved, see Harry Specht, "Disruptive Tactics," *Social Work* 14 (April 1969): 5–15.

12. Alan Klein, *Society, Democracy and the Group* (New York: Woman's Press and William Morrow, 1953): 329–30.

13. Garvin and others, in *Individual Change*: 288.

Chapter 9

The Evaluation of Group Work Practice

A growing idea in social work is that the "practitioner" should become a "practitioner-researcher." One reason for this is political—the current emphasis on accountability. Funding sources and legislative bodies have raised questions about whether the funds for social programs are well spent, which has led to the requirement that workers collect and report data on the outcome of their activities. While the purpose of this is to ensure that funds are routed to the most effective activities, thus benefitting more people, this unfortunately is not always the result of evaluative efforts.

A reason for difficulties in performing an evaluation is the current state of knowledge regarding measurement of the outcomes of social work intervention. An exception is the rapid development of the field of behavior modification, which has led to many reliable devices for measuring behavioral change. Not all intervention goals, however, are conceptualized as changes in discrete behaviors. Goals are sometimes described in terms of emotions, attitudes, self-evaluations, the qualities of one's decisions, and institutional changes. While practitioners and researchers are working to create valid and reliable measures of *all* phenomena related to social work objectives, there are still weaknesses in their products as well as disagreements among practitioners as to appropriate types of measurement.

Another problem with the current approach to accountability is that the type of data to be collected is often imposed by the agency upon the worker, at times with little regard for the worker's concerns regarding the variations that exist among clients. Workers, therefore, do not always take seriously data collection for program evaluation. Many group workers known to the author record data on agency forms with little thought because they do not identify with the agency's purposes and methods of evaluation.

Group workers, like all social workers, experience the difficulties with such current evaluative technologies. This does not militate against our conviction that workers' evaluation of their practice should be an essential component of their activity, and that all workers must struggle to overcome the barriers to such practice that exist through inadequacies in evaluative technology and approaches inappropriately imposed by the agency. The reasons for such evaluation go beyond the concern that resources should be allocated to effective programs. The worker also has an obligation to the group members. They have a right to examine whether their investment in the group work process has attained their goals.

Furthermore, the worker has a responsibility to practice in effective ways. Workers, consequently, must know which procedures they employ to facilitate individual change are the most effective. When workers apply procedures to change group and environmental conditions to attain individual goals, they must also know whether those "work." Thus the requirement we place on workers, as professionals, is that they must employ the interventions most likely to help members with the least investment of time and energy by all parties.

In the term "practitioner-researcher," we have purposely placed the word "practitioner" first. The interests of practitioners must be in serving the members of the group. If taking responsibility for the effectiveness of that service leads to a better understanding of the procedures employed—and in some instances to insights into human behavior—that is valuable but secondary to offering responsible and accountable service. Thus the practitioner should not employ questionnaires or other instruments or subject members to any stress unless these are required to serve those members. When practitioners desire to do research, as such, members should be informed about this as a separate issue that they can accept or reject on its own merits.

It follows from these comments that all relevant parties should be involved in determining the nature and extent of an evaluative procedure. First and foremost, the group members should be helped to determine what they wish to know about the effects of group services. Second, the workers should consider what information will help them be responsible to the members as well as lead to better practice. Agency requests for information from workers or even members should not conflict with or impede these requirements.

In determining how to evaluate group work practice, the worker must decide (with proper involvement of members and significant others) on the design of the evaluation and on the instruments to be used. Furthermore, the worker must gather evaluative information not only in relationship to the members but to the group and to the environment when these systems are targets of intervention. We will, therefore, separately consider issues of design and measurement as these apply to individual members, the group, and systems outside of the group.

Evaluation of Individual Change of Group Members

Evaluation Design

The design of an evaluation consists of plans as to when and from whom information will be collected, as well as the type of information that will be sought. These plans, in turn, are based on how the information will be analyzed to determine the effects of service.

To identify whether individuals have benefitted from group work service, a measurement must be made of their relevant circumstances and behaviors prior to and after the group work experience. In addition, depending on the situation, additional measurements must be made during the group work process and some time after it has terminated.

The measurement of the status of a member's problems or concerns prior to group work service is referred to as a *baseline.* The member, then, seeks to improve this measure as a result of group participation. An appropriate baseline requires that members decide what they wish to change as a result of group experience and what their change goals are. Examples of some ways used by group members to establish individual baselines are as follows:

Example: A member of a group of college students measured, for three classes, how anxious he felt when he spoke out. He used a scale in which zero represented complete calm and one hundred the most anxiety he has felt.[1]

Example: A member of a parent's group counted how many times she criticized her son for each of three consecutive days.

Example: A member of an assertiveness group measured his degree of assertiveness using the Rathus scale.[2]

Example: A member of a career decision group indicated that twice previously he thought he had made the right career decision but had withdrawn from training programs before they started because of doubts about his decision.

Example: A member of a gay "coming-out" group said that he had gone home twice in the past month to tell his parents about his "gayness" but left without accomplishing this.

Technical issues regarding baseline measurements are beyond the scope of this text. A major technical issue relates to the number of baseline measurements that should be made to ensure that the measure represents the *typical* behavior of the group member. The reader can consult several texts that explain, in detail, the criteria for an appropriate baseline.[3] Because of difficulties in securing baseline data, some workers ask members retrospectively about baseline data.[4]

In addition to the frequency of measurements, another decision must be made as to whether effectiveness will be evaluated in terms of each individual or for the group as a whole. There is a long tradition of evaluating group and individual treatments by examining their effects on individuals. The presentation of case studies are instances of this. In such case studies, the practitioner asserts the value of his or her approach by showing that it has helped specific persons. This method, without a doubt, advanced knowledge about many techniques and will continue to do so. The measures were qualitative in that they described the person's situation before and after treatment.

One of the newest designs for evaluating change efforts is also focused on the individual case, but quantitative rather than qualitative measures are employed. These are usually referred to as "single subject designs" and include a baseline measure as well as subsequent measurements. Because of the quantitative nature of the measurements, statistical procedures are usually employed to rule out some of the causes of the change that lie in events other than the group experience. For example, an anxious member may, without treatment, experience a gradual lessening of anxiety. During treatment, this progress may occur more rapidly. Relatively simple statistical procedures can be used to determine the likelihood that a change in the rate of progress is due to something other than the group intervention.[5]

There are a number of different kinds of single case designs, each with a rationale for its use.[6] One of the most common designs is the AB design in which a baseline measurement is made followed by a measurement after (and sometimes during) the intervention. Another is a multiple baseline design in which baseline measures are made on some behaviors while treatments occur for others. Variations of this latter design include measuring baselines and changes that involve different members in the group or different situations for the same member. Another common design involves obtaining a baseline followed by several types of interventions, with measurements secured after each intervention. This last design helps identify the relative potency of different interventions, especially if one utilizes them with different members and in different sequences.

A problem for group workers with some of the designs is that what is done with one member will affect others. It is, therefore, difficult to separate the effects of an intervention in the group from the effects members have on each other. Nevertheless, it is still valuable to know if members are making progress, even when the variable responsible for the progress cannot be determined with certainty.

A major issue for group workers who utilize a variety of techniques, not primarily behavioral, is how to measure baselines and changes that are not thought of in terms of specific behaviors that can be counted. These include the quality of one's communications, decisions, satisfactions with self, and perceptions of self. Measures exist for all of these phenomena, and new ones are now being created. The lack of measures, therefore, cannot be a reason for failing to evaluate individual progress.[7] Rose provides a number of examples of measurements of changes in group members that were examined through single-subject designs. These included leadership behaviors, emotional responses, and information-giving responses.[8]

Practitioners will occasionally use control group designs[9] in which the worker compares members who received a particular form of service with those who received an alternative form or no service at all. The value of this approach is that reasons for change, other than the specific intervention, can be ruled out. The practitioner's problem with such designs is that they require procedures that are time consuming and sometimes difficult to achieve, such as random assignment of members to experimental and control group. In addition, data analysis problems are caused by premature termination of members from groups and the influences of members on each other.

In rating individual behaviors to evaluate the effects of group work, the worker can utilize a number of different data sources. One is the member's *self report*. In this instance, the members count their own behaviors, rate their own feelings or attitudes, or indicate the situations in which they experience some form of difficulty. Another is the *worker's observation* or *judgment*. The worker or other group members can count how often the member speaks, rate the degree of assertiveness of the member's statements, or note whether the member speaks of personal material in the group. *Outside observers'* ratings can be employed for the same purpose, and these observers, with the permission of the members, can either sit in on meetings or review tape recordings. The worker can also use records kept by others such as school teachers, parents, or employers, with permission of the member.

Measurement Techniques

Workers must be familiar with a variety of measures, including the following:[10]

Behavioral Counts.   Behavioral counts include the number of times a member engages in a desired act such as completion of homework assignments, absences from school, initiation of conversation with acquaintances, or expressions of affection. Many devices have been developed to facilitate counts, such as mechanical counters and charts.[11]

Goal Attainment Scaling.   Goal attainment scaling is a procedure for measuring clients' progress in attaining goals.[12] As can be seen in the completed form in Table 9.1, a scale is developed for all goals of each client. The scale consists of five levels, ranging from the most favorable to the most unfavorable outcome with relationship to the goal. The mid-point of the scale represents the "expected" level of success. When this approach is used in groups, the group members can help each other define each level and rate outcomes in terms of these levels.

Kiresuk and Garwick have developed statistical procedures that create goal attainment scores for clients.[13] These scores can be used to help the group worker identify which types of groups are the most helpful to their members. Workers can examine the conditions found in successful and unsuccessful groups as a way of developing a better understanding of the most effective sets of group experiences in relationship to members' attributes, problems, and so forth.

We have also used goal attainment scales to evaluate members' achievements when the members were very low functioning and capable of only minimally participating in creating scale points. We worked with the members to help them identify their "expected level of success" and created the other levels without full member participation. We recognize the limitations of this but have yet to devise another solution to such problems in developing the scale.

Self Ratings on Emotional States.   An emotion for which members often seek help is anxiety. This discomfort is experienced by members with phobias or problems when performing such tasks as asking a person for a date or answering questions posed by a teacher. Practitioners have found considerable reliability in asking members to rate their own degrees of anxiety on a scale of zero to one hundred.[14] Such scales have also been used for irritation, anger, and congeniality.[15]

Value Clarification Ratings.   Members often seek to clarify and affirm their values as a result of group experience. Some of the instruments utilized for value clarification exercises can also be used to determine baseline as well as changes in the values of members. One example of this is the "values grid" (Table 9.2). The members place the value issues relevant to them in the issue column. For example, in one adolescent group, the members listed "declaring pride in being black," "what it means to be a man or woman," and "how honest I should be with people I am close to." Members check the seven columns in terms of the following questions:

1. Are you *proud* of (do you prize or cherish) your position?
2. Have you *publicly affirmed* your position?
3. Have you chosen your position from *alternatives*?
4. Have you chosen your position after *thoughtful consideration* of the pros and cons and consequences?
5. Have you chosen your position *freely*?

TABLE 9.1 Goal Attainment Follow-Up Grid

Program using GAS: Intercity Head Start
Client Mrs. B.
Date of scale construction 8-1-73
Follow-up date 9-7-73

Levels of predicted attainments	Scale Headings and Scale Weights			
	Scale 1	Scale 2	Scale 3	Scale 4
Most unfavorable outcome thought likely	Mrs. B. reports angrily yelling at Jimmy daily or more often during last week in August.	No action on or discussion of Mrs. B.'s loneliness.	No discussion or action about returning to clinic.	
Less-than-expected success	Mrs. B. reports angrily yelling at Jimmy more than three times but less than daily during last week in August.	Mrs. B. discusses her loneliness but cannot make plans to deal with it.	Mrs. B. is discussing her reaction to the clinic but has not formulated plans to return.	
Expected level of success	Mrs. B. reports angrily yelling at Jimmy no more than three times during last week in August.	Mrs. B. is discussing her loneliness and making plans to join a group.	Mrs. B. has discussed her reaction to the clinic and plans to secure a return appointment.	
More-than-expected success	Mrs. B. has discontinued angrily yelling at Jimmy but has not discovered another way to discipline him.	Mrs. B. has initiated contacts with a group.	Mrs. B. has telephoned the clinic for a return appointment.	
Most favorable outcome thought likely	Above, and Mrs. B. is using another form of discipline before becoming angry with Jimmy.	Mrs. B. has attended one group meeting.	Mrs. B. has been into the clinic for a return appointment.	

From *Social Work Processes* by B. Compton and B. Galaway. Copyright © 1994, 1989 Wadsworth Publishing Company; © 1984, 1979, 1975 by The Dorsey Press. By permission of Brooks/Cole Publishing Company, a division of International Thomson Publishing Inc., Pacific Grove, CA 93950.

TABLE 9.2   Value Grid

Issue	1	2	3	4	5	6	7
1							
2							
3							
4							
5							

Taken from Sydney B. Simon, Leland W. Howe, and Howard Kirschenbaum, *Values Clarification: A Handbook of Practical Strategies for Students and Teachers* (New York: Hart Publishing Company, Inc., 1972), p. 35.

6. Have you *acted* on or done anything about your beliefs?
7. Have you acted with *repetition*, pattern, or consistency on this issue?[16]

Ratings on Skills in Understanding Self and Situation.   A goal of group services for members may be to help them learn how to understand and make rational decisions regarding behavior or situations. After the group experience is over, their improved ability to analyze situations and make decisions will help the members cope better with problem situations. A number of approaches previously discussed present the members with ways of accomplishing this, including problem solving and behavioral analysis. Scales can be used to evaluate the ability of the member to use any of these approaches. The member can apply the scale to his or her own process, or other members can use it as a basis for interviewing the members to assess their cognitive effort. Some questions, for example, that can be used to assess members' skills in problem solving are the following:

1. Has the member sought information relevant to the problem? For example, if the problem is finding a job, has the member found out about the types of jobs most available for persons with his or her training and abilities?
2. Has the member identified the alternatives available to him or her? Do these alternatives include all the most important or relevant ones? Has the individual used the information generated in question 1 to identify alternatives?
3. Has the member evaluated the alternatives using criteria such as the following?

   a. the alternative with the most likelihood of helping the member achieve his or her goal
   b. the alternative with the fewest disadvantages or costs
   c. the alternative most consistent with the member's values

4. Has the member chosen the alternative he or she evaluated most favorably?
5. Has the member developed or begun to develop a plan to implement the alternative?

These questions can be answered with either a "yes" or "no," or they can be rated on a zero to five scale with zero standing for absence of the behavior and five representing its presence to the fullest degree. Admittedly such a scale does not represent the kind of specificity used in formal research, but it does present information that will help the members and the worker judge whether a rational approach to problem solving has been utilized and is, therefore, likely to be a part of the way members will now approach problems.

Task Accomplishment. In many groups, including task-centered ones, the member seeks to attain goals by accomplishing tasks. We have slightly modified the instruments developed by Reid and Epstein for use with such groups.[17] To evaluate client task completion, we developed a form to be completed after each session. Within each space allocated on the form for each group member, the following information is requested: the task or the subtask to be completed by that session; the obstacles encountered by the member in accomplishing the task; the plan that the member has devised at that session to overcome the obstacles; who suggested the task (worker, member, other members); and ratings of the member's commitment to the task and the degree to which the task was accomplished.

Reid has also developed an instrument to measure progress made by clients in solving problems.[18] This instrument allows the client and the worker to choose from among six types of scales the one most appropriate for the client's situation. The scales differ in the types of measurements required from fully quantitative to fully qualitative. The instrument can also be used to measure members' problem reduction in groups.

Psychological Instruments. Many instruments developed by psychologists and other behavioral scientists, as well as social workers can be used by group work practitioners. Their use does not require highly specialized training. Increasingly, in fact, social workers themselves are developing evaluation and assessment instruments compatible with social work objectives and methods. Fischer and Corcoran have performed an important service for group workers, as well as for all other social workers, by compiling many of these instruments and providing data on their psychometric properties and usefulness.[19]

Some of the scales presented by Fischer and Corcoran are especially appropriate for group work, and we list them below together with the volume and page number on which the instrument might be found in the Fischer and Corcoran text. All of these instruments can be self-administered, and the first eight are devised for use with children.

1. Adolescent Coping Orientation for Problem Experiences (**I**, 401)
2. Assertiveness Scale for Adolescents (**I**, 407)
3. Behavioral Self-Concept Scale—for children (**I**, 417)
4. Children's Beliefs about Parental Divorce (**I**, 441)
5. Children's Loneliness Questionnaire (**I**, 449)
6. Depression Self-Rating Scale—for children (**I**, 464)
7. Hare Self Esteem Scale—for children (**I**, 472)
8. Index of Peer Relations (**I**, 484)

Evaluation of Changes in Group Conditions

As discussed in Chapter 5, the group worker seeks to modify group conditions and help the members to do so to create a group conducive to attaining members' goals. A variety of procedures were presented for the worker to accomplish this. Workers, therefore, should evaluate whether their activities lead to desired changes in the group. Often these group changes will be self-evident. At other times, the worker will seek a reliable means of measuring group changes so as to evaluate the effectiveness of group work techniques and to reinforce members for cooperating in their use.

Measurement Techniques

We shall now discuss some of the approaches that should become familiar to group workers for measuring changes in group conditions.

Group Recording.   Group workers, as part of responsible practice, will write a record after each meeting. Sometimes, when the worker wishes to engage in a thorough analysis of factors that contributed to a particular group outcome, she or he will write a *process record*. In this record, the worker presents the most significant events of the meeting. It is almost impossible (in terms of time spent, if nothing else) to record every word spoken. Instead, the worker selects the statements made by members and workers that most reveal the role played by each in determining the direction taken during the session, how the individuals coped with events, or how group conditions evolved. Inevitably, the worker will have to form a judgment as to relevant statements. If workers wish consultation based on more "objective" data, they often seek permission of the group members to electronically record the session.

The following is an example of a segment of a process record from a group of adults whose goals related to improving their interpersonal relationships:

The group members were discussing the idea that many of them did not know how to be assertive. Sam said that he had been left behind when his colleagues at work went out together for lunch. Mary asked him what he was doing at the time. He said that he was doing some filing. She asked him to pretend that she was one of his co-workers and to act the way he had been behaving at the time. He did this and afterwards I (the worker) asked the group to give him feedback. Jill said that he seemed to be avoiding eye contact with the others in the office. Bob noted that when Mary walked past him, he bent over even farther. The worker asked Sam what kind of message he may have been sending to others. Before Sam could answer, Barbara said that she had similar problems and she didn't know why Sam was getting all of the attention. I wondered why Barbara raised that issue right now.

A less time-consuming type of recording is of *critical incidents*. This requires the worker to write a process record but only of an incident that happened during the full group session. The worker believes such an incident should be closely examined for the information it offers about an event that either affects the whole group or some part of it.

Most frequently, the worker engages in *summary recording*. Through this format the worker summarizes the main events of the session and includes a few direct quotes from members or workers. Toseland and Rivas present a typical form for such recording,[20] consisting of the following items: group name; dates of beginning and ending of group; worker's name; session number; members present and absent; purpose of group; goals of session; activities at session; worker's analysis of meeting; and future plans.

We have devised a form to be used when workers try to develop new group work technologies. Prior to the meeting, the worker prepares a list of the activities he or she has planned for the session with details of the techniques to be used. Each activity is numbered, as well as the group work recording form. The worker is asked to record after the appropriate number whether the activity was conducted as planned, how the activity was modified, and how successful the activity was. The form also has a place to record critical incidents related to the use of the technology as well as issues that were encountered in this use.

Still another type of group recording makes use of codes to describe the sequence of events in a group meeting. An example of this type of instrument follows.

Group Work Recording Form

Practitioner's Name: _____ Group Name: _____ Session #: _____

Date of Meeting: _____ Time of Meeting: From _____ To _____

Members Present:

1. Practitioner's goals for group session (comment as to whether these are acknowledged by members):

2. Practitioner's goals for individuals during session (comment as to whether these are acknowledged by members):

Codes*	Episode 1 Time:	Episode 2 Time:	Episode 3 Time:	Episode 4 Time:	Episode 5 Time:
Content Codes					
Intervention Codes					
Type of Process Codes					

* Codes will be created by the agency; the following are illustrative: content = individual's problem behavior, group condition, group planning, nonverbal program; interventions = interpretations, problem solving, reinforcement, modeling; type of program = discussion, presentation, game, creative project, exercise, problem solving, role play.

3. Practitioner's agenda for session (comment on how this relates to members' agenda):

4. Process:

In space below, briefly describe incidents and significant interactions among members or between members and worker and indicate in which episodes interaction took place:

5. Major obstacles, if any, to attaining goals during meeting:

6. Report of evaluative data collected during meeting:

7. Plans for next meeting:

8. Overall assessment of session:

The major objectives of the session were accomplished *for* the following proportion of members:

_____ Completely	_____ All
_____ Almost completely	_____ Most
_____ Partially	_____ About half
_____ To a slight degree	_____ A few
_____ Not at all	_____ None

Behavioral Counts.   We began our discussion of evaluating individual changes with behavioral counts, largely because of the simplicity of this form of measurement. For similar reasons, such counts can also often be used to assess changes in group conditions. Many changes that group workers seek to achieve in groups are manifested in specific behaviors of members that can be defined and counted on a tally sheet. For example, the workers and the group may seek to increase certain classes of member behaviors for all members, such as expressions of feelings, self-disclosure statements, requests for help from others, arrivals on time to the meetings, declarations regarding one's values, or verbal reinforcements to others. Either the worker, an outside observer, or a member can keep a record of all such acts and can report the results to the group. This represents a group condition in that such behaviors are partially under the control of group norms that call for either expressing or inhibiting them. Group members and workers, when evaluating their groups, will often seek to change the frequency with which certain behaviors are expressed so the effectiveness of the group will be enhanced.

Measurements of Group Structures.   Since the basic tool in group work is the communication among members and between members and the worker, the communication structure—who talks to whom about what—is often the target of change. In Chapter 5 we presented a number of examples of ways to assess communications structures that can be used to evaluate whether efforts to change such structures are effective. One of the simplest techniques presented is a tabulation of the sequence of member and worker statements (M M M W M W M M M W). This can be used to indicate whether there is an increase in member-to-member as compared to member-to-worker interactions simply by dividing the number of Ms by the number of Ws.

Some devices used to change group conditions can also be used to measure changes. Rose, for example, described a procedure to help a group become more aware of its pattern of offering reinforcing remarks instead of punishing remarks.[21] Members placed poker chips in a can, using one color to indicate feeling reinforced and another to indicate feeling punished. While the chips were used to signal subjective experience, they can be counted to evaluate a change in this type of communication in the group.

Rose has also developed a system for assessing content expressed by one member to another. He developed the following content categories: suggestion-opinion-giving response; questions; responses to questions; self-suggestion responses; negative affect; positive affect; and information giving.[22] The observer coded each remark in terms of who said it, who it was directed to, and the category into which it fit. This allowed the worker to tabulate who spoke most frequently, who was spoken to most often, and which types of comments were most frequent. Depending on member and worker concerns, any one of these as well as other potential tabulations might be used to select goals for changes in group conditions and then to monitor changes.

To assess changes in a group's sociometric structure, some workers rely on observations of subgroups, while others have used standard sociometric questionnaires in which members are asked with whom they choose to work or to whom they felt closest. Such questionnaires can provoke a great deal of anxiety, however. Yalom reports, nevertheless, asking each member to rate all members of the group in popularity, apparently without serious harm to the members.[23] These approaches can be used to assess changes in the number of isolates and the composition of subgroups.

Workers may also wish to monitor changes in the power structure of the group, particularly when members are influenced by others in the group in dysfunctional ways. Some members, also, may have had little influence on the group, causing damage to their self-esteem and hindering their integration into group activities. One way to assess changes in this pattern is to record responses to members' ideas or suggestions. These responses can be coded as (1) support or agreement; (2) disagreement; or (3) not relevant (for example, changed subject or ignored statement). All responses are not coded; only those made in relationship to directions, suggestions, or new ideas. Some members do not contribute any of these and, at least by this measure, are low in this manifestation of power.

Measurement of Group Processes.   One of the most important group processes is problem solving, and workers will seek to assess changes in the group's problem-solving capacity. We previously presented a means of evaluating the group's handling of problem-solving incidents as an exercise (see exercise at end of Chapter 5). The instrument presented there was utilized as follows: tape recordings were made of group meetings and were replayed to identify problem-solving episodes. The scale was used to rate each of these episodes. Changes in problem-solving processes were examined both from within the meetings and over several meetings. Occasionally a group that engages in effective problem solving regresses. The worker in these situations will examine the content of the problem as well as other events in the group to diagnose the source of the difficulty.

Another crucial type of process, also a form of problem solving, is the process illumination activity discussed in Chapter 5. Although this is an essential part of most approaches to group psychotherapy, we have not found any research evaluating its impact as a specific and discrete tool. We do have several suggestions, however, for evaluating this procedure. Members whose interpersonal processes have been examined in this way can be asked, after the procedure has been utilized, to note in a personal journal what they have learned about their responses to the other person and about the other's responses. Subsequent "processing" of their interactions can also be noted in the journal. The worker or an observer can also make notes on the types of learning they assumed took place. Periodically workers can examine the log, with the permission of the member, to assess the kind of learning accomplished. We hope this kind of exploratory work will help workers develop more systematic ways of studying the effects of process illumination.

The process of changes in attraction of members to each other and to the group, a major component of cohesiveness, is essential. A successful group depends on the members' attendance and investment. The workers should, therefore, obtain feedback from members as to their reactions to the group at specific meetings as well as over longer periods of time. A two- or three-question instrument can be completed just before members leave in which they record how strongly they desire to return (for example, on a seven-point scale from "not at all" to "very much") and the activities or discussions during the meeting they found most and least useful. Yalom describes a cohesiveness scale that he and his colleagues used on which members rated the following items (on five-point scales).[24]

1. How often do you think your group should meet?
2. How well do you like the group you are in?
3. If most of the members of your group decided to dissolve the group by leaving, how would you like an opportunity to dissuade them?

4. Do you feel that working with the group you are in will enable you to attain most of the goals in therapy?
5. If you could replace members of your group with other "ideal group members," how many would you exchange (exclusive of group therapists)?
6. To what degree do you feel you are included by the group in the group's activities?
7. How do you feel about your participation in, and contribution to, the group work?
8. How do you feel about the length of the group meeting?
9. How do you feel about the group therapists?
10. Are you ashamed of being in group therapy?
11. Compared to other therapy groups, how well would you imagine your group works together?

This scale can then be totaled for each person and a group average computed. The worker should calculate the group median rather than mean so than the statistic is not strongly affected by a few members who may be extremely positive or negative. Changes in group cohesiveness over time can be examined to identify the need for or the consequences of interventions aimed at this phenomenon.

Workers should also assess the phase of development of the group. This is usually done through the examination of one's impressions of various group conditions. In Chapter 5 we presented an instrument for collecting data about group development. It can be used by workers to confirm their impressions as well as to identify aspects of the group that are impeding development, such as ambiguity of purpose, antagonisms among members, dysfunctional structures, or inappropriate choices of activities.

Rose has developed another way of measuring group processes.[25] At the end of the session, he presents members with a questionnaire with items that the members can respond to by circling a point on a scale. The following are examples of such items: How useful was today's session for you? Describe your involvement in today's session; rate the extent of your self-disclosure of relevant information about yourself or your problem; how important to you were the problems or situations you discussed (others discussed) in the group today? Circle the number on the scale that best describes the interrelationships among group members and leaders in this group. Circle all the words that best describe you at today's session (e.g., excited, bored, depressed, interested, comfortable); how satisfied were you with today's session?

Measurement of Shared Attributions.   As discussed in Chapter 5, the group affects the way members view events. The worker cannot assume, however, that a group discussion of the cause of some event accurately reflects how each individual views it. A number of members, for example, may have remained out of the conversation. Do they agree with what is being said? Are they afraid to voice disagreement? Are they suspending judgment to hear what others think? Consequently, workers will sometimes ask members privately to write their perceptions of the causes of an event or their values regarding it. If the worker has asked the group to discuss its understanding of the event, this can be compared to members' individual responses. Similarities and differences in what individuals say privately and publicly will tell a great deal about conditions, such as willingness of members to honestly share opinions and ability of some members to control others' opinions.

Social-Psychological Instruments.   Instruments developed by social scientists can also be used, with some adaptation, by practitioners for evaluating group changes. The practitioner who desires to measure change in some group dimension can usually locate such instruments by consulting one of the standard texts on the sociology of groups.[26] Some examples of instruments that can be used are Bales's for observing interactions,[27] Byrne's for assessing members' similar activity preferences,[28] and Crosbie's for charting members' statuses (for example, power and prestige).[29]

Evaluation of Environmental Changes

The basis for evaluating an environmental change, when the aspect of the environment targeted is some specific policy or resource, may be self-evident. Evidence that the policy has been changed can easily be secured—for example, if the member has had a welfare grant increased or a school has established a new curriculum. At other times, the environmental change the members are seeking may be harder to identify because it relates to attitudes of organizational participants or to patterns of interaction within the system.

Measurement Techniques

Some ways to assess environmental changes are to draw upon official reports, members' experiences, and interviews with informants, or to administer appropriate instruments. We shall describe each of these sources.

Official Reports.   Some reasons to examine these are to determine if policies have changed, if resources are being used differently, or if the way services are being delivered has been altered. Such documents include annual reports, budgets, service descriptions, and statistical reports.

Member Experiences.   Members involved in the same organization can compare their experiences. This is appropriate if the change sought is in the behavior of the organization toward these members, such as the amount of reinforcement for students provided by a teacher. Another example of this occurred in a group in a hospital setting. The members sought more courteous attention from the nursing staff. Members agreed to keep records of the responses of nurses. This was subsequently shared at a meeting between the group members and representatives of the nursing staff, when it was decided to present this data at a meeting of all the nurses.

Interviews.   Some organizational manifestations can best be examined by trained observers through sensitive interviews with key personnel. An example of a phenomenon measured this way was the imposition of destructive labels on group members, a form of negatively stereotyping them. Another occasion requiring such interviews is when individuals in the environment act in undesirable ways toward group members and are able to continue this through informal support from others in their system. An example of this was when a school counselor advised all black students not to consider going to college.

A student brought this issue to the attention of her group, and the members decided to interview their teachers to find out how aware they were of this advice. At a later time, they interviewed the teachers again to find out if any actions had been taken to prevent this type of discrimination.

Structured Instruments.   The group, the worker, or both can choose to use an already developed instrument to measure changes in environmental conditions. For example, Moos has developed a number of scales to measure environmental conditions that impact participants.[30] These conditions, which include such dimensions as the degree of structure, the freedom to express one's beliefs, and the presence of conflict, are examined by asking organization members to rate items on a questionnaire. Group members can use this instrument to evaluate changes in such environments as school rooms, hospital wards, residential treatment milieux, or even communities.

Guerney, in a training program for use in groups to enhance relationships, developed a number of scales to measure changes in relationships, such as an "interpersonal relationship scale" and a "relationship change scale."[31] Items in these scales can be used to assess changes in the quality of relationships, even when the specific procedure developed by Guerney is not utilized. These changes, because they are interactional, reflect not only the behavior of the group member but the responses of significant others. Such measure may be used when these others are part of the group work process, as in couples' groups or when a group member is working on relationship issues involving people not in the group.

Example: Members in a group of high school students were being helped to stay in school and to be more successful. For baseline data, the worker utilized the school grades of the members during the previous semester; their responses to a brief questionnaire developed by the worker regarding their attitudes toward school; and the proportion of homework assignments they had completed the first two weeks the group met. During these first weeks, the worker helped the members become more acquainted with each other and did not attempt to modify the members' school behaviors. The worker asked the members to record their assignments daily and to check those that were finished. These same measures were utilized when the group had met for two months and when the group terminated at the end of four months. Several group process issues emerged during these four months. One was the attendance of members during the first meetings. Several times during these months the worker distributed a modification of the cohesiveness scale previously described. The worker discovered an increase in cohesiveness as the members became more committed to the group's goals and as changes were made in the group's program to make the group more attractive. At one point, also, some members less committed to the group's goals heavily influenced others. The worker asked the members separately to list the members of the group who most influenced them. The results of the survey were presented to the group, which led to a thoughtful discussion on how and why members were influenced by peers. The same questionnaire submitted later showed a number of changes in who influenced whom that the worker believed were conducive to the members' attaining their goals. The means of helping the members included securing the teachers' support. A few teachers had negatively labeled the members, and their lack of encouragement was demoralizing. The group invited these teachers to sit in on several meetings to learn about members' efforts. Afterward, members who encountered these teachers in classes kept a "log" of transactions. The logs were presented in group meetings to help members assess changes brought about by these interventions with the teachers.

Summary

This chapter began with a general discussion of the current emphasis on accountability in social work. While some undesirable consequences of this emphasis were described, we favor the concept of the practitioner-researcher. In group work this requires the worker to be able, with the cooperation of the members, to assess changes in individuals, group conditions, and the environment of the group. The chapter, therefore, included a discussion of some of the measures the group worker can employ to evaluate changes in each of these entities. In addition, some form of recording should be maintained for each group session. A sample recording form was presented.

Group Work Recording Exercise

Goals

1. To understand the components of group work practice recordings.
2. To develop accuracy in recording group sessions.

Procedure

1. Trainees review and discuss Recording of Group Sessions in this chapter.
2. Trainees observe an example of a group session. This can be a role play, a tape, a film, or a written, detailed account of a group work session. (For the latter purpose, the extended examples in Chapters 11–16 can be utilized.)
3. Each trainee completes the group work recording form presented in this chapter.
4. The teacher or trainer leads a discussion in the training group or class based on how each person has responded to each item on the form. Differences in responses are noted and discussed as a means of increasing members' skills in utilizing the form.

Endnotes

1. This is referred to as a "subjective units of disturbance scale." For details, see Joseph Wolpe, *The Practice of Behavior Therapy*, 2nd ed. (Elmsford, N.Y.: Pergamon Press, 1973): 120.

2. S.A. Rathus, "A 30-item Schedule for Assessing Assertive Behavior," *Behavior Research and Therapy* 11 (1973): 398–406.

3. See, for example, Martin Bloom, Joel Fischer, and John G. Orme, *Evaluating Practice Guidelines for the Accountant Professional*, 2nd ed. (Boston: Allyn & Bacon, 1995): 328–344.

4. Ibid: 469–70.

5. For a discussion of statistical procedures that can be applied by practitioners with little knowledge of

statistics, see S. Jayaratne, "Analytic Procedures for Single Subject Designs," *Social Work Research and Abstracts* 14 (Fall 1978): 30–40. For an analysis of technical issues in the use of such designs in social work, see Joel Fischer, *Effective Casework Practice* (New York: McGraw-Hill, 1978): 88–102. The same author also discusses what he terms "objectified case studies": 102–108.

6. For a comprehensive presentation of single case designs, see M. Bloom, Fischer, and Orme, *Evaluating Practice*: 345–478.

7. For a recent and authoritative discussion of the measurement of individual change as a result of treatment, see Michael J. Lambert and Allen E. Bergin, "The Effectiveness of Psychotherapy," in *Handbook of Psychotherapy and Behavior Change*, 4th ed., eds. Allen E. Bergin and Sol. L. Garfield (New York: John Wiley, 1994): 143–89.

8. Sheldon Rose, *Group Therapy: A Behavioral Approach* (Englewood Cliffs, N.J.: Prentice Hall, 1977): 66–72.

9. Readers interested in applying such designs should consult texts on the subject such as by D.T. Campbell and J.C. Stanley, *Experimental and Quasi-Experimental Designs for Research* (Skokie, Ill.: Rand McNally, 1963).

10. For an excellent discussion of the training of practitioners who can utilize appropriate outcome measures, see Martin Bloom. "Incorporating Objective Outcome Measures into Competency Training," in *The Pursuit of Competence in Social Work*, eds. Frank W. Clark and others (San Francisco: Jossey-Bass, 1979): 111–22.

11. For a comprehensive discussion of counts used in group work, see Rose, *Group Therapy*: 43–46.

12. For further details on this approach, see Thomas J. Kiresuk and Geoffrey Garwick, "Basic Goal Attainment Procedures," in *Social Work Processes*, 2nd ed., eds. Beulah Roberts Compton and Burt Galaway (Homewood, Ill.: Dorsey Press, 1979): 412–21.

13. Ibid.

14. Wolpe, *The Practice of Behavior Therapy*: 100.

15. T.M. Sherman and W.H. Cormier, "The Use of Subjective Scales for Measuring Interpersonal Reactions," *Journal of Behavior Therapy and Experimental Psychiatry* 3 (1972): 279–80.

16. For many such instruments, see Sidney B. Simon, Leland W. Howe, and Howard Kirschenbaum, *Values Clarification: A Handbook of Practical Strategies for Teachers and Students* (New York: Hart Publishing Co., Inc., 1972).

17. William Reid and Laura Epstein, *Task Centered Practice* (New York: Columbia University Press, 1977): 288.

18. William Reid, *The Task Centered System* (New York: Columbia University Press, 1978): 272–93. In this book Reid presents an early version of the scales. The elaboration of these scales referred to here is in an as-yet-unpublished document.

19. Joel Fischer and Kevin Corcoran, *Measures for Clinical Practice: A Sourcebook*, 2nd ed., Vol. 1, *Couples, Families and Children*; Vol. 2, *Adults*. (New York: The Free Press, 1994).

20. Ronald Toseland and Robert Rivas, *An Introduction to Group Work Practice*, 2nd ed. (Boston: Allyn & Bacon, 1995).

21. Rose, *Group Therapy*: 142.

22. Ibid.: 50–51. These categories are similar to those used by Bales to study group interactions; see Robert F. Bales, *Interaction Process Analysis: A Method for the Study of Small Groups* (Reading, Mass.: Addison-Wesley, 1950).

23. Irvin D. Yalom, *The Theory and Practice of Group Psychotherapy*, 4th ed. (New York: Basic Books, 1995): 60–61.

24. Irvin D. Yalom, *The Theory and Practice of Group Psychotherapy*, 3rd ed. (New York: Basic Books, 1985): 54.

25. Sheldon D. Rose, "Use of Data in Identifying and Resolving Group Problems in Goal Oriented Treatment Groups," *Social Work with Groups* 7 (2) (Summer 1984): 23–26.

26. See, for example, Howard L. Nixon II, *The Small Group* (Englewood Cliffs, N.J.: Prentice Hall, 1979); and Stephen Wilson, *Informal Groups: An Introduction* (Englewood Cliffs, N.J.: Prentice Hall, 1978).

27. Bales, *Interaction Process Analysis*.

28. D. Byrne, *The Attraction Paradigm* (New York: Academic Press, 1971).

29. Paul V. Crosbie, "Effects of Status Inconsistency: Negative Evidence From Small Groups," *Social Psychological Quarterly* (2) (June 1979): 110–25.

30. Rudolf H. Moos, *Evaluating Treatment Environments: A Social Ecological Approach* (New York: John Wiley, 1974).

31. Bernard G. Guerney, Jr., *Relationship Enhancement* (San Francisco: Jossey-Bass, 1977).

Chapter 10

The Group and Endings

What the end of a group experience means to participants must be understood by workers so they can be helpful. Much of the future impact of the experience is determined at this stage. If the termination process is successful, members will be more likely to transfer the learning in the group to other life situations, to enter into other group experiences when the need arises, and to remember the group with positive feelings rather than with guilt or anger. In this chapter we shall discuss the group termination phenomena that workers must understand and the tasks they must undertake for a "good" termination experience.

Meanings of Endings

In many ways all endings have some things in common. This is true whether the ending is of a relationship with a single person or a group; of a relationship in which all parties simply separate, or one in which someone has died. Some have even speculated on similarities when one loses a treasured possession or even part of one's self as in surgery or disability. In all of these events, the person has invested energy in the situation, may have expressed affection, and has participated in an ongoing experience with the person or object.

After the loss, the individual has the task of withdrawing this energy investment, of mourning for the lost person or object, and of establishing a new equilibrium in which the person, group, or object no longer plays the same role except in memory. From the earliest days of life, people must cope with loss. Young children whose parents leave their field of vision are uncertain of the parent's return until this has been repeated a number of times. When a parent leaves for work, this is experienced as a loss, at least until the child understands the reasons for this absence. Playmates move away, teachers change, and sooner or later—often first with pets—the permanency of death must be dealt with.

Thus coping with loss is an essential part of life, perhaps one that creates some sense of tragedy, and life cannot be lived to its fullest until one comes to terms with the inevitability of endings. It is essential that the group worker *understand* these issues and use the ending of the group as an occasion to help the members add to *their understanding.*

Somewhat different processes will take place, depending on when the group will end. Some groups do not have a fixed time for ending. In these, various members may leave while the group goes on—either because they have accomplished their purposes or have given up hope of doing so. Some groups may end at the same time for all members when it is agreed that optimum benefits have been attained. Probably most groups conducted by social workers have a fixed number of sessions, whether these be short-term for a few months or long-term for, say, a school year.

Unless there are strong reasons to the contrary, such as uncertainty as to group purpose or the complexities of the time it takes to change personalities, we prefer a time limit to groups—whether it is short or long term. This is because of our belief that time limits mobilize the energy and the planning of activities by participants to achieve their goals—if the time limits are reasonable.[1] Other things being equal, we also favor a short time rather than a long one because of ideas such as those advanced by Reid and Epstein, namely, that people are most motivated to receive help when they experience disequilibrium in their lives and are most likely to terminate when equilibrium has been restored.[2]

Groups that have time limits, particularly short-term groups of eight to twelve sessions, start the termination process early, perhaps from their beginning. Members know the date of the last meeting, even if (as frequently happens) they deny this or try to negotiate an extension. Activities are planned with an awareness of this time frame. The depth of relationships is affected, also, by this awareness. Thus any discussions of relationships or choice of member goals are held with an implicit or explicit sense of the available time. Since the date of the ending is known in advance, members are not surprised when the worker raises issues around planning for the last sessions.

Groups that have no advance determination of the length and that are terminating because the goals have been attained pose a different issue. Members are more likely to deny that they are ready for termination, and they will raise questions as to why the worker has decided to terminate. They must adjust to an event whose timing was, at least initially, ambiguous or unknown.

As we have seen, there are differences between the termination of groups with established time periods and those in which the ending was determined later. Nevertheless, if the experiences have been positive and members have accomplished many of their goals, there is more in common in the way the worker facilitates the termination process in these two situations than in situations when the group was unsuccessful. Another dissimilar event is when termination was imposed by unanticipated circumstances such as the loss of the worker from the agency. Another termination is when members enter and leave at different times, although planned, as in so-called "open groups."

Worker Tasks

First we shall discuss the worker's tasks in groups when the group experience was generally viewed as positive and when all members terminate simultaneously. We shall return, at the end of the chapter, to a discussion of termination tasks under a variety of other circumstances. In the former circumstances the worker helps the members as follows:

To evaluate the group in relationship to achievement of its goals.

To understand and cope with their feelings regarding termination.

To maintain the beneficial changes resulting from the group experience.

To utilize the skills, attitudes, and knowledge gained through the group in a variety of circumstances.

To seek out and utilize new services when appropriate.

There is no established order to any of these tasks. In each group the nature of the members' experiences will determine whether accomplishing one task will naturally lead to another. For example, in an evaluation of one group, as criticisms were offered, angry feelings were expressed. On the other hand, a discussion of new situations in which acquired skills would be appropriately used led to positive expressions. The worker, therefore, will usually plan with the members to accomplish these tasks in an order and in a way that makes sense to the group. Even after this process has begun, changes will take place in the termination plan because of unanticipated issues that arise. To help the reader apply the principles of termination planning, we have included a termination exercise at the end of this chapter.

In groups that have only met for a few months, a major emphasis on termination tasks will usually occur during the last two or three meetings. Long-term groups may devote part of several more sessions to termination issues.

Evaluation

The last chapter was devoted to presenting many ways that changes in individuals, groups, and the environment can be measured. Of concern here is the way these or other instruments and procedures will be used by workers as part of the termination process. One aspect of this process is a decision as to which formal sources of information will be utilized in the group as part of termination. The evaluative instruments and design, for purposes of accountability, will already have been determined. The issues here are which findings will be examined *by the group members* and how this will take place.

Members' Evaluation of the Group

The worker should review the instruments used and their purposes. The members, on the basis of the issues they have decided are relevant for their termination concerns, will select, from the data available, the specific information to discuss. This discussion will emphasize the meaning of the information to the members and the reasons they perceive for their successes and failures in the group. These reasons are seldom produced by the questionnaires and instruments themselves.

Example: In an assertiveness training group, the members discussed the changes in each member (on an assertiveness scale); all of these changes constituted an improvement, but some members' gains were greater than others. One member with a small increment talked about the severe criticism he still received from his employer when he asserted himself. Another member with a much greater gain spoke of the encouragement she had received from her friends as she became more assertive with her family.

An important part of the evaluative process is the free and unstructured discussion of members' personal changes. This includes things they liked and did not like about the group. Such discussion is invaluable to the worker, as many dimensions of change can be identified that have not been included in any instrument and that can help the worker plan for subsequent groups. The aspects of the experience that members believe caused their changes also will suggest potent aspects of the group experience that were not part of the worker's strategy.

A worker, for example, who attributed most of the members' changes to the kinds of techniques he used, such as role plays and demonstrations, was surprised to learn that the members thought many of their gains were due to his acceptance, liking, and concern for them. In contrast, a worker who attributed change to the supportive atmosphere of the group was equally surprised to learn that the most helpful thing to them was the specific advice they received on how to train their children. There is no certain way of knowing whether the members' or the worker's perceptions of why changes took place were most correct, but the ideas of the members should be seriously considered.

Similarly, when the members discuss what they liked and disliked about the group, they will frequently comment on dimensions not formally measured and perhaps unpredicted. Thus one group discussed at length an experience they had when a blizzard prevented their leaving the agency and they had to "camp out" there overnight. The things they learned about each other when discussion was unstructured, the small ways they helped each other with such problems as making plans for children and spouses, and the stronger identification they had with the group after the experience demonstrated a great deal to the worker about the "causes" of the excellent outcomes of that group. While the worker could not "program" blizzards, he did decide to consider a "marathon" session in similar groups in the future.

Members' Evaluation of the Worker

An important component to evaluation, not considered yet, is an evaluation of the worker. Workers should not wait until the termination of the group to ask for feedback from members on their activities, and in long-term groups workers should ask for this several times. Most workers do not yet do this directly, but it is our conviction that this is a requirement for responsible practice and that workers should be trained to include this with other evaluative activities. Asking for a personal evaluation is, of course, anxiety provoking for most, if not all, workers because of a desire to be regarded highly, a fear of negative criticism, and a concern that undesirable traits unknown even to the workers may be uncovered. Workers, however, who face these concerns and ask for an evaluation will demonstrate that they can take feedback in the same way as they expect members to. Workers also have an opportunity to model constructive ways of handling both criticism and praise.

The problem is how to ask for an evaluation by members. Ideally, the kind of trust built up between members and the worker will allow members to take responsibility for their critique and still be free to offer it sincerely. They can respond to written questions and discuss their answers openly. There will be times, however, even in effective groups, when the worker and the members will decide together that the most useful responses will be anonymous.

Some questions that workers can ask to receive feedback on their work are the following:

1. What are some of my actions you find most and least helpful?
2. What actions would you like me to take that are not being taken?
3. Are there personal qualities of mine you find helpful or not helpful (for example, ways of speaking, timing of interventions, sense of humor, ways of expressing self)?
4. How well do you think I understand what you are thinking and feeling? How do I communicate that?
5. How honest do you believe I am with you?
6. Do you experience me as supportive and caring?
7. How do you think I respond to members of a gender or ethnic culture different from my own?

It is important for workers to remember that members will find offering this type of feedback difficult. There are many social conventions against giving honest responses to these kinds of questions, and this is compounded by the emotional meaning workers usually have for members. This makes it particularly difficult for members to express criticism. Thus in such discussions the topic can subtly shift to a discussion of the group's program, the agency's inputs, or the general type of service offered. This shift can also be a response to a sense of the worker's discomfort. When the worker, however, clearly and honestly asks for evaluation, it is likely to be forthcoming.

Understand and Cope with Feelings

As indicated in the opening paragraphs of this chapter, people have many feelings with which they find it difficult to deal during endings. They must learn to handle these feelings for several reasons. One is that each time a person copes with feelings regarding endings, he or she will undoubtedly acquire strengths useful in coping with future endings. Second, unresolved feelings about an experience such as group work can hinder the member's ability to remember and utilize the learning acquired through that experience.

All losses engender similar feelings, although these feelings may vary in sequence and in intensity. Kübler-Ross, for example, in her important work on death and dying, describes the sequence of reactions when one learns of impending death.[3] We believe that these feelings are present to some degree whenever any ending is faced. The first response she notes is that of denial, which almost always occurs when the worker broaches the subject of the group's ending. Members may not deny that the group will end, but they frequently do deny their feelings about this. They manifest this by continuing to engage in whatever activities were before them when the subject of termination was raised, or they may state that they do not have feelings about the group's ending or that they have already dealt with these feelings. Another manifestation of such denial is seen in members who miss meetings after termination is first discussed or who diminish their group participation. Workers, particularly in short-term group or groups they deem less successful, may join in this denial and underestimate the meaning of the relationships, the activities, and the identification of members with the group.

In dealing with denial, workers can acknowledge to the members that endings are difficult and that feelings about them are also hard to express. They can ask the members to recall other endings of relationships; since those were more distant, members may initially be more able to express feelings experienced in those situations. Some workers have introduced a period in which members mill about the meeting room saying goodbye to other members as well as to the worker; a variation of this is to rotate around the group asking members to formulate a farewell statement. This type of experience elicits expressions, on verbal and nonverbal levels, of feelings that can be explored.

Kübler-Ross describes another reaction—anger. In groups this is often expressed at the agency that established time limits, at the group (and indirectly the worker) for not having accomplished more, and even at one's self for not having fully achieved one's goals. Anger can also be shown by members who become overly critical of the worker, thus rejecting him or her before they are rejected. This emotion at termination is difficult for members and workers. Workers may feel guilt because of their sense of responsibility for what happened in the group; members will fear that positive aspects of the experience will be lost because of their anger. Nevertheless, a group that has encouraged an honest expression of feeling throughout its existence cannot do an "about face" at this point. The legitimacy of the feelings must be acknowledged through the worker's admitting that imperfections of the group or one's self or both do make one angry. The important question is what the members will "do" with the anger. Ultimately, the anger must be channeled so that the member works to make future situations more responsive to the member's needs and the member more effective on his or her own behalf.

The third reaction described by Kübler-Ross is "bargaining." In groups, members who react this way seek to postpone the endings of the group or to create new experiences that may not be appropriate. In a sense, this may be one way the member channels anger and thus is a first step in coping effectively with it. The worker should continue to empathize with the members' desires to continue the group and the feelings that have elicited that solution. If the worker continues to be firm on plans for ending, however, more effective means of coping with anger over termination are likely to emerge.

Depression, according to Kübler-Ross, is another stage of this process. While we do not find that these stages appear discretely or consecutively in groups, depression often occurs after a phase of denial and bargaining. It is manifested in a lack of energy for the final activities of the group, a recounting of sad events or failures that occurred earlier, and even in direct emotional expression such as tears. We believe this is a period of withdrawal of energy from the group and of mourning, and is a psychological necessity. When it is not denied but is allowed full expression, it usually leads to a return of energy to perform the other tasks necessary for termination. The members invest energy in these tasks in a phase analogous to the one Kübler-Ross describes as "acceptance."

Some members respond to the feelings about termination through regression. They will behave in ways that they did earlier in the life of the group. Members in one group, for example, began to manifest relationship problems that had presumably been resolved. Members of a children's group increased their quarreling and cooperated less in activities than they had at the meeting before termination was discussed. While regression is a defense in times of stress, in groups it has the added function of demonstrating that members still need each other, the worker, and the group.

In a sense, this discussion of some of the feelings at termination suggests that they are all "negative" or "painful." If the group has been successful, there are also several positive feelings manifested. Members will experience pleasures at having attained their goals, mastered obstacles, and remained in the group through the difficulties. Members also inevitably experience some relief that the time investment and expense of attending meetings will end. They may feel some guilt for this latter emotion, yet in the continuing spirit of disclosure they can also assert pleasure that these costs will cease.

As can be seen, the feelings toward endings are ambivalent, and this typifies any change. During the group, it is hoped that members come to understand ambivalence, and that this can be deepened as they explore their feelings toward termination. An ability to work through ambivalence is necessary during all transitions, and this may be one of the most significant learnings that occur at the group's end.

Much of the "dual" nature of termination responses is reflected in Garland, Jones, and Kolodny's discussion of "flight" during the termination phase.[4] This can be a "nihilistic flight" or a "destructive reaction to separation" such as "rejecting and rejection-provoking behaviors," or a "positive flight" such as when "constructive moves are made toward 'self-weaning' from the group." The latter "includes finding new groups, activities, work interests, friends, etc., outside the group while continuing as a member."

Maintain Changes

The problem of helping the client maintain changes after the end of the helping process is a general one. Research into all forms of change efforts shows that a significant proportion of the people participating in the effort do not maintain their change. This has led to increasing attention to maintenance of change.[5] A major barrier to this is that members' ability to hold onto changes is not only a function of how the change was produced, as the strongest reverses often result from the negative impact of the environment. Friends and relatives may reinforce older ways of behaving. Formal organizations such as schools and places of employment may punish the new behaviors. Even without these negative forces, the members may still be uncertain of acting in new ways.

The worker, therefore, as termination approaches, must apply techniques to help the members deal with those forces that can undo the beneficial effects of the group. Some of these have been discussed already but bear repetition here. One principle for accomplishing this is *overlearning*. This means that members have the opportunity to test out a number of times what they have learned before the group ends. If the termination plan includes a reduction of the frequency of meetings, members can assign themselves to a number of "trials" of new behaviors between these meetings.

Workers will also discuss the resistance members may meet in the environment; other members, familiar with each other's situation, can do the same. This has several effects. For one thing, members will be less likely to become discouraged when "backsliding" takes place. They also should engage in problem solving to deal with these barriers. Such warnings are analogous to "paradoxical instruction," also. Some members have a tendency, for psychological reasons, to undermine their own progress, particularly if it has been recognized by others. It is harder to revert to this kind of negativism when continued progress *as well as* regression are predicted.

Approaches to helping that involve work with representatives of all of the members' relevant systems are emphasized by "network" theorists, who are most concerned about the kinds of environmental issues just discussed.[6] While there is much to commend total "network" approaches, research does not clearly indicate when they are required, especially if environmental issues have been extensively considered by group members.

Some group members' problems are precisely that they do not have supportive networks to help sustain changes. In these cases, the best way to help members maintain their gains is to facilitate their forming or joining support groups after the group work experience has ended. Sometimes the professionally led group itself will be continued without such leadership by the members for the same reasons. Some criticize these efforts on the grounds that group work has created a dependency on itself rather than on autonomy. We do not agree with this criticism. Most well-functioning people are able to draw on supportive and reinforcing networks consisting of family, peers, colleagues, or fellow members of church and other community groups. Many "graduates" of the group work experience do not have these social assets, and there is nothing intrinsically demeaning for them in seeking support from self-help groups. Increasingly, group-based programs have responded to this principle.[7]

The concept underlying this section is that maintaining progress often depends on securing continuing reinforcement for it. It is hoped that this will come from the members' natural environment. They will often have to deliberately ask for reinforcement, however, even if this *is* a sad commentary on how unlikely we often are to praise each other. One of the final exercises in the group can be to help members role play ways of asking for recognition from significant others. The anxiety such requests often cause and the assumption that one is then devoid of humility can be overcome and can enable the members to make a small contribution to the creation of a society in which norms favoring positive statements properly outnumber those favoring negative ones.

Utilize Skills in a Variety of Circumstances

Helping the members utilize what they have learned in the group in various situations will also help them maintain their gains. This process of generalization begins within the group itself. Members who have relationship problems, for example, often begin to try out new ways of interacting with other group members. Nevertheless, the purpose of joining a group is not to learn to adapt to the group or even to learn how to secure changes in it but to acquire personal and social changes in one's natural environment. Therefore, the worker must help the members transfer what they have learned to other appropriate situations.

There are several ways the worker can help the members in this regard. One way is to vary, even within the group, the contexts in which members use their skills. This can be done by taking trips with the group into environments, when possible, and when it is not, by simulating such environments through role plays and similar devices.

Example: In a group of developmentally disabled youths meeting under the auspices of a community mental health program, members had been learning the skill of asking for information and clarifying information that was not clear. During the final meetings of the group, the members took trips to a job program, a health service, a vocational school, and a department store. Before these trips, the group members discussed the information they would seek in each setting. Afterward, the members returned to their group meetings to discuss their experiences and to identify the common elements in their responses to each situation.

Since each environment in which a member uses a skill is in some respects unique, members must be able to solve the problems posed by these differences. Therefore, there is scarcely a group in which it is not appropriate to seek to enhance the members' problem-solving skills.

In addition, members must not only be able to "act"; they must understand how to analyze situations and to explain why each situation calls for the solution that it does. Thus in some way all groups must seek to add to the members' understanding of human behavior. If members understand the principles that govern their actions, they will be able to apply these actions in the broadest range of circumstances. This ability to understand behavior has even broader ramifications, as Yalom points out:

> *And so it is with psychiatric patients: fear and anxiety which stem from uncertainty of the source, meaning, and seriousness of psychiatric symptoms may so compound the total dysphoria that effective exploration becomes vastly more difficult. Thus, didactic instruction, through its provision of structure and explanation, has intrinsic value and deserves a place in our repertoire of therapeutic instruments.*[8]

The worker will utilize this principle of cognitive understanding throughout the group, but the ending is a good time to reinforce it to prepare members to apply broadly what they have learned. There are a number of therapeutic systems described in this book that explicitly provide for teaching a causal framework to members; these include positive peer culture and some approaches to behavior modification. In another sense, this is also true for ego psychological and other cognitively oriented systems whose goal is to increase members' insights.

Utilize New Services

Members will often seek out new services after the group ends as a logical sequel to their participation in the group. Thus in a group to help unwed mothers make some decisions regarding raising their children or placing them for adoption, some members sought services to help them acquire child-rearing skills; others wished services to help them resume their vocational and educational careers. In the last meetings of the group, the resources to meet these needs were discussed. The worker as well as members shared their knowledge of the agencies providing these services.

Giving knowledge about resources should be more than a simple presentation of information. In the group of unwed mothers just referred to, each member discussed her specific needs in relation to available services. She also was helped to present her expectations of the service, her fears regarding it, and any barriers she anticipated in its use. The members and worker presented their ideas as to the likelihood that these expectations would be met. Ways were also sought to alleviate anxiety about the service and to overcome the barriers. In some cases the worker and in other cases the "buddies" within the group offered to provide support and additional information as the member coped with applying for and making use of the projected resource.

Reduce Cohesion

During the first phases of the group, the worker seeks to increase the cohesiveness of the group, but this process is reversed during the termination phase. Members must be helped to become less attracted to the group and, when appropriate, more attracted to alternative relationships. The worker, therefore, also reverses the application of principles for attaining group cohesion. For example, instead of increasing the frequency with which members have contact with one another, this may be reduced by having meetings less often and/or for a shorter time. Some groups will taper off with a meeting every other week or once a month. The worker may place less emphasis on resolving conflicts within the group and may not call attention to commonalities of experiences or attitudes except as these relate to coping with termination. This may not be true in group psychotherapy, when this type of process is maintained until the very end.

Ceremonies

Transitions in social institutions are often marked with ceremonies. These include graduations, weddings, farewell parties, and even funerals. The function of these events is to clearly demarcate one status from another, to express aspirations, to give final rewards, to allow for the expression of sentiment, to provide group support for change, and to emphasize the positives even of sad occasions. The last meeting of the group, consequently, is often the occasion for a ceremony.

The elements used in closing ceremonies for social work groups include special refreshments, gift giving, "mock" diplomas, "last words" from members, group pictures, short speeches by the worker, "rituals," or a beloved song sung together. All of these fulfill one or more of the functions just listed.

To be most meaningful, the ceremony should be planned by some or all of the group members together with the worker. This does not preclude some "surprise" elements such as "diplomas" injected by the worker or a special planning committee. Members may also add spontaneously as the ceremony is in progress.

Special Termination Issues

The discussion of termination presumed that the entire group ended; alternatively, one member may leave and the group still continue. This occurs in groups that meet indefinitely although members join for periods that coincide with their needs—so called *open-ended* groups. Another example of this is a time-limited group in which a member leaves for personal reasons such as a geographical move or even dissatisfaction with the group.

A modified termination process occurs, even when one member leaves. Unless this termination is appropriately responded to, the results can be negative for the same reasons as if the entire group ended without dealing with termination. This includes reinforcing what the member has learned in the group, working with feelings about leaving, transferring the learning to new situations, and moving toward new resources if necessary. For these reasons, the worker will encourage the member to attend at least two meetings after he or she decides to leave. The first of these sessions usually is devoted to feelings about leaving; the second to the reinforcement and transfer issues.

In addition to the value accruing to the member who leaves, there are benefits to all the other members. When a termination process does not occur, all members may worry about whether they are really valued by their peers and if their departure will be ignored. Members, moreover, need an opportunity to express their feelings of loss of the departing member. Finally, each member who leaves provides a preparation and a rehearsal for how other members will deal with their departures from the group.

Nevertheless, times may occur when a member does leave abruptly. Members should be given an opportunity to discuss their feelings of rejection. They may also wish to contact that person, perhaps by phone, to express some of their thoughts and feelings about the termination.

A special case of the single person leaving is the departure of the worker, usually because he or she is also terminating from the agency. Members will often experience this as rejection or as a punitive response to ways they have behaved in the group, even when they know rationally that this is not the case. Members, therefore, will need several sessions to discuss their reactions to the worker's leaving, and at least some of these sessions should involve the new worker. This is because, even after the worker leaves, members are likely to discuss their responses. Depending on the nature of the group and the quality of the relationship with the worker, this ending will include an evaluation of the worker, expressions of appreciation, and even a ceremony.

Terminations are particularly difficult when the members and/or the worker view the group as unsuccessful in achieving its major objectives. Nevertheless, an absence of appropriate processes around that kind of termination can also compound the negative effects on the group by exaggerating them, by confusing responsibility, and by making it difficult for members to seek out group experiences that will be beneficial to them.

When the group is unsuccessful, members should still evaluate it so that specific reasons for failure are identified. Members can then seek group experiences devoid of those dimensions. Some frequent reasons for failure are poor group composition, lack of readiness or commitment of members, lack of resources from the agency, negative responses from the environment, unrealistic or inappropriate goals, and poor leadership from the group worker. Lack of success is seldom due to only one reason, and the task of the worker is to prevent a displacement of all the blame onto a single variable.

After discussing the issues just described, members will usually discover some positive elements overlooked in the group that can be reinforced. This will allow members, also, to express, without guilt or overstatement, feelings regarding departing individuals they have liked, as well as relief that the group has ended. Such an approach to ending even successful groups allows for a rational approach to selecting better, alternative experiences.

Sometimes a group "peters out" with fewer and fewer members attending. In this case, the worker should ask the members to attend a formal ending to the group. This accomplishes all of the goals just described for unsuccessful groups. It is clear that the group has ended, so feelings of members are responded to, reasons for failure of the group are clarified, and members are helped to make alternative plans. In rare cases, the reasons for the group's failure are successfully identified, and the group starts again with more likelihood of success.

Another special issue is posed by "open-ended" groups, such as those in hospitals, in which members may only be present for a few meetings. These should be treated as "one-session" groups in which each session concludes with a brief termination discussion in which members evaluate the session, comment on what they did or did not "get" from it, and, if they know they are leaving, say goodbyes.

Summary

This chapter began with a discussion of the meaning of endings and an application of this to group situations. Specific tasks of the worker were described as these apply to the endings of relatively successful groups; these include dealing with feelings, evaluating the group, reinforcing gains, promoting transfer of learning, and making appropriate referrals to new resources. General issues in termination were also discussed, such as reducing cohesiveness and planning ceremonies. In conclusion, this chapter presented ideas on termination of individuals when the group continues as well as on termination processes in unsuccessful groups.

Termination Exercise

Goals

1. To learn to identify member responses to group termination.
2. To acquire skills in helping group members cope with termination.

Procedure

(This exercise is most effective when utilized with a training group that is actually terminating. Others must simulate this.)

1. Participants review this chapter and discuss it.
2. Participants divide into four subgroups. Each subgroup is assigned a task as follows: Subgroup A plans an evaluation procedure for the entire group; this can apply to the group thus far, or if the group only convened for this exercise, for this session only. Subgroup B plans a procedure to help the group members deal with feelings about termination. Subgroup C plans a procedure(s) to help the group maintain and transfer something the members have learned thus far. Subgroup D plans a termination ceremony for the group.

3. Each subgroup facilitates the group's participation in the procedures it has devised. The order can be determined by the trainer, by the subgroups, through negotiation, or by the group as a whole.
4. This termination process is assessed utilizing the accompanying termination assessment form.
5. The group discusses how the termination process they have experienced might be used in some way with other groups, as well as what modifications might be required with such groups.

Termination Assessment Form

Evaluating the Group Experience

1. Check whether the following dimensions were discussed.

    _____ Whether the activities were appropriate to goals.

    _____ Whether the interpersonal relationships in the group were conducive to attaining goals.

    _____ Whether the members' investment in the group was conducive to attaining goals.

    _____ The relationship of the worker's performance to goal attainment.

    _____ A summary of the individual members' goal attainments.

    _____ Relationship of agency conditions to goal attainment.

2. Discuss each of these dimensions of assessment in terms of the adequacy of the process.

Dealing with Feelings

3. Was denial of feelings about termination present? How was it dealt with?
4. Were there feelings of sadness? How were they dealt with?
5. Were there feelings of anger? At whom were they directed? How were these dealt with?
6. Were there feelings of pleasure regarding the ending of the group? How were these responded to?
7. If ambivalence was present, How was it dealt with?

Maintenance of Change

8. Check which of the following were employed.

    _____ Overlearning.

    _____ How to cope with a negative environment.

    _____ How to develop a supportive environment.

    _____ Other (specify).

9. Discuss how well each was employed and with what likely effects.

Generalization

10. Check which of the following were employed.

_____ Varying the context of the group experience.

_____ Enhancing understanding of general principles.

_____ Giving assignments to practice skills outside the group.

_____ Other (specify).

11. Discuss how well each was employed and with what likely effects.

Referral

12. Were suggestions made for future experiences that will be appropriate to the members' needs? (Specify.)

13. Were members helped to examine how they will apply for such experiences? (Specify.)

14. Were members helped to anticipate any barriers to the use of such experiences?

15. Were members offered any support from the worker or other group members in gaining access to such experience or overcoming barriers to their use?

Endnotes

1. The author has always been interested in the ideas regarding the meaning of time in the helping process developed by the "functional" approach to social work. See Ruth Elizabeth Smalley, *Theory for Social Work Practice* (New York: Columbia University Press, 1967): 142–51. Another approach to the time dimension may be found in Arnold P. Goldstein, Kenneth Heller, and Lee B. Sechrest, *Psychotherapy and the Psychology of Behavior Change* (New York: John Wiley, 1966): 280–86.

2. William Reid and Laura Epstein, *Task Centered Casework* (New York: Columbia University Press, 1977): 28.

3. Elisabeth Kübler-Ross, *On Death and Dying* (New York: Macmillan, 1969).

4. James A. Garland, Hubert E. Jones, and Ralph Kolodny, "A Model for Stages of Development in Social Work Groups," in *Explorations in Group Work,* ed. Saul Bernstein (Boston: Boston University School of Social Work, 1965): 44.

5. G.A. Marlatt, *Relapse Prevention: A Self Control Program for the Treatment of Addictive Behaviors* (Seattle: Univ. of Washington Alcoholism and Drug Abuse Unit, 1980).

6. R.V. Speck and C.L. Attneave, *Family Networks* (New York: Pantheon, 1973).

7. Examples are the Synanon communities, the community-based programs developed by agencies using positive peer culture, and the types of services developed by Fairweather. For the latter, see George W. Fairweather and others, *Community Life for the Mentally Ill: An Alternative to Institutional Care* (Chicago: Aldine, 1969).

8. Irvin D. Yalom, *The Theory and Practice of Group Psychotherapy,* 4th ed. (New York: Basic Books, 1995): 10.

Chapter *11*

Working with Groups for Identity Development

In Chapter 2 we discussed the purposes assigned by agencies to the groups they serve. To assist in this analysis, we utilized a typography that consisted of (1) identity development; (2) skill attainment; (3) social control; and (4) rehabilitation.

This was followed by Chapters 3 to 10, which presented general principles and procedures, along with some variations, for working with groups. To elaborate more fully on these variations, we now present the next six chapters—the first four are devoted to the four categories in our typology. One chapter deals with work with oppressed groups and one with task-oriented groups such as committees. Each chapter will conclude with an extended practice example to offer additional insights on how groups with different purposes are conducted.

In this chapter, we shall present ways of working with groups when the purpose of identity development is at the forefront, particularly when the worker wishes to help the members determine their values, norms, and aspirations in situations where these are in flux, in conflict, or largely absent.

When we first conceptualized identity development (which we previously called "anomie reduction") as one of the major functions of group service, we did not realize how pervasive this function was. In subsequent use of this material in teaching, the students were able to identify aspects of anomie reduction in their practice with all groups. This is probably because, as one writer states,

> All societal roles and practices are open to suspicion. Conventional sex roles are questioned for the limitations they place on individual expressiveness. The Anglo's domination of industry and education is questioned for racist practices and elitist control. Government and the courts are suspect. Formulas and principles of welfare and taxation are challenged. No longer are conventional marriages and single careers the norm; private medicine doesn't work; the environment is deteriorating at an unacceptable rate; and all hidden forms of influence,

whether from the private sector or from the government, are being viewed for the limitations they pose to individual freedom and democratic values.[1]

No wonder that members of groups struggle with normative issues.

Beyond the fact that the material in this chapter pertains, to some degree, to all groups, as we indicated in Chapter 2, some groups are established primarily to resolve normative concerns. These groups are most likely to focus on people who, at a particular time, have become strongly aware, for political or social reasons, of their identity issues. As of this writing, related groups with which we have had contact have been devoted to men's, women's, homosexuals', youth's, and ethnic minorities' concerns. In addition, some of the approaches have been adapted for groups of expectant fathers, employees, students, the elderly, the handicapped, and the socially militant. Thus, for purposes of semantic simplicity, we shall use the phrase *identity development group* to refer to groups specifically formed for this purpose as well as all groups that at some stages of their development focus on this purpose.

Many of the techniques used by such groups have come from "consciousness-raising" and "values-clarification" programs and, to a lesser degree, from the encounter movement. While we shall discuss a range of approaches to identity development, we shall draw heavily from these programs.

In this, as well as the following chapters, we have organized our presentation around the basic tasks of work with groups, namely, those occurring before the group meets (for example, selection of members, composition of the group), during group formation (for example, clarification of purpose, choice of strategy), when the group acts to attain its objectives (for example, choice of techniques and targets for change), and when the group is evaluated and terminated (for example, planning for next experiences, choosing the evaluation instrument).

Pregroup Tasks

As Culbert states, the people in a consciousness-raising group—and we believe in all identity development groups—"should have a common relationship to the social system or structure serving as the focus of their discussion."[2] He gives, as an example, a group in which married women discussed their family roles. In this group all members were married, and he argues that if the group included single women or men, this would have diffused its focus.

Workers, therefore, recruiting for such groups have a conception of the type of consciousness-raising purpose of the group, and members are screened for their compatibility with this. We have found, beyond this compatibility, that heterogeneity is valuable in the way the members have defined their relationship to the role. Thus a group of men seeking to cope with changing masculine roles found it beneficial to enroll some members who were "gay" and some who were "straight." When members discussed their experiences as males at different stages of their lives, the similarities and differences between the "gay" and "straight" men helped each to clarify many of their conceptions of masculinity. Furthermore, this group was composed of men of different ages—the youngest being nineteen and the oldest fifty—and different statuses—ranging from cook to college professor. Because of this compositional range, the similarities and differences in their experiences helped to illuminate many of the issues they discussed.

The fact that the men's group just described "worked" was, in part, due to the fact that they broadly defined their consciousness-raising purpose as dealing with men's roles. Had they initially, or later, decided the primary focus was narrower (for example, the role of husband or of gay person), the most desirable composition would have been of persons with the same role.

When identity development activities occur in groups primarily established for other purposes, how well they are handled will depend on the composition of the group. If the members seeking to clarify their roles and values share role and value concerns with some other members, these can be dealt with in the group—if opposition to such consideration is absent. Opposition may arise if the others find this process threatening or irrelevant.

Thus, in one social skills group of university students, a lesbian worked on some of her beliefs about her role because several other women in the group identified themselves as lesbians and from their experiences were able to help her clarify some of her issues. The other members of the group, whose life styles were different, were not too naive, hostile, or uninterested to impede this process. On the other hand, a gay man in another group, when he dealt with analogous issues, had to respond to the curiosity of some members and the discomfort of others. The worker subsequently helped him find another group that was more supportive when he dealt with his sexual orientation.

Identity development activities are best conducted in groups of between eight and twelve members. A smaller group, while providing for a great deal of intimacy, is impeded when one or two members have to miss a meeting because a few absences in a group of this size are strongly felt. On the other hand, larger groups prevent members from receiving support from each other as they relate a general topic to individual experiences.

The identity development group should begin with a clear idea as to the number of sessions it will hold. Two patterns are possible: either a short term or an indefinite term. The short-term (six to twelve sessions) experience is typical of a group whose focus is on a circumscribed role such as "working mother," "coming out gay," or "expectant father." The long, indefinite-term group is one in which the focus is so broad as to incorporate the whole range of men's or women's roles. In the latter group, the members should agree after the second or third meeting to evaluate how satisfactory the composition is, that is, whether they have sufficient compatibility, homogeneity, heterogeneity, and size for their purposes. When there are major problems in these aspects of composition, the worker should help the group terminate and reform or seek changes in membership.

Group workers have organized and facilitated identity development groups, particularly of the short-term variety. Long-term groups frequently arise in the community out of the needs of their members or are recruited as part of the development of social movements. In the latter case, group workers are called on as consultants by all or some of the members. Long-term groups can also be the outgrowth of short-term, worker-led groups that decide to continue (on a leaderless basis) with occasional consultation. In that event, the group will have to choose members to fulfill coordinator and recorder functions, and these should rotate so no one is overly burdened with these tasks or uses them to avoid a more intensive involvement in the group.

Group Formation Tasks

Some assessment and screening is usually accomplished prior to the beginning of the group. This process ascertains whether the person can function as a group member; that is, reveal aspects of self to others, engage in problem solving in a group, and accept help from others. The commitment of the individual to clarifying the role(s) relevant to the group's purpose is also examined as well as personal values in relationship to the role. This initial assessment is essential in determining whether the individuals have been appropriately referred to the group and how they will affect and be affected by its composition.

During group formation, the process of assessing the members' identity concerns will continue. In this type of group, in particular, efforts to understand internal barriers to defining one's values and roles as well as barriers from the environment will be undertaken in the formation phase and will continue throughout the life of the group. The ability to look at both of these dimensions is important. Culbert found, in his examination of consciousness-raising groups, that the duality in assessment can be approached through a general discussion of what members feel is "off" in their interaction with some system. This discussion is facilitated by asking questions such as the following: "In what ways could this feeling be a clue that the system expects something from me that does not seem natural or consistent with my self-interests? In what ways could this feeling be a clue that something which seems natural enough to me is considered inappropriate or inadequate by the system?"[3]

Culbert further noted that many people are reluctant to identify the way the "system" has contributed to their problem and that they will, consequently, blame themselves and their inadequacies for their role-related problems. He recommends confronting this issue and suggests an exercise in which members relate instances "where they accepted the blame or responsibility for something that went wrong only to receive a later indication that they were not at fault."[4]

It has been our experience that the opposite also occurs. Members project the blame onto the environment rather than realize that they compounded their problems when they failed to take moral stands and avoided experiences that would help them make moral decisions.

Another major aspect of assessment in these types of groups is the sort of personal identity the person has as well as the one he or she may be seeking. These identity issues have often been suppressed or confused by environmental forces. To "uncover" identity processes, members will often relate their "life stories" to the role in question.

Example: In a men's consciousness-raising group, each member told how he had viewed himself at various stages of his life in regard to the concept of "maleness" and how this self-presentation was viewed by family, friends, and others. The men reflected on such issues as how they wanted to express emotions, how some of them wanted to engage in activities not usually defined as "masculine," and how they experienced friendships with other men. They asked each other questions that helped to open some long "forgotten" hopes and experiences. Because they shared a common cultural heritage, as men in our society, their questions to each other brought out highly relevant material.

The type of discussion adds to an assessment of how each member had made important role choices previously and whether such choices led to satisfaction or frustration. Value conflicts still to be resolved can also be uncovered in this way. An examination of previous decision-making patterns illuminates the levels of self-awareness experienced by each member, his ability to engage in problem solving, and how he used or did not use relationships with others to work out problems relevant to his role. These dimensions can also be clarified as the members "process" whether and how to deal with such issues when they interact with each other. In such discussions, also, members will come to understand the kinds of role models they have, have not had, or still seek.

In addition to such people-oriented assessment, the members and the worker will engage in environment-oriented assessment to understand the nature of the environmental conditions experienced by members, and the environmental supports and changes required for clarifying one's norms and pursuing relevant goals. This is accomplished through looking at the norms in the member's personal situations and determining whether they are ambiguous, unacceptable to the member, or conflicted. Examples include traditional norms in one's family or workplace that are not acceptable and normative conflicts in one's community, school, or peer group. The member may even report experiencing punishment in these systems for considering new role-related behaviors.

As the members begin to determine their values in identity development groups, they will seek support from their environments. This requires the group to help the members determine which systems will be supportive, which can be changed to provide support, and whether the member can, with the help of other group members, even create new opportunity structures ranging from support groups to new conditions of employment.

During the group formation phase, in addition to assessment, the members will seek to clarify group purpose. This starts with a decision as to how the roles to be discussed in the group will be defined. Thus, in a men's consciousness-raising group, a discussion took place on whether all issues of concern to the members as men would be discussed or whether some were beyond the purview of the group. This determination of the scope of the group will also help the members review the appropriateness of any previous decisions such as the number of times the group will meet. Individual goals should also be defined at this stage so that their attainment can be measured and ultimately the effectiveness of the group evaluated. In a women's group, for example, one member developed the goal of making a decision as to what she thought should be her obligations in her marriage. Another member set as her goal a determination as to what kind of lesbian life style would fit her personality and her needs.

In the formation phase the members will also consider the general types of procedures they plan on using to achieve their goals, even though their ideas on this may change as events unfold in the group. They can be told by the worker that the following are the most common types of procedures:

Exercises to help them become more aware of their own beliefs, wants, and preferred life styles

Experiences to help them develop their self-concepts

Problem-solving discussions, particularly around choices about which they are ambivalent

Group discussion in which each member shares current and developing beliefs with others so that members will have a number of models available to expand their basis for choice

Process-oriented discussions so that members may better see how they present themselves as well as how they use others for support or change

Discussions of their life situations so they may compare their perceptions of reality with perceptions held by others

Goal Pursuit Tasks

The workers, in choosing techniques to help the members, will make decisions on targets to be affected by these interventions. For the person experiencing problems with personal beliefs, the internal target is most frequently an attitude. Workers, therefore, will draw on their knowledge about how attitudes are formed and how attitude conflicts are resolved. For example, we often modify our attitudes by our understanding of the world and how our behaviors affect it. The workers, therefore, will direct their attention to the kinds of cognitions that help form attitudes. For example, one group, in which prejudice against racial minorities was an issue, examined information on the accomplishments of members of that minority group as well as the damage to its members through lack of educational opportunity and exclusion from job markets.

Our attitudes are also linked to our emotions. Members in the group just mentioned feared members of the minority in question, but through discussion of their experiences, were able to see the irrationality of these fears. This led to a willingness to meet with some minority group members to learn more about their concerns and consequently to further reduce their fears.

In an identity development group, the members, after they have clarified their attitudes and the forces that have produced them, will usually seek to change aspects of their environments that are in conflict with their new values or that hinder achievement of objects based on such values. Members will decide to confront the actions of others who deny them opportunities to live according to their values; they will also seek to create opportunities for themselves or to challenge the ways they are prevented from gaining access to these opportunities. As an example, members of a gay group were more determined after a consciousness-raising group experience to challenge people who express stereotypes about gay persons and to demand their rights to hold jobs and to secure promotions based on their skills rather than on their sexual orientations.

Culbert presents a model for development of consciousness-raising groups that can be used to identify some of the major techniques used for identity development. His first stage is incorporated in our discussion of group formation tasks in such groups, when members are helped to identify aspects of systems that are discrepant with their individual needs. Culbert's second stage is "understanding ourselves and the system."[5] In this phase, he recommends that members work to develop a better understanding of themselves, that is, "how we work and what we need" as well as of the systems with which they interact.

In the process of analysis of self and relevant systems, members sometimes hold stereotyped perceptions or make inferences from their existing picture of reality. The worker should seek to offset this limited way of thinking by asking members to examine their concrete experiences rather than their "pet theories." The members can discuss how such experiences relate to defects in their social situations as well as to incorrect or limited views of themselves. This process is enhanced when members ask themselves the following types of questions: "If what I am feeling now (about my situation or my values or my needs) is an example of a more basic issue, what would that be? What is it about my qualities and the organizations, agencies, and other systems I have contact with that could have produced some of the conflicts I am experiencing?"[6]

Members discussing such questions may discover both similarities and differences among themselves. When only a few people identify a particular conflict, this may indicate that the issue is related to their needs and abilities; when a larger number of group members discover similarities, this will usually indicate dysfunctions in their environments.

One of the exercises that can be used to help members gain a clearer idea of how their social behaviors indicate their needs is "Role Nominations." In this exercise, members are given a list of various "roles" such as initiator, encourager, and dominator. The members check off the roles that have been enacted by each of the group members during group meetings. The "nominations" for each member are then tallied, and a group discussion of the results is held.[7]

Another exercise for this purpose is "Adjectives." In this activity, members are asked to think of the person with whom they have the most satisfactory relationship and to write three adjectives describing that person. Members then do the same for the person with whom they have the least satisfactory relationship. After this, the group worker explains that this can also tell a great deal about the values of the members. The members, usually in dyads, discuss what they have learned about themselves from this exercise.[8]

An understanding of relevant systems can be enhanced through answering questions such as the following:

1. What do you think your (boss, wife, teacher, and so on) expects of you and other people in the system?
2. How powerful is the person referred to in question 1 compared to others, including yourself?
3. How strongly does that person want to retain you as a member of the system?
4. Diagram the system in terms of its subsystems, for example, the people most closely allied to one another in the system, and the people most antagonistic to one another.

Culbert states that, in the third stage of a consciousness-raising group, the members should develop a better understanding of their relationship with the system. This should grow out of the previous stage when members increased their knowledge of both themselves and the system. He sees this understanding facilitated by response to the following types of questions.[9]

1. What are the goals we hold for our interactions with the system and what means do we use to attain them?
2. How do you think the system views you?
3. How do we influence the system and how does it influence us?

A major function of group discussion of these questions is to point out the assumptions members make in their answers. Sometimes this will require the group members to confront the individual regarding any resistance to examining such assumptions.

Example: In a men's consciousness-raising group, a member stated that his wife expected him to make the major family decisions; she became quite upset when he refused to do so. The members pointed out that there was a series of assumptions here about what his wife "really" wanted and why she became upset. One member stated that he had had a similar pattern and later found out that his wife feared that he planned on leaving her when he refused to continue making decisions; she actually resented his power but feared being left alone even more.

The fourth stage, according to Culbert, is one of "formulating alternatives."[10] The ability to do this should flow from a better understanding of member-system transactions and related assumptions. Specifically, "We do this by noting how assumptions which have been characterized by our relationship with the system are inconsistent with what we have learned about our own needs, interests and ideals."[11] These alternatives, logically, can include changes in the system or in our behavior with reference to the system. In the example of the husband who thought he made too many decisions, the alternatives he listed included (1) developing a different pattern of decision making in the system, such as working toward consensus on issues; (2) engaging in mutual problem solving; and (3) changing his relationship to the system by refusing to make decisions and explaining the role he would like to have in the family. Group members are helpful in this process because of their ability to suggest alternatives. They can also help members analyze the consequences for themselves as well as for others of carrying out each alternative.

The final stage of such a group is "affecting the lives of others."[12] Culbert makes the excellent point that effective consciousness-raising requires that the member secure the support of others outside of the group in this endeavor. This requires that these outside people, to some degree, have their "consciousness raised." Women in a consciousness-raising group will require that men see how they also are oppressed by stereotyped male roles; gay persons will require "straight" people to see the limitations in some definitions of that role (for example, narrow definitions of male and female "behaviors"); adolescents will require that relevant adults question "adult" roles that are too rigid and authoritarian or even too flexible and seductive. The same can be said of the "alter" group in relationship to any role that serves as the focus of consciousness-raising.

In this last stage of the consciousness-raising group, the members will help each other plan how to receive the aforementioned support and change. This can often be initiated by what Culbert calls "friendly dialogue," which can even lead to others seeking support for a reexamination of their positions through formation of their own groups. He also believes that, in this stage, members need support to work for long-term institutional changes in ways that guarantee the rights of others to do the same in their own interests.

Evaluation

One of the major aspects of evaluating the effectiveness of an identity development group is determining whether members have clarified values related to the role dealt with in the group. To effect this, members can decide the values around which they experience the most conflict. At early meetings and at subsequent points in the life of the group, they can rate the certainty of their value stance.

Example: One group, devoted to helping adolescents with confusion on sexual issues, developed questions such as the following:

Do you believe that people of your age, if they have "mature feelings," should have sexual intercourse if they wish?

_____ yes   _____ no

How certain are you of this belief?

_____ Very certain

_____ Somewhat certain

_____ Slightly certain

_____ Not certain at all

Members can also make ratings on additional scales to indicate how likely they are to declare their beliefs and act on them. Members can also indicate whether they have identified changes that they wish to make in themselves or their situations to actualize their values. Progress in accomplishing such changes can be charted using some of the measures described in Chapter 9.

On a group level, members can rate whether specific exercises, discussions, or meetings have helped with any of the preceding situations. The effectiveness of such events can also be assessed by using a value assessment instrument prior to and following the event.

An Example

A group of nine men came together through a series of mutual friends to examine aspects of the male role. They were dissatisfied with some of the ways they had been leading their lives, which they attributed to the changes taking place in sex roles in our society. They sought help from a local community mental health agency and were assigned a group worker from the agency staff to help facilitate their group. The following are excerpts from some group meetings.

First Meeting.   The men began the meeting with a "round" in which each man spoke of his feelings about coming to the group. Some of these feelings included fears about confidentiality, eager anticipation about what the group could become, anxiety about being a group composed only of men, and doubts about what such a group would accomplish. There was some "cross talk," but it was limited and guarded. The group worker spoke empathically about their feelings and acknowledged that these were realistic in a group such as this. He gave recognition to the members for taking the risk in coming and speaking openly about feelings.

Much of the first meeting was then spent negotiating group operating procedures such as meeting times, length of meetings, and rules about absences. The purposes of the group were also discussed, such as the idea that this was not a "therapy" group, although the members expressed some ambiguity and confusion about the differences between this group and therapy. Some of the ideas around which there was a consensus were that the group was to help clarify what they wanted to be like as men; that they would have to discuss their relationships with women as well as other men; that this would entail self-disclosure; and that they wanted feedback from each other as well as an opportunity to compare experiences. It was also evident, by the end of the meeting, that a few of the men thought of themselves as "gay," several as "heterosexual," and at least two as possibly "bisexual." Some others had lived their lives as heterosexuals but were not sure what their feelings were about other men as friends.

The men discussed how they would like to conduct their next meeting. The worker suggested that they spend some time telling about their lives so that they might get to know each other better. When the worker asked at the end of the meeting how the members thought the meeting had gone, they expressed positive reactions. He also asked if the members were committed to continuing the group, which was also strongly supported.

Second Meeting.   At the second meeting, one of the men was not present, arousing speculation as to the meaning of his absence. The group again began with a "round." Several men spoke about how enthusiastic they were after the last meeting and how eager they were for this one. One member spoke of some anxiety about the variety of sexual orientations in the group. There was little response to this, and the worker indicated that this might be a "scary" topic and that the group should discuss this further when they were "ready."

The group spent the bulk of the meeting with two members telling their "stories." The first to speak, Bob, was thirty years old and a professional psychologist. He talked about his family composition as he was growing up and about the sadness he still felt about his father's death when he was an adolescent. He indicated that he was married and had recently become a father of a son and that this had caused him to think a lot about himself and *his* father. He offered a number of recollections of his father—some very positive, although he also spoke of situations when his father had been uncaring or even hostile to him. With some anxiety, he spoke about a homosexual "affair" he had in college before he was married. He had, however, discussed this with his wife and had reached an agreement with her that he would seek no sexual experiences with either sex outside of marriage. This was said somewhat blandly, which was commented on by one of the members. Almost all of the members asked Bob questions about his life or briefly indicated that they had had similar experiences or feelings.

Sixth Meeting.   By the sixth meeting, all of the members had told their "stories." One member had dropped out, explaining that he did not have time for the group, although several members thought he was intimidated by the frank tone of the meetings. One of the members said he still was not sure what the other members thought "masculinity" meant. When others echoed this concern, the worker suggested several exercises that could help. The worker had brought a large pad of newsprint, and he asked members to suggest adjectives often applied to men. The list generated included "strong," "unemotional," "aggressive," and "athletic." The worker asked the men to suggest adjectives they thought applied to themselves, whether or not these were on the first list. The new list included "tender," "artistic," "unsure," and "funny." A lengthy discussion then took place about the similarities and differences between the lists and the reasons for these.

Eighth Meeting.   At the eighth meeting, one member, Jim, said that he had a serious problem and that he wanted to know what the rest of the members thought about it. He had been having an "affair" with a woman that his wife did not know about. With the help of the worker and the members, he talked about some of his reasons for the affair; these included his desire to "still be free"; his belief that people should act on their feelings; and his dissatisfactions regarding his relationship with his wife. The other members asked Jim questions to clarify the situation, such as his sources of dissatisfaction with his wife and his expectations regarding the other woman. Ultimately, the discussion moved to consideration of ways he could change his relationship with his wife as well as the implications of carrying out various alternatives.

The worker asked the members to consider whether there were some general issues in Jim's situation that affected all of them. This led to a discussion of the values and consequences of monogamous and nonmonogamous relationships.

During the discussion of Jim's problem, one member, Harold, became quite critical of the self-centered way he thought Jim was handling his life. This led to a hostile exchange between Jim and Harold, and it was obvious to the worker that the members were fearful such anger could "bust up" the group and that this kind of issue was likely to arise at this stage of a group's development. The worker, therefore, supported a discussion of the members' feelings and values regarding conflict and expressions of anger. While time constraints prevented this discussion from continuing too long, the members agreed this was an important topic for them.

Analysis.   In this sample of some of the issues in a men's group, many of the principles previously discussed are illustrated; these include the effects of the similarity in role concerns and small size on what became a cohesive group. The group also began in a fairly typical way to become acquainted with each other and to share role concerns. The worker was supportive during the formation period through his use of empathic responses and his identification of issues for discussion. When necessary, he supplied programmatic experiences to facilitate group development. He was aware of process issues such as the conflict that arose between Jim and Harold and the fears generated by early disclosure of intimate material. He also was aware when one person's input reflected universal concerns, such as the constraints placed on individuals through their relationships. The group still had not progressed to where members could emphasize alternatives in their goals for themselves and their "systems" and work toward these, but that clearly was the group phase they were approaching.

Summary

In this chapter, we reviewed the nature of identity development groups and described their similarity to groups referred to as consciousness-raising. We discussed the worker's tasks in preplanning such groups, including decisions on composition and specific definitions of purpose. The phase of group formation was then considered, and we described the assessment issues most prevalent in identity development groups. In discussing the phases when goal attainment is at the forefront, we used a paradigm developed by Culbert to conceptualize the phases present in consciousness-raising and, perhaps, in all identity development groups. Some issues in evaluation of identity development groups were described, followed by a brief case example of one such group.

Endnotes

1. Samuel A. Culbert, "Consciousness-Raising: A Five Stage Model for Social and Organizational Change," in *The Planning of Change*, 3rd ed., eds. Warren G. Bennis and others (New York: Holt, Rinehart & Winston, 1976): 231.

2. Ibid.: 233. Because of the relevance of consciousness-raising activities for identity development groups, we shall be making many references to the consciousness-raising experience.

3. Ibid.: 236.

4. Ibid.: 237.

5. Ibid.

6. These questions are similar to some posed by Culbert, *Consciousness-Raising*: 238.

7. For details on this exercise, see J. William Pfeiffer and John E. Jones, eds., *A Handbook of Structured Experiences for Human Relations Training*, II, rev. (LaJolla, Calif.: University Associates, 1974): 72–75. The reader can consult this series of annual handbooks for many other useful group exercises.

8. For details on this exercise, see J. William Pfeiffer and John E. Jones, eds., *Handbook of Structured Experiences for Human Relations Training*, V (LaJolla, Calif.: University Associates, 1975): 114–15.

9. Culbert, *Consciousness-Raising*: 239–41.

10. Ibid.: 241–42.

11. Ibid.

12. Ibid.: 242–44.

Chapter *12*

Working with Groups to Enhance Skill Attainment

The skill attainment purpose of groups is to help members fulfill the requirements of roles that they aspire to or are already in. This might be a role of student, parent, spouse, employee, friend, or retired person. Examples of groups related to anticipated roles are those for people approaching retirement or graduation or parenthood. Examples of groups for people already in roles and experiencing difficulties in fulfilling role requirements because of personal behaviors, barriers present in the situation, or both, are those for school children with classroom difficulties, for parents with problems raising their children, and for teenagers without friends. Skill attainment groups, therefore, may be thought of as prevention-oriented compared to other types of groups.

The skill attainment purpose is sometimes the major one fulfilled by the group. To some degree, however, it is present in all groups. Therefore, the approaches to group work described in this chapter may be appropriately used whenever this issue predominates.

Several strategies are used in groups with skill attainment purposes, and they shall often be referred to in this chapter. These strategies are social skills training, task-centered group work, and behavior modification in groups.[1] All these approaches have educational components, an emphasis on skill, and a concern with helping the member identify and contract for specific changes that will enhance personal functioning. Social skills training groups usually focus on specific components of social skills such as assertiveness, communication, and initiating and maintaining relationships. The techniques for training include presentation of models, discussion of principles, role playing, and homework assignments. Task-centered work involves helping members select a task that will ameliorate a problem. Behavior modification in groups helps members understand social-learning principles and apply these in their lives. These social-learning principles include the modification of circumstances under which a behavior takes place or the likely consequences of behaving in specified ways—consequences that may be pleasant or aversive.

Pregroup Tasks

One principle in groups with a skill attainment function is that members should have similar relevant roles. This is because the strategy for work with such groups has a strong educational component; this can best be accomplished when members can be served by similar or common educational experiences, when they can accomplish tasks in the same sequence, or when the commonalities in members' roles facilitate the use of the group as a support system. Common environmental barriers may also be overcome if the members act together.

The worker, in assessing clients prior to the first meeting, will seek to learn the roles likely to be targeted by group members. This may require some prioritizing of their concerns prior to the beginning of the group. Thus an individual who sought help with parenting functions as well as assertiveness with her employer was asked to indicate which of these caused her the most concern. Since it was the parenting issue, she was invited to join a parents' skill-training group.

Prior to the first meeting, the worker should also assess the skills already possessed by the person in fulfilling the role because, while some homogeneity in this respect is not essential, it is desirable. Potential members also may vary in their skills which can enrich the group. The group will have problems in establishing cohesiveness and developing a coherent program, however, if the differences in skills are vast. As an example, a member of one social skills group had always been very shy and had very few friends. Another member had many relationships but experienced considerable difficulty in handling conflicts that arose in them. The former person required elementary training in initiating and sustaining conversations, while the latter did not—it was in later phases of relationships that his problems occurred.

Skill attainment groups are usually time-limited, short-term groups that meet from ten to twenty times. Because they usually prepare members for specific roles, their content is focused and their educational approach often allows for something analogous to a "curriculum." This short-term framework can be made more feasible if members are prepared for the group prior to the first meeting. In task-centered groups, for example, the worker will help the members define the problem that concerned them as well as the role to which the problems are related. Then the initial activity of the group will be to clarify and reaffirm the relevant roles as well as the problems to be resolved—although the latter are sometimes modified as members experience the reality of the group. If this work is not done in advance, the short-term plan for the group is sometimes unrealistic.

Example: In the preparation of a group of young adults with problems in separating from their families, each prospective member was helped to clarify how he or she wished to work on functioning as an independent adult. One member defined the problem as handling parents imposing advice on him; another as establishing a separate residence against parental opposition; a third as helping the family be less dependent on him for advice and direction. (This group provides the extended example used later in this chapter.)

In short-term groups, if the types of worker interventions are known in advance, these should also be explained to the members. In a task-centered group, members receive an explanation of the task concept. They are told that they will be helping each other identify and work on tasks related to their problems. In assertiveness groups, members are often given "handouts" on the meaning of an assertive philosophy and are told about the sequence of activities (that is, learning about the meaning of assertion, assessing their own interactions, practicing, and then applying *new ways* of interacting).

When the intervention to be used is known, this will also have an impact on how members will be selected for the group. Some people will be able to make use of planned formats, while others will not. This issue can be assessed by noting carefully the response of the prospective member during the worker's explanation. The worker can always opt to modify the format. Also, initial interviews will have disclosed that for some members one format will be more useful and appropriate than another.

If the skill attainment group has a fairly structured program, the group can accommodate a larger number of members than other groups. Some groups devoted to parent training, for example, will enroll as many as fifteen to twenty members. The worker can still, when appropriate, subdivide the group into "buzz groups" for further discussion of selected topics. The larger group can also be used by people who are fairly adequate in their role functioning, such as many parents, college students, employees, and trainees. On the other hand, if the group members are young or vulnerable in other ways, or the technology calls for discussion and feedback, a size of about seven to ten members will be best. An example of this was a group we categorized as a skill attainment group: a group of developmentally disabled young adults seeking to learn how to meet their sexual and affectional needs in socially acceptable ways. Even though a "training" format was used, the amount of personal support and problem solving required in the group necessitated a small group.

In the formation of any type of skill attainment group, the worker must be aware of stereotypes and biases that may develop. Gambrill and Richey have investigated a number of these as they relate to gender issues in social skills training.[2] Men and women entering a group may present a socially desirable image rather than one that truly meets their needs. Men may underestimate their social anxiety, and women may overestimate their assertiveness since both of these responses are subject to gender stereotypes. Social workers involved with social skills groups may mistakenly expect men, more than women, to emphasize reduction of social anxiety since women might be defined as more emotional and excitable. Still another set of stereotypes cited by Gambrill and Richey relates to sexual orientation:

> *For example, lesbian women may join a social skills group to increase contacts with other women, not with men, or their goals may be related to career advancement and not be relationship focused. The sexual orientation of group members may not be at all obvious. This discretionary visibility (whether sexual orientation is disclosed) may mislead a trainer into making faulty assumptions about desired goals. Reluctance to disclose a deviant sexual orientation may be increased by failure of the trainer to overtly recognize alternative life style.[3]*

This means that group workers must be sensitive to members' wishes regarding appropriate social behaviors other than traditional views of how men, women, blacks, whites, or members of any other group are *supposed* to behave.

Group Formation Tasks

In the first stage of group development, even though the purposes and procedures to be used in the group have been discussed individually, they should be discussed again in the group-as-a-whole. Members who did not "hear" everything will then have another opportunity to understand and react to the plans for the group. It is also likely that when members actually see who is present and hear something of their "story," they will want to modify the concerns they intended to bring to the group. The opposite can also happen: members who were reluctant to discuss some aspects of their lives, at least initially, when confronted with the actual group composition may be more ready to do so because their similarity to other members reduces anxiety about reactions of other group members to their "deficiencies" or "weaknesses."

The amount of problem specification that takes place in a skill attainment group will be related to the strategy the worker plans on using. If the group is similar to what Radin calls a "socioeducation" group[4] (for example, certain types of family life education), it may be sufficient for the worker to understand the major tasks called for by the role and to check this out with the group. Thus a worker in a parent education group will already have in mind the development of skills in discipline, self-care, preparation for schooling, and so on, and will ask the group members whether these are, in fact, on their "agenda." In contrast, in a task-oriented group the worker will help the members to provide a fairly detailed description of their "problems" so that each member can be helped to develop tasks appropriate to their circumstances.

In behaviorally oriented, skill-training, and task-centered groups, a further assessment of the members' skill attainment concerns will take place so that interventions will be appropriate to these. In a behavioral group, this assessment will include a specification of: (1) the "antecedent conditions" in situations in which the member wishes to be able to act in a specified manner, as well as (2) the consequences the member receives or will receive when he or she behaves appropriately or inappropriately. A considerable literature exists on ways members can help each other complete this type of behavioral analysis.[5] Because members share many similar experiences, they are often astute in suggesting antecedents and consequences to each other. The possibility of setting up role plays can also help members engage in this type of assessment in the group.

In task-centered groups, there is less emphasis on assessment; rather the members help each other devise tasks to reduce problems. The process that most closely corresponds to assessment is that of designing a task suitable for the person to accomplish, given his or her motivation, personal capacity, and the realities of the situation. After a task has been chosen, the members will—with the help of the worker—help each other assess the barriers to accomplishing those tasks the members may encounter within themselves and in their environments.

Brim presents a useful framework in assessment relevant to skill attainment. It can be used in a variety of social skill training situations. Specifically, he states, "There are three things a person requires before he is able to perform satisfactorily in a role. He must know what is expected of him (both in behavior and in values), must be able to meet the role requirements, and must desire to practice the behavior and pursue the appropriate ends. It can be said that the purposes of socialization are to give a person knowledge, ability, and motivation."[6] This is summarized by Brim in a six-cell table as follows:[7]

	Behavior	Values
Knowledge	A	B
Ability	C	D
Motivation	E	F

In discussing this table, Brim explains that "Cells A and B indicate respectively that the individual knows what behavior is expected of him and what ends he should pursue; E and F indicate that the individual is motivated to behave in the appropriate ways and to pursue the designated values; C and D indicate that the individual is able to carry out the behavior and hold appropriate values."[8] Some ways the group and the worker can assess the member relevant to Brim's formulation are now given.

Cell A.   The member is asked to describe the behavior that he or she thinks is appropriate to the situation; alternatively, the members can be shown examples of appropriate and inappropriate behavior to see if they recognize what is called for in the situation.

Cell B.   The member is asked what the goals or objectives of the behavior are.

Cell C.   An examination is made of the member's ability to perform the behavior. This can be accomplished through the members either describing to the group how they acted in the relevant life situation or role playing a simulated version of the situation as the other members and worker identify their degree of skill.

Cell D.   As Brim indicates,[9] some people are "unable" to hold certain values because of "conflict within the personality." This is illustrated through the example of a son who did not pursue the value of going to college because he perceived this as placing him in competition with his father's record.[10] Group workers deal with many group members who have difficulties holding desired values because of psychological and social conflicts. Often these must be resolved by the members before they can invest themselves in skill attainment activities.

The assessment of the inability to hold particular values is a subtle process. The sign of this often comes from the member's nonverbal cues. A member may proclaim commitment to a goal or a value while acting uncomfortable or showing inappropriate expression of emotion. Other members may see, in the member's behavior in the group or outside of it, that the individual's commitments are lacking or in conflict.

Cells E and F.   Members should examine whether there are any reinforcers in the member's natural environment for engaging in the appropriate behaviors or for proclaiming the goals and values that will support these behaviors.

This type of assessment will help members and workers plan appropriate activities for skill attainment. If, for example, values or motivation are lacking, the group's attention to increasing the members' abilities may be fruitless.

An analogous assessment of the environment must take place in skill attainment groups. Members are unlikely to work very hard to adapt themselves to roles that there will be no opportunity to pursue. School children who perceive that their teachers will not give them the help they need; trainees in job programs who know about racial or sex discrimination or a recession in the relevant industry; elderly people who are aware their families do not wish them to be active in the community—these people will be frustrated by programs geared only to these behaviors and skills. These systems can be assessed by examining the experiences members and others have had with such environments. On occasion, also, members will be asked by the group to test out the opportunities in relevant systems available for group members.

In examining opportunity structures, members should perceive whether role steps are defined and properly paced. Earlier we referred to a group of developmentally disabled young adults who were helped with affectional and sexual behaviors. In addition to their learning how to deal with such situations, appropriate opportunities had to be permitted them, such as social occasions with the other sex, dating, and ultimately, for some, engagement and marriage. These "steps" were not defined by their parents and caregivers or graded in any way. Thus some members were given too much responsibility for social contacts and others too little. The worker, with the help of group members, undertook an assessment of this, and as a result, meetings were held with people in the environment who could bring about the necessary changes for clarifying and pacing such opportunities.

Based on these types of assessments, the worker and members will choose targets for the group's activities. As we discussed in reference to Brim's work, these targets may be any combination of members' behaviors, attitudes, and cognitions (knowledge) required for the roles the members seek to fulfill. Along with this, we have pointed out the futility of such role preparation when the environmental opportunities for role performance are limited. Thus associated aspects of the environment must also be targeted for change.

In a group of school children experiencing learning problems, the group worker and the members targeted the members' skill of paying attention to the teacher as well as the members' level of motivation for school success. In addition, the school was deficient in its opportunity structures in that remedial instruction to help these children "catch up" was lacking. The worker helped the members compose a petition to their teacher and the principal in which this service was requested.

Also, during the formation period of the group, the members are helped to determine their skill attainment goals. Almost always, in such groups, it is possible to attain a high level of precision in such formulations, and this accomplishment, itself, goes a long way toward enhancing socialization processes in the group.

Goal Pursuit Tasks

One of the most frequently used procedures in social skills groups is behavioral rehearsal. In this activity the worker helps the members role play or in other ways simulate the behaviors they seek to possess. The following are some of the steps in this process:

1. The member, through play or description, presents an example of the way the situation is customarily handled.
2. Members, with the help of the worker, suggest changes in the way the member acts. These changes are often guided by general principles the group has learned. Examples of these from assertiveness training are "giving and receiving compliments" and "carrying on social conversations."[11]
3. The member has an opportunity to clarify suggestions from the group and to plan how he or she will act.
4. A member of the group is chosen to play the "alter" in the role play and is briefed by the member learning the behavior.
5. The role play is enacted.
6. After the role play, members *first* state the positive aspects of the performance. Members then make suggestions for improvements.
7. The member should plan occasions (homework assignments) outside the group to try out the behavior. At subsequent meetings, the member should report on this. Additional modifications and rehearsals may then be required.

Another major procedure in skill attainment groups is modeling. A number of different people can model behaviors that the member desires to learn. Members who have successfully mastered the behavior can demonstrate it in role plays or can describe how they handled situations outside the group. The worker can also demonstrate behaviors. Members may select people outside of the group whose behaviors they desire to emulate. Workers can also play tapes and films that present good examples of handling situations relevant to the members' concerns.

In task-centered groups, any of the preceding procedures can be used to help accomplish tasks. The philosophy underlying task-centered work, however, calls for the maximum involvement of the group members in selecting their own tasks. The worker will illustrate the task concept by appropriate examples so that members will understand what is required. In our experience, the first members to select tasks do so slowly. The process, however, serves as a model for members who subsequently choose their tasks more quickly. In a homogeneous group, members may also select similar tasks, which is another reason for the acceleration in this process with time.

Rooney describes some innovative approaches for helping group members define tasks and accomplish tasks.[12] In working with a group of high school youths, he proposed that members list their tasks as well as their progress on these tasks on long sheets of paper. These lists were then placed on the walls. He, as the worker, modeled this technique by creating his own list of tasks, such as activities he had promised to carry out to help the members achieve their goals. Members also formed a "buddy system" and worked in pairs to select means of overcoming barriers to task accomplishment.

During the task accomplishment phase, members are helped with their tasks as follows: they can rehearse them through group role playing or through verbally reviewing with other members how they plan to handle specific situations. They also will secure support from other members for carrying out their tasks. This support can be supplied as members empathize with each other regarding their feelings about their tasks, as they reinforce one another with praise or even through awarding "tokens," and as they encourage one another to "keep on."

Problem-solving activities will also be used as members encounter problems in carrying out their tasks. The customary problem-solving phases of collecting information, identifying alternatives, evaluating alternatives, and carrying out the most desired alternative will, consequently, be used in such task situations.

"Coaching" is another approach used to help members carry out tasks. It can also be used in analogous situations in other kinds of skill attainment groups.[13] Coaching involves helping the member create a series of intermediate goals, secure information from other members on task activities, obtain support when it is needed, ask for advice, and even request that the worker or other members be present when the member works on the task in the actual life situation.

In behavioral groups used for skill attainment purposes, a major emphasis is placed, throughout the life of the group, on helping members define precisely their problems in skill attainment and monitor changes through such measures as behavioral counts. Members are assisted in helping each other develop behavioral change plans through acquiring an understanding of social-learning theory. In adult and other literate groups, this can be done by helping members read and understand texts designed for the lay person.[14]

As in task-centered groups, members of behavioral groups are often given homework assignments. These involve either monitoring behaviors or trying out approaches to behavioral change. To enhance this, workers can issue assignment forms to members to keep in individual notebooks. Assignments are recorded as well as the effects of carrying out the assignment. These personal accounts also can reinforce the members' participation in the program.

The worker will also train the members in a variety of behavioral change procedures. These include choosing appropriate schedules of reinforcement and reinforcers as well as procedures for altering dysfunctional thought processes and communication patterns.[15]

The sequence of activities in social skills training groups has been fairly standardized. First sessions are spent describing and planning subsequent ones. A sequence of skills is taught through exercises and "homework" assignments. Opportunity is provided for members to describe or enact experiences related to the skills and to engage in problem solving. An assertiveness training group, for example, might offer exercises in the first meetings to teach members how to say "yes" and "no," how to initiate social conversations, how to identify personal rights, and how to assert these rights.[16]

Because of the problems some members have in learning and applying these skills, group workers have sought to understand how to overcome many obstacles, such as members' thought patterns that interfere with their ability to carry out desired behaviors. Members undergoing social skill training, therefore, should be taught how to recognize these patterns,[17] which include these statements people make to themselves: "one must have love all of the time from significant people," "one's life is bad when it does not go your way," "the solutions to life's problems should be found quickly," and "one cannot overcome the effects of past misfortunes."

When members find it difficult to apply some aspect of skill training to carry out a task or to perform a behavioral assignment, the worker and members can ask about the person's thoughts under those circumstances. When these serve as barriers to success, the member can be taught to make other self statements that will facilitate forward movement. For example, Lange and Jakubowski present a list of self statements that can help a person deal better with anger, such as "This is going to upset me but I know how to deal with it," or "Getting upset won't help."[18] While this approach may appear simplistic to some readers, its effectiveness has been well documented.[19]

Similarly, people involved in skill attainment experiences will often be hindered by their emotional responses. Often these responses consist of anxiety in the face of trying out skills, but they can also be excessive anger, jealousy, or sadness, the latter related to failure in carrying out tasks. Workers in such groups, therefore, must know how to respond empathetically to such emotions and to help members deal with them. Lange and Jakubowski, for example, describe several relaxation procedures in assertiveness training groups.[20]

Because skill attainment groups are so often oriented to educational procedures and task accomplishment, the worker should sometimes provide for a release of tension or a change of pace. Thus some of the "rounds" described in the previous chapter, in which members share their feelings at the moment, are appropriate. Members may also benefit from a "half-way-through" party or other social occasion. Rose, for example, describes a social skill training group for fourth and fifth grade boys that met twice a week for half-hour sessions for ten weeks.[21] At the first meeting, members were given a cookie on entering and a token for sitting down. The children worked for tokens to be exchanged for such prizes as match box cars. When individual reinforcers were gradually withdrawn, group rewards included a field trip to the university to make a video tape and a picnic at the local park.

In the earlier days of group work, most workers worked in community centers and settlement houses. These agencies provided skill attainment (that is, socialization) experiences through club activities and special interest groups (for example, arts and crafts, dramatics). These groups attained their goals through the worker's facilitation of group development and group decision making and the selection of activities appropriate to the members' development tasks. While we are not offering a detailed discussion of group work in such situations, we believe that many of the procedures we have described throughout this book, and particularly in the chapters on identity development and skill attainment, are useful to facilitate the members' acquisition of skills in such groups.

Evaluation

In behaviorally oriented groups, workers will help members evaluate their success in skill attainment through devices previously described, such as behavioral counts, self reports of coping with targeted situations, and reports by significant others. The latter can include behavioral checklists completed by teachers, employers, and parents. Rose, for example, has developed a children's behavior code employed by observers in the child's academic classroom and gym class.[22] In one project, Rose also used charts showing the number of behavioral assignments completed by each child.

Reid and his colleagues have developed a scale for evaluation of task-centered groups.[23] The problems on which members are working are listed, with changes rated on a 10-point scale ranging from "problem greatly aggravated" to "problem no longer present." The mid-point of the scale ("5") represents "no change"; smaller numbers represent degrees of problem aggravation, and larger numbers represent degrees of problem alleviation. In the interest of reliability, workers secure these ratings from the client and a collateral person and also make their own ratings.

Lange and Jakubowski discuss a number of measures for evaluating assertiveness training that can also be used for a broad range of social skills training groups. One category of measurement is so-called "paper-and-pencil" measures. Examples of this are the College and Adult Self-Expressions Scales[24] and the Gambrill-Richey Assertion Inventory.[25] Behavioral measures can also be used, such as examining the behavior of members during role plays. The worker can create these although Lange and Jakubowski also cite some that have already been developed.[26] When such role plays are used, raters are trained to assign scores to the member along such dimensions such as eye contact, length of conversation, loudness, and appropriateness of affect.

An Example

A group of three men and two women were organized into a group by a staff member of the counseling service of a university. All of these members had come to the agency asking for help with issues involving their emotional separation from their parents. The worker believed that a task-centered approach would help these members attain the role of an adult rather than a "child" in their "families or origin." Prior to the first meeting, the worker had ascertained that these clients wanted to work on this problem. They were willing to join a task-centered group after this approach was explained to them. The following are excerpts from several group meetings.

First Meeting.   At the meeting, the members introduced themselves by name and told a little about their courses of study, their home communities, and their families. The worker explained again what a task-centered group was, and some further questions about this approach were raised and answered. The worker suggested that members tell each other about their family concerns. The first member to speak, Jack, described his parents and particularly his father as only being able to converse with him if they were offering him advice. Another man, Bill, described the pressures he received from his family to get married. Sally was about to graduate and wanted help to resist pressures from her parents to live with them when she returned to her home community. Phil stated his problem as dealing with his family's expectancy that now that he was the first family member to go to college, he could solve *all* the outstanding problems in his family. The worker encouraged the members to ask each other questions so that they could better understand each other's situations. This was done, although members primarily sought out similarities and differences in each other's family situations. The worker ended the meeting by suggesting that the topic of the second meeting should be to identify change goals for each member.

Fourth Meeting.   The two intermediary meetings were devoted to helping each member list long- and short-term goals. One purpose of this fourth meeting was to help members select tasks that would help them reach their goals.

Jack, whose problem was his "advice-offering parents," volunteered to "go first." His short-term goal was to discuss this problem with his parents in such a way that they would understand the kind of relationship he wanted with them, which was one in which each party would both give and receive advice. This type of goal obviously led to a definition of this task as conducting such discussions with his parents.

In the process of helping Jack develop this goal and task statement, the main problem of the group members was the tendency to hastily make suggestions as to how Jack should solve his problem. The members also asked Jack many questions irrelevant to the purpose of defining goals and tasks. The worker used this situation to continue to educate group members about the model; in this case, he continued to define and illustrate what goal and task statements were. (In other task groups, the worker has role played this process with a co-worker.)

The remainder of the meeting was spent developing tasks for the other group members. The process did quicken as members learned more about the nature of such tasks.

Sixth Meeting.   At the previous meeting, Jack had discussed with group members the kinds of statements he would make to his parents. At this meeting, the worker suggested that he role play these statements. Two members of the group agreed to role play the parents; by this time, they had heard enough from Jack that they thought they could do this realistically. The role play commenced, and after about five minutes Jack seemed at a loss for words. The role play was stopped, and the worker asked Jack to talk about his reactions. Jack indicated that he was feeling uncomfortable. After a little more reflection, he said that in some ways he was worried about how his "parents" were reacting. Sally wondered if he was concerned if his parents would still like him after this. Phil commented that perhaps he thought that his parents would begin to feel useless and old and that Jack would feel bad about being responsible for this. Jack said that both of these comments made sense. He wondered if the role players might have some feelings about what it was like to be his parents. A discussion then took place with the role players about their reactions. After this continued for a while, the worker asked if it was possible for Jack to ask for feedback from his actual parents on what they were feeling.

During this meeting, two other members asked for similar help with the planning of how to fulfill their tasks. Another two members briefly reported on their first steps in accomplishing their tasks, and they were given support and encouragement from the other members.

Analysis.   This example illustrates a number of processes typical of skill attainment groups. The educational components are clear as members learn about tasks associated with attaining adult status in their families. Members also work at establishing clear goals related to their roles. Since all members experienced similar problems, they provided optimum levels of support and empathy to each other. The homogeneity of the group allowed members to work in unison at the various processes required by task-centered work. The group composition also provided many opportunities for members to experience vicariously the consequences of carrying out similar tasks.

Summary

In this chapter we discussed the techniques and concepts that most pertain to skill attainment groups. We noted that three approaches are frequently used in such groups: behavior modification, social skills training, and task-centered work. Pregroup tasks were discussed, such as group composition and member preparation. The ways members are assessed in skill attainment groups were portrayed, as well as specific assessment issues when each of these major approaches is employed. The techniques workers use in the middle phase of the group were described, such as coaching, behavioral rehearsal, modeling, and reinforcement. The evaluation devices used by practitioners of these approaches were listed. The chapter concluded with a case example from a task-centered group.

Endnotes

1. An introductory discussion of these shall be presented in this chapter. For more detailed discussions of task-centered group work, see Eleanor Tolson, William Reid, and Charles Garvin, *Generalist Practice: A Task Centered Approach* (New York: Columbia University Press, 1995): 221–308. For behavioral approaches in groups, see Sheldon Rose, *Group Therapy: A Behavioral Approach* (Englewood Cliffs, N.J.: Prentice Hall, 1977). One detailed account of an aspect of social skills training is by Arthur J. Lange, and Patricia Jakubowski, *Responsible Assertive Behavior* (Champaign, Ill.: Research Press, 1976).

2. Eileen Gambrill and Cheryl Richey, "Gender Issues Related to Group Social Skills Training," *Social Work with Groups* VI (3/4) (Fall/Winter 1983): 51–66.

3. Ibid.: 58.

4. Norma Radin, "Socioeducation groups," In *Individual Change Through Small Groups*, ed. Paul Glasser, Rosemary Sarri, and Robert Vinter (New York: Free Press, 1974): 89–104.

5. See Rose, *Group Therapy*, pp. 26–40; H. Lawrence and M. Sundel, "Behavior Modification in Adult Groups," *Social Work* XVII (1972): 34–43.

6. Orville G. Brim, Jr. and Stanton Wheeler, *Socialization After Childhood: Two Essays* (New York: John Wiley, 1966): 25.

7. Ibid.

8. Ibid.: 25–26.

9. Ibid.: 26, footnote.

10. Ibid.: 41.

11. For exercises to teach these two skills, see Lange and Jakubowski, *Responsible Assertive Behavior*: 74 and 77, respectively.

12. Ronald Rooney, "Adolescent Groups in Public Schools," in *Task-Centered Practice*, eds. William J. Reid and Laura Epstein (New York: Columbia University Press, 1977): 168–82.

13. Anselem Strauss, "Coaching," in *Role Theory: Concepts and Research*, eds. B. Biddle and E. J. Thomas (New York: John Wiley, 1966): 350–53.

14. See, for example, Wesley C. Becker, *Parents Are Teachers: A Child Management Program* (Champaign, Ill.: Research Press, 1971).

15. See Rose, *Group Therapy*: 86–102, for a discussion of these and other procedures.

16. For descriptions of these exercises, see Lange and Jakubowski, *Responsible Assertive Behavior*: 69–113.

17. Many workers draw on the techniques of Albert Ellis for such cognitive changes; see A. Ellis, and Windy Dryden, *The Practice of Rational-Emotive Therapy*. (New York: Springer Publishing Co., 1987).

18. R.W. Novaco, *Anger Control: The Development and Evaluation of an Experimental Treatment* (Lexington, Mass.: Heath, 1975), as quoted in Lange and Jakubowski, *Responsible Assertive Behavior:* 150–51.

19. Ibid.

20. Lange and Jakubowski, *Responsible Assertive Behavior*: 169–72.

21. Sheldon D. Rose and Alison Roessle, "A Social Skill Training Group for Fourth and Fifth Grade

Boys," *Behavior Group Therapy* 1 (5) (September 1979): 2–12.

22. Ibid.

23. See "Task-Centered Group Recording Guide III: Final Session," School of Social Service Administration, rev. (Chicago, Ill.: University of Chicago, March 27, 1977).

24. J.P. Galassi, J.C. Delo, M.D. Galassi, and S. Bastein, "The College Self-Expression Scale: A Measure of Assertiveness," *Behavior Therapy* 5 (1974): 165–71.

25. Eileen D. Gambrill and Cheryl A. Richey, "An Assertion Inventory for Use in Assessment and Research," *Behavior Therapy* 6 (1975): 350–62.

26. R.M. McFall and A.R. Marston, "An Experimental Investigation of Behavior Rehearsal in Assertion Training," *Journal of Abnormal Psychology* 76 (1970): 295–303.

Chapter *13*

Working with Groups in Social Control Situations

In the two previous chapters, we presented some ways to work with groups whose members are in transition from one role to another or from one stage of a role to a later stage. As we stated previously, members of such groups are being helped with socialization tasks and, as such, are usually viewed as healthy, nondeviant, or prosocial members of the society. Their group activities are considered by many, including the members themselves, to be educational and voluntary. The group experience may be thought of as prevention in that the members are learning to cope with situations that often cause emotional illnesses and dysfunctional or illegal behavior in those who cannot cope.

In this chapter and the next, we shall describe how group workers facilitate groups for members viewed by society in opposite ways to the ones to which we have just referred, perhaps because of a failure in such socialization. Thus the latter members are characterized as criminals or delinquents on the one hand or as mentally or emotionally ill on the other. The group is considered as "treatment" or "rehabilitation" more often than as education. The overall function is one of *resocialization*.

At times the members recruited for such groups do not yet share some or all of the goals the agency has identified in offering such group services. Part or all of the group, in fact, may never move to this commonality of purpose with the agency. We have termed this phenomenon "working with groups in social control situations." The social control aspect is justified by the agency in that society, through legislative processes, has established the social control function and has created judicial and executive procedures to determine the individuals to whom it should apply. Thus people who break the law are placed on probation or sent by the courts to training schools or prisons. In an analogous manner, people who behave in bizarre ways or in ways dangerous to themselves or others can also, by judicial decree, be placed in mental hospitals or other psychiatric facilities.

The current term for these people is "involuntary clients."[1] In our discussion of these clients elsewhere, we point out that understanding their problems from an ecological point of view does not differ in many respects from understanding any other clients' problems. Thus we see socially deviant behavior as a product of *both* the individual's history and of her or his social context.[2] An important example of this is the association between being a member of an oppressed minority group and the likelihood of being incarcerated.

Blacks and members of certain other groups are overrepresented in arrests, convictions, and prison populations, even though studies indicate there is little relationship between race and crime. Thus law breakers are more likely to be treated aversively when they are members of such groups.[3]

Rooney, drawing upon social-psychological ideas, defines an involuntary relationship as containing one or more of the following elements:[4] (a) a person feels forced to remain in it because of physical or legal coercion; (b) the cost of leaving the relationship for the person is too high; (c) the person feels pressured to act differently in the relationship than she or he wishes to act.

There is some debate among social workers as to whether the term "client" should be applied to such individuals. We chose to refer to such group members as clients because we believe that practitioners are required to act in some way to benefit them, even if these members do not see what is done as beneficial. Admittedly there is an element of condescension in this formulation, but we think this is inevitable.

We also find that most involuntary group members have a degree of ambivalence regarding the group, although they may resist the group because it is imposed on them. On the other hand, they often recognize that the group may benefit them and, thus, experience conflict about this. This fits in with the ideas of *reactance theory*, which deals with the way people respond when their ability to do as they wish is infringed.[5] It is possible that the involuntary group member will become a voluntary one as he or she gets to know the social worker and the other group members better, comes to trust their sincerity, and sees these relationships as a means to accomplish personal goals.

Social workers should be aware of a number of legal issues in their work with involuntary clients in groups. One of these is *due process*, which means that individuals "are entitled to due process of law before they can be deprived of life, liberty, or property."[6] A case can be made that requiring group treatment deprives liberty unless all the protections of due process have been observed.

Another legal issue is *informed consent*. This requires that clients be given explanations of group treatment and consent to it. This consent must be based on an understandable explanation of group work, and how to do this is something group workers should further develop.

Based on these issues, we have developed a set of principles for work with involuntary clients:[7]

1. Respect the client's right to reject group work and "take the consequences."
2. Explain the rationale for group work, the group work methods to be utilized, and the evidence for the effectiveness of group work as fully as possible. Many of these clients have not been treated as intelligent beings; reinforcement of their awareness of their own abilities to learn and understand will help them approach future situations as opportunities to learn effective and socially acceptable solutions to problems.

3. Choose as many ways as possible to involve the involuntary client in decision making in the group, such as prioritizing issues for consideration, selecting problems on which to focus, or selecting among group approaches.
4. Recognize the right of group members to work toward changes designed to improve the relevant systems such as the service agency or other agencies.
5. Above all, recognize that the group member is an individual and not a clone of every other prisoner or patient (or whatever other term applies).

We do *not* believe that social work as a professional activity is controlled solely by the social mission of correctional or psychiatric institutions. This is similar to the work of teachers, doctors, or psychiatrists in such settings who supply professional services to "inmates" or "patients" in the interests of their individual growth and health needs. Such services do, however, complement the social control functions of the agency by making it more likely that the participants will be able to meet their own needs in socially acceptable ways.

Working with groups in these types of social control situations is closely related to the type of work with groups that we have termed "rehabilitation," which shall be discussed in the next chapter. Thus when the purpose of the group, as we conceive it, has been achieved and the members have identified the commonality between their desires and the goals of the agency, presumably they will seek help in attaining these mutually held objectives; the function of the group then becomes one of resocialization—for roles that are "alternative" in contrast to the previous ones. It is also possible that a "common ground" between the members' and the agency's purposes will not be found and that members will resist participation in the group, even after an extended period. In these cases, there may be no viable group work purpose that can be achieved. There are many measures, however, which we shall discuss later in this chapter, that workers can take to avoid such an impasse.

Ethical issues, in addition to those described earlier in this chapter, confront the workers in these situations. One is whether they should ever impose changes on a member. This is not a simple matter because there is a thin line between *coercing* a member and *urging* a member to consider alternative values and behaviors that the worker thinks will be beneficial. The complicating factor here is the power the agency wields contrasted with the power of the member—especially when the agency controls the client's access to discharge from the agency, thus the client's freedom. The worker is, in reality as well as in the perception of the member, associated with such power. The client's willingness to participate in the group, for example, may be used for or against him or her in a discharge proceeding.

In addition, the worker can be caught between two values: one is the self-determination in which members choose their own goals; the other is the respect the worker holds for the worth of the individual—what the individual is and may become—and this latter may justify strong measures to involve the member in activities that the worker believes could enhance or even save the individual's life.

There are no easy answers to such questions, and all workers, especially in social control settings, must struggle with them every day. We believe that the workers must discuss their dilemmas in this regard with members, especially if they expect the members to reciprocate and share *their* conflicts. Also, worker honesty in this regard is a first step in helping members protect themselves from improper pressures.

Another struggle for workers is to avoid being inappropriately co-opted by the agency, especially when the program is more custodial than therapeutic. For example, we interviewed some inmates of a federal prison regarding their experiences with social workers, including those facilitating inmate groups. One social worker was criticized by the inmates because they felt he had accepted the guards' attitude toward prisoners during a session. An example they gave was that when a prisoner spoke to this worker of his desire for a pass to visit his seriously ill wife, the social worker was unreceptive and communicated his belief that prisoners were always trying to "con" the system and, therefore, the request was not merited.

Another ethical issue arises when the clients in a social control situation are diagnosed as psychotic or developmentally disabled or not of legal age. We believe that in these situations, when the members are incapable of taking responsibility for themselves, the worker must consult with the families of such members regarding goals. Every effort, however, must always be made to secure informed consent. The worker might even consider establishing an advisory group of clients with whom to consult on procedures for protecting client rights in group situations.

As in all other chapters devoted to a specific type of group (Chapters 11–16) we emphasize that some groups are established primarily to fulfill a specific function such as a social control function, usually in correctional settings. On the other hand, many agencies form groups in which social control represents one of several functions. An example of this is the use of groups in some school settings. A school, concerned about disruptive behavior (such as students ignoring teacher requests, committing vandalism, or committing aggressive acts against other students), may form groups for stopping this behavior in addition to supporting the education of the members. The presence of such "mixed" goals can pose difficulties for group members as they negotiate the purposes of the group with the worker. Sensitive negotiation skills as well as clear and honest statements from the worker are essential in such situations.

The strategies for group work in social control situations must address several common conditions. Group members are likely to be involuntary, at least at first. Although group attendance is seen as leading to some external benefit, such as a recommendation for parole or probation, it does not mean that the member "really" wishes the group experience; however, the group worker must respond to this issue as a first task. While any individual change effort will meet with some resistance, even in voluntary situations, groups in social change situations often encounter this phenomenon.

A second condition is that members' behavior is socially deviant. This means that their behavior has been fostered by the social forces that promote deviance: denial of access to social resources such as jobs and education; pressure from deviant peers, the imposition of derogatory labeling, and so forth. Social control groups must confront these conditions that make it difficult, if not impossible, for the member to leave the deviant role. These conditions are often greatly present in poor communities and among those oppressed by virtue of their ethnicity. Social control groups must operate in ways that recognize these social conditions.

When groups are conducted in an institution for criminals or delinquents, the members are likely to be affected by the *inmate code*. This norm among inmates requires the individual to uphold his or her solidarity with other inmates by withholding information about them and by supporting them in any encounter with staff. As a result, members of groups in these settings resist discussing their reactions to each other in group meetings. Inasmuch as these reactions are the core of many group work approaches, workers must find ways of helping members confront this code.

If the barriers caused by the inmate code are to be surmounted, there must be a commonality of group and agency purposes. Correctional institutions are often coercive and punitive, and this can undermine the development of self-disclosure and confrontation in the group. The worker, consequently, must "humanize" the correctional setting.

The group can play a role in this humanization. For example, the author consulted in a state prison with a worker who sought to train inmates as group workers for other inmates. The process included lobbying the prison administration to secure legitimacy for this approach, then conducting a pilot program. Because of the success of the program, several guards were also trained as group workers, and some groups were co-led by an inmate and a guard, both supervised by the worker. This gradually led to a different and more positive attitude of guards to prisoners, and each group began to see the other as individuals rather than as clones.

Even in benign settings with social control functions, members will often resist a reconsideration of their values and behaviors. The strategies employed by group workers in such situations involve the creation of a strong and supportive group in which members are aware of their caring for each other. In this climate the members will employ techniques with one another that are confrontive and direct. A great deal of controversy exists, however, among group workers regarding interventions that involve strong confrontations.

Pregroup Tasks

A major factor in selecting members for and composing groups in social control situations is the nature of potential group members' existing group interactions. The interactional and social-psychological conception of deviance utilized in our approach to group work holds that such antisocial behavior is maintained by their interactions with their families and their peer groups, particularly the latter.

This view requires the worker to examine the peer group interactions of potential group members. Frequently the worker will attempt to work with the peer group itself as a "natural" group. This is the approach taken in such services as street gang work with delinquent adolescents.[8] In residential institutions with delinquent adolescents, the group, for group work purposes, is often the living group such as the "cottage" because this is where delinquent norms may be maintained.

In any case, in a pregroup assessment the worker will seek to determine the members' subcultural identifications. Members will be asked about the groups they belong to and the activities of such groups. The kinds of behavior the members condone should be investigated. Particularly important to note are the possible conflicts among the group members regarding their beliefs. This may indicate whether some motivation for change can come from such peer groups.

Motivation to either examine one's values and behaviors or to change them is also assessed during pregroup interviews. Few potential members are likely to have strong motivation for change or, if they have, to admit it to authority figures. Nevertheless, such motivation will help the group achieve the agency's objectives, and the presence of it in some members will facilitate consideration of alternative life styles in the group. The worker can assess this by asking the potential members about times they may have considered alternative goals, how they might now respond to new opportunities, and whether family members or other people in their social network are likely to support their entry into new roles.

A problem in group composition has been that the population in an organization such as a prison may not allow for much heterogeneity among members in life experiences, behaviors, and values. Members will, therefore, reinforce each other in their commitments to deviance. This does not preclude the use of groups, however. The worker can confront members about their adherence to such beliefs when the group has developed sufficiently to support members in dealing with such confrontation constructively. This type of confrontation, however, usually requires the members to be involved in other programs in the agency so that staff and participants in all programs can work together to promote a consideration of new roles.

Even under optimal conditions, however, the group composition will sometimes work against the achievement of the agency's objectives. A technique that workers have used to offset this is to "seed" the group with people who have been in the program long enough to have begun the process of personal change. Such "members" provide important models of how to overcome the pull of past social forces.

Groups that help members consider alternatives in their lives as well as attain related roles are usually not short-term groups but may involve members for many months. They may also be "open-ended" in that members "graduate" to new group experiences as they become ready. It is also possible to have a planned sequence of groups—the first one, to orient the members to the program and to promote a willingness to consider its values; the second, to help members make appropriate choices regarding their careers and begin to pursue them; and the last, either to facilitate termination from the program or to provide a supportive type of follow-up.

Members in many such programs are not prepared in any detail for the group because of the importance of helping members place most of their dependence on the group rather than on the worker. The group itself constitutes the strongest force for a reconsideration of norms. For this reason, also, such groups may not be as small as other social work groups and may have as many as ten to fifteen members. This allows for some members to be selected as models and for additional changes for heterogeneity, yet the group is not so large that a member becomes "lost."

Group Formation Tasks

In discussions of group development in this chapter, we draw from the guided group interaction material, cited previously, as a model of how groups may develop in social control situations. Based on our reading and experience, we believe there are general elements of development in most groups of this sort. As the reader will find in reviewing the literature cited here, there is considerable empirical support for this approach.

When a group is started in a social control situation, it is often hard work to overcome the initial distrust and hostility displayed by the members toward the worker and the agency and sometimes toward each other. Empey and Erickson describe a number of techniques used in the initial stages of a guided group interaction experience that are relevant to other social control situations as well.[9] They assume that members will behave in a manner that is "erratic and defensive" and, therefore, "the concern of a group leader should be with fostering interaction among group members and instilling some confidence that it might eventually be effective and rewarding.[10]

The recommended techniques are those, therefore, that will "foster and reward interaction" and that will teach members "that whatever interaction took place in a group and whatever progress was made, would depend on them, not just staff."[11] This is accomplished by showing sincere interest in what members say and by avoiding stereotyped responses often made by workers in these settings, such as "the stern disciplinarian, the loving father, the kindly friend, or the all-wise doctor." In a sense, this requires the worker to behave somewhat ambiguously which includes *not* declaring all of the rules and procedures to be followed in the group but casting these issues back to the members. This is in direct contrast to what workers do in skill attainment groups.

In social control groups, the members often seek formulas for the group and for their tenure in the agency. They will ask what they should be doing in the group and how this relates to their "stay" in the agency, particularly if it is a residential one and they have been committed there. Workers in guided group interaction programs are taught to redirect these questions back to the members for *their* ideas.

Another technique to encourage interaction and to set the stage for a willingness to use the group for problem solving is to ask the members to tell their "stories" (their histories) and to talk about their interests and feelings about the program. This also helps members find out from the group worker whether he or she will be understanding, supportive, and nonjudgmental.

The worker inexperienced with such groups will fear that the kinds of processes just described will continue indefinitely and that nothing worthwhile will be accomplished. The experience of such programs as guided group interaction is that members become bored with this activity and see that it, in itself, will not lead to discharge from the program. The members are then ready to consider using the group for problem-solving activity. The worker promotes this next phase by helping the members reflect on what they have been doing and why their inputs have been shallow. While a change in the group may not happen quickly, such discussion does prepare members to invest their energy in seeking the commonality between their needs and the agency goals.

Workers will receive much information during this formation period, however, that will help them assess the members. Such procedures as the members telling their "stories" will give information about the kinds of norms they are committed to and how these norms relate to their present and past social relationships. Whether members experience conflict about their deviance can be examined as well as their knowledge about the role alternatives and opportunities available to them.

Attention must also be paid to assessing the social barriers faced by the members. These include the effects of racism as well as of "deviant" labels placed upon them. Means will have to be sought to cope with these barriers.

Helping members choose new personal goals in social control-oriented settings must often be paralled by seeking changes at an agency level. Members who view the agency as unresponsive to their needs are unlikely to use the services of that agency to reexamine their own lives. The members have chosen their deviant careers in response to a lack of environmental opportunities and an unsympathetic environment, and an agency that recreates this will fail in accomplishing its purposes.

The assessment processes during this formation period must thus include an evaluation of agency conditions detrimental to group members. When this is done in good faith, it will encourage the members to look *also* within themselves for sources of their difficulties. The conditions frequently targeted in these circumstances are the resources the agency supplies the members (educational programs, recreation, physical facilities), the responsiveness of the staff to member concerns, the degree to which members can participate in agency decision making, the agency's procedures for disciplining members (use of punishment, arbitrary or excessive penalties, favoritism), and sexist and racist attitudes.

As implied by the preceding discussion, the development of the contract in social situations is more problematic than in any of the others we have outlined because it requires members to voluntarily reconsider and then change basic values. *This process only occurs when the agency is responsive to member concerns.* The intervention target thus must include the transactions occurring between the individual, the group, and the agency. After each participant in the interaction has made some changes, a contract for further client change becomes a realistic option.

Goal Pursuit Tasks

As we have stated, Empey and Erickson present a model for the development of guided group interaction groups that can be drawn on for other social control oriented groups. There are some distinguishing features of their type of treatment, however, that are not present in other programs, including that when guided group interaction is used as the treatment approach, the setting is frequently residential. The Provo, Utah, program was an exception in that the participants were assigned on the basis of a judicial process but lived in the community and only spent part of each day at the program center. Program features included group meetings and a paid work program, school attendance, or both.

The Provo program, like others of its kind, employed little overall formal structure to communicate to the boys that release from the program was simply a matter of conformity to the rules. The ambiguity created by this lack of structure, it was hypothesized, created anxiety that members turned to the group to relieve; it also elicited members' typical coping mechanisms and stimulated creativity in solving problems.

Because the boys were involved with each other outside of the group as well as in it, the group became the vehicle for dealing with many behaviors the boys observed and with which they confronted each other. The salience of the group was enhanced by granting it the power to help decide when each boy would be released. This was linked with whether the boy had worked on his problems in the group and had been open and honest with other members.

Earlier in this chapter, we described the formation period in such groups. This period ends as the members become frustrated with unproductive uses of the group and consider using the group for problem solving. Empey and Erickson refer to the next stage, then, as "stereotyped problem solving."[12] Members begin to raise concerns but are still well defended in how this is done. They ask questions they think they are expected to ask, and they give answers of similar quality.

The group worker during this period must be patient. Too early a confrontation will reinstitute the members' defensiveness and mistrust. On the other hand, the worker must be sensitive to genuine problem statements in contrast to the "role playing" of problem-solving processes members believe are of interest to the staff members.

The members' behavior during this period may appear, therefore, to be contradictory. Members are tentatively and ambivalently testing out the problem-solving potential of the group. Because this is a social control situation, steps in the direction of problem solving by some group members are seen by others as "giving in" to workers or currying favor with them, and members will criticize each other for this. Thus this phase is also marked by group conflict, and the worker is in a more strategic position if he or she mediates it rather than bears the brunt of it.

Empey and Erickson note that this type of conflict is intensified in those institutional settings into which members bring events that have occurred outside of the group— members' antisocial acts, for example, which may have affected other group members. As they state:

> *When a group encounters such problems, basic loyalties, basic beliefs, and commitments are subject to strain. Boys are torn between their own self-interests and those of others. In a prison, a rule that is enforced by staff as well as offenders is that everyone should do his own "time," and not mess with the "time" of others. Some of the same behavior can be expected in a community program. The pressures against those who would assume a reformer's role is [sic] considerable. That is why group members at this stage of development cannot be expected to run much risk in dealing with the problems that emerge.*[13]

The worker's role in responding to this type of situation must involve recognizing how difficult a period this is for members. What is at stake here, when members begin to discuss each other's behavior, is their choice between antisocial and prosocial norms. As members wrestle with the issues of their evaluation of each other's behavior, they begin, as Empey and Erickson point out, to take responsibility for making judgments rather than being solely the targets of judgments made by "authority." This conflict also results in members directing hostility displaced from each other to the worker.

Empey and Erickson remind the reader that discussion of behavior in this phase introduces members to the "reformation role"; this begins to make the group a "medium for change" and is a modification of the traditional staff-client relationship. The overall dynamic, therefore, is still that of building an effective group rather than of solving basic problems.[14]

The next phase in the group emerges as members begin to challenge each other's characteristic defenses. As Empey and Erickson wisely note, "Delinquents, like anyone else, do not enjoy a group in which daily interaction is characterized by perpetual tension, though they may not know what to do about it."[15] The alternative the worker encourages is greater openness and honesty to "get beyond existing facades." The important ingredient here is timing. Too premature a pressure toward openness can coalesce the group around a strongly antisocial member as protection against the strong feelings that emerge.

If these issues are resolved to a sufficient degree, the phase that follows is termed by Empey and Erickson "awareness of individual differences and alternatives." In this stage, members start to move away from stereotyped reactions to each other, and beliefs regarding "individual differences and needs" emerge. This is accompanied by more openness regarding oneself and one's reactions to others in the group. Even this, however, is frightening, so this phase is marked by reactions such as reaffirmation of the value of deviant behavior. This conflict can also be reflected in the emergence of subgroups that represent each point of view.

Despite these continuing conflicts in the group, the presence of more members committed to openness allows for an investment in problem solving around current issues. The members who involve themselves this way will feel rewarded, and the worker can help them share their satisfactions with the others. This is correlated with the group's beginning to perceive each member as unique rather than as a stereotype.

Because of the openness that has surfaced, the worker will bring problems to the group that affect the members. This will include such day-to-day issues as nonattendance of members and problems being experienced in other components of the agency's program, such as its school or vocational facilities.

Empey and Erickson call the next phase "group awareness,"[16] as its objectives are to increase the members' understanding of "group structure and process and to maximize group problem solving." The explanation for this emphasis is that since much of deviance is a *social* phenomena, an understanding of *social* processes is an important treatment goal.

The natural processes of the group support this phase in that members become concerned about the group as an entity. This interest is facilitated by the worker who actually, but in nontechnical terms, teaches about such group phenomena as unwritten norms, leadership, and sources of power in the group. This new "sophistication" will also help the member understand the workers' actions and even criticize them.

Thus in this phase, while members continue to solve individual and group problems, they will do so with a better understanding of the barriers to this process posed by group phenomena. This understanding also motivates the members to improve the operation of the group, such as by creating new group norms.

The final stage is termed "integration of group and program structure."[17] Empey and Erickson recognize that this phase might not be reached by many groups, but when it does occur, members help prepare new groups as well as take responsibility for the continuing development of the agency's services. In addition, members seek to extend the prosocial norms of the group into the other institutions of the community.

As an argument against the notion that the kind of group development described here is too idealistic for "real" work with delinquents, Empey and Erickson cite research based on one thousand recorded group sessions representing ten different groups. In this investigation it was found that "when groups remain closed, there was some rather clear-cut evidence that a developmental process does take place—a process in which therapist participation decreases, group-centered comments increase, greater member-risks occur in which candid and confrontive statements are made, and nontask-oriented comments decrease. The analysis revealed that this process is better described in terms of a developmental trend than in terms of sharply demarcated stages."[18] In this discussion, the authors state that movement may include regressive shifts as well as forward ones. The worker under such circumstances must identify themes and directions rather than look for group changes that are without ambiguity or that cover all members at the same time.

The group phases just outlined fit partly into our concept of a social control function and partly into a rehabilitation function. As we stated earlier, it is unlikely that a social worker will think of the former without the latter. In view of the back and forth movement of the group described by Empey and Erickson, at any given moment some members may be settling on efforts to change themselves, while others are still considering whether to formulate such a contract between themselves and the group. The continued pull from anti-social peers and others keeps the social control function of the agency ever present as a force in the members' lives.

The foregoing material represents a model of how groups with social control functions are likely to evolve. Practitioners with such groups, however, have used a variety of inter-ventions drawn from different theoretical orientations. How these affect the group's devel-opment is not well understood and should be the target of further investigation. Workers with such groups can develop their own specific approaches by consulting a literature that includes experiences in social control settings with analytic,[19] behavior modification,[20] problem-solving,[21] and therapeutic-community[22] technologies.

Evaluation

In consonance with our concept of group work in social control situations as functioning to secure agreement among agency, group, and client on client goals, we have sought to identify ways of evaluating the attainment of such agreement. We reserve for the next chapter on "rehabilitation" the issue of evaluating personal change in clients of psychiatric, correctional, and similar institutions with control functions *after* agreement about goals has been reached.

Because one of the steps in fulfilling the function of groups in social control settings is to secure the commitment of the member to the group, it is a vital component for eval-uation. Workers should carefully monitor such variables as meeting attendance, prompt-ness in attending meetings, and the proportion of members who actively participate in meetings, even if such participation is hostile. We believe that the issue of contract is cru-cial in these groups. Workers, therefore, should monitor when each member has arrived at a contract regarding goals with the worker, group, and agency. This also implies that "behavioral agreement" with the contract should be examined. Workers can create simple log sheets in which deviations from the contract on the part of member (perhaps of the agency, too) are recorded and then examined by the worker to help determine the future of the group.

Most groups related to this function must also be concerned about the honesty and openness of members because this is essential to a viable contract. Workers can develop "climate" questionnaires to evaluate the attainment of this condition. These consist of ques-tions in which members rate the trust they place in other members and the worker, the like-lihood that the group will help them, the amount of support they feel from the group, and the freedom they have to say what is actually "on their minds." Such questionnaires are usually completed anonymously. Because of members' fears about confidentiality, they may even request that a trusted person outside of the group, tabulate and report the findings.

An Example

An example of issues that workers encounter in social control groups is shown in this excerpt of a meeting in a prison.[23] As can be seen, the group had progressed past the phase of group formation and had entered the middle phase of development. The group was composed of twelve men (eight black and four white) whose offenses included murder, armed robbery, and rape. The group had been meeting for four months.

The group worker had an eclectic orientation toward his work. He used many of the approaches described in this book, including techniques related to analytic as well as behavioral theories. An innovation he had created for this group and others is the use of an inmate as a co-worker. Such inmates had been selected and trained by him based on their participation in groups in which they demonstrated capabilities for helping others. The worker is Dr. S. and the inmate co-worker is F.

At the meeting, two new members were present for the first time: Bill and Ted. They had learned from informal discussions with group members outside the group that they were expected to tell something about their "problems" and background at this meeting. This had been reinforced in a screening interview they held with the worker. Bill began talking when the group convened as if he had been cued to do this. He stated that his offense had been armed robbery, but that his was not the usual case. He had come from a "good" family and had not been in trouble as a teenager. He had been married when he was seventeen to a woman he loved and with whom he had a close relationship. He had received training as a musician and earned his living playing with bands. The long times he had to be away from home stressed his marriage. His wife wanted him to come home more. Because of her loneliness, she began to see other men. Eventually they were divorced. He found a new woman who was well-off financially and did many nice things for him but wanted to be able to depend on him in return. After a heated argument about this, he took her driving in her car and, with every intention of returning it, made her get out of the car at gunpoint. He was very surprised, consequently, when he was confronted by the police and arrested.

The other men in the group asked Bill many questions such as why he had a gun and why the woman had called the police. Bill responded that he always carried a gun to defend himself and that this woman was simply very angry with him. The other members expressed disbelief and indicated that Bill was not taking any responsibility for what had happened. He continued to make defensive statements, and another member, Frank, told him that in the group he would learn how to face what he did to bring trouble upon himself.

Ted then told his story without any prompting. He had been involved in a series of burglaries since he was a young teenager. When he was seventeen (about three years before), he and a "rap-buddy" (partner in committing crimes) burglarized a store. While it was in progress, the owner of the store apprehended them and drew a gun. Ted grabbed a hammer and hit this man on the head. The man was in a coma and was expected to die. His "rap-buddy" snitched on him, and he was arrested. The buddy was not sentenced but Ted was given "seven to fourteen." The victim survived, but due to the seriousness of the crime, Ted was tried as an adult and placed in an adult institution.

Ted indicated he had a problem with violence, and several members asked him to elaborate on this. He said he had been involved in at least a dozen fights in the last facility he had been in. Consequently, he had been placed in solitary confinement a number of times. His first fight occurred when his "rap-buddy," in jail on another charge, had been transferred to the same institution in which Ted was a prisoner. Ted said that he was justified in attacking the buddy, but that he was wrong in his earlier attack on the person he had robbed. He explained that several other fights had occurred as he sought to ward off homosexual advances.

F. commented that Ted presented himself as a "victim" forced by others to be violent. Within this institution, it was clearly understood that "victim" meant that one abdicated responsibility for one's own actions. Ted did not respond to this, and the theme was picked up by several other men. One commented that he thought Ted was a danger to other people and was not ready for release to the community. Another asked Ted if he still would attack his "rap-buddy." Ted said he wouldn't because this matter was now settled.

At this point, group discussion to define "snitching" took place for about five minutes. Several members indicated that they had concluded that it was not "snitching" if you told the truth about something, even if this implicated others in a crime. These men agreed that snitching meant telling lies that falsely implicated others when the liar was the culprit. This discussion was an outgrowth of Ted's criticism of his "rap-buddy" for snitching.

A black man in the group (Ted is white) asked Ted about his recent actions to relieve himself from his work assignment in the kitchen. Ted stated that he did not like kitchen work. The black member said that he knew Ted had been relieved of this assignment by writing a letter to the supervisor stating that he was being "pressed" by others on this work detail and that he could not handle this pressure (probably a reference to his known violent reactions). He continued by stating that Ted had manipulated a situation for his own benefit in a way that could cause others to suffer. He pointed out that since Ted was white and the others on the detail were black, the charge of the white man would be believed, as it was often alleged that most black inmates harassed the whites. Ted denied this charge, and a lengthy discussion ensued in which black members (supported by one white member) sought to convince Ted of the results of his actions. One member also pointed out that this discussion was related to the earlier point that Ted saw himself as "victim" when he actually provoked others.

At this point, the session was about to run past its allocated time. Dr. S. indicated to Ted that his anger at others and the way he handled it may have been the result of some of his earlier experiences, perhaps family ones. He asked Ted to think about this and to present some of these thoughts at a future meeting.

This example illustrates several processes typical of groups in social control settings. We see the new members encouraged to tell their stories as a way of introducing themselves to other members, initiating interactions, and identifying problems to be worked on in the group.

Even though this was Ted's first meeting, the other members perceived that he was open to some confrontation. It is also likely that this confrontation took place because his actions were not only harmful to himself but to his fellow inmates. That this was not a beginning group is evidenced by the members' willingness to confront one another and to deal with such problems as racism in the institution. The inmate code usually prevents such confrontation unless members have begun to abandon it during group sessions. Members, also, are not likely to deal with such issues as racism unless they have become convinced that the group is a place where issues can be dealt with effectively.

Summary

In this chapter we discussed the character of group work in social control situations. The function of the group when the social control function is dominant is to help the members seek out the common ground between their goals and those of the group and the agency— perhaps even of the larger environment. This is a difficult and sometimes long-term process in which the agency must also indicate a willingness to change itself to relate more to member needs. The major worker skills in this situation are mediating among members, group, and agency.

At times, however, members need much support to enter into this process as well as to increase their motivation to do so. This motivation is sometimes increased by workers through their use of confrontation, their support of intermember confrontation, their reminders of the short- and long-term consequences of behavior, and their heightening of anxiety through the use of ambiguity.

A general model for the development of such groups and the workers' changing roles in different phases of the group was drawn from experiences with delinquents in a guided group interaction program. That program identified phases moving from the group-building efforts to the stereotyped and then more individualized forms of problem solving. Research was cited as to the validity of this concept of group development. This chapter concluded with an illustration of a prison group.

Endnotes

1. For a recent extensive discussion of these kinds of clients and how their involuntary status affects work with individuals, families, and groups, see Ronald H. Rooney, *Strategies for Work with Involuntary Clients* (New York: Columbia University Press, 1992).

2. Charles Garvin and Brett Seabury, *Interpersonal Practice in Social Work,* 2nd ed. (Boston: Allyn & Bacon, in press), Chapter 7.

3. Warren Netherland, "Corrections Systems: Adult" in *Encyclopedia of Social Work*, 1, 18th ed., ed. A. Minahan (Silver Spring, MD: National Association of Social Workers, 1987).

4. Rooney, *Involuntary Clients*: 4.

5. Ibid.: 129–36.

6. Ibid: 40.

7. Garvin and Seabury, *Interpersonal Practice in Social Work*, Chapter 7.

8. Irving Spergel, *Street Gang Work* (Reading, Mass.: Addison-Wesley, 1966).

9. Empey and Erickson, *The Provo Experiment*: 96–103.

10. Ibid.: 96.

11. Ibid.: 103–35.

12. Ibid.: 103.

13. Ibid.: 104.

14. Ibid.: 106–7.

15. Ibid.: 111.

16. Ibid.: 119–25.

17. Ibid.: 134.

18. Ibid.

19. R. Rappaport, "Group Therapy in Prison: A Strategic Approach," in *Group Counseling and Group Psychotherapy with Rehabilitation Clients*, ed. Milton Seligman (Springfield, Mass.: Thomas, 1977).

20. H. Novotny and J. Enomoto, "Social Competence Training as a Correctional Alternative," *Offender Rehabilitation* I (1976): 45–55.

21. G. Kassebaum, D. Ward, and D. Wilner, *Prison Treatment and Parole Survival: An Empirical Assessment* (New York: John Wiley, 1971).

22. Harry Wexler, Gregory Falkin, and Douglas Lipton, "Outcome Evaluation of a Prison Therapeutic Community for Substance Abuse Treatment," *Criminal Justice and Behavior* 17 (1) (1990): 71–92.

23. This example was also reported by the author in Charles D. Garvin, "Resocialization: Group Work in Social Control and Correctional Settings," in *The Group Workers' Handbook: Varieties of Group Experience*, ed. Robert K. Conyne (Springfield, Mass.: Thomas, 1985): 128–31.

Chapter 14

Working with Groups for Rehabilitation

In Chapter 12 we discussed the use of groups to help members perform better in their roles. We indicated that such people are usually defined as "normal" and that their group activities have educational foci. Another category of people also seeks to attain new roles or fulfill the requirements of existing roles; they, however, are currently performing in ways regarded as "sick" or "deviant." They have a double burden then: to overcome the forces that make it difficult to relinquish their previous positions as well as to acquire new behaviors, insights, and ways of coping with desired roles.

An example is schizophrenics in a mental hospital. As they develop skills to cope with life stresses, they must also overcome forces in the family, the community, and the workplace that define them as "sick." An effective group program must be focused on both of these dimensions: the adaptation to new roles as well as the overcoming of conflicts between the new and the old.

There are major differences and similarities in the situations of the various people who fall within this aspect of group work. In general terms, for example, a psychotic child or adult in a hospital, a prisoner in a training school or reformatory, and a client of a family counseling agency are faced with acquiring new roles while coping with the effects of the old ones. Nevertheless, the psychological and social dynamics in each case are quite different, as reflected in the ways workers deal with such members. Thus psychotic persons have few adaptive mechanisms and must be helped to develop them. Prison inmates may "act out" when stressed and must be helped to control their behavior and deal with stress differently. Each of these "dynamics" calls for different interventions with the individual as well as with the group and will be commented upon in this chapter.

Because of the extensive discussion of work in correctional and other social control settings in the last chapter, we shall give more weight in this one to psychiatric settings. We believe that some concerns and processes in a correctional setting are similar to those in a psychiatric setting when the former is oriented to rehabilitation and once the social control issues have been, at least partially, resolved with members. This also recognizes that it can be the operation of social factors that determines whether *some* people "end up" in prison or a mental hospital.

In discussing approaches to helping individuals in groups, we shall cite five types. The first, referred to by Rose as a "minimal skill training group," involves training people in social skills that they may almost totally lack and that are necessary for any kind of functioning outside of a psychiatric or other institution. These are similar to the social skills training approaches described in Chapter 12; yet are contrived to take into consideration the needs and abilities of emotionally impaired persons. A second is the activity-oriented group for people not able to function in "talk" groups. The third, typically considered "group psychotherapy," is for people who possess basic social skills and a considerable degree of reality testing but who need help overcoming persistent patterns of responding to situations in self-defeating ways. The fourth is the transition group for people leaving such settings. The fifth, the so-called "patient government group," is designed to help people learn participatory democracy skills that exist (or should exist) in all communities. Such groups are formed in institutions to give patients a way of participating in making rules, planning programs, and solving organizational problems.

In all of these cases, however, work is required to alter environments that maintain people in "deviant" roles, although, in some, the individual and the group may be able to act more on their own behalf than others. In any case, individuals in these groups will experience conflict among the demands of differing systems and must be helped to cope with these conflicts in functional ways.

Pregroup Tasks

An assessment before the beginning of the group will include an identification of the roles with which the person seeks help. In a mental hospital or after-care program, those roles emphasized tend to be associated with peers, family, and employment. For people who are severely impaired, the roles may be even more functional such as "information seeker" (for example, asking directions), "consumer" (for example, making a purchase), or "initiator of relationships" (for example, making the acquaintance of someone else).

Since the purpose of the compositional principle often is to secure members with similar levels of social functioning, this attribute must be assessed prior to starting the group. Some people in psychiatric settings have experienced a deterioration in their behavior, and the worker may have to secure historical information from the prospective member as well as significant others. Such information includes the kinds of social interactions in which the client has engaged at different phases of his or her life and how well these were managed. For example, the worker will ask whether the individual has had friends during previous periods, whether they were of both sexes, and what activities were engaged in with these friends. This helps the worker compose groups of people with similar skill levels, even if these skills are not manifested currently. The skill level of the group will also determine the techniques the worker employs.

Goldstein, Sprafkin, and Gershaw have developed and tested skill survey instruments that can be used.[1] One version is for the staff to complete, the other for clients. On the survey, the rater indicates the level of skill on a five-point scale ranging from "never good at using the skill" to "always good at using the skill." Thirty-six skills are listed, such as "starting a conversation," "listening," "expressing anger," "apologizing," "following instructions," and "decision making."

If the worker seeks to develop a minimal skill training group, a specific number of sessions is usually planned. The number varies, however, based on the level of social competence of the members. Even within this type of planning, the worker can establish either a continuous training experience or divide it into segments with in-between periods when members work on the skills they have already developed without attempting new material. More research is needed on the effectiveness of such varying arrangements. Group psychotherapy experiences in which members are helped to develop insight into their behavior while also trying out new behaviors in the group can, in contrast, last at least a year. Transition groups may meet only three to five times. Patient government groups are ongoing.

In any case, members should be prepared for the group experience. In one type of minimal skill training, "structured learning therapy," potential members are informed of the skills that may be taught in the group. The skill checklist developed by therapists using that approach can communicate to potential members what some of the group purposes may be.

Goldstein and his colleagues consider that the client may not be able to comprehend the checklist, in which case it can be administered by the worker as a questionnaire. In any event, the worker should discuss the skills that may be taught, describe the procedures that will be used at meetings (to be presented later in this chapter), and contract with the individual regarding skills he or she is interested in pursuing. People invited to join the group are given a "trainee's notebook," which includes details regarding times and places, rules on attendance and participation, and a description of the therapeutic procedures. The notebook includes pages for notes on each session as well as records of homework assignments and progress made on these.

In Chapter 3 we presented Yalom's procedure for preparing members for group psychotherapy. Some of the issues he clarifies for members are appropriate to any group experience. Several things he tells members, however, are unique to the group psychotherapy experience. One is his preparation of members for analysis of "process" by telling them that they must be "honest and direct with their feelings in the group at that moment, especially their feelings toward the other group members and the therapists."[2] Frustration and confusion during the first dozen meetings are predicted. The difficulty many people have in expressing feelings in group psychotherapy sessions is described, as well as "the tendencies of some to withdraw emotionally, to hide their feelings, to let others express feelings for them, to form concealing alliances with others."[3]

The long-term nature of group psychotherapy is also explained to members by Yalom as a product of changing behavior and attitudes created over many years. Rules are explained that may be required in group psychotherapy but not in other group experiences with other members outside the group. The members are told that such relationships may impede rather than enhance therapy because "friendships among certain group members may prevent them from speaking openly to one another in the group" because of loyalties that develop to those relationships.

Both minimal skill training and psychotherapy groups are usually small, consisting of five to seven members. The amount of individualization and support necessary for resocialization experiences requires this size. Activity-oriented and transition groups can sometimes be larger, depending on how their activities are structured. Patient government groups may be large, depending on the number of units that must be represented.

Group Formation Tasks

After the initial assessment prior to the first group meeting, additional and often more complex assessments take place, which may continue throughout the group's life. In selecting individualized goals during group formation, one of the first concerns is the forces at play in each member's life that maintain dysfunctional patterns. This is because during the time the group meets, plans will have to be made to change these forces, to provide the member with better means of coping with them, or both. These forces include those from families and peer groups that reinforce antisocial patterns as well as those stemming from social institutions such as schools and places of employment that do the same.

These interactions are assessed by asking members to describe reactions of significant others to their problems and actions. Because of the frequent similarities in the members' circumstances, they can help each other identify these reactions. Also, the worker may have other information from the agency regarding family, peer, and organizational responses that can be contributed to this analysis.

As members, in the beginning meetings of the group, clarify their goals for participation in the group and review situations that hinder their goal attainment, the worker and other members should note how the members indicate they cope with identified conflicts. Some members are able to engage actively in problem-solving conflicts and decision-making efforts, while others deny conflicts, minimize them, or are overwhelmed by them. In such cases, the worker and others will help the members remove such barriers to their effort to attain alternative, more functional roles.

Once the member has begun to accomplish tasks to attain his or her goals in view of forces promoting old roles and behaviors, the type of relevant assessment is similar to that conducted in skill attainment groups. As stated in Chapter 12, when the worker's interventions are composed of behavioral modification techniques, an assessment will specify the "antecedent conditions" of the member's behavior as well as the consequences of acting in functional or dysfunctional ways. This assessment should include information on the types of behaviors and attitudes also described in Chapter 12, that is, the member's knowledge, ability, and motivation with regard to both behavior and attitudes.

The availability of opportunity structures is also an essential element of moving from dysfunctional to functional role performance and must also be ascertained. For example, people released from mental hospitals or other psychiatric rehabilitation programs must be able to find jobs, secure needed services, and obtain training. The group should examine whether these are available to the members. Members can be coached on how to approach these resources, and the group can plan group actions to make them more accessible. An assessment of such opportunities is, therefore, an integral requirement for group work services. The patient government group should be primarily devoted to improving the agency's or institution's opportunity structures.

The targets of group work intervention in rehabilitation situations are thus similar to those we described previously for skill attainment situations, namely, the member's knowledge, skill, and motivation for performing designated roles. The essential difference, however, is that *the conflicts encountered in moving out of deviant positions must be addressed.*

The resocialization aspects of such groups have other effects on group processes during group formation. Some members may continue to respond with either resistance or ambivalence to the social control aspects of the agency. This can be manifested in some members opposing others in the group who wish to adapt in new ways. The entire group may also occasionally move into a resistive mode more typical of social control situations. This may be a response to either pressures from the environment or to overwhelming anxiety about the changes taking place. Whitaker and Lieberman, in their model of group psychotherapy, discussed in Chapter 5, present an analytical framework also pertinent to understanding the formation period of rehabilitation.[4] They indicate that members will experience wishes regarding their personal outcomes, which are termed the "disturbing motive." While members may have different wishes, these become linked by the process of communication and association. In a similar fashion, some of the fears regarding these wishes also become linked, which Whitaker and Lieberman term the "reactive motive." These two motives form the "focal group conflict" for which, at any given time, the group seeks a solution. These solutions may either be facilitating or hindering.

During the formation period of rehabilitation groups, members will wish that their relationships become gratifying, their activities be less likely to get them into trouble, or their strivings be met with success. This feeling of hopefulness can be shared by all group members. On the other hand, fears will also be felt—that the group will represent another promise that is broken, that the members and the worker are not sincere in their offers to help, that the hindering forces of the environment will be more powerful than the group, or that the members, themselves, will lack sufficient motivation or wisdom to help themselves.

Hindering solutions in this kind of conflict will include persistent efforts to test the group without really investing in it, a denial of the reality of the conflict taking place, a false sense of optimism in the face of problems, or a projection of the conflict onto others. Facilitating solutions should include the willingness to pursue the desired goals while still seeking to overcome barriers, and a commitment to ask for help from others in this process as well as offer it. This can only be achieved, however, as the worker and the members engage in an examination of the focal conflicts in the formation period and the solutions that emerge.

Goal Pursuit Tasks

Workers will combine sets of procedures to correspond to the unique requirements of each group. However, it is most feasible in this chapter to describe separately those procedures that pertain to minimal skill training, group psychotherapy, transitional, activity-oriented, and patient government groups. When these are integrated, it may be because members are able to use techniques they were not ready for earlier, or because the worker discovered gaps in skills that required departing from the planned approach.

Minimal Skill Training Groups

One model of a minimal skill approach is "structured learning therapy," developed by Goldstein and his colleagues.[5] This set of procedures was designed for people who function too poorly to be discharged from or remain out of mental hospitals. Under existing treatment programs, such people sometimes spend years in psychiatric facilities, during which they become even less able to function in the community.

Structured learning therapy, which has an impressive record of effectiveness,[6] combines elements of modeling, role playing, social reinforcement, and transfer of training techniques. The authors thoroughly examined the research related to each of these processes and developed a group training approach combining the most effective formats.

The modeling component includes securing the members' attention through physical and other arrangements that avoid distracting stimuli. Retention of the behaviors observed in the model is enhanced by helping the members conceptualize the behaviors observed by learning a list of principles and relating these to a demonstration of related behaviors. The investigators assert that anxiety associated with the behaviors can also be reduced by having the models demonstrate a relaxed way of performing the skill.

The role-playing component is enhanced in the following ways: The members have a choice whether to take part in the role playing, although they are asked to role play skills they had committed themselves to acquire. They are also given an opportunity to improvise in the role plays. Finally, they are given verbal praise and other signs of approval for taking part.

The reinforcement principles that are part of structured learning therapy are that reinforcement follows immediately after the desired behaviors, that reinforcement is contingent on the desired behaviors, and that reinforcement is on an intermittent schedule (that is, randomly determined).

Transfer of training is enhanced by teaching principles of behavior to members as well as providing models of the behavior. In addition, members are given opportunities to practice the behavior under varying circumstances, including "homework" assignments related to performing the behaviors to be learned.

Structured learning therapy sessions are held as often as three times a week. The setting for meetings is similar to a classroom in that members sit at tables placed at either end of the worker's table and perpendicular to it. This leaves space at the opposite end of the worker's table for role plays. This physical arrangement indicates to members that they are learners, encourages their receptivity to learning, and prepares for their involvement in later learning experiences.

After the initial meeting in which members become acquainted with each other and learn about the meeting format, the subsequent meetings utilize a common structure. They include a definition of the skill to be learned (for example, "starting a conversation") and the reasons for the skill. Members are given a "skill card" that outlines the "learning points" for that skill. The learning points, for example, for starting a conversation are as follows:

1. Choose the right place and time.
2. Greet the other person.
3. Make small talk.

4. Judge if the other person is listening and wants to talk with you.

5. Open the main topic you want to talk about.[7]

After the learning points are reviewed, a demonstration tape of a role play is shown. While the role play unfolds, the worker points on a chart to the learning points exemplified by the action at that moment. Following this, the members discuss their reactions to the role play, giving the worker additional opportunity to resolve ambiguities and to provide encouragement for the next step, in which the members themselves role play the skill. When these "rehearsals" are over, the role players are given feedback by other members and by the worker. A format for providing such feedback is also supplied in the text. It includes such points as asking the "co-actor" in the role play how he or she was made to feel, asking the "audience" how well the learning points were followed, and asking the "main actor" for self-evaluation; meanwhile, the worker provides appropriate feedback for all desired responses.[8]

The final phase of the meeting is devoted to determining homework assignments. Each group member is asked to try out in the institution the skill that was learned in the group. Since the in-group role plays are based on people and incidents drawn from actual member situations, in most cases the member is asked to carry out the assignment in those same situations. The member's notebook contains pages in which the homework assignment is noted, along with the member's description of what happens and his or her evaluation of it. At the subsequent meeting, time is set aside, usually at the beginning, for discussion of these reports. Goldstein and co-workers note, however, that people who function very poorly will not be asked to do this much writing; presumably reports are oral. The Goldstein, Sprafkin, and Gershaw text contains much information also on how to help members develop complex skills such as job seeking, handling both positive and negative marital interactions, and dealing with crisis situations.

Group Psychotherapy

Group psychotherapy for rehabilitation is hard to specify because the procedures are seldom well spelled out and there is a lack of consensus on what the process is. There is also much variance in outcomes, and the variables that account for this are not clear.[9] The group psychotherapy literature presents it as a long-term process in which people become aware of their dysfunctional interactional patterns through feedback from group members and the worker. They are then able, in the group, to explore new ways of relating, which is facilitated by forces in such groups that are strengthened by worker activities.

One such force is a norm of openness in discussing one's feelings about oneself and others. The worker reinforces the existence of this norm through modeling it as well as encouraging it in others. The worker also helps members understand the value of the norm and confronts the group when members violate it. Another norm the worker supports is that members should continually monitor the functioning of their group and should seek to identify and resolve antitherapeutic group conditions through problem-solving activity. These group conditions include antagonistic subgroups, the abuse of power by members, and group climates that inhibit the members' progress (for example, depressed or hostile emotional tone during a session).

The worker in a group psychotherapy situation also tries to maintain a "here and now" focus. This means that member concerns regarding events in their "outside" lives or in their past are related to patterns in the group that represent contemporary manifestations of these issues. The following are some examples of this from psychotherapy groups:

Example: A member in one group psychotherapy session said, "My mother always dominated me." In response, the worker questioned, "Do you see anyone else in the group that you have some of the same feelings about?" In another group, one member said, "I wish that I could tell my wife when I want her help," to which the worker responded, "Is there anyone in the group that you would like to ask for help?"

The value of such "here and now" focus is to help members see how their current interactions are a continuation of dysfunctional patterns in the past. Members can explore, as we have said, new ways of acting in the group as a safe environment for such testing. They should be helped by the members and the worker to try out this "interpersonal learning" in their other life roles. The worker's interventions for this purpose are not always as abrupt as the few examples just given. For some members, the worker will support a "there and then" focus so that the issue the member describes can be delineated clearly for both the member in question and for others.

In group psychotherapy, the worker will also use procedures analogous to those used in individual psychotherapy. The difference for the skillful group worker is that it is not only the worker who utilizes the procedure. Members are also helped to use these processes appropriately with each other. One such procedure, for example, is interpretation. In discussing interpretation, some workers adopt a specific framework for making interpretations such as psychoanalytic theory, in which an interpretation is defined as an action "through which the therapist makes material previously unconscious in the patient, conscious for him in a meaningful and affective way."[10] Some group therapists give a broader definition of interpretations, namely, as views of the causes of behavior that contrast (for whatever reason, including unconscious processes) with the views of those events already held by the member. The member is exposed to "cognitive dissonance" between old and new ideas, which is then resolved by changing one's thoughts and/or behaviors.[11]

The skillful worker will not present interpretations to members and will limit such presentations among members until a good deal of preparation takes place. This preparation includes a slow and careful effort to help the member see that the two events whose connection is to be asserted through an interpretation do exist independently (for example, anger toward mother and toward wife), and that manifestations of one are regularly associated with the other. Unless this slow process occurs, the member is likely to deny any but the most simple and obvious patterns. Psychologically oriented group members are often prone to make "quick" interpretations, often as a means of competing with each other and the worker. Once this kind of behavior is "processed," however, members, through their knowledge of each other, will develop and share many insights regarding each other's behavior.

As we indicated in Chapter 3, workers engaged in group psychotherapy in inpatient settings frequently work with groups in which members attend for only a week or two, after which they are discharged from the hospital and continue their treatment in the community.

Yalom has developed a model for work with such groups.[12] In this model, the worker helps the members select a highly specific and immediate goal that they can attain within a single meeting. This goal identification also helps the member be clear about what he or she should continue to work to achieve in subsequent treatment after discharge from the hospital.

The group sessions begin with an explanation by the worker of the purpose of the group, namely, to help members work on problems related to relationships with other people. Each member is then helped to identify a goal for the meeting, and the worker is highly active in helping the member to set a goal attainable in that time frame. Examples of such problems are "to seek feedback on whether others find me hostile," "to initiate a relationship," "to learn how to refuse a request," or "to continue to relate when I feel anxious and eager to withdraw."

After each member has targeted a goal, the worker supports interactions among members in which each can work on that goal. This can often happen simultaneously within the same conversation; some members can be trying out new ways of interacting while others are receiving feedback.

The meeting concludes with a review by the worker of what has been accomplished. This is often enhanced by observers whose presence is known to the members, who have been told that at the end of the meeting such observers will give feedback on their observations of interactions among members. The members are also given an opportunity to briefly react to the observer's comments. The observers utilized by Yalom are usually trainees in one of the mental health professions.

This model is employed with "higher functioning" patients who can sustain this amount of verbal interaction, even though some may be delusional or may even manifest bizarre behavior. Yalom presents another model for lower functioning hospital patients in which the worker makes use of structured activities.

Activity Groups

The third type of alternate role attainment group is an activity-oriented group. These groups are formed in residential institutions, community-based institutions, and halfway houses for both children and adults to help group members whose functioning cannot be enhanced on primarily a "verbal" level (that is, through discussion and problem solving). Such people are usually excluded from "group psychotherapy" such as that just outlined. These groups use a variety of program media to attain their goals. See Chapter 5 for a full discussion of such media. The following are examples of how such tools are used.

Arts and Crafts.   Members are given opportunities to work with clay, paints, cloth, and other materials. These media help them express emotions, communicate ideas to others, and enhance their sense of creativity and individual accomplishment. Such projects may either be individual or involve cooperation among group members, depending on the effects the worker desires on group and interpersonal processes.

Games and Sports.   Members can be helped to assume roles related to their goals for being in the group by playing games (for example, assertive roles); this helps them deal with interpersonal issues (for example, competition and cooperation) and release tensions. These are obviously only a few of the benefits of this type of activity.

Cooking and Other Forms of Food Preparation.   These activities often meet the needs of members to nurture and be nurtured. They elicit concerns over these behaviors, which are then "worked on" in the group.

Music and Dance.   These activities are valuable in helping members express emotions, feel unity with others, and, in the case of dance, improve body image and a sense of one's physical self.

Trips.   Members can travel as a group to a variety of places to learn skills and communicate concerns. Groups have gone to restaurants, stores, museums, amusement parks, and zoos.

Dramatics.   This activity ranges from role plays to improvised as well as formal dramatic activities. Drama can help members learn more about roles of concern to them, communicate repressed ideas and feelings, and practice new behaviors. Learning the actual skills involved in acting and producing a drama can also boost self-esteem.

Transition Groups

The next type of rehabilitation group is the transitional group. Institutions will form groups for people about to be discharged to the community. Such groups focus particularly on helping members cope with community and family forces that can pressure them to return to their dysfunctional ways of adapting. Of particular importance in these groups is helping members explain their institutionalization or treatment in appropriate ways. The group will also help members make specific plans for work and living arrangements and for social and supportive interactions.

The important consideration in planning such groups is to begin them sufficiently in advance of discharge so they can fulfill their proper function. This will include the review of and in some cases the development of appropriate individual goals. The techniques used in such groups include rehearsal activities through role playing, homework assignments for members who have temporary "passes" into the community, educational programs, group trips, and opportunities for problem solving. Not the least of the critical tasks for such a group is to help members express and overcome ambivalence regarding leaving the institution. Members will, on the one hand, desire the autonomy, sense of accomplishment, freedom, and opportunity to develop themselves by a return to the community. On the other hand, they may be leaving a "safe" environment, one in which they can be relatively dependent and in which less responsibility may have been expected of them because they were defined as "sick." It is rare for this ambivalence to be totally resolved, yet the balance must be tilted for any chance of a permanent return to the community.

Patient Government Groups

Group workers have facilitated patient government groups for many years. They are usually established in institutions to help patients participate in institutional decisions that affect them, the rules of the institution, and its program. These groups are sometimes used to mediate disputes between patients and staff and among patient groups.

Patient government groups are usually modeled on a legislative body. Members are elected by constituent groups such as wards or cottages. Within the group, members take responsibility for all the leadership positions. Ideally, the staff member functions as a facilitator and consultant to the group.

The major task required of the group worker is to train the members in skills required for their respective roles. This includes member skills in agenda planning, problem solving, decision making, and encouraging maximum participation of all "representatives." Problems in such groups arise when the decisions the group is permitted to make are not "real" and members lose interest in the group. It is also possible that the members of the group have been ill prepared to carry out their roles, thus creating strong feelings of frustration among members and staff alike. When properly charged and constituted, such groups can contribute to feelings of worth and power for the members. When the groups are artificial, they can add instead to the feelings of unreality and impotence that already plague the members.

Evaluation

Several measures intrinsic to structured learning therapy help workers to evaluate it. These may also be used for similar minimal skill training experiences. First, group members are required to keep a trainee's notebook that calls for a series of self-evaluations. These consist of a narrative report of what happened when members carried out their homework assignment, a listing of the "learning points" followed, and an overall rating of how well the skill was performed (excellent, good, fair, poor). Workers can examine the learning points followed and the ratings for evidence of group effectiveness. The narrative report can be used to substantiate the members' ratings as well as their claim to having followed specified learning points.

The schedule we described earlier that is used to assess members' entering skills can also be used as an "after" measure by both members and staff. It can help workers compare groups that have been more and less effective to determine with whom the training has worked best and for whom additional ways of helping should be devised.

Yalom, in his discussion of the need for the practitioner to evaluate the outcomes of group psychotherapy, suggests that the beginning group psychotherapist develop an understanding of the complexity of outcome evaluation by interviewing people who have terminated. He states, "It is a very valuable exercise for the student to attempt to evaluate the degree of change, the nature of change, the mechanisms whereby the group experience effected the change, and the contributing role of other factors in the patient's environment. The exercise becomes richer yet if the student has available a tape of the initial interview to which he and the patient can listen."[13]

Yalom criticizes approaches for evaluating group member progress that depend on instruments not specific to the members' treatment goals. He concludes:

Clinicians fail to heed or even to believe research in which outcome is measured by before-and-after changes on standardized instruments. And with good reason, for abundant research and clinical evidence indicates that change means something different to each patient. Some patients need to experience less anxiety or

hostility; for other patients, improvement would be accompanied by greater anx-
iety or hostility. Even self-esteem changes need to be individualized. It has been
demonstrated that a high self-esteem score on traditional self-administered ques-
tionnaires can reflect either a genuinely healthy regard of self or a defensive pos-
ture in which the individual maintains a high self-esteem at the expense of self-
awareness. These latter individuals would, as a result of successful treatment,
have lower (but more accurate) self esteem as measured by questionnaires.[14]

Yalom also stresses that the effectiveness of group therapy should not be determined using the same criteria as those used for individual therapy. As he states:

I suspect that, although group and individual therapies may be equivalent in
overall effectiveness, each modality may affect different variables and have a dif-
ferent type of outcome. For example, group therapy graduates may become more
interpersonally skilled, more inclined to be affiliative in times of stress, more
capable of sustaining meaningful relationships, or more empathic, whereas indi-
vidual therapy patients may be more self-sufficient, introspective, and attuned to
inner processes.[15]

In an analogous manner, workers should evaluate the outcomes of activity groups in terms compatible with the reasons the activity was chosen. If a game was used to help members become less stressed in competitive situations, means should be devised to secure self-reports as well as observations of the members' responses to competition. If an art project is chosen to help members become more comfortable with disclosure, the number of self-disclosure statements before and after the experience should be counted. If a musical session is held to increase group cohesiveness and member comfort, these variables should also be measured before and after the activity.

It is also important to plan a follow-up after members have completed a transition group. This can be accomplished by interviewing members after the group in reference to the purposes of the group. If the group was established to help members take steps to find employment, their employment plans should be examined both before and after the group. If members are to be helped explain the facts of their treatment appropriately, they can be asked how they would handle this both before and after the group. Through such devices, the techniques used in such groups will be improved and our knowledge of the value of such experience enhanced. Patient government groups can be evaluated by assessing the quality of group decisions as well as member satisfaction with them. Leadership skills of members should also be assessed.

Since we stated that a unique aspect of all these groups is to help members reduce the conflict between old and new roles, this dimension should be examined. When the group ends, one way of doing this is to ask members about some of their perceptions and attitudes regarding previous roles. Examples of such questions are as follows:

1. Are there people who approved of the ways you acted before you entered the group, ways in which you no longer act? How do you feel about them now?
2. If you meet a person who tries to get you to perform [a "deviant" act] or makes you feel you want to do this, what would you do? How would you feel?

An Example

This example is from a transition group formed to help adolescents about to leave a residential treatment center.

First Meeting. As the meeting began, Tim said that John should tell the group what had happened to him on his last visit home. The worker asked John if he wanted to do so, and John said that he did. He had gone to his former school to apply for readmission. While he was there, a boy asked him where he had been for the past term. When he said he had been in a hospital, the boy responded that he hoped it was not one of those places for crazy kids. John was so upset after this conversation that he went home without registering for school. The worker said that he could see how difficult this was for John. He asked if any of the other members had had something like that happen to them. Rick said that when he was last home, several of his old friends seemed unwilling to talk to him when he approached them on the street. Tim added that when he was home and relatives were visiting his parents, they also seemed to avoid talking to him. The worker said that a number of the members had similar concerns about family and friends. He asked if any of the others had thought of ways of handling this.

Jack said he did not like to talk to anyone about "this place." Al said that he told people he was just away at school. He planned on telling the local school, when he returned home, that the school he had been going to had lost his records. Tim thought Al would be in for a lot of trouble if the school ever found out he was lying. Al responded by saying that it would be a lot better than people finding out where you had been. Rick thought, on the other hand, that it might be possible to explain things to people in a way they would understand. The worker summarized the ideas presented and said that he recognized that John still did not have an answer as to what he could have done when he went to the school.

The worker said that he had some tape recordings of how members of groups like this one had talked to peers as well as relatives or people in school about where they had been. He asked if the boys would like to hear these so they could discuss some of the alternatives they could use. He added that this might help John decide what he wanted to do. The members all agreed this was a good idea, so the worker played the first tape in which a boy was talking to his friend "back home." He told his friend that he had been upset about a lot of things that had happened to him. He had gone to a special school where they help young people learn how to handle their problems without becoming so upset. The school employed doctors and social workers as well as teachers, but this did not mean that you were "crazy."

John thought there were some ideas on this tape he could use. He was not sure, however, about telling others about "seeing doctors." The worker asked the boys what they thought about this, and there was a lot of discussion about doctors seeing you when you are sick and whether they were thought of as "sick."

The worker said that he could see there was a lot more about this they wanted to discuss, so perhaps they could go on with it at the next meeting, as the time was up. He also had more tapes they could hear and discuss.

Analysis. In the incident just described, we can see the conflicts the boys face in interactions between their "sick roles" and the roles they seek to assume when they leave the institution. The worker had not yet helped the boys recognize this conflict, as such. He had, however, responded to their feelings so that they would be more able to deal with them. He also sought to increase their skill in overcoming obstacles to performing their new roles, as well as their understanding of what had happened to them while in placement. The group was developing as a supportive and safe place to deal with these issues. Not the least of the facets of this experience was that the worker saw the members as competent to cope with the difficult problems they faced. He used models in the form of tapes at this meeting, but planned to move to such action-oriented approaches as role plays in which the members practiced ways of handling similar situations.

Summary

In this chapter, we presented the issues members confront in groups devoted to helping them move from "sick" or "deviant" roles into more functional ones. Of particular importance was the recognition of the kinds of conflicts encountered in this situation and the role of the group in helping members cope with such conflicts. In addition to discussing assessment issues and the ways groups are formed in the light of these, we discussed a range of types of groups fulfilling the purposes of rehabilitation. These groups were categorized as those supplying minimal skill training, those devoted to group psychotherapy, those utilizing activity bases, those conducted at the point of transition to the community, and those involving patients in governance. The means of evaluating such groups were described, and an example of a transitional group was presented.

Endnotes

1. Arnold P. Goldstein, Robert P. Sprafkin, and N. Jane Gershaw, *Skill Training for Community Living: Applying Structured Learning Therapy* (Elmsford, N.Y.: Pergamon Press, 1976): 166–73.

2. Irving D. Yalom, *The Theory and Practice of Group Psychotherapy*, 4th ed. (New York: Basic Books, 1995): 283.

3. Ibid.: 284.

4. Dorothy S. Whitaker and Morton S. Lieberman, *Psychotherapy Through the Group Process* (New York: Lieber-Atherton, Inc., 1965): 14–40.

5. Goldstein, Sprafkin, and Gershaw, *Skill Training.*

6. Ibid.: 126–45.

7. Ibid.: 83.

8. Ibid.: 50–51.

9. For a recent compilation of such research, see Richard L. Bednar and Theodore J. Kaul, "Experiential Group Research: Current Perspectives," in *Handbook of Psychotherapy and Behavior Change: An Empirical Analysis*, 4th ed., eds. Allen Bergin and Sol L. Garfield (New York: John Wiley, 1994): 631–63.

10. Robert J. Lange, *The Technique of Psychoanalytic Psychotherapy* (New York: Jason Aronson, 1973): 451–511.

11. Leon Festinger, *A Theory of Cognitive Dissonance* (New York: Row, Peterson, 1957). For applications to a theory of interpretation, see Leon H. Levy, *Psychological Interpretation* (New York: Holt, Rinehart & Winston, 1963).

12. Irving Yalom, *Inpatient Group Psychotherapy* (New York: Basic Books, 1983).

13. Yalom, *Group Psychotherapy*: 530.

14. Ibid.

15. Ibid.

Chapter 15

Working with Oppressed People in Groups

Throughout its history, group work has made a contribution to people experiencing social oppression. At some times this contribution was less than other times, as during reactionary periods in the larger society or in the profession of social work. We believe, however, that social work has a special commitment to those who are oppressed, and in this chapter we will focus on practice issues related to this commitment. We have sought to raise issues of this type throughout the book but wish to highlight them here.[1]

We define oppression as the destructive effects of social institutions on people when such institutions damage their identities, denigrate their life styles, and deny them access to opportunities. This oppression becomes social oppression when it is based on attributes people share. The most apparent examples are the sexism directed at women and the racism directed at members of ethnic groups such as blacks, Latinos, Native-Americans, and Asian-Americans. Others who experience such oppression are members of sexual minorities such as gay men and lesbians, age groups such as the elderly, handicapped people, those stigmatized by a label such as "mental patient" and "offender," individuals from nontraditional families, and the working and nonworking poor. Even then, this is a partial list, which can be extended by reflecting on the frequent creation of self-help groups for those who experience rejection from human service institutions.

Goldenberg presents an excellent description of oppression:

> *Oppression is, above everything else, a condition of being, a particular stance one is forced to assume with respect to oneself, the world, and the exigencies of change. It is a pattern of hopelessness and helplessness, in which one sees oneself as static, limited, and expendable. People only become oppressed when they have been forced (either subtly or with obvious malice) to finally succumb to the insidious process that continually undermines hope and subverts the desire to "become."[2]*

The kinds of oppression that are experienced by the individuals we have listed include the poor schools often found in black neighborhoods, the poverty found on many Indian reservations, the antagonism displayed by many teachers when a Latino or Asian-American child speaks in a language other than English, the probing questions directed at a female applicant regarding her responsibilities for her children, the gay man or lesbian passed over for promotion, and the fully qualified older adult who is encouraged to retire.

Still other examples are the physically handicapped person whose school library is not accessible to wheelchairs, the ex-offender or mental patient who has been abandoned by friends and family, and the single parent who finds that schools, workplaces, and other "opportunity structures" are unnecessarily stressful because of rigid schedules and policies. Poor people are also stigmatized by educational and social institutions in ways that perpetuate their poverty cycle.

There are good reasons for the use of group work by socially oppressed people. They often wish to offer support to and secure support from others in a similar status. Under this circumstance, the oppressed person may wish to join a homogeneous group in respect to the oppressed status or seek membership in a heterogeneous group to overcome the isolation produced by the oppression. In either case, the oppressed person is likely to want help in learning to cope with or to change social institutions. Often, the member may want the group to take some action because she or he recognizes that many people acting together possess more power than an individual to change social conditions.

The motivation and skills to change oppressive situations are related to what is frequently termed *empowerment.* In a book that has made a major contribution to our understanding of this, Solomon defines empowerment as

> *. . . a process whereby persons who belong to a stigmatized social category throughout their lives can be assisted to develop and increase skills in the exercise of interpersonal influence and the performance of valued social roles. Power is an interpersonal phenomena: if it is not interpersonal it should probably be defined as "strength." However, the two concepts—power and strength—are so tightly interrelated that they often are used interchangeably. In any event, the transformation of the abstraction of power into an observable reality will be the dominant theme of the chapters that follow.*[3]

Groups can facilitate empowerment in ways not available to other social work modalities. With reference to Solomon's emphasis on skills, members can help each other learn how to assert themselves, how to select and implement appropriate change strategies, and how to defend themselves against retaliation. They can learn these things as they seek to mold the group as well as institutions in the environment to their needs. The relationship that exists between being empowered in the group and in the larger society should be reinforced by the worker. Members, for example, may play a passive role with respect to change processes, particularly those that involve conflict, as these occur in the group. They can be helped to "work out" this withdrawal in the group to avoid such withdrawal outside of the group.

Workers can enhance empowerment through groups by applying the following principles: members must understand that the group is *their* group and that they are responsible for its direction. This does not mean that they may not have to deal with policies and

procedures of the agency, but they must be helped to see how they can affect these procedures and what the consequences are of violating them. Then the members can decide to
take on these consequences, and the worker can help members assume this responsibility.

Members are also empowered when they understand that their lives are affected by
environmental forces but that they have the responsibility and the capacity to change that
environment. Sue analyzes this by distinguishing between *locus of control* and *locus of
responsibility*.[4] The former dimension refers to the individuals' attributions as to the causes
of events that affect them: an "external locus of control" is one in which the individual
believes that his or her life is primarily affected by random external events, while an "internal locus of control" is one in which the individual believes his or her life is primarily
affected by events under his or her control. The empowered individual does not take
responsibility for the oppressive circumstances he or she faces but is able to see how these
have been created by historical as well as current structural circumstances.

The locus of responsibility dimension differs from locus of control in that it refers to
the one who has responsibility to work for change in an oppressive environment. The person with an external locus of responsibility expects others to do this, while the person with
an internal locus of responsibility understands that he or she must take part in such change
efforts. In brief, then, the empowered individual has an external locus of control orientation with an internal locus of responsibility. The ways for workers to facilitate this are
drawn from the consciousness-raising orientation we described in Chapter 11.

Group workers seeking to help members understand the forces affecting their lives, as
well as their capacity for changing them, can learn much from the writings of Brazilian
educator Paulo Freire.[5] Freire presents many of his ideas in the context of programs he
developed to reduce adult illiteracy in Brazil. He concluded that adults will be enhanced
in becoming literate if they connect literacy to the idea that culture is created by human
beings and can be altered in the same way. This connection is developed through the emergence of a *critical consciousness* in which people come to understand the forces that maintain their oppressive social circumstances, whether these forces occur in their schools,
workplaces, or communities. The highest form of critical consciousness is referred to by
Freire as *critical transitive consciousness*. He defines this:

> The critically transitive consciousness is characterized by: depth in the interpre-
> tation of problems, by the substitution of causal principles for magical explana-
> tions; by the testing of one's "findings" and by openness to revision; by the
> attempt to avoid distortion when perceiving problems and to avoid preconceived
> notions when analyzing them; by refusing to transfer responsibility; by rejecting
> passive positions; by soundness of argumentation; by the practice of dialogue
> rather than polemics; by receptivity to the new for reasons beyond mere novelty
> and by the good sense not to reject the old just because it is old—by accepting
> what is valid in both old and new.[6]

Group workers seeking to enhance empowerment will provide opportunities to further
members' critical consciousness. Examples of this are as follows:

A group worker in a support group for abused women helped them examine the
many ways society makes it possible for men to abuse women. These included the

nonresponsiveness they initially experienced when they asked for help and the "message" many received from their families that they were responsible for how they were treated by men.

A group worker in a mothers' group composed of black women who were raising children in the absence of a male partner discussed with them the penalties their families faced from the welfare system when they sought to create two-parent families.

A newly assigned group worker in a group of elderly members found that the group had officers who had been appointed by her predecessor. She was told by that worker that the members would be upset if they faced a competitive election. She returned to the group and initiated a discussion of this. She helped the members to examine the many times that others assumed they wished to be told what to do when this was untrue. The members also came to realize that others often stated this as the reason when actually they wished to keep things "simple" for themselves.

As we described in Chapter 2, the agency context for group work service has a major influence upon that service, particularly true for work with oppressed people. Many of our agencies, themselves, commit institutional forms of racism as well as institutional biases against members of the group oppressed for reasons other than race. Chesler describes these biases in regard to blacks,[7] although they undoubtedly occur for all the other oppressed groups we have listed. These are (1) blaming the victim; (2) focusing on the pathology rather than on the strength of the victim; (3) blaming cultural values of the victims for their detrimental situations; (4) using racism to maintain the status quo; (5) assuming that members of the group will remain dependent permanently.

Consequently, the agency that seeks to serve oppressed people and understand the social basis of their oppression will certainly not confine its services to one-to-one or even group forms but will expect its workers to act as brokers and advocates for clients. This means that the agency will allow workers time for such activities, will hire workers oriented in this way, and will train workers to be more effective agents for social change. As Pinderhughes has pointed out, there is a correlation between workers who seek to empower themselves and those who seek to facilitate clients in this process.[8] Furthermore, workers with and on behalf of group members who try to change oppressive conditions will encounter conflict, and the agency will have to support workers when this happens or workers are likely to reduce these types of activities that are essential for change to occur.

The agency that provides a good environment for change does not "colonize" the oppressed group but encourages its members to participate at all levels of agency decision making:[9] these include the governing boards of private agencies and the advisory boards of public ones. Members of the oppressed group will also be recruited through affirmative action procedures for all levels of staff. The most direct consequences for these "noncolonial" policies is that information will be readily available regarding the group, stereotypes will be challenged, and role models will be present for members.

It can be anticipated that most agencies that seek to effectively serve oppressed people will find that they have some shortcomings related to the kinds of conditions we have just described. The agency should, consequently, seek feedback from members regarding these dimensions and help in changing them. Agency good faith is demonstrated when it does this.

Pregroup Tasks

Any planning of group services for oppressed people must be done jointly with those who are similarly oppressed—with individuals who actually will become members of the group or with those in a similar status. This principle is consistent with the goal of empowerment since, from the beginning, actions affecting oppressed people are taken *with* rather than *for* them. At times, also, the agency (often together with group representatives) will undertake a needs assessment of a sampling of relevant people within the agency's catchment to determine the needs to be met through group services. This needs assessment can be conducted through such devices as a door-to-door survey or "hearings" held in the agency or a "neutral" spot in the community.

This type of beginning led one agency to provide family-type programs for Latinos within the neighborhood, rather than separate family members from one another. Another agency in a Chinese-American neighborhood developed a series of educational activities for youth who wished to learn more about their history and culture. Still another institution in a largely black area organized a series of youth-oriented programs to help members deal with school- and occupation-related problems.

Agencies concerned about oppression not based on ethnicity have established still other services. One agency created a group for former prison inmates who wished to help each other deal with employment issues. The group members also wished to change ex-offenders' image in the community. A university counseling service conducted a needs assessment with several gay men and lesbians, then established several "coming out" groups to help members clarify identity issues for themselves and consequently to decide how and when to express this identity to others such as family members and friends. In addition, the counseling service sponsored a conference for parents of homosexuals, a "defense" committee to respond to charges of harassment of homosexuals in the university, and a planning committee for gay and lesbian social centers.

As we indicated earlier in this chapter, preparation of agency staff should precede the first group meeting. Unless the agency is largely composed of members of the targeted population, a process of staff consciousness-raising should take place. This might include learning about the needs of the group as well as its history and current situation.

Elsewhere, we categorized the information that workers should have to offer effective service to oppressed groups.[10] Briefly, our categories are the following:

1. Communications.   This refers to the language utilized by the group members and the rules as to who speaks to whom and about what. The language may be Spanish, Chinese, or Native American; a nonstandard form of English such as black-English; or the argot used by some homosexuals or members of a criminal subculture. The group worker should be familiar with the language or be prepared to compensate for this through, for example, the use of an indigenous person as a co-facilitator. The rules regarding communications processes and structures are important to know since they will affect how the worker thinks about group composition or how the group will react to topics introduced by the worker.

2. Habitat.   This refers to how members are likely to view as well as utilize their physical space, where the worker and the members decide to hold their meetings, and how the space for the meeting is arranged. There could be problems, for example, if the agency held a meeting of an almost exclusively Catholic group of Latinos in a local Protestant church; yet, it could be an asset to conduct this meeting in the local Catholic church attended by the members. Some ethnic group workers might prefer the typical circle arrangement for group meetings, while another group might be more comfortable when the worker locates himself or herself in a way that denotes a different status.

3. Social Structure.　This refers to the social stratification of the larger oppressed community with which the members identify. When speaking of an ethnic group, this includes the structure of the family, economic, and social institutions of the ethnic group. Other oppressed groups also have internal structures, as described by Kassebaum, Ward, and Wilner in their discussion of a prison.[11] Within this setting, prisoners were categorized as "square johns," "right guys," "con-politicians," and "outlaws." Another example is that of the gay male subculture in which distinctions may be made between those who wear female clothes and those who do not, those who dress in leather and those who do not, and so forth. The worker must understand these categories, as they will also have implications for group composition, group goals, and the interactions that arise among members once the group has begun.

4. Socialization.　This refers to how the individuals associated with the oppressed group are helped to enter into social roles that exist within their culture and to learn the behaviors required for these roles. Examples of this are the roles associated with stages of the life cycle unique to each ethnic group, such as the preparation for puberty ceremonies found in many Native-American tribes. The purposes developed for groups by oppressed people often are to further this type of socialization.[12] Workers should also be sensitive to occasions when members may wish to use the group to alter a socialization pattern. This is often found in women's groups in which the members seek to change the roles traditionally assigned to women in the family, community, and workplace.

5. Economy.　This refers to how the group is affected by the economic institutions and practices of the larger society, as well as the internal economy within the oppressed group. Ethnic groups such as blacks, Latinos, and Native-Americans have been systematically exploited by the economic institutions of the society, as attested to by their income and occupational distributions. The same has been true of women. Homosexuals, the elderly, and ex-offenders find it difficult to succeed in many occupations because of prejudice against them. It is hard, therefore, to imagine a group composed of members of these populations that does not, in some way, deal with issues related to economic factors.

6. Beliefs and Sentiments.　This refers to the belief systems that emerge as people with similar concerns or destinies interact. These beliefs are embedded in the religion, folklore, literature, "sayings," music, and poetry that group members identify as their own. These beliefs have great impact on selection of partners for intimate relationships, discipline of children, behavior toward others who are and are not in the in-group, and treatment of illness (both mental and physical). This does not imply that all people who consider themselves part of the group will think alike but, rather, that some beliefs will be more characteristic of one group than another. For example, members of many Native-American groups will hold the value that it is inappropriate to insist on a change in another's behavior and that it is essential to respect another's privacy and independence.[13] Group workers, in this case, should emphasize group approaches in which members have an opportunity to observe others as models rather than being offered unsolicited advice and direction.

In keeping with the empowerment focus of all work with oppressed people, the potential members of the group or others in a similar status should participate in pregroup tasks such as deciding on group composition, size, format, and purpose. There is no one preferred condition: decisions on these matters will depend on the purposes chosen as a basis for initial planning. As we have suggested, many purposes will require that the group be homogeneous in that all members experience oppression in similar ways: as blacks, women, poor people, and so forth. On some occasions, these members may wish to interact with others from a different social situation to receive feedback, learn how to assert themselves, or create a coalition for social change. The latter may be an important strategy when several groups discover that they have an adversary in common.

The above planning steps may require that an agency change its image in the community. The agency should seek publicity for its program in the media and should utilize existing networks. An example of this was a new agency to serve gay men and lesbians. The agency arranged interviews on television for its staff, who were then also invited to speak to local gay and lesbian groups. Posters on agency services were placed in gay bars and businesses. Physicians and other health services were contacted, as well as a local church that had been established by and for homosexuals.

Group Formation Tasks

Some aspects of formation that may be prolonged for other types of groups occur rapidly in groups of similarly oppressed people. Members assume (although this may not always be a fact) that they have had similar experiences, perceive things in a similar way, speak the same language, and may even know many of the same people. In fact, they may already be acquainted with one another. Members are likely, therefore, to be ready to "get down to business."

That business will initially consist of determining individual and group goals. As in any other group, this involves assessing the relevant circumstances. As a result, members may discover that their previous experiences have not been as similar as they had thought and that some of their values and goals may differ. These issues should either be reconciled or members should seek a way to proceed with multiple agendas.

One value to which we subscribe with reference to such groups is that individual and group goals should be chosen with consideration for their effects on others who are similarly oppressed. This is because of the negative social and political implications of some individuals making gains at the expense of others. When some blacks, disabled people, or women become symbols of how open the opportunities are for social mobility, this can be used to deny opportunities to others. This phenomenon of "tokenism" has many insidious consequences. An example of this was when several gay group members sought employment in a firm boycotted by the gay community. Their energies were then drained into struggling within the gay community rather than into creating job opportunities.

As the worker and members consider their goals and the means to attain them, they must assess member competencies, particularly as these relate to creating environmental changes. This places the emphasis on member strengths and member learning. This perspective is highly compatible with that of Maluccio,[14] who views the member as a learner and assessment as a process of determining competence rather than deficits. We believe that this perspective, especially with regard to oppressed people, removes many barriers between members and worker and reduces resistance.

Because of the focus on coping with an oppressive environment, members will assess their relevant environments as part of the goal-setting process. This assessment will include such factors as what investment people make in the environment status quo, how decisions for change are made and who can make them, who in the environment has the power to influence the decision makers and how they may be reached (the existence of allies), and what is likely to make others in the environment aware of the need for change.

It is important for members to assess the likelihood of some form of retribution for the change effort, and what this retribution might be. There is seldom a situation in which people can work for change without risks, and members should learn this "fact of life." Nevertheless, they can choose when and how to take risks—an important principle to learn.

Goal Pursuit Tasks

When the group members are working to attain their goals, they will engage in two types of activities: those to increase their competence and those to bring about change in their environment. In this chapter we shall describe how to increase their competence. The approaches to bring about environmental changes were described in Chapter 8.

As we stated in the introductory section of this chapter, an important aspect of becoming empowered is to increase one's critical consciousness. This can be done through several procedures, one of which is for members to review their life stories. The focus of this review should be upon how past experiences have caused members to devalue themselves in inappropriate and destructive ways. In one group, for example, some Latino members spoke of how the response of others to their use of Spanish led to feelings of inferiority rather than of pride in their culture. In another group, women members discovered how the response of others to their assertiveness inhibited the expressions of their own needs and interests.

Another approach to consciousness-raising is for members to examine their current interactions with people who do not share their oppressed status (blacks with whites, women with men, gays with straights, and so forth) and to identify how they respond to these in powerless ways. It often helps to examine these interactions in light of the concept of "false consciousness," which refers to an acceptance of the values of one's oppressor when this is dysfunctional to meeting one's own needs. Examples of this are black people who believe that blacks are unmotivated, poor people who believe that those without material resources are entirely responsible for their lack of opportunity, women who believe that others of their gender are happy and content to be dependent on men, and handicapped people who believe they do not have the right to seek intimate relationships.

All of these myths must be challenged as part of the empowerment process. Values-clarification exercises are a way of accomplishing this, as they help members examine their values and evaluate them critically. A useful type of exercise is to choose some statement and ask members to rate how they agree or disagree with it (5–strongly agree; 4–agree; 3–neutral; 2–disagree; 1–strongly disagree). Members then join other members who have made the same rating and discuss in that subgroup why they think as they do. Subgroups report to each other their reasons, and the entire group discusses the issues that have surfaced through this process. Workers can draw upon a substantial literature of values clarification to discover appropriate exercises.[15]

In addition to consciousness-raising, members must be helped to acquire skills directly associated with competence in securing a more humane environment. One important category of such skills is *assertiveness*. This behavior is derived from the idea that all human beings have the right to express their needs, wishes, and feelings in ways that do not infringe on the rights of others,[16] even though people associated with all oppressed groups are likely to have been discouraged or even punished for being assertive. A number of authors have focused on helping women regain their assertiveness. This type of specialized investigation of how to help oppressed people, in view of their unique circumstances, should be extended.[17]

Other skills that members may seek to acquire relevant to their empowerment are how to engage in constructive confrontation, how to appropriately express anger, how to negotiate, and how to present information to support one's position. Workers can also help members learn how to defend their rights aggressively when this is made necessary by the intransigence of an adversary. This involves identifying vulnerable positions of others, eliciting help from people who have authority over an adversary, and threatening legal action.

Negotiation skills are particularly important. As described by Ury and Fisher,[18] the successful negotiator must bargain in ways that recognize each person's *interests* rather than *positions*. An interest is what each party seeks to receive from the interchange, while a position is a specific "solution" that an individual seeks to defend. For example, if a group member has a child with special educational needs, having these needs met is an interest, while having them met through an assignment to a specific program is a position. The school's desire to secure needed services for each child while minimally disrupting existing arrangements is an interest; meeting the needs of the aforementioned child through a tutoring arrangement is a position.

Fisher and Ury also describe how successful negotiators seek to separate relationship issues from substantive ones, help participants perceive each other's situations accurately, respond to feelings, and try to create innovative solutions. All of these skills can be taught to group members through simulation of actual or illustrative situations during group sessions.

While treatment groups often adopt a "blame the victim" posture, this does not contradict the idea that all of the techniques described in this book may be required by oppressed people if by treatment we mean help in modifying one's behaviors, cognitions, or affects that hinder the member from attaining his or her goals. Thus someone who is oppressed may need help to improve the quality of his or her relationships, reduce a feeling of depression or anxiety, or raise a sense of self-esteem. While becoming an active social change agent (and, we hope, achieving some success) may ameliorate these problems, this is not inevitable. The agency, however, that offers treatment to oppressed people will be unlikely to think in terms of pathology or view the coping behaviors of oppressed people as signs of "illness." It will not degrade people by the loose application of labels.

Workers will help members select suitable social action projects: those that will enhance members' competence to cope with the environment, raise their self-esteem, and teach skills in working with others. These projects must not be too insignificant or too ambitious. Early group workers were noted for the energy they brought to improving garbage collection or securing stop signs at busy intersections. During the 1960s, workers went to the other extreme and encouraged members to join rent strikes, welfare department sit-ins, and picket lines without warning these members about the likelihood of retaliation and the ability of the targeted institutions to procrastinate. Many group members in recent decades, on the other hand, did participate in voter registration drives, which helped members see immediate results (a newly registered voter) while increasing their investment in political processes. We hope that while members may not have affected election results in the short run, this did not erase the beneficial effects of their activity.

Another activity for these members is to create a network with others who share similar concerns. The workers role is to facilitate the ways oppressed individuals can communicate with and support one another. The worker helps members locate others who may wish to join their group or form additional groups, and also helps members become knowledgeable about interacting with other groups and organizations.

Many years ago, as a group worker in a settlement house, I was approached by a group of young black women to sponsor their "club," which they had named "Better Human Relations Builders." They wanted to do something to combat racism but were not sure how to proceed. I helped them contact the National Association for the Advancement of Colored People, as well as other organizations, for program ideas and support. A highlight of the year we spent together was our attendance at a civil rights rally, where the members first experienced the large movement of which they were becoming a part.

Nothing we have stated is meant to imply that oppressed people should always be isolated in groups with others in a similar status. Homogeneous groups are often valuable because of the support they provide, their concern for a reaffirmation of identity, and the energy they can bring to social-change activities. An oppressed person may join a group with others who are not oppressed in the same way. This can be valuable for all as members discover how oppression diminishes the oppressor as well as the oppressed and as all explore the true meaning of justice.

Evaluation

One of the most important ways to measure the outcome of a group experience involving oppressed people should be whether they have been empowered. As we indicated earlier, empowerment involves increased skills to influence others and perform valued social roles.

Skills to influence others are demonstrated in specific situations. One way, therefore, to measure them is to ask members about situations in which they sought to use influence and the kinds of influence they employed. Categories such as the following could be utilized: reward, coercion, expertise, reference to one's position, or the respect one receives. For some evaluation purposes, it may be sufficient to know that the member has sought to influence situations in which he or she previously would have behaved passively.

Another way of measuring social influence is with an assertiveness scale. One that has been frequently used was devised by Gambrill and Richey.[19]

Members can also role play situations in the group and can be evaluated by other group members. The ratings will focus upon behaviors targeted in the group, such as persistence in presenting one's argument; resistance to discounting, discourteous, or rejecting behavior of the "other"; appropriate and ethical increases in aggressiveness; or the selection of a strategy appropriate to the situation.

If members have been focusing on self-esteem or identity issues, an evaluation measure appropriate to these should be employed. Workers can use or adapt measures of self-esteem or self-efficacy developed by such investigators as Nugent and Thomas[20] or Sherer and his colleagues.[21] Measures of identity can also be devised in which members are asked about their feelings of status as a member of an ethnic group, as a woman, as a gay person, and so forth. They can also be asked about the frequency with which they interact with others in a similar status, partake of relevant cultural and educational offerings, or attend relevant events.

Since empowerment "begins" in the group experience itself, the worker should gather data on whether this has been manifested. This includes the following:

1. Have group members developed some form of structure through which they can take responsibility for their group? Is this structure working as planned?
2. Have group members initiated goals and activities or do they depend on the worker for this?
3. Do members express their beliefs and intentions regarding the group or do they signal otherwise by not paying attention to events in the group, speaking about irrelevant matters, attending infrequently, and so on?
4. Do members challenge agency actions that interfere with group autonomy?

It is also important to evaluate whether members are developing their critical consciousness. One way to do this is to note, when examples of oppression are presented in the group, whether members analyze the social forces at play, who profits from the oppression, and the psychological consequences of the oppression. It is essential to note whether members even identify instances of oppression or whether they personalize these as proof of their own inadequacy, immorality, or fate.

An Example

This example is from a group of seven young black women who were meeting in a school setting. Their group worker was also a black woman, who was a graduate student in a school of social work. The members of the group had not been doing well in school; several had been involved in fights with other youths. Two members of the group were mothers of infants being cared for by their own mothers. The following events took place in the seventh meeting of the group.

Meeting.   Mary had been elected president of the group at the previous meeting. She entered the meeting this week about ten minutes after the others had arrived and immediately began talking to Lisa about a teacher who had thrown her out of class that day. Several members criticized her for coming late, especially since she was their president. It appeared likely that a real confrontation was in the offing. I (the worker) interrupted and said that I thought what was happening resulted from their not having been given much opportunity to learn to govern themselves in group. Perhaps, also, Mary had some feelings about her new responsibility that had something to do with how she was acting.

Alicia said I was right. Even when she had been a member of the school's student council, the sponsoring teacher had conducted the meetings. Cecelia gave another example of a club in a neighborhood community center in which the staff member assigned to the group had always "been in charge." Mary said that this had always been how it happened to her. She admitted that she was nervous and had come close to skipping this meeting. Frankie said that it didn't matter to her—wasn't it the job of the staff to run things? Mary responded that this wasn't right. They would never learn how to do things for themselves if this always happened, which was why she was in the group.

I thought this was a good time to move things on, so I suggested we talk more about the job of the president so that Mary, as well as future presidents, could do it well and not be so nervous. I added that they might always be a "little nervous" but could still do the job. For example, whenever I came to a meeting, I was always a little tense about how things were going to go and about whether I would be as helpful as possible.

I then wondered if they wanted to talk about this topic of the president's tasks. All of the members said they did. Mary said that T. J., who had been elected secretary, could write down their suggestions. I said I thought this was a good idea and that these suggestions could be put on the blackboard (we were meeting in a classroom) so we could think about them. An animated discussion then took place in which such items were listed: saying when it was time for the meeting to begin, calling on each person to speak, insisting that members raise their hands when they wanted to talk, reminding members not to speak when they were not called on, and asking the members at the beginning of the meeting to make a list of what they were going to talk about that afternoon.

After this discussion, Mary said she could start to practice these things by asking us to make a list of what we wanted to talk about for the rest of the meeting. Mary wanted to talk to everyone regarding what to do about having been thrown out of class. No one else had any suggestions for topics, so we decided to discuss the issue and then have our refreshments. T. J. said that Mary probably had brought this on herself, as she usually did by cussing or fighting. Alicia immediately answered that she knew the teacher always looked for a chance to pick on a black student. I commented that we were making a mistake by either blaming ourselves or someone else without getting all the facts first. Lisa said that was right, and she asked Mary to tell exactly what happened.

In the subsequent discussion, we learned that Mary had been using curse words in class but only because she felt provoked when the teacher said, "You all never do your work"; Mary interpreted this as an attack on all black students. This led to a spirited discussion that we had to end before any conclusions were reached because the meeting time had come to an end. I suggested that Mary put this topic on her list for the next meeting. I also asked if she wanted to meet with me after the meeting to discuss what she was going to do about the class in the meantime. She said that she did.

Analysis.   As we have indicated throughout this chapter, a major issue for work with oppressed people is empowerment. We see this manifested at the beginning of the meeting as the worker supported the members in setting up a structure for governing their own group. This structure, however, had not yet begun to work, as Mary was uncomfortable and unskilled in her position. The worker addressed both of these issues while taking the opportunity to increase all of the members' competence in fulfilling a leadership role.

In addition, the worker sought to increase the critical consciousness of the group by discussing Mary's classroom problem and helping them to learn how to assess both their own responsibility for events and the forces present in the actual situation. This process was begun and is likely to continue for some time with reference to Mary's situation, as well as to situations encountered by other members. A challenge to the worker will be how to help the members conceptualize this kind of analysis so they can use it beyond the specific situation under consideration. While this assessment process might take place in any type of group, it is important to note that the issue of racism was raised here—this offers the group an opportunity to learn more about how to understand and deal with that reality.

Summary

In this chapter, we discussed the special aspects of group work with socially oppressed members. Such oppression was defined as "the destructive effects by social institutions on people when such institutions damage their identities, denigrate their life styles, and deny them access to opportunities" based on "attributes they share with others." We identified a number of populations to which this applies, such as many ethnic groups, women, and sexual minorities.

We discussed empowerment, attributions regarding themselves and their environments, lack of critical consciousness, and the conditions present in agencies serving them—all common issues facing members. Following this, we described typical issues facing such groups in their various phases. This included joint planning between agency and group representatives in the pregroup phase, as well as preparing agency staff in this phase; assessing member competency and environmental conditions in the formation phase; and devloping alternative strategies for the goal pursuit phase such as skills training, consciousness-raising, social action, and creation of support from a network.

Evaluation issues were discussed with reference to all of these types of interventions, including measurement of critical consciousness, social competence, and empowerment. We concluded the chapter with an example of a group of young black women coping with issues of empowerment and critical consciousness.

Endnotes

1. Since the previous edition of this book, much work has been done on how to work with oppressed people in groups. See, for example, Judith A.B. Lee, *The Empowerment Approach to Social Work Practice* (New York: Columbia University Press, 1994): 208–61; Lorraine M. Gutiérrez, "Using groups to empower Latinos: A preliminary analysis, in *Proceedings of the Eleventh Annual Symposium of the Association for the*

Advancement of Social Work with Groups, Montreal (1989); Judith A.B. Lee, ed., *Group Work with the Poor and Oppressed* (New York: Haworth, 1989); Margot Breton, "Toward a model of social groupwork practice with marginalized populations," *Groupwork* 4(1) (1991): 33–47; Margot Breton, "Liberation theology, group work, and the right of the poor and oppressed to participate in the life of the community," in *Group Work Reaching Out: People, Places, and Power*, ed. James A. Garland (New York: Haworth, 1992): 257–70.

2. Ira Goldenberg, *Oppression and Social Intervention* (Chicago: Nelson-Hall, 1978): 2.

3. Barbara Solomon, *Black Empowerment* (New York: Columbia University Press, 1976): 6.

4. Derald W. Sue, *Counseling the Culturally Different: Theory and Practice* (New York: John Wiley, 1981): 74–80.

5. Paul Freire, *Education for Critical Consciousness* (New York: Seabury Press, 1973).

6. Ibid.: 18.

7. Mark A. Chesler, "Contemporary Sociological Theories of Racism," in *Toward the Elimination of Racism*, ed. P. Katz (New York: Pergamon, 1976): 21–72.

8. Elaine Pinderhughes, "Empowerment for our Clients and for Ourselves," *Social Casework* 64 (June 1983): 331–38.

9. For an excellent discussion of "colonization" as this process has implications for social agencies, see Robert Blauner, "Internal Colonialism and Ghetto Revolt," *Social Problems* 16 (Spring 1969): 393–408.

10. Charles Garvin and Brett Seabury, *Interpersonal Practice in Social Work: Processes and Procedures* (Englewood Cliffs, N.J.: Prentice Hall, 1984): 321–29.

11. G. Kassebaum, G. Ward, and D. Wilner, *Prison Treatment and Parole Survival: An Empirical Assessment* (New York: John Wiley, 1971).

12. For an example of this, see E.D. Edwards, M.E. Edwards, G.M. Daines, and F. Eddy, "Enhancing Self-Concept and Identification with 'Indianness' of American Indian Girls," *Social Work with Groups*, 1(3) (1978): 309–18.

13. E. Daniel Edwards and Margie E. Edwards, "Group Work Practice with American Indians," *Social Work with Groups* 7 (Fall 1984): 12.

14. Anthony Maluccio, *Promoting Competence in Clients* (New York: The Free Press, 1981).

15. See, for example, Howard Kirschenbaum, *Advanced Value Clarification* (LaJolla, Calif.: University Associates, 1977).

16. See Chapter 8 for information on assertiveness training.

17. See, for example, Sue Slipman, *Helping Ourselves to Power: A Handbook for Women in the Skills of Public Life.* (New York: Pergamon, 1986); Pamela Butler, *Self-assertion for Women: A Guide to Becoming Androgenous* (San Francisco: Canfield Press, 1976); Pauline McVicar and Al Herman, "Assertiveness, self actualization, and locus of control in women," *Sex Roles* 9 (4) (1983): 555–62.

18. Roger Fisher and William Ury, *Getting to Yes: Negotiating Agreement Without Giving In* (New York: Penguin Books, 1981).

19. Eileen Gambrill and Cheryl Richey, "An Assertion Inventory for Use in Assessment and Research," *Behavior Therapy* 6 (1975): 350–62.

20. W.R. Nugent and J.W. Thomas, "Validation of the self-esteem rating scale," *Research on Social Work Practice* (1993): 191–207.

21. Mark Sherer, James E. Maddux, Blaise Mercandante, Steven Prentice-Dunn, Beth Jacobs, and Ronald W. Rogers, "The self-efficacy scale; Construction and validation," *Psychological Reports* 51(1982): 663–71.

C h a p t e r *16*

Working with Committees and Other Task Groups

Social workers participate either as facilitators or members in many types of groups. Throughout this book, we have primarily emphasized groups whose members have joined the group to attain personal goals. Group workers may be involved with other groups as part of their professional work and can use their knowledge of group processes to help those groups achieve their purposes. Because there are differences as well as similarities in the ways workers can help these two types of groups, we have included this chapter on committees and other task groups.

While there may be a wide range of groups in which social workers are involved, the two major categories are (1) staff groups created in the agency to enhance the agency's functioning and (2) community groups created outside of the agency that benefit "classes" of clients (such as the "elderly," "handicapped," "poor," and "homeless"). The staff groups include staff administrative meetings, teams, committees with specific charges such as to recommend a new policy or program, and in-service training. Community groups include councils consisting of representatives of several organizations, social action groups acting to change social conditions, and committees created as components of a neighborhood organization devoted to social planning and neighborhood development. Each type of agency or community group has unique requirements that go well beyond the scope of this chapter; consequently, we shall broadly describe some of the ways of facilitating these two somewhat general sets of groups.[1]

As a general term for the types of groups we shall be discussing, we use *task group*. Toseland and Rivas define these as groups "that are used to find solutions to organizational problems, to generate new ideas and to make decisions." They add that "Task groups can have three primary purposes: (a) meeting client needs, (b) meeting organizational needs and (c) meeting community needs."[2]

It is important for the reader to recognize that it is not always possible to draw a clear line between individual change groups and task groups. Sometimes a worker will create a task group composed of agency clients because of the therapeutic benefits for those clients. An example of this is the patient government group we discussed as part of rehabilitation in Chapter 14. On the other hand, community organizers engaged in "grass roots" work with people in a community may encounter group members who seek to discuss personal problems during committee meetings, and the other group members may decide to deal with these to a limited degree.

Nevertheless, it is useful to maintain a distinction between individual change and task groups and to be aware of the difficulties that arise when the line becomes blurred. These difficulties consist of a failure of the group to accomplish its mission because of individual needs; intragroup conflict; loss of members frustrated by group ineffectiveness; and a lack of help to members seeking it because there is, in fact, no mandate for treatment to occur.

While we shall become more specific in this chapter as to the procedures employed in task groups, we shall also point out some general similarities and differences between task and individual change groups. As the reader will see, the differences may at times be relative rather than absolute, depending on the specific task or individual change group under consideration.

First is the structure of the meeting. Many individual change groups have an agenda, but it is often "loose" and consists of a series of topics. An exception is a skills training group with a highly structured meeting plan. Virtually all task groups have a specific agenda for the meeting, and we shall describe important considerations for creating this agenda later in this chapter.

Second, many agenda items in a task group call for specific decisions as to actions to be taken. The less formal "topics" in a treatment group may or may not lead to specific actions, and when the discussion is of an individual's behavior, that individual may or may not enact the recommendations made by others in the group.

Third, task groups usually have a formal process of decision making such as majority rule and voting procedures. These procedures are seldom used in individual change groups where decisions, if they are made, are often through group "consensus."

Fourth, especially as a task group increases in size, there may be formal rules as to how members are "recognized" to speak, how "motions" for action may be made, and so forth.[3] Individual change groups are much more likely to be conducted informally.

Fifth, members are usually selected for an individual change group based on their individual needs as well as on how their participation will help meet others' needs. Members are selected for a task group almost exclusively in terms of the composition most likely to help the group achieve its mission.

Sixth, individual change groups always insist on confidentiality. Task groups, on the other hand, usually create minutes of meetings, which may be required to be made public.

Last (and certainly not least), the role of the group worker is likely to be different. In an individual change group, the worker has a central position as a group facilitator. In a task group, the group worker may simply be another member or the formal chairperson, or may "staff" a group that has a chair as well as other appointed "officers." The role of "staff" to a group has unique requirements that we shall also describe later.

Task groups go through the same phases as any other group; therefore, we shall continue our discussion utilizing the same phase structure employed in the preceding chapters on practice variations.

Pregroup Tasks

As with any group, the purpose for which it is formed will help determine many other conditions such as group composition and size. The purpose is usually determined by the agency or community organization that creates the group and is often communicated to the potential group members in written form. This is often referred to as the group's *mandate.* When the group begins to meet, the members usually review this mandate and, if it is unclear, ask for clarification.

As we stated earlier, the composition of the group should be determined by the human resources the group will require to accomplish its purposes. These resources include both the attributes of members as well as their location in the organizational structure. Thus, if a task group is to plan a fund-raising event, it should include people capable of planning the event and carrying out the tasks related to it such as publicity, budget, and recruitment of workers. If another task group is to assess the health needs of a community, it should include representatives of various age groups, ethnic groups, social classes, and both genders.

Various compositional problems are likely to occur in task groups. One that arises in an agency is whether different levels of the agency hierarchy should be represented, such as line staff, supervisors, and administrators as well as people from various departments. Again, the purpose of the group will help the convenors make this decision, and the effect of the presence or absence of any contingent should be considered. Another is the presence of individuals in the group who are in conflict as individuals or in conflict by virtue of membership in groups that are at conflict. The likelihood of conflict does not, in itself, militate against including any individual. The convenors, however, will have to consider how to help the group cope with this issue—a topic we shall consider later.

A phenomenon that convenors must consider is that of the "hidden agenda." This refers to task group members with personal goals they wish to pursue in the group, but which they do not express openly because these goals are not directly related to the purpose of the group and may even be contrary to it. A hidden agenda may also relate to the member's identification with another group that he or she may officially or unofficially represent. The convenor—as well as any subsequent officer, staff person, or facilitator—can make some informed guesses about hidden agendas and, on the basis of this, come to some conclusions about group composition or, at least, how this will be dealt with once the group has begun.

The convenor of a group in an agency will also be cognizant of how the group's composition relates to the "informal" system of the organization. The informal system represents relationships among staff that arise from their interactions with each other rather than from formal job requirements. Thus staff form relationships with each other at lunch, around the coffee machine, or after duty hours. Staff may use the informal system to create cooperative arrangements not mandated by the agency or, in contrast, to complain about the agency and to hinder its efforts. The convenor should try to understand how the group's composition intersects with the informal system and, consequently, how members are likely to want to use the group.

Often the convenors will seek volunteers for the group rather than appoint specific individuals because of their role in the agency. This most often occurs in community organizations who seek to recruit people in the neighborhood for active roles in meeting community needs. There are several ways to do this. We think the least effective ways are through a newspaper announcement, posters in businesses, or a circular sent out to people on a mailing list. Individuals are unlikely to respond to these anonymous approaches unless the issue is a "hot" one as, for example, after some crisis has occurred in the community or in response to an issue that people think will seriously affect their well-being (e.g., a fire has demonstrated the lack of safety of dwellings, or a factory is to be built that makes the community a less desirable place to live).

Instead, a personal form of appeal is better. This can be in the form of home visits in the community, telephone calls, speeches before local groups, or a table in a shopping center with staff or volunteers present. Ideally, also, a professional staff person should be teamed up with indigenous community members with whom recruits can identify. As a further guarantee of meeting attendance, the staff member or a volunteer should call the community resident to remind her or him of the meeting. If transportation, baby-sitting, or fears of coming alone are manifest, some plan should exist to address these needs. The measures will ensure that the bane of the organizer's life—a meeting called to which no one comes—will not occur.

The size of the group will also be related to its purpose. We have found, when the purpose of the group is to create a plan to be considered subsequently by a large, representative body, that the smallest group that can bring the required knowledge and experience to the task is best. On the other hand, if the group must accomplish a task that requires the support and approval of a wide range of people, the most representative group is best, even if it is fairly large (more than fifteen people). A large group may have to subdivide into smaller task forces to accomplish its mission.

Some task groups with a range of purposes or steadily evolving purposes may be created for either a long or indefinite period. Otherwise, if there are only a few purposes, the group should be created for a limited time. This will help recruit members who may be willing to commit their energies to a short-term group but hesitate to take on long-term commitments.

The role of staff members should also be clarified in advance so that prospective members can adapt to this. There are several roles performed by trained group workers:

1. *Member:* The worker may simply be a member of the group. Examples of this are staff committees and representative community groups.
2. *Officer:* The worker may hold office in the group, such as its chair or secretary.
3. *Staff:* This is a position frequently held by the group worker. In this situation, the group has officers and members whose roles are separate from that of the worker who is not a member. According to Tropman,[4] the roles of the staff person are as follows:

resource person
consultant
technician
catalyst
enabler
tactician
assistant to the chair

Since the role of *staff* may be an unfamiliar one, we shall discuss it now in detail. The staff person usually functions as an aid to the chair, although he or she may, at times, be assigned to help other group members accomplish their tasks. In relationship to the chair, the staff person will secure information, analyze options, make recommendations, and suggest strategies. The staff person will usually consult with the chair about the agendas for coming meetings and notify members of these. The staffer is also likely to prepare the minutes of previous meetings and to distribute these with the agenda of the coming one. The staffer will maintain the group's files and make them available to members as needed.

An important factor in holding productive meetings is the way the agenda has been constructed. The agenda lists in order the topics to be considered at the meeting and sometimes indicates how much time is to be allocated to each. Tropman recommends the following order:[5]

1. Enter brief, agenda-relevant minutes.
2. Make informative announcements.
3. Decide on less controversial items.
4. Consider most difficult item.
5. Break.
6. Talk over "for discussion only" items.
7. Consider the least difficult item(s) and call for adjournment.

Tropman recommends that less controversial items be handled first, as they help participants develop confidence and "open up." By then (about one third of the way through the meeting), latecomers will have arrived and those who have to leave early will still be present. The energy level of members will be high.

After a difficult item has been dealt with, members may need a "break," either a time to stretch or a longer period when members might refill their coffee cups. A more relaxed discussion of items that do not yet require action might take place. Tropman believes that some quick, noncontroversial items may be resolved just before the close of the meeting so that it ends on a high note of success, especially if earlier items involved controversy and tension.

Group Formation Tasks

During the first group meetings, the major issues will be purpose, membership, structure, operating procedures, and work plan. We shall discuss each of these in turn.

The purpose of the group, often referred to as its mandate, should be the first topic considered. The agency or community organization that convenes the task group will specify, usually in writing, the mission of the group. This may also be derived from the minutes of the meeting at which the group was proposed. If the group worker is appointed as a staff person for the task group, he or she will be expected to clarify the group's mandate. Otherwise, a staff person or officer of the "parent" organization could be invited to attend the group's initial meeting for this purpose. Along with this clarification, the group should be informed of other expectations of the "parent," such as the resources it will supply as well as those the task group should secure on its own; the time within which outcomes should be produced; the reports that the task group should submit to the parent (or other groups) and at what intervals; and any other constraints placed on the task group.

The individuals invited to join the task group may have some objection to the mandate created by the "parent." This should be recognized and discussed. Many task groups have foundered due to conflicts between them and the organization because of a failure to consider reactions to initial mandates.

At times, the parent organization will have determined the membership of the task group as well as its officers after consultation with the person designated as the task group chair. The members of the task group should have the right to ask for and receive information as to the basis for this selection. Sometimes the task group will have the responsibility of adding additional members as needed and of selecting some or all of its officers. In this latter circumstance, existing members should assess how many members and what kinds of officers the group will need to accomplish its purposes. They will then have to plan ways to recruit additional members.

Groups should also discuss the attributes and experiences they require in their officers, which will often help members be more objective in selecting such persons. They should also determine the length of time officers will serve. We have not found it desirable to have officers rotate after one or a few meetings unless a staff person will provide continuity for the group.

Structural decisions must then be made, including when and where the group will meet, how meetings will be called, how members will be notified of meetings, what the responsibilities of members are, and how many members must be present for business to be conducted (that is, the size of a quorum). How decisions will be made (by majority vote, consensus, two thirds) should also be clarified as well as whether the group will use formal procedures such as those embodied in *Robert's Rules of Order*.[6]

Many groups find it useful to discuss group norms at an early meeting. These might include the following:

1. The responsibility members have to notify the group if they cannot fulfill a responsibility they have assumed or if they wish to withdraw from the group.
2. The way members may help one another to remain task oriented.
3. Whether the group is willing to engage in "process" discussions in which members seek to assess how well the group is functioning as a group and how its deliberations may be improved.
4. Whether members should feel free to disagree publicly with majority decisions of the group if they were not in the majority. This can also be an issue for a group officer— even the chair—who does not agree with the majority of members in the group.

During the formation period, if the group has several purposes or one complex purpose, it should develop a work plan. This includes whether the group will divide itself into subcommittees that will work on a different purpose or aspect, and whether a time period should be established during which the group will work on each purpose. If the group must accomplish a series of complex steps to complete its work by a specific date, the members may wish to employ a procedure like the Program Evaluation and Review Technique (PERT).[7] This technique helps members create a chart by starting at the "end" with the final product and due date and working backward, listing each prior task and when it must be accomplished for the group to meet its deadline.

Goal Pursuit Tasks

A major part of the activity of most task groups is problem solving. Anyone who seeks to facilitate task groups should understand the ways groups can best engage in problem solving, as we described in Chapter 5. In addition to the procedures we described there, several additional ones are often used in task groups.

Brainstorming as well as other procedures we shall describe are means of overcoming two major blocks to effective problem solving. One is that people tend to think in ways similar to those they have used in the past, even when these are not productive. The other is that some members of groups have higher status than others, so their ideas tend to be accepted, while those of lower status members tend to be rejected. Some means must be used, therefore, to encourage groups to look at ideas generated by all group members, not just a select few.

Brainstorming involves asking members to provide possible alternative solutions to the group problem without any evaluation as to the positives or negatives until all the solutions have been listed. These are often written on a blackboard or newsprint so members can review all possibilities without immediately linking them to the specific member who made them. A brief discussion usually precedes the introduction of brainstorming in groups unfamiliar with it. Members are informed that people often withhold creative solutions for fear that others will regard them as too "way out." Group members must get past this informal censorship to tap their most creative capacities. The brainstorming session is then introduced by stating several "rules" that apply.

Another means of generating new ideas is to encourage members to draw upon analogies as a way of relating thoughts about a different situation to the problem at hand. Gordon[8] and Prince[9] have done much work in showing how this method works.

The worker, in utilizing analogies, will first explain to the members that he or she is introducing a different means for considering an issue. When approval has been secured for this, the worker will ask the question, "How is this situation like . . . ?" This sentence may be completed with a noun that refers to an external real situation, a fantasy, or the persons themselves.

An example of this occurred in a staff committee trying to understand a particularly difficult family situation. The chairperson asked, "How is the M. situation like a horserace?" Some of the answers provided by the staff present were the following:

Everyone is trying to outdistance the other, even if the other is hurt in the process and even if he or she has to resort to "dirty tricks."

In this effort, each person remains in the same track.

Each person is looking for cheers from the "audience."

There are a few clear "front runners" and the others have little hope of obtaining what they want.

In the process of "running," many family members have "forgotten" why they are in the race.

After this list was completed, the group discussed each comparison further as well as the implications it held for helping the family. The group members stated that they had come up with many new ideas. The skill of the chairperson lay in providing an analogy with the potential to help the members generate such thoughts.

Several procedures have been developed to help members focus on objective factors rather than on personal ones. (This is referred to in the social-psychological literature as a "process loss.") One is the *Delphi Method.* As described by Zander,[10] the first step in a "Delphi" is for the members to complete a questionnaire about their opinions, usually devised by the group worker. The results are reported to participants as part of a second questionnaire, in which members are also asked to react to the results of the first questionnaire. During this process, new ideas may be generated, and these are added to the subsequent questionnaires.

The Delphi procedure is particularly useful when group members come from different backgrounds or professions. Because of the anonymity it guarantees, members react to the ideas rather than to their judgments about whether people from a particular group are likely to have good ideas. It was called Delphi (after the site of the oracle in ancient Greece that foretold the future) because it is often used to pool the individuals' predictions about the future when these individuals possess different yet valid types of information.

The author utilized this method, for example, as part of a project to predict the likely goals for mental health services so that staff development could be future oriented rather than primarily "catching up with yesterday."[11] Readers can consult the work of Dalkey for details on how to set up a Delphi.[12]

Still another method for facilitating problem solving in groups is the *Nominal Group Technique.* Toseland and Rivas,[13] who have experimented with the technique, recommend that it be used with six to nine people (so that larger groups should be divided). Before the meeting, the worker writes a clear statement of the problem on a work sheet and duplicates this sheet for every participant. Members are asked to work individually at first by writing their ideas about or responses to the problem on the sheet.

After sufficient time for each member to write something, the worker proceeds to the next step. Each member, in turn, is asked to provide one idea, which the worker writes on a large pad of newsprint or on a blackboard. Members are explicitly prevented from giving all of their ideas at once. They are encouraged, however, to think of new ideas by building on those presented by others. The worker continues calling on each person, in turn, in additional rotations until all the ideas have been listed. Members, however, do not criticize each other's ideas at this point.

The next stage involves clarifying the ideas listed, after which the group is helped to rank order the ideas. Members are asked to list the best five (or four or six, or whatever the worker thinks will produce a suitable range of alternatives) on cards. These "votes" are then listed on the chart. The items that have received some predetermined number of votes can then be further ranked by members to create a "short list." Further discussion should take place if there are major discrepancies in the rank ordering of different members in order to clarify the basis for such disagreements. Research on and description of Nominal Group Technique is available in the work of Delbecq and his colleagues.[14]

Toseland and Rivas note still another approach to the use of task groups referred to as *Quality Circles and Quality Improvement Teams.*[15] Quality circles are composed of employees who convene voluntarily to create solutions to work problems. Quality Improvement Teams are an outgrowth of an approach referred to as *Total Quality*

Management. While Quality Circles are typically made up of staff members from the same work unit, Quality Improvement Teams may be made up of employees from different departments and agency levels who are appointed by management.

The agency may appoint an individual to coordinate the work of Quality Circles and to train the members in some of the techniques discussed earlier in this chapter. These circles typically have six to eight members.

Toseland and Rivas utilize the work of Kinlaw in describing the steps for quality improvement used by Quality Improvement Teams, as follows:[16]

1. Understanding the opportunity or problem.
2. Defining the specific improvement target.
3. Designing strategies to reach the target.
4. Designing data-acquiring strategies.
5. Designing a process to use the data.
6. Deciding how the project will be managed.

In addition to introducing such devices as brainstorming, Delphi, and nominal group technique, workers who seek to facilitate task groups will be on the lookout for several problems that hinder the work of such groups: lack of interest, uneven verbal input, and restraints on discussion. Zander, in a summary of the techniques used by facilitators to deal with these problems, suggests the following.[17] Lack of interest can be countered by posing an interesting issue that members will want to discuss; by raising issues in ways that require interaction among members; by providing an experience for the group that will raise interest in the topic (such as a field visit or an interesting speaker); and by making sure that topics placed on the agenda have been suggested by members.

Verbal input can be made more even by creating small subgroups to develop points of view about different aspects of the topic, by highlighting differences of opinion, and by appointing a member or members to observe and report on the group's process. Members can also be asked in advance to prepare a statement about their point of view. Participation is enhanced when members are given a brief period of silence to consider their point of view and even to make a few notes.

When the discussion appears to lag, the facilitator can summarize the points made thus far or can ask if a member or the chair would be willing to do this. The facilitator can indicate unresolved issues or those about which there are differences. This also may be the point when the worker introduces one of the techniques we discussed in another chapter.

Earlier in this chapter we made reference to *Robert's Rules of Order.* In small task groups, it is unlikely that the members will wish to draw upon all the formal rules embodied in such parliamentary procedure. Burghardt recommends a modified version for groups that must frequently make formal decisions.[18] In this version, group members operate by making and seconding motions; calling or moving the "question" to end debate on the issue; making amendments to motions; and making procedural motions.

When the group is considering an issue, the chairperson can ask, or the facilitator can suggest, that someone "make a motion." This requires stating in clear terms the action that member wishes the group to take. If there is support for the motion, it is "seconded." If not, another person usually states a different motion on the issue.

After the motion has been made and seconded (and usually recorded by the secretary for the minutes), the chair calls for discussion on the motion. When anyone thinks that all points of view have been expressed, that person can either "call for" or "move" the question. In the former case, the chair will ask if there are any objections to "calling the question"; if not, the motion will be voted on. If the member has "moved" the question, a vote is taken as to whether the group is *ready to vote on the issue itself.* If a majority votes in favor of *this* motion, the main motion is then voted on.

Sometimes it appears likely that a motion will be passed if it is modified. An individual can then "move" to amend the motion in some way. The original maker and seconder of the motion will often agree with the amendment, which is then incorporated in the original motion as a "friendly amendment." If it is not agreed to in this way, the amendment must be voted on by the members (before they vote on the original motion), and it is only incorporated if the majority agrees to it.

Procedural requests (usually referred to by the member who makes them as *points of order*) include requests for information about the topic, the time remaining in the meeting, or other pertinent issues. Procedural motions include motions to "table the motion" and to adjourn the meeting. The move to "table" is often made when the member thinks that the group should have more time to think about the issue or to get more information. When the motion has been presented by a subcommittee, those members are usually expected to secure more information, rethink the issue, and so forth. Points of order may be handled by the chair if he or she thinks them appropriate. Procedural motions are voted upon and passed by the majority of the group present.

As we have stated earlier, the group members should decide in their first meetings how and to what degree they wish to use such decisional procedures. The important thing is that they are tools for groups to use in the ways they think will best expedite their deliberations. In large groups, however, *Robert's Rules of Order* are usually adhered to more firmly than in small groups, and members may have to be instructed in their use.

Evaluation

In general, many of the procedures described in Chapter 9 that relate to changes in group or environmental conditions can be used in task groups. In addition, a number of procedures can be used to assess the unique aspects of such groups. Tropman, in a series of exercises at the end of his succinct discussion of effective meetings, provides items that could be used by workers, observers, or members to evaluate aspects of their groups.[19] Some of those we have found most useful from his work as well as our own are the following:

1. Membership

    1.1. Does the group represent all of the interests that it should?
    1.2. Does the group consist of members that cover the range of skills the group requires to accomplish its mission?

2. Mission

    2.1. Is the purpose of the group clear?
    2.2. How well do members agree with the purpose?

3. Task Group Functioning

3.1. How well do the members know their membership roles?

3.2. Do you think the group makes good decisions?

3.3. How well are all members involved in decision making?

3.4. Does the group operate on the basis of an agenda?

3.5. Do members have an opportunity to contribute to the agenda and are they notified of its content before meetings?

3.6. Does the agenda take into consideration the proper placement of important and/or controversial items so that members become involved in the meeting yet are not too exhausted to give proper consideration to them (usually in the middle third of the meeting)?

3.7. Have members accepted and do they effectively employ procedural rules that help them make decisions?

3.8. Does the group employ procedures to help members be more creative and objective in decision making?

4. The Staffer Role

4.1. Does this person provide information to the chair and the members that they need?

4.2. Does this person give technical assistance or training?

4.3. Does this person help in the creation of an agenda and its distribution in a timely fashion?

4.4. Does this person help members analyze choices?

4.5. Does this person help to set the stage for the meeting (set-up of room, availability of materials that are needed)?

4.6. Do racism or sexism have an impact on the interactions among members?

5. The Chairperson

5.1. Does this person prepare for meetings in advance?

5.2. Does this person act impartially?

5.3. Does this person conduct meetings in an orderly fashion?

5.4. Does this person work with staff person[s] when they are assigned?

5.5. Does this person model good committee behavior for members (such as promptness, good listening, objectivity, preparation such as reading reports in advance of meeting)?

The above points are meant to be suggestive and can be added to in numerous ways or modified by creating rating scales (for example, ranging from "5"—accomplished at a high level, to "1"—totally missing). Members can use selected items by completing questionnaires during a meeting, by holding an open discussion on appropriate points, or by appointing different individuals or subgroups to assess different aspects of group functioning.

An Example

The following is an example of part of a meeting of a "block club" organized in the neighborhood of a community center. The center hoped eventually to create such clubs in all of the blocks in its area. The purpose of the block clubs is to help the residents identify and work toward ways of making their block a better place to live. This might require members of several or all of the block clubs to work together for community-wide change. For that purpose, the center had created a block club federation, and each individual group selected two representatives to attend the federation. This meeting was to be the fifth for this group.

Meeting between Staffer and Chair.   Immediately after the fourth meeting, Ms. J., the block club worker who was trained in group work and who had her Master's degree, met with Ms. F., who had just been elected the chairwoman of the club. They talked about how things were going in the group and about the agenda for the next meeting. Ms. F. said that she was worried because none of the Latino residents had attended any of the meetings (Ms. F. was black). The worker, who was also black, had visited the homes of several Latino residents prior to the first meeting and had called them before each meeting, but to no avail. Ms. J. and Ms. F. decided that this should be one of the items on the agenda of the next meeting.

They also discussed the survey that Ms. J. had made of block concerns when she visited the residents. Those mentioned most frequently were the number of robberies in the neighborhood, the fights between teenagers from different ethnic groups, the lack of any medical services in the immediate neighborhood, the many days the school had been closed for teacher meetings thereby causing working parents to have child care problems, and the threat that a number of apartment buildings in the block would be torn down so the city could build a new fire station. Ms. J. and Ms. F. thought that the next meeting should select the group's first project.

Ms. F. said she didn't know how to handle Mr. Y., who had attended every meeting. Every chance he had he complained about the poor reception on his television. The other members resented his interruptions because these had little to do with the purposes of the meeting. Ms. J. suggested that Ms. F. explain to the members that when they were discussing a particular point on the agenda, she would have to interrupt anybody not speaking on that topic. She also suggested that since Mr. Y. was a custodian at the local school, he could be told that the group would value his opinions about how the children in the neighborhood behaved when this topic was discussed.

Based on this discussion, Ms. J. wrote down the following agenda and agreed to have it distributed from door to door. Several members of the club said that their children would do this chore.

Agenda for Fifth Meeting

1. Introduction of new members
2. Minutes of the fourth meeting
3. Information about a fund-raising event sponsored by the federation
4. Decision regarding a group project
5. Discussion regarding how representative the block club is
6. Decision regarding how frequently the group will meet
7. Selection of temporary representatives to the Federation

Meeting.   Eleven people attended the fifth meeting of the group, including two Latinos. Since the previous meetings never had more than nine in attendance, this was an improvement. Ms. F. called the meeting to order and asked the worker, who had taken the minutes of the previous meeting, to read them. After this, she asked if there were any additions to the minutes, but none were made. Ms. F. then introduced Mr. H., Mr. O., and Ms. T., who were attending for the first time. She had approached them before the beginning of the meeting and had obtained their names, addresses, and phone numbers.

Following this, Ms. F. called on the worker to explain about the fund-raising event. The worker explained that it was a bake sale and that the federation hoped that as many residents as possible from each group would bake and donate cakes. Mr. Y. said he didn't see how anyone in his family could bake a cake with all of the rumbling caused by street repairs. He then rambled on about this. Ms. F. said that the group could decide to take this up as an issue, but that this wasn't the time to discuss it at any length.

Ms. F. then stated that the group should begin to decide on its projects. She called on the worker to tell about the neighborhood survey. While she was doing this, Mr. P. asked whether the survey was any good inasmuch as he had never been asked his opinion. The worker explained that she did visit homes at various times of the day and evening so that different family members could be interviewed, and that she had talked to about 40 percent of the families on the block. She was sorry she had missed Mr. P.; however, he would have a good chance to give his opinions now.

The worker listed the topics suggested by the residents as well as the responses to questions about what they would like to see improved in the neighborhood. She suggested a way of selecting the ones to work on first by allowing each person to pick three topics and then voting on them. First, she suggested, they could discuss each one to clarify what the issue was. Afterwards, they could create committees around the topics that had received the largest vote so that people could work on the topic about which they had the greatest concern.

The above presentation and discussion took about a half-hour, while the clarification and selection took another hour. This left a half-hour of the two-hour meeting for the last three items on the agenda. Space here does not permit further details on this meeting.

Analysis.   This excerpt demonstrates several aspects of work with a task group. In this example, the group worker is functioning as staff person for the committee. In this role, she provides support for the chair and fulfills tasks between meetings that will help the group to function. We see that a major part of her work involves helping the chair prepare the agenda and securing information for the committee—in this case, the results of a survey.

We see that the worker helps the chair and the group to keep a *task focus* rather than a focus on meeting individual needs. On the other hand, she does help the group draw upon the strengths of members so that individuals will find the group rewarding. She also is concerned that the group maintains the interest of the members by focusing upon concerns of theirs related to the overall purpose of the group. She provides techniques that will help the group make decisions, such as the approach she used to prioritize neighborhood concerns. Individual motivation is also maintained by having each member select his or her favorite issue to work on.

Summary

In this chapter we discussed how workers facilitate task groups in the agency and in the community. These ways draw upon the same small-group knowledge base as that utilized with treatment groups. Because, however, the focus is on accomplishing a task rather than on changing the situations of individual members, the ways of facilitating such groups involve some techniques not customarily employed in treatment groups.

We followed the same outline as that drawn upon in the previous chapter and described pregroup, formation, goal pursuit, and evaluation processes. The pregroup activities include a decision by the agency or community organization that creates the group as to its purpose or mandate; they also include staff training, decision making, or carrying out of an activity such as fund raising or publicizing events. Another pregroup activity is choosing members for the group or determining that the chairperson and possibly a few others will do this. Major compositional issues are to ensure that the group represents the right factions and includes members who possess the range of expertise necessary to accomplish the group's purpose. If the group is to recruit its own members, an effective means of attracting people must be used. Another important issue is to determine whether the group worker will be a member, officer, or staff person of the group.

During the group's first meetings, members will clarify the group's purpose and will negotiate any disagreements they have about this with the agency or community organization. They will also deal with membership issues if they are expected to expand the group's size. They will resolve structural issues such as choosing officers, and they will clarify how decisions will be made, such as whether they will employ formal parliamentary procedure. A work plan and time schedule will also be devised.

As the group moves on to accomplish its purposes, it will have to devise means for reaching decisions as objectively and creatively as possible. For these reasons, workers have employed the methods of brainstorming, Delphi questionnaires, Nominal Group Technique, and using analogies. These procedures for overcoming apathy and uneven participation during meetings were described in this chapter.

Following this discussion of goal pursuit methods in task groups, we presented a list of items for evaluating the functioning of task groups. The chapter ended with an example of a task group created by a community organization program.

Endnotes

1. Readers interested in more extensive discussions of work with different types of task groups can consult John E. Tropman, *Effective Meetings: Improving Group Decision Making* (Beverly Hills: Sage, 1980) and Steve Burghardt, *Organizing for Community Action* (Beverly Hills: Sage, 1982).

2. Ronald W. Toseland and Robert F. Rivas, *An Introduction to Group Work Practice*, 2nd ed. (Boston: Allyn & Bacon, 1995): 29.

3. Task groups often use what has been referred to as parliamentary procedure such as that embodied in H. Robert, *Robert's Rules of Order* (Glenview, Ill.: Scott Foresman and Co., 1970).

4. Tropman, *Effective Meetings*: 52.

5. Tropman, *Effective Meetings*: 67.

6. See footnote 3.

7. D. Cook, *Program Evaluation and Review Technique: Application in Education*, Cooperation

Research Monograph 17 (Washington, D.C.: United States Office of Education, 1966).

8. W. Gordon, *Synectics: The Development of Creative Capacity* (New York: Harper & Row, 1961).

9. G. Prince, *The Practice of Creativity* (New York: Harper & Row, 1970).

10. Alvin Zander, *Groups at Work* (San Francisco: Jossey-Bass, 1977): 78–79.

11. Charles Garvin, "Training and the Future of Mental Health Services: Steps Towards a Service Society," in *The Michigan Study of Mental Health Continuing Education*, ed. A. Lauffer (Ann Arbor: School of Social Work, The University of Michigan, 1977): 31–50.

12. N.C. Dalkey, "The Delphi Method: An Experimental Study of Group Opinion," *Management Science* (June 1969).

13. Toseland and Rivas, *An Introduction to Group Work Practice*: 337–41.

14. A. Delbecq, A. Van de Ven, and D. Gustafson, *Group Techniques for Program Planning: A Guide to Nominal Group and Delphi Processes* (Glenview, Ill.: Scott, Foresman and Co., 1975); A. Van de Ven and A. Delbecq, "Nominal versus Interacting Group Processes for Committee Decision-Making Effectiveness," *Academy of Management Journal* 9 (1971): 203–12.

15. Toseland and Rivas, *An Introduction to Group Work Practice*, 2nd ed.: 345–48.

16. C.D. Kinlaw, *Continuous Improvement and Measurement for Total Quality: A Team Based Approach* (San Diego, Calif.: Pfeiffer, and Homewood, Ill: Business One Irwin, 1992); cited in Toseland and Rivas, *An Introduction to Group Work Practice*, 2nd ed.: 347.

17. Alvin Zander, *Making Groups Effective* (San Francisco: Jossey-Bass, 1982): 42–43.

18. Steve Burghardt, *Organizing for Community Action* (Beverly Hills: Sage Publications, 1982): 54–57.

19. Tropman, *Effective Meetings*: 93–109.

Bibliography

Acosta, F.X., and J. Yamamoto, "The Utility of Group Work Practice for Hispanic Americans," *Social Work with Groups* VII (1984): 63–73.

Anderson, Carol M., *Schizophrenia and the Family: A Practitioner's Guide to Psychoeducation and Management.* New York: Guilford Press, 1986.

Antze, P., "The Role of Ideologies in Peer Psychotherapy Organizations: Some Theoretical Considerations and Three Case Studies," *Journal of Applied Behavioral Science* 12 (1976): 323–46.

Back, K.W., *Beyond Words: The Story of Sensitivity Training and the Encounter Movement.* New York: Russell Sage, 1972.

Bales, Robert F., *Interaction Process Analysis: A Method for the Study of Small Groups.* Reading, Mass.: Addison-Wesley, 1950.

———. "Task Roles and Social-Emotional Roles in Problem Solving Groups," in *Readings in Social Psychology*, 3rd ed., eds. E.E. Maccoby, T.M. Newcomb, and E.T. Hartley: 437–47. New York: Holt, Rinehart & Winston, 1958.

Bednar, Richard L., and Theodore J. Kaul, "Experiential Group Research: Current Perspectives," in *Handbook of Psychotherapy and Behavior Change: An Empirical Analysis*, 2nd ed., eds. Sol L. Garfield and Allen Bergin: 769–816. New York: John Wiley, 1978.

Beninati, Joseph, "Pilot Project for Male Batterers," *Social Work with Groups* 12 (2) (1989): 63–74.

Berman-Rossi, Toby, and Irving Miller, "African-Americans and the Settlements During the Late Nineteenth and Early Twentieth Centuries," *Social Work with Groups* 17 (3) (1994).

Berne, Eric, *Transactional Analysis in Psychotherapy.* New York: Grove Press, 1961.

Bernstein, Douglas A., and Thomas D. Borkovec, *Progressive Relaxation Training: A Manual for the Helping Professions.* Champaign, Ill.: Research Press, 1973.

Bernstein, Saul, ed., *Explorations in Group Work.* Boston: Boston University School of Social Work, 1965.

Bertcher Harvey, *Group Participation Techniques for Leaders and Members*, 2nd ed., Thousand Oaks, Calif.: Sage, 1994.

Bertcher, Harvey J., and Frank Maple, "Elements and Issues in Group Composition," in *Individual Change through Small Groups*, eds. Martin Sundel, Paul Glasser, Rosemary Sarri, and Robert Vinter: 180–202. New York: Free Press, 1985.

Berzon, B., Charles Pious, and R. Farson, "The Therapeutic Event in Group Psychotherapy: A Study of Subjective Reports by Group Members," *Journal of Individual Psychology* 19 (1963): 204–12.

Bettelheim, Bruno, *A Home for the Heart*. New York: Knopf, 1974.

Bion, W.R., *Experiences in Groups*. New York: Basic Books, 1959.

Blauner, Robert, "Internal Colonialism and Ghetto Revolt," *Social Problems* 16 (Spring 1969): 393–408.

Bloch, Sidney, and Eric Crouch, *Therapeutic Factors in Group Psychotherapy*. New York: Oxford University Press, 1985.

Bloom, Martin, Joel Fischer, and John G. Orme, *Evaluating Practice: Guidelines for the Accountable Professional*, 2nd ed., Boston: Allyn and Bacon, 1995.

Borgers, Sherry B., and Randy W. Koenig, "Uses and Effects of Modeling by the Therapist in Group Therapy, *Journal for Specialists in Group Work* 8 (3) (1983): 133–38.

Breton, Margot, "Liberation Theology, Group Work, and the Right of the Poor and Oppressed to Participate in the Life of the Community," in *Group Work Reaching Out: People, Places, and Power*: 257–70. New York: Haworth, 1992.

———. "Toward a Model of Social Groupwork Practice with Marginalized Populations," *Groupwork* 4 (1): 33–47.

Brim, Orville G., Sr., and Stanton Wheeler, *Socialization after Childhood: Two Essays*. New York: John Wiley, 1966.

Brody, C.M., *Women's Therapy Groups: Paradigms of Feminist Treatment*. New York: Springer, 1987.

Burghardt, Steve, *Organizing for Community Action*. Beverly Hills: Sage, 1982.

Burrow, T., "The Basis of Group Analysis," *British Journal of Medical Psychology* 8, Pt 3 (November 1928): 198–206.

Butler, Pamela, *Self-assertion for Women: A Guide to Becoming Androgenous*. San Francisco: Canfield Press, 1976.

Butler, S., and C. Wintram, *Feminist Groupwork*, London: Sage, 1991.

Cartwright, Dorwin, and Alvin Zander, eds., *Group Dynamics: Research and Theory*, 3rd ed., New York: Harper & Row, Pub., 1968.

Chesler, Mark, "Contemporary Sociological Theories of Racism," in *Toward the Elimination of Racism*, ed. P. Katz: 21–72. New York: Pergamon, 1976.

Chu, J., and S. Sue, "Asian/Pacific Americans and Group Practice," *Social Work with Groups* VII (1984): 23–36.

Churchill, Sallie R., "Social Group Work: A Diagnostic Tool in Child Guidance," *American Journal of Orthopsychiatry* 35 (April 1965): 581–88.

Clark, Frank W., and others, eds., *The Pursuit of Competence in Social Work*. San Francisco: Jossey-Bass, 1979.

Cloward, Richard A., and Lloyd E. Ohlin, *Delinquency and Opportunity*. Glencoe, Ill.: Free Press, 1969.

Compton, Beulah R., and Burt Galoway, eds., *Social Work Processes*, 5th ed., Pacific Grove, Calif.: Brooks-Cole, 1994.

Cook, D., *Program Evaluation and Review Technique: Application in Education*. Cooperation Research Monograph 17. Washington, D.C.: United States Office of Education, 1966.

Corsini, R., and B. Rosenberg, "Mechanisms of Group Psychotherapy: Processes and Dynamics," *Journal of Abnormal and Social Psychology* 51 (1955): 406–11.

Coyle, Grace L., *Studies in Group Behavior*. New York: Harper & Row, Pub., 1937.

———. *Group Experience and Democratic Values*. New York: Women's Press, 1947.

———. *Group Work with American Youth*. New York: Harper & Row, Pub. 1948.

Croxton, Tom A., "The Therapeutic Contract in Social Treatment," in *Individual Change through Small Groups*, eds. Martin Sundel, Paul Glasser, Rosemary Sarri, and Robert Vinter: 159–79. New York: Free Press, 1985.

Culbert, Samuel A., "Consciousness Raising: A Five Stage Model for Social and Organizational Change," in *The Planning of Change*, 3rd ed., eds. Warren G. Bennis and others: 231–45. New York: Holt, Rinehart & Winston, 1976.

Dalkey, N.C., "The Delphi Method: An Experimental Study of Group Opinion," *Management Science* (June 1969).

Davis, Allen, "Settlements: History," in *Encyclopedia of Social Work* 2: 1175–80. New York: National Association of Social Workers, 1971.

Davis, Larry, "Essential Components of Group Work with Black Americans," *Social Work with Groups* VII (1984): 97–109.

Davis, Larry, and Enola Proctor, *Race, Gender, and Class: Guidelines for Practice with Individuals, Families and Groups.* Englewood Cliffs, N.J.: Prentice Hall, 1989.

Delbecq, A., A Van de Ven, and D. Gustafson, *Group Techniques for Program Planning: A Guide to Nominal Group and Delphi Processes.* Glenview, Ill.: Scott Foresman and Co., 1975.

Dewey, John, *How We Think.* Lexington, Mass.: Heath, 1933.

Edwards, E.D., M.E. Edwards, G.M. Daines, and F. Eddy, "Enhancing Self-Concept and Identification with 'Indianness' of American Indian Girls," *Social Work with Groups* I (1978): 309–18.

Edwards, E. Daniel, and Margie E. Edwards, "Group Work Practice with American Indians," *Social Work with Groups* 7 (Fall 1984): 7–22.

Ellis, Albert, and Windy Dryden, *The Practice of Rational-Emotive Psychotherapy.* New York: Springer Publishing Co., 1987.

Empey, LaMar, and Maynard L. Erickson, *The Provo Experiment: Evaluating Community Control of Delinquency.* Lexington, Mass.: Heath, 1972.

Ezriel, H., "Psychoanalytic Group Therapy," in *Group Therapy*, eds. L.R. Wolberg and E.K. Schwartz: 191–202. New York: Intercontinental Medical Book Corporation, 1973.

Fairweather, George, and others, *Community Life for the Mentally Ill: An Alternative to Institutional Care*, Chicago: Aldine, 1969.

Fairweather, George W., ed., *Social Psychology in Treating Mental Illness: An Experimental Approach.* New York: John Wiley, 1964.

Falloon, I., "Interpersonal Variables in Behavioral Group Therapy," *British Journal of Medical Psychology* 54 (1981): 133–41.

Falloon, I., P. Lindley, R. McDonald, et al. "Social Skills Training of Out-Patient Groups," *British Journal of Psychiatry* 131 (1977): 599–609.

Festinger, Leon, "Informal Social Communication," *Psychological Review* LVII (1950): 271–82.

Fischer, Joel, *Effective Casework Practice.* New York: McGraw-Hill, 1978.

Fischer, Joel, and Kevin Corcoran, *Measures for Clinical Practice: A Sourcebook*, 2nd ed., Vol. 1, *Couples, Families, and Children*; Vol. 2, *Adults.* New York: The Free Press, 1994.

Fisher, Roger, and William Ury, *Getting to Yes: Negotiating Agreement Without Giving In.* New York: Penguin Books, 1981.

Flowers, John V., "The Differential Outcome Effects of Simple Advice, Alternatives, and Instructions in Group Psychotherapy, *International Journal of Group Psychotherapy* 29 (1979): 305–16.

Flowers, John V., Curtis D. Booraem, and Karen A. Hartman, "Client Improvement on Higher and Lower Intensity Problems as a Function of Group Cohesiveness," *Psychotherapy: Theory, Research, and Practice* 18 (2) (1981): 246–51.

Follett, Mary Parker, *The New State*, New York: Longmans, 1926.

Framo, James, "Symptoms from a Family Transactional Viewpoint," in *Progress in Group and Family Therapy*, eds. Clifford Sager and Helen Kaplan: 271–308. New York: Brunner/ Mazel, 1972.

Freire, Paulo, *Education for Critical Consciousness.* New York: Seabury Press, 1973.

Galinsky, Maeda, and Janice Schopler, "Warning: Groups May be Dangerous." *Social Work* 22 (1977): 89–94.

Gambrill, Eileen, and Cheryl A. Richey, "An Assertion Inventory for Use in Assessment and Research," *Behavior Therapy* 6 (1975): 350–62.

———. "Gender Issues Related to Group Social Skills Training," *Social Work with Groups* VI (Fall/Winter 1983): 51–66.

Garfield, Sol L., and Allen Bergin, eds., *Handbook of Psychotherapy and Behavior Change: An Empirical Analysis*, 2nd ed., New York: John Wiley, 1978.

Garvin, Charles, "Education for Generalist Practice: A Comparative Analysis of Current Modalities," in *Teaching for Competence in the Delivery of Direct Services*. New York: Council on Social Work Education, 1976.

———. "Training and the Future of Mental Health Services: Steps Toward a Service Society," in *The Michigan Study of Mental Health Continuing Education*, ed. Armand Lauffer: 31–50. Ann Arbor: University of Michigan School of Social Work, 1977.

———. "Group Process: Usage and Uses in Social Work Practice," in *Individual Change through Small Groups*, eds. Martin Sundel, Paul Glasser, Rosemary Sarri, and Robert Vinter: 203–25. New York: Free Press, 1985.

———. "Resocialization: Group Work in Social Control and Correctional Settings," in *The Group Worker's Handbook: Varieties of Group Experience*, ed. Robert Conyne: 113–34. Springfield, Mass.: Thomas, 1985.

———. "Work with Disadvantaged and Oppressed Groups," in *Individual Change through Small Groups*, eds. Martin Sundel, Paul Glasser, Rosemary Sarri, and Robert Vinter: 461–72. New York: The Free Press, 1985.

Garvin, Charles D., William Reid, and Laura Epstein, "A Task-Centered Approach," in *Theories of Social Work with Groups*, eds. Robert W. Roberts and Helen Northen: 238–67. New York: Columbia University Press, 1976.

Garvin, Charles D., and Brett Seabury. *Interpersonal Practice in Social Work: Processes and Procedures*. Englewood Cliffs, N.J.: Prentice Hall, 1984.

Garvin, Charles D., and others, "Group Work Intervention in the Social Environment," in *Individual Change through Small Groups*, eds. Martin Sundel, Paul Glasser, Rosemary Sarri, and Robert Vinter: 273–93. New York: Free Press, 1985.

Garvin, Charles D., and Paul H. Glasser, "Social Group Work: The Preventative and Rehabilitative Approach," in *Individual Change through Small Groups*, eds. Martin Sundel, Paul Glasser, Rosemary Sarri, and Robert Vinter: 35–49. New York: Free Press. 1985.

Garvin, Charles D., and Beth Reed, "Small Group Theory and Social Work Practice: Promoting Diversity or Recreating Inequities, in *Human Behavior Theory: A Diversity Framework*, ed. Roberta Greene. New York: Aldine de Gruyter, 1994.

Garvin, Charles D., and Beth G. Reed, "Sources and Visions for Feminist Group Work: Reflective Processes, Social Justice, Diversity, and Connection," in *Feminist Visions for Social Work*: 41–69. Washington, D.C.: NASW, 1995.

Geller, Janet A., "Reaching the Battering Husband," *Social Work with Groups* 1 (Spring 1978): 27–38.

Glasser, Paul H., and Charles D. Garvin, "An Organizational Model," in *Theories of Social Work with Groups*, eds. Robert W. Roberts and Helen Northen: 75–115. New York: Columbia University Press, 1976.

———. "Social Group Work: The Organizational and Environmental Approach," in *Encyclopedia of Social Work* II: 1338–50. New York: National Association of Social Workers, 1977.

Glasser, Paul, Rosemary Sarri, and Robert Vinter, eds., *Individual Change through Small Groups*. New York: Free Press, 1974.

Glassman, Urania, and Len Kates, *Group Work: A Humanistic Approach*. Newbury Park, CA: Sage, 1990.

————. "The Technical Development of the Democratic Humanistic Norms of the Social Work Group." New York: Adelphi University School of Social Work, no date (Mimeographed).

Goldenberg, Ira, *Oppression and Social Intervention*. Chicago: Nelson-Hall, 1978.

Goldstein, Arnold, Kenneth Heller, and Lee Sechrest, *Psychotherapy and the Psychology of Behavior Change*. New York: John Wiley, 1966.

Goldstein, Arnold P., Robert P. Sprafkin, and N. Jane Gershaw, *Skill Training for Community Living: Applying Structured Learning Therapy*. Elmsford, New York: Pergamon Press, 1976.

Gordon, W., *Synectics: The Development of Creative Capacity*. New York: Harper & Row, 1961.

Gutierrez, Lorraine M., "Using Group to Empower Latinos: A Preliminary Analysis," in *Proceedings of the Eleventh Annual Symposium of the Association for the Advancement of Social Work with Groups*. Montreal, 1989.

Hanmer, Jalna, and Daphne Statham, *Women and Social Work*. Houndmills, Basingstoke, Hampshire, and London: Macmillan Education Ltd., 1988.

Hartford, Margaret E., *Working Papers toward a Frame of Reference for Social Group Work*. New York: National Association of Social Workers, 1962.

————. *Groups in Social Work*. New York: Columbia University Press, 1972.

————. "Group Methods and Generic Practice," in *Theories of Social Work with Groups*, eds. Robert W. Roberts and Helen Northen: 45–74. New York: Columbia University Press, 1976.

Hasenfeld, Yeheskel, "Organizational Factors in Service to Groups," in *Individual Change through Small Groups*, eds. Martin Sundel,

Paul Glasser, Rosemary Sarri, and Robert Vinter: 294–309. New York: Free Press, 1985.

Heil, Richard A., "A Comparative Analysis of Therapeutic Factors in Self-Help Groups." *Dissertation Abstracts International* 53 (8B) (1993): 4373–4.

Hill, W.F., "Further Considerations of Therapeutic Mechanisms in Group Therapy," *Small Group Behavior* 6 (1975): 421–9.

Ho, M.K., "Social Group Work with Asian/Pacific-Americans," *Social Work with Groups* VII (1984): 49–61.

Hoehn-Saric, R. and others, "Systematic Preparation of Patients for Psychotherapy: Effects on Therapy Behavior and Outcome," *Journal of Psychiatry Research* II (1964): 267–81.

Howe, Irving, *World of Our Fathers*. New York: Simon & Schuster, 1976.

Hurvitz, N., "Peer Self-Help Psychotherapy Groups and their Implication for Psychotherapy, *Psychotherapy: Theory, Research, and Practice* 7 (1970): 41–9.

Hynes, K., and J. Werbin, "Group Psychotherapy for Spanish Speaking Women," *Psychiatric Annals* VII (1977): 622–7.

Jourard, S., *The Transparent Self*. New York: Van Nostrand, 1971.

Kahn, M.H., and K.E. Rudestam, "The Relationship Between Liking and Perceived Self-Disclosure in Small Groups," *Journal of Psychology* 78 (1971): 78, 81–5.

Kaiser, Clara A., *The Group Records of Four Clubs*. Cleveland: Western Reserve University, 1930.

Kapp, F.T., G. Gleser, A. Brissenden, et al. "Group Participation and Self Perceived Personality Change," *Journal of Nervous and Mental Disease* 139 (1964): 139, 255–65.

Kassebaum, G., D. Ward, and D. Wilner, *Prison Treatment and Parole Survival: An Empirical Assessment*. New York: John Wiley, 1971.

Kaye, J.D., "Group Interaction and Interpersonal Learning," *Small Group Behavior* 4 (1973): 424–48.

Kelley, Harold H., and John W. Thibaut, "Group Problem Solving," in *The Handbook of Social Psychology*, 2nd ed., eds. Gardner Lindzey and Elliot Aronson: 1–101. Reading, Mass.: Addison-Wesley, 1969.

Kelly, Jeffrey A., "Group Social Skills Training, *Behavior Therapist* 8 (5) (1985): 93–5.

Killilea, M., "Mutual Help Organizations: Interpretations in the Literature," in *Support Systems and Mutual Help: Multidisciplinary Explorations*, eds. G. Caplan and M. Killilea. New York: Grune and Stratton, 1976.

Kinlaw, C.D., *Continuous Improvement and Measurement for Total Quality: A Team Based Approach*. San Diego, CA: Pfeiffer and Homewood, Ill.: Business One Irwin, 1992.

Kiresuk, Thomas J., and Geoffrey Garwick, "Basic Goal Attainment Procedures," in *Social Work Processes* 2nd ed., eds. Beulah R. Compton and Burt Galaway. Homewood, Ill.: Dorsey Press. 1979.

Kirschenbaum, Howard, *Advanced Value Clarification*. LaJolla, CA. University Associates, 1977.

Klein, Alan F., *Society, Democracy, and the Group*. New York: Morrow, 1953.

———. *Effective Group Work*. New York: Association Press, 1972.

Konopka, Gisela, *Therapeutic Group Work with Children*. Minneapolis: University of Minnesota Press, 1949.

———. *Social Group Work: A Helping Process*, 2nd ed., Englewood Cliffs, N.J.: Prentice Hall, 1972.

Kübler-Ross, Elisabeth, *On Death and Dying*, New York: Macmillan, 1964.

Land, E.C., "A Comparison of Patient Improvement Resulting from Two Therapeutic Techniques," *Dissertation Abstracts* 25 (1964): 628–9.

Lang, Norma C., "A Broad Range Model of Practice with the Social Work Group," *Social Service Review* 46 (1972): 76–89.

———. " A Comparative Examination of Therapeutic Uses of Groups in Social Work and in

Adjacent Human Service Professions: Part II—The Literature from 1969–1978," *Social Work with Groups* 2, (2) (Fall 1979): 197–220.

Lange, Arthur J., and Patricia Jakubowski, *Responsible Assertive Behavior.* Champaign, Ill.: Research Press, 1976.

Laqueur, H., H. Laburt, and G. Morong, "Multiple Family Therapy: Further Developments," *International Journal of Social Psychiatry* (1964) Congress Issue: 70–80.

Lawrence, Harry, "The Origins of Social Group Work" (unpublished manuscript, p. 13), quoted in Scott Briar, "Social Casework and Social Group Work: Historical Foundations," in *Encyclopedia of Social Work* II: 1241. New York: National Association of Social Workers, 1971.

Lawrence, Harry, and Martin Sundel, "Behavior Modification in Adult Groups," *Social Work* 17 (1972): 34–43.

Lee, Judith A.B., *The Empowerment Approach to Social Work Practice.* New York: Columbia University Press, 1994.

Lee, Judith A.B., ed., *Group Work with the Poor and Oppressed.* New York: Haworth, 1989.

Lewis, E., "Regaining Promise: Feminist Perspectives for Social Group Work Practice," *Social Work with Groups*, 15 (2/3) (1992): 271–84.

Lieberman, Morton A., "Group Methods," in *Helping People Change*, eds. Frederick A. Kanfer and Arnold P. Goldstein: 433–86. New York: Pergamon Press, 1975.

Lieberman, M.A., I. Yalom, and M. Miles, *Encounter Groups: First Facts.* New York: Basic Books, 1973.

Lieberman, Morton A., and Lonnie R. Snowden, "Problems in Assessing Prevalence and Membership Characteristics of Self-Help Group Participants, in *Understanding the Self-Help Organization: Frameworks and Findings*: 32–49. Thousand Oaks, CA: Sage, 1994.

Lindeman, Eduard C., *The Community.* New York: Association Press, 1921.

London, Perry, *Behavior Control.* New York: Harper & Row, Pub., 1971.

McCorkle, Lloyd W., Albert Elias, and F. Lovell Bixby, *The Highfields Story*. New York: Holt, Rinehart and Winston, 1958.

McGrath, Joseph E., *Groups: Interaction and Performance*. Englewood Cliffs, N.J.: Prentice Hall, 1984.

McVicar, Pauline, and Al Herman, "Assertiveness, Self Actualization, and Locus of Control in Women," *Sex Roles* 9 (4): 555–62.

Mahoney, Michael J., *Cognition and Behavior Modification*. Cambridge, Mass.: Ballinger Publishing Co., 1974.

Maluccio, Anthony, ed. *Promoting Competence in Clients*. New York: The Free Press, 1981.

Marlatt, G.A., *Relapse Prevention: A Self Control Program for the Treatment of Addictive Behaviors*. Seattle: University of Washington Alcoholism and Drug Treatment Unit, 1980.

Martin, Garry, and Joseph Pear, *Behavior Modification: What It Is and How to Do It*, 4th ed., Englewood Cliffs, N.J.: Prentice Hall, 1992.

Martin, P.Y., and K.A. Shanahan, "Transcending the Effects of Sex Composition in Small Groups," *Social Work with Groups* VI (1983): 19–32.

Meadow, Diane, "Connecting Theory and Practice: The Effect of Pregroup Preparation on Individual and Group Behavior," No Date (Mimeographed).

Meichenbaum, Donald, *Cognitive-Behavior Modification: An Integrative Approach*. New York: Plenum Press, 1977.

Meichenbaum, D.H., J.B. Gilmore, and A.L. Fedoravicius, "Group Insight Versus Group Desensitization in Treating Speech Anxiety," *Journal of Consulting and Clinical Psychology* 36 (1971): 420–21.

Mickiewica, Adam, "Therapeutic Factors in AA and Al-Anon Groups," *Polish Psychological Bulletin* 25 (1): (1994): 59–73.

Middleman, Ruth, *The Non-Verbal Method in Working with Groups*. New York: Association Press, 1968.

Middleman, Ruth R., and Gale Goldberg, *Social Service Delivery: A Structural Approach to Social Work Practice*. New York: Columbia University Press, 1974.

———. "Social Work Practice with Groups," in *Encyclopedia of Social Work*, 8th ed., ed. A. Minahan: 714–729. Silver Spring, M.D. Practice with Groups National Association of Social Workers, 1987.

Mills, Theodore M., *The Sociology of Small Groups*. Englewood Cliffs, N.J.: Prentice Hall, 1967.

Moos, Rudolf, *Evaluating Treatment Environments: A Social Ecological Approach*. New York: John Wiley, 1974.

Moreno, J.L., *Psychodrama* (rev. ed.). Beacon, N.Y.: Beacon House, Inc., 1964.

Murphy, Marjorie, *The Social Group Work Method in Social Work Education*. New York: Council on Social Work Education, 1959.

Netherland, Warren, "Corrections Systems: Adult," in *Encyclopedia of Social Work*, 18th ed., ed. A. Minahan. Silver Spring, Md.: National Association of Social Workers, 1987.

Newsletter, W.I., "What Is Social Group Work?" in *Proceedings of the National Conference on Social Work*: 291–9. Chicago: University of Chicago Press, 1935.

Northen, Helen, *Social Work with Groups*. New York: Columbia University Press, 1969.

———. "Psychosocial Practice in Small Groups," in *Theories of Social Work with Groups*, eds. Robert W. Roberts and Helen Northen: 116–52. New York: Columbia University Press, 1976.

Novotny, H., and J. Enomoto, "Social Competence Training as a Correctional Alternative," *Offender Rehabilitation* I (1976): 45–55.

Nugent, W.R., and J.W. Thomas, "Validation of the Self-Esteem Rating Scale, *Research on Social Work Practice* 3 (1993): 191–207.

Ozbay, Huluk, Erol Koka, Emine Ozturk, and Serpil Gungor, "Therapeutic Factors in an Adolescent Psychodrama Group," *Journal of*

Group Psychotherapy, Psychodrama, and Sociometry 46(1) (1993): 3–11.

Papell, Catherine P., and Beulah Rothman, "Social Group Work Models: Possession and Heritage," *Journal of Education of Social Work*, 2, (2) (Fall 1966): 66–77.

————. "Relating the Mainstream Model of Social Work with Groups to Group Psychotherapy and the Structured Group Approach," *Social Work with Groups* 3(2) 1980: 5–23.

Parloff, Morris B., Irene E. Waskow, and Barry E. Wolfe, "Research on Therapist Variables in Relationship to Process and Outcome," *Handbook of Psychotherapy and Behavior Change: An Empirical Analysis*, 2nd ed., eds. Sol L. Garfield and Allen Bergin: 233–82. New York: John Wiley, 1978.

Perls, Fritz, R.F. Hefferline, and Paul Goodman, *Gestalt Therapy*. New York: Julian Press, 1951.

Pfeiffer, J. William, and John E. Jones, eds., *A Handbook of Structured Experiences for Human Relations Training*. LaJolla, Calif.: University Associates, 1974 (issued annually).

Philpott, T.L., *The Slum and the Ghetto: Immigrants, Blacks, and Reformers in Chicago, 1880–1930*. Belmont, Calif.: Wadsworth Publishing Co., 1991.

Pincus, Allen, and Anne Minahan, *Social Work Practice: Model and Method*. Itasca, Ill.: F.E. Peacock, 1973.

Pinderhughes, Elaine, "Empowerment for our Clients and for Ourselves," *Social Casework* 64 (June 1983): 331–8.

Prince, G., *The Practice of Creativity*. New York: Harper & Row, 1970.

Rakos, Richard F., *Assertive Behavior: Theory, Research, and Training*. London, New York: Routledge, 1991.

Rappaport, R., "Group Therapy in Prison: A Strategic Approach," in *Group Counseling and Group Psychotherapy with Rehabilitation Clients*, ed. Milton Seligman: 115–31. Springfield, Mass.: Thomas, 1977.

Rathus, S.A., "A 30-Item Schedule for Assessing Assertive Behavior," *Behavior Research and Therapy* 11 (1973): 398–406.

Redl, Fritz, and David Wineman, *Controls from Within*. New York: Free Press, 1956.

Reid, William, *The Task-Centered System*. New York: Columbia University Press, 1978.

Reid, William, and Laura Epstein, *Task-Centered Casework*. New York: Columbia University Press, 1972.

————. *Task-Centered Practice*. New York: Columbia University Press, 1977.

Richmond, Mary, "Some Next Steps in Social Treatment," *Proceedings of the National Conference of Social Work, 1920*: 254–8. New York: Columbia University Press, 1939.

Robert, H., *Robert's Rules of Order*. Glenview, Ill.: Scott Foresman, and Co., 1970.

Roberts, Robert W., and Helen Northen, eds., *Theories of Social Work with Groups*. New York: Columbia University Press, 1976.

Rohde, Renate, "The Group as an Effective Medium for Working with Children of Chemically Dependent Families, *Journal for Specialists in Group Work* 18 (4) (1993): 182–8.

Rooney, Ronald, "Adolescent Groups in Public Schools," in *Task-Centered Practice*, eds. William J. Reid and Laura Epstein: 168–82. New York: Columbia University Press, 1977.

————. *Strategies for Work with Involuntary Clients*. New York: Columbia University Press, 1992.

Rose, Sheldon, *Treating Children in Groups*. San Francisco: Jossey-Bass, 1972.

————. *Group Therapy: A Behavioral Approach*. Englewood Cliffs, N.J.: Prentice Hall, 1977.

————. "Use of Data in Identifying and Resolving Group Problems in Goal Oriented Treatment Groups," *Social Work with Groups* VII (Summer 1984): 23–36.

————. *Working with Children and Adolescents in Groups*. San Francisco: Jossey-Bass, 1987.

————. *Working with Adults in Groups: Integrating Cognitive Behavioral and Small Group Strategies*. San Francisco: Jossey-Bass, 1989.

————. "Putting the Group Into Cognitive-Behavioral Treatment, *Social Work with Groups* 13 (3) (1990): 71–83.

Rose, S.D., J.J. Gayner, and J.L. Edelson, "Measuring Interpersonal Competence," *Social Work*, 22 (1977): 125–9.

Rose, S., and C. LeCroy, "Group Treatment Methods," in *Helping People Change*, 4th ed., eds. F. Kanfer and A. Goldstein. New York: Pergamon Press, 1991.

Sarri, Rosemary, and Maeda Galinsky, "A Conceptual Framework for Group Development," in *Individual Change through Small Groups*, eds. Martin Sundel, Paul Glasser, Rosemary Sarri, and Robert Vinter: 70–86. New York: Free Press, 1985.

Schopler, Janice, and Maeda Galinsky, "Meeting Practice Needs: Conceptualizing the Open-Ended Group," *Social Work with Groups* VII (1984): 3–21.

———. "Group Practice Overview," in *Encyclopedia of Social Work* II: 1129–42. Washington, D.C.: National Association of Social Workers, 1995.

Schopler, Janice H., Maeda Galinsky, and Mark Alicke, "Goals in Social Group Work Practice: Formulation, Implementation, and Evaluation," in *Individual Change through Small Groups*, eds. Martin Sundel, Paul Glasser, Rosemary Sarri, and Robert Vinter: 140–58. New York: Free Press, 1985.

Schulman, Evaline D., *Intervention in Human Services*, 2nd ed., St. Louis: C.V. Mosby, 1978.

Schutz, William, C., *Firo: A Three Dimensional Theory of Interpersonal Orientations*. New York: Holt, Rinehart & Winston, 1958.

———. *Here Comes Everybody*. New York: Harper & Row, 1971.

Schwartz, William, "The Social Worker in the Group," in *New Perspectives on Service to Groups*: 7–29. New York: Columbia University Press, 1961.

———. "Neighborhood Centers and Group Work," in *Research in the Social Services: A Five Year Review*, ed. Henry S. Maas: 130–91. New York: National Association of Social Workers, 1971.

———. "Social Group Work: The Interactionist Approach," *Encyclopedia of Social Work* 2: 1252–63. New York: National Association of Social Workers, 1971.

———. "Between Client and System: The Mediating Function," in *Theories of Social Work with Groups*, eds. Robert W. Roberts and Helen Northen: 171–97. New York: Columbia University Press, 1976.

———. "Social Work with Groups: The Search for a Method," in *Social Work: The Collected Writings of William Schwartz*, ed. Toby Berman-Rossi. Itaska, Ill.: Peacock, 1994.

Shaffer, John B.P., and David Galinsky, *Models of Group Therapy and Sensitivity Training*, Englewood Cliffs, N.J.: Prentice Hall, 1989.

Shalinsky, William I., "The Effects of Group Composition on Aspects of Group Functioning" (unpublished DSW dissertation, Western Reserve University, 1967).

Shaw, Marvin E., *Group Dynamics: The Psychology of Small Group Behavior.* New York: McGraw-Hill, 1976.

Sherer, Mark, James E. Maddux, Blaise Mercandantem, Steven Prentice-Dunn, Beth Jacobs, and Ronald W. Rogers, "The Self-Efficacy Scale: Construction and Validation," *Psychological Reports* 51 (1982): 663–71.

Sherman, T.M., and W.H. Cormier, "The Use of Subjective Scales for Measuring Interpersonal Reactions," *Journal of Behavior Therapy and Experimental Psychology* 3 (1972): 279–80.

Shulman, Lawrence, "Scapegoats, Group Workers, and Pre-emptive Intervention," *Social Work* 12, (2) (1967): 37–43.

Siporin, Max, *Introduction to Social Work Practice.* New York: Macmillan, 1975.

Slavin, Roberta L., "The Significance of Here-and-Now Disclosure in Promoting Cohesion in Group Psychotherapy," 50th Annual Conference of the American Group Psychotherapy Association, *Group* 17 (3) (1993): 143–50.

Slavson, S.R., *Creative Group Education.* New York: Association Press, 1937.

Slipman, Sue, *Helping Ourselves to Power: A Handbook for Women in the Skills of Public Life.* New York: Pergamon Press, 1986.

Smalley, Ruth E., *Theory for Social Work Practice.* New York: Columbia University Press, 1967.

Solomon, Barbara, *Black Empowerment.* New York: Columbia University Press, 1976.

Somers, Mary Louise, "Problem Solving in Small Groups," in *Theories of Social Work with Groups,* eds. Robert W. Roberts and Helen Northen: 331–67. New York: Columbia University Press, 1976.

Spergel, Irving, *Street Gang Work: Theory and Practice.* Reading, Mass.: Addison-Wesley, 1966.

Studt, E., S. Messinger, and T. Wilson, *C-Unit: Search for Community in Prison.* New York: Sage, 1968.

Sue, Derald, *Counseling the Culturally Different.* New York: John Wiley, 1981.

Sundel, Martin, Paul Glasser, Rosemary Sarri, and Robert Vinter, eds., *Individual Change through Small Groups,* 2nd ed., New York: Free Press, 1985.

Thibaut, John W., and Harold H. Kelley, *The Social Psychology of Groups.* New York: John Wiley, 1959.

Tolson, Eleanor Reardon, William J. Reid, and Charles D. Garvin, *Generalist Practice: A Task-Centered Approach.* New York: Columbia University Press, 1994.

Toseland, Ronald, and Max Siporin, "When to Recommend Group Treatment: A Review of the Clinical and Research Literature," *International Journal of Group Psychotherapy* 36 (2) (1986): 171–201.

Toseland, R., C. Rossiter, T. Peak, and G. Smith, "Comparative Effectiveness of Individual and Group Interventions to Support Family Caregivers, *Social Work* 35 (3) (1990): 209–19.

Toseland, Ronald, and Robert Rivas, *An Introduction to Group Work Practice.* 2nd ed., New York: Macmillan, 1995.

Traux, C.B., R.R. Carkhuff, and I. Rodman, Jr., "Relationships between Therapist Offered Conditions and Patient Change in Group Psychotherapy," *Journal of Clinical Psychology* 21 (1965): 327–29.

Traux, C.B., J. Wittmer, and D.G. Wargo, "Effects of the Therapeutic Conditions of Accurate Empathy, Non-possessive Warmth, and Genuineness on Hospitalized Mental Patients During Group Therapy," *Journal of Clinical Psychology* 27 (1971): 137–42.

Trecker, Harleigh B., ed., *Group Work: Foundations and Frontiers.* New York: Whiteside Inc., 1955.

———. ed., *Group Work in the Psychiatric Setting.* New York: Whiteside, Inc., 1956.

Tropman, John E., *Effective Meetings: Improving Group Decision Making.* Beverly Hills: Sage, 1980.

Tropp, Emanuel, "Social Group Work: The Developmental Approach," *Encyclopedia of Social Work* 2: 1246–52. New York: National Association of Social Workers, 1971.

———. "Developmental Theory," in *Theories of Social Work with Groups,* eds. Robert W. Roberts and Helen Northen: 198–237. New York: Columbia University Press, 1976.

Tschuschke, Volker, and Robert R. Dies, "Intensive Analysis of Therapeutic Factors and Outcome in Long Term Inpatient Groups," *International Journal of Group Psychotherapy* 44 (2) (1994): 185–208.

Van de Ven, A., and A. Delbecq, "Nominal versus Interacting Group Processes for Committee Decision-Making Effectiveness," *Academy of Management Journal* 9 (1971): 42–43.

Vinter, Robert D., "Group Work: Perspectives and Prospects," in *Social Work with Small Groups*: 128–49. New York: National Association of Social Workers, 1959.

———. "Analysis of Treatment Organizations," *Social Work* 8 (1963): 3–15.

———. "Social Group Work," in *Encyclopedia of Social Work*: 715–24. New York: NASW, 1965.

———. "The Essential Components of Group Work Practice," in *Individual Change through Small Groups,* eds. Martin Sundel,

Paul Glasser, Rosemary Sarri, and Robert Vinter: 11–34. New York: Free Press, 1985.

———. "Program Activities: An Analysis of Their Effects on Participant Behavior," in *Individual Change through Small Groups*, eds. Martin Sundel, Paul Glasser, Rosemary Sarri, and Robert Vinter: 226–36. New York: Free Press, 1985.

Vorrath, Harry, and Larry Brendtro, *Positive Peer Culture.* Chicago: Aldine, 1974.

Walters, Marianne, "A Feminist Perspective in Family Therapy," in *Gender and Power in Families*, eds. Rosine Jozef Perelberg and Ann C. Miller: 13–33. London and New York: Tavistockl/Routledge, 1990.

Weigel, R.G., N. Dinges, R. Dyer, et al., "Perceived Self-Disclosure, Mental Health, and Who Is Liked in Group Treatment," *Journal of Counseling Psychology* 19 (1972): 47–52.

Weiner, M.F., *Therapist Disclosure: The Use of Self in Psychotherapy.* Boston: Butterworths, 1978.

Weiss, B.J., "The Development of Cohesiveness in Marathon Growth Groups," *Dissertation Abstracts International* 32 (1972): 6065B.

Wexler, Harry, Gregory Falkin, and Douglas Lipton, "Outcome Evaluation of a Prison Therapeutic Community for Substance Abuse Treatment," *Criminal Justice and Behavior*, 17(1) (1990): 71–92.

Wheeler, Inese, Kathleen O'Malley, Michael Waldo, and James Murphy, "Participant's Perception of Therapeutic Factors in Groups for Incest Survivors, *Journal for Specialists in Group Work* 17(2) (1992): 89–95.

Whitaker, Dorothy Stock, and Morton A. Lieberman, *Psychotherapy through the Group Process.* New York: Atherton Press, 1965.

Williamson, Margaretta, *The Social Worker in Group Work.* New York: Harper & Row, 1929.

Wilson, Gertrude, "From Practice to Theory: A Personalized History," in *Theories of Social Work with Groups*, eds. Robert W. Roberts and Helen Northen: 1–44. New York: Columbia University Press, 1976.

Wilson, Gertrude, and Gladys Ryland, *Social Group Work Practice*, Boston: Houghton-Mifflin, 1949.

Wolpe, Joseph, *The Practice of Behavior Therapy*, 2nd ed., Elmsford, N.Y.: Pergamon Press, 1973.

Yalom, I.D., *Inpatient Group Psychotherapy*, New York: Basic Books, 1983.

———. *The Theory and Practice of Group Psychotherapy*, 3rd ed., New York: Basic Books, 1985.

———. *The Theory and Practice of Group Psychotherapy*, 4th ed., New York: Basic Books, 1995.

Yalom, I.D., P.S. Houts, S.M. Zimerberg, et al. "Prediction of Improvement in Group Therapy," *Archives of General Psychiatry* 17 (1967): 159–68.

Zander, Alvin. *Groups at Work.* San Francisco: Jossey-Bass, 1977.

———. *Making Groups Effective.* San Francisco: Jossey-Bass, 1982.

Index